THE SHELL MONEY OF THE SLAVE TRADE

AFRICAN STUDIES SERIES   49

OTHER BOOKS IN THE SERIES

THE SHELL MONEY
OF THE SLAVE TRADE

JAN HOGENDORN

Department of Economics, Colby College

and

MARION JOHNSON

Centre of West African Studies, University of Birmingham

The right of the
University of Cambridge
to print and sell
all manner of books
was granted by
Henry VIII in 1534.
The University has printed
and published continuously
since 1584.

CAMBRIDGE UNIVERSITY PRESS

CAMBRIDGE

LONDON   NEW YORK   NEW ROCHELLE

MELBOURNE   SYDNEY

Published by the Press Syndicate of the University of Cambridge
The Pitt Building, Trumpington Street, Cambridge CB2 1RP
32 East 57th Street, New York, NY 10022, USA
10 Stamford Road, Oakleigh, Melbourne, 3166, Australia

First published 1986

Printed in Great Britain at the University Press, Cambridge

British Library cataloguing in publication data

Hogendorn, Jan S.
The shell money of the slave trade. – (African studies series,
ISSN 0065-406X; 49)
1. Slave-trade – Africa – History   2. Cowries
I. Title   II. Johnson, Marion, 1914–
382'.44'096   HT1322

Library of Congress cataloguing in publication data

Hogendorn, Jan S.
The shell money of the slave trade.
(African studies series; 49)
Bibliography: p.
Includes index.
1. Shell money. 2. Cowries. 3. Slave-trade – History.
4. Slave-trade – Africa. I. Johnson, Marion, 1914–
II. Title. III. Series.
GN450.5.H64 1986   380.1'44'096   85-25511

ISBN 0 521 32086 0

CE

It is very singular that ... the contemptible shells of the Maldives prove the price of Mankind, and contribute to the vilest of traffic in negro lands; but so it is.

(Fragment attributed to L. A. Flori in the H. C. P. Bell
Collection,
Sri Lanka National Archives, 25.16.42C.)

What we call Money being arbitrary, and its Nature and Value depending on a tacit Convention betwixt Men, these (cowrie) shells, in several Parts of Asia and Africa, are accounted current Money, with a Value assigned to them. This is established by a reciprocal Consent, and those who are pleased to shew a Contempt of them, don't reflect that shells are as fit for a common standard of pecuniary Value, as either Gold or Silver; they certainly forget that they themselves are obliged to do what they ridicule and take them for ready Money.

"Dutch Gentleman's" pamphlet (in the British Museum),
*Voyage to the Island of Ceylon on Board a Dutch Indiaman
in the Year 1747.*
London, 1754, pp. 19–20.

Contents

Maps

Tables and chart

Preface

Both Marion Johnson and Jan Hogendorn first became interested in the cowrie shell money of West Africa while living and working there, some 5,000 airline miles from where the shells had actually originated. Marion Johnson, trained in monetary economics at Oxford, was resident in the Gold Coast during 1937–39, but only began her inquiry into the cowrie currency much later, during a four-year stay from 1962 to 1966 in now-independent Ghana. While undertaking research on trade routes at the University of Ghana, Legon, she noted the frequent references by nineteenth-century travellers to the existence of a shell-money standard. Little specific attention had been directed to the cowrie currency since the ambitious German works of the turn of the century, so, with four notebooks filled with material on the subject, she wrote the articles published by the *Journal of African History* in 1970 that ten years later furnished the impetus for this volume.[1] Work on the cowrie required treatment of the Muslim gold *mithqal* and the "trade ounce," the eighteenth-century standard of value with no circulating equivalent, used with such frequency along the West African coast. Two further articles resulted from this research.[2] Most of the writing was done at the Centre of West African Studies, University of Birmingham, where she has been for the past fifteen years.

In 1980 Jan Hogendorn took leave from the Department of Economics, Colby College, as Research Associate in the same center. Trained in development economics at Wesleyan University in the U.S.A. and at the London School of Economics, he had first encountered cowries in the great Kano market during the mid 1960s while carrying on the fieldwork for his Ph.D. dissertation on the Nigerian groundnut trade. He did not suspect how far these shells had travelled until he read Marion Johnson's articles in the *Journal of African History*. By this time he was developing an interest in the relation between African indigenous moneys and the slave trade, reflected in an article, also in the *Journal of African History*, that appeared four years after Johnson's essays on the cowrie.[3] It was at Birmingham that the idea was conceived for a jointly authored book on the cowrie currency.

The shell money of the slave trade

That work of four years, involving field and archival work in Europe, Africa, and Asia, is now complete.

The authors could not have done it without help. Grants from both the U.S. and U.K. Social Science Research Councils, the Mellon Foundation, and the Colby Social Science Grants Committee allayed most of the financial worry. Several able student research assistants found employment on this project, their scepticism as to whether there really was a shell money overcome by the excitement of studying a trade so strange, so long-lasting, and geographically so wide-ranging.

In the Netherlands, Floris Klinkenberg of the University of Leiden served for a long period as Hogendorn's research assistant in the national archives at The Hague, and his careful work is gratefully acknowledged. Floris turned up much more material than is included in this volume, as can be seen in his subsequent master's thesis at Leiden,[4] and he was chiefly responsible for the research effort in the Netherlands. Assistance was also rendered by J. Valkenberg at Leiden.

Lynn Garrett of the Centre of West African Studies, Birmingham, and Joanne Lynch of Colby College worked in Britain as researchers at the Public Record Office, Kew. Joanne Lynch concentrated on the European aspects of the cowrie trade, eventually becoming co-author of a recently published article.[5]

At Colby College in the U.S.A. the supply of student assistants was sufficiently liberal to allow for a division of labor. Kathy Dornish helped in translating German and transcribed the tapes from the fieldwork. Shellie Stoddard prepared the tables and diagrams. Virginia Bushell checked bibliographical references, travelled to Widener Library at Harvard when necessary, and in general managed the inter-library ordering of works not available at the college. Colby's Kelly McPhail checked details of the life and habitat of the cowrie in Australia and Hawaii. Jill Lord undertook the computer editing and printing of the original drafts. Proof-reading was assisted by Christie Emond, Kelly McPhail, and Faith Delaney, and Faith was in charge of the final production of the manuscript. Some of these students put in two years on these tasks.

In the academic and business communities, many individuals gave support and encouragement. Help of a personal nature came from more people than are named here, but the following must have special mention.

Australia: S. Arasaratnam of the University of New England.

Canada: Paul Lovejoy of York University.

Denmark: James Heimann of Copenhagen University, whose lengthy letters were full of interesting points, and whose own published research on the cowrie (from the perspective of an anthropologist) is cited frequently in this book; Kristof Glamann of the Carlsbergfondet.

Ghana: the late Thomas Hodgkin of the Institute of African Studies, Legon, who made facilities available to Marion Johnson at the time of her work there; and Ivor Wilks, who was generous with help and encouragement. Jane Guyer was helpful, and Daniel McCall told us personally of his very recent encounters with the still-circulating cowrie currency in Ghana. A number of other Ghanaian informants provided assistance.

India: Om Prakash of the University of Delhi; Phirov Sukhadwala of Coin Shellcrafts House, Bombay.

Maldive Islands: Mr. Hussein Haleem of the Maldive Mission to the United Nations in New York City made the initial contacts in Male for Hogendorn. The Hon. Abdula Hameed, Minister of Provincial Affairs, made it possible to visit atolls that were ordinarily off-limits to foreigners, and the officials of his ministry were indispensable in making travel arrangements to areas where boats did not run to schedule. Mr. D. Abdul Hameed, Principal of the Majeediyya School in Male, supplied a student translator of Divehi, the local language, while the Director of Information and Broadcasting, Mr. Hassan Maniku, and his assistant, Mr. Ahmad Shahiku, helped to provide access to official customs records. In the merchant community, Mr. Abdullah Faiz of Kalegefanu Enterprises, Mr. I. M. Didi of the firm of that name, Mr. A. H. H. Maniku, Mr. Mohamed Ahmad, and Mr. Adam Shariff (the latter two helped with translations) gave of their time.

Netherlands: Pieter Emmer, Femme Gaastra, Robert Ross, Leonard Blussé, and George Winius of the Centre for the History of European Expansion, University of Leiden, made research in the Netherlands a pleasant experience. In particular Pieter Emmer made it possible for Hogendorn to obtain the services of Floris Klinkenberg as research assistant. Also at Leiden, P. van Emst volunteered useful information. Frank Perlin of Erasmus University, Rotterdam, was helpful with questions concerning Indian monetary history.

Nigeria: John Lavers of Abdullahi Bayero University, Kano.

Sri Lanka: the Director and staff of the Sri Lanka National Archives assisted in supplying materials from the Dutch colonial period and from the H. C. P. Bell Collection.

United Kingdom: the staff of the University of Birmingham's Centre of West African Studies, including especially the former director, John Fage, the present director, Douglas Rimmer, and A. G. Hopkins, were uniformly helpful and considerate. A number of colleagues and students at the centre have also shared information with us. W. F. Holmstrom of the Department of Zoology at Birmingham gave us our first introduction to the life and habitat of the living cowrie. Polly Hill of Cambridge University provided personal information.

United States: Ralph Austen of the University of Chicago, Philip D. Curtin at Johns Hopkins, Henry Gemery at Colby (co-author with Hogendorn of a number of articles on African moneys), Harvey Feinberg of Southern Connecticut State College, Patrick Manning of Northeastern University, John Richards of Duke University, and John Willis of Princeton University provided advice and encouragement. Joseph C. Miller of the

University of Virginia was generous of his time in making available information about the Portuguese period, and also made it possible for Marion Johnson to do some of the writing in Charlottesville during 1984. Lore Ferguson of the Oak Grove-Coburn School helped with translations of nineteenth-century German works. We were well treated by the specialists on the cowrie in life, the malacologists on the staffs of the American Museum of Natural History, New York City, and the Academy of Natural Sciences, Philadelphia. In New York, Walter Sage went beyond courtesy, answering questions by phone or letter and once even driving nearly 400 miles for a critique of the manuscript. William Emerson, Curator of Molluscs at the American Museum, also lent his support. At the Academy in Philadelphia, Virginia Orr Maes answered questions which at the start must have seemed elementary to her; also at the Academy, Curator of Malacology Robert Robertson and Clyde Goulden of the Ecology Department gave assistance. G. Boss and Gary Rosenburg of the Mollusc Department, Museum of Comparative Zoology, Harvard University, also provided advice. William Dunkle, Data Librarian of the Woods Hole Oceanographic Institute, assisted with information on Indian Ocean water temperatures. Finally, at Colby's Miller Library the inter-library loan department, especially Sonny Pomerleau, seldom failed to find a scarce item. The typing was done at Colby by Karen Bourassa.

Our thanks to the *Journal of African History, Slavery and Abolition*, and *Itinerario* for allowing portions of published material to be included.

ORTHOGRAPHIC NOTE

When a spelling appears often in quotations from earlier authors, we have sometimes adopted it for the sake of uniformity. Cases in point are Bornu, instead of the now much-used Borno, and Ashanti instead of Asante. Translations of quotations into English are sometimes provided without additional notice; this will be clear from the note references.

NOTE ON CURRENCIES OTHER THAN COWRIE

Where a value is quoted in British pounds sterling (£), shillings (s.), and pence (d.) we have often for the reader's convenience provided a decimal equivalent to the £ s. d. Before decimalization, there were 20 shillings to the pound, and 12 pence to the shilling. In the eighteenth century the troy ounce of gold was reckoned at £4, but in West Africa the official valuation in the nineteenth century was £3 12s. 0d. (72 shillings) to the troy ounce. The margin was supposed to allow for all expenses of transmission to England. Merchants and traders in West Africa considered £1 equivalent to four silver dollars, or five shillings each, but the official value of the silver dollar was only 4s. 2d. (50 pence); the French 5-franc piece was valued at about 3s. 9d. (45 pence). The German mark was equivalent to one shilling. There

xiv

were 20 stuivers to the Dutch guilder; £1 equalled about 10 guilders.[6] The Indian rupee's exchange rate with sterling was standardized by the East India Company at 2s. 6d. in 1660–1676, 2s. 3d. in 1677–1705, and again at 2s. 6d. in 1706–1760. The rupee sank in the nineteenth century. It was valued at 2s. down to about 1873, but after silver depreciated, it went as low as 1s. before stabilizing at 1s. 4d. in 1899.[7]

Introduction

The shell money of the slave trade consisted of thousands of millions of little cowrie shells, most of them fished in the lagoons of the far-off Maldive Islands of the Indian Ocean. They came to West Africa in a journey lasting a year or more, shipped initially by Arab merchants who took them to North Africa for export across the Sahara, and later by the European trading companies who carried them to Lisbon, Amsterdam, or London as ballast. Thence they were shipped by the barrel-load to the West African coast, where they were an indispensable currency before, during, and after the slave trade, in purely quantitative terms overshadowing all others.

Of all the so-called "primitive moneys," this cowrie currency of West Africa (and parts of Asia as well, although that is not our focus) is arguably the most important, the most interesting, and the most modern.[1] Cowrie-money was not really primitive at all. It seems so only to eyes grown so familiar to dates, faces, and nationalities stamped on coins that they can conceive of no alternative. It was a "general-purpose money" that served as medium of exchange, unit of account, store of value, and standard for deferred payment. For a very long period of time, the shells were actually better suited to transactions of extremely low value than were metallic coins, because it was all but impossible to mint a coin with worth as low as an individual cowrie. (The smallest British coin just before the colonial period was the farthing, equal to one quarter of a penny. It was about the same value as 25 to 32 cowries in southern Nigeria.) The shells were used for large transactions as well, up to half a million sometimes changing hands at one time. Understandably, a great variety of indigenous counting systems evolved, geared to the needs of non-literate but intensely commercial peoples.[2]

In one respect, the cowrie currency was exceptionally "modern" in a manner not even equalled by the great international currencies of the twentieth century. During the heyday of the pound sterling before World War One, or the U.S. dollar after that time, neither ever circulated very widely in the marketplaces of other countries. Yet the "primitive" cowrie crossed dozens of frontiers – round about the year 1800 a pocketful of shells could have been easily spent as money in coastal Burma or Timbuktu, in Benin or Bengal, on long stretches of the Ganges or the Niger. They were used in the territories of several strong central governments and in hundreds of smaller polities as well, carried as cash by Muslims and Hindus and animists. Stamped with no nationality, yet after many a border-crossing recognizable at once as ready money, the cowrie shell had more modern traits than it is usually given credit for.

Those who inquire more closely into the history of the sea-shell money in West Africa find an unexpectedly sombre story, because the cowrie was so intimately connected to the slave trade. This unpleasant link to slavery occurred because the cowrie was the money which sellers of slaves demanded in exchange for the export of their unfortunate wares. Thus, to the extent that slaving was motivated by a desire to hold increased stocks of money, cowries were an expensive currency indeed, with social costs far beyond the nominal cost of their importation. (The modern literature on slavery in Africa has attained large size. In this volume we discuss neither the institution of slavery, nor the long process of change that slavery underwent in its African setting, nor the slave trade as such.[3])

Of all the goods from overseas exchanged for slaves, the shell money touched individuals most widely and often in their day-to-day activities. Especially at the low end of the income distribution, people who never owned another import would frequently have used the cowrie currency in local markets for their purchases of food and other necessities. Of all the ramifications of the slave trade, the resulting inflow of cowries would have had perhaps the most universal effect, over the widest geographical area, on the common people of West Africa.

The need to export in order to purchase stocks of money was in concept identical to the principle under which the later colonial currency boards operated. Some aspects of West Africa's cowrie currency area were quite different from the colonial monetary systems, however. One substantial dissimilarity was that the shell money was in effect inconvertible: neither the North African merchants who brought them across the Sahara, nor the Europeans who later brought them by sea, would take them back again. Once paid in, they were never again paid out, and the statement of "Dutch Gentleman" in our epigraph is not strictly accurate if it implies that foreigners would ever settle a balance of payments surplus in their favor by carrying away cowries. (Then again, a British or American penny is almost equally inconvertible, as anyone knows who has ever tried to exchange foreign coins at bank or airport.) Another difference was that the cowrie was often part of a multiple currency system in its zone of circulation, serving as small change alongside gold, slaves, and (latterly) dollars, shillings, francs, and the like, which were the higher denominations of the monetary system.[4] A final difference concerned seigniorage, the profit accruing to government when currency costs less to produce than the value at which it is put into circulation. There was ordinarily no seigniorage as

2

such when the cowrie entered Africa. A profit, as on any other item of merchandise, may well have accrued to the initial producers in the Indian Ocean or to European buyers and shippers (we examine profitability in chapter 9), but this would not seem to fit the standard definition of seigniorage. Seigniorage might still have occurred if governments (or merchant groups) within West Africa could have exploited a monopoly position to keep shells scarce and thus put them into circulation at a price above that at which they were acquired. There are hints of this in the discounting of the Dahomean monarchy, and the speculations of treasury officials in Bornu after 1849, but leaky frontiers and ease of smuggling would no doubt have made the maintenance of such seigniorage very difficult.

In one last respect, the cowrie could very well serve as an object lesson in a money and banking class of today. Dramatically and convincingly, near the end of its life as a working money it suffered a hyperinflation that demonstrates nicely the wide application of both the Quantity Theory of Money and Gresham's Law. The Quantity Theory of Irving Fisher states that the stock of money (M) multiplied by the number of times that money is spent each year (velocity, V) must equal the annual value of all transactions, PQ, where Q is the number of transactions and P is the average price level. $MV = PQ$. When an economy is growing, Q rises and therefore, with V relatively constant, the stock of money M can also rise without affecting the level of prices. But should M expand much more rapidly than Q, the theory predicts the likelihood of rises in P, i.e. inflation. The cowrie currency conforms to the predictions of this theory remarkably well. As long as the small shells from the atolls of the Maldives were the only ones imported to West Africa (true for half a millennium at least), the limited growth rate in M did not significantly outrun the growth of the domestic economy, so that the value of the cowrie expressed in goods was relatively stable. But when the East African variety of the cowrie suddenly was poured into West Africa by European traders in the years after 1845 (see chapters 6 and 9 for details), it generated a hyperinflation that ultimately destroyed the usefulness of the shell money standard (which by that time was mainly associated with the palm-oil trade, and not with slaving).[5] At the same time, Gresham's Law – "bad money drives out the good" – was in full operation. The East African shells were much cheaper than the smaller variety produced in the Maldives; wherever they proved acceptable, they were paid out by the importing merchants to the point that the shells from the atolls virtually disappeared in some areas.

The great cowrie inflation was not the only example of a "primitive" money badly depreciated by oversupply; the copper and brass currencies of Africa were much eroded by improved manufacturing techniques in Europe, and similar advances in the fabrication of wampum beads ruined that famous American Indian currency.[6] But the cowrie inflation is best documented, and demonstrates clearly how Fisher's rule and Gresham's

Law both apply in a world far removed from the coins, paper, and bank deposits for which they were formulated.

In the chapters that follow we examine West Africa's shell money in a format that is both geographical and chronological. The first seven chapters concentrate on the demand and supply of cowries – why they were wanted, where they came from, and how they got to Africa – emphasizing the changing nature of the trade from the sixteenth to the nineteenth centuries. The next two chapters discuss their zone of circulation in West Africa, their values, methods of counting, the economics of the trade, and the cowrie hyperinflation. Our last chapter examines the decline and eventual demonetization (without compensation to the last holders) during the colonial period, and the surprising survival of the shells as money, still used in at least one area as a way to evade currency controls. It concludes by examining the economic transformation in the Maldives where the shells were produced. Indeed they still are produced, though not for use as money; new markets have been found, and the fishing still goes on as it has done for a thousand years and more.

1

The cowrie

The "contemptible shells of the Maldives" which "prove the price of Mankind" are money cowries, *Cypraea moneta*. The word cowrie is taken direct from the Hindi and Urdu *kauri* and has a Sanskrit origin.[1] The Latin name *Cypraea* derives from the island of Cyprus where Aphrodite (Venus) was worshipped as a goddess of fertility. Many peoples are said to have seen in the long slender orifice of the shell's underside the "one entrance into life," in the delicate phrasing of Grafton Elliott Smith.[2] A cowrie worn around a woman's neck was supposed to promote conception and ease childbirth.

The little live gastropod is singularly unappealing at close quarters. Its tiny body, striped, somewhat dark in color and definitely slimy, appears to exude from its shell. It is an omnivore with graceless eating habits, consuming with its ribbon-like tongue (*radula*) algae, polyps, some corals, and animal detritus such as half-consumed fish or excrement. Sexes are separate, and reproduction efficient enough to supply vast quantities – entirely suitable for a fertility symbol. It is quite variable in size, adults ranging from less than half an inch to over an inch and a half in length.[3] (The larger examples were always less acceptable as money because by boosting weight per unit they increased transport costs.) About three-quarters of an inch was a typical length for shells in the trade.

Young shells are toothless and have a large aperture on their underside that narrows with adulthood. The function of the teeth that line this aperture is uncertain, but possibly concerns feeding, cleaning, or the evasion of predators.[4] In terms of money and trade, the inhabitant of the shell is an unwelcome intruder. Only with its demise and the decay of its body is the shell revealed as lustrous, creamy-white with a slight hint of yellow, easily reflecting light and altogether attractive.[5]

The slightly asymmetrical shell, resembling that of a tortoise in miniature, and standing about a quarter of an inch high, slips and slides easily along a hard surface. That makes it an obvious plaything and gambling counter.[6] Its attractive appearance leads to understandable use in decoration that has lasted to this day. Its easy portability meant it could be carried vast distances from its habitat, and the "added charm of novelty touched with mystery" no doubt helped to give the cowrie its place in religious ritual as a charm, an amulet, or as a "giver of life."[7]

There are other traits, though, that are more central to our story. It can be accurately traded by weight, by volume, or by counting. For such a light object, about 400 to the pound, it is very solid and thus extremely durable. It does not seem to fade as rapidly as other species, and there is no obvious difference between shells purchased in West African markets today (most of which must have come from the Indian Ocean a century and more ago) and shells seen during the Maldive fieldwork that were alive within the year. Even though very light in weight, they can be compared in durability to metal coins, and are difficult to break. In a tumbler we rotated a sample at a speed promoting abrasion; more than thirty hours later, when the experiment was stopped, there was still no apparent wear. In a "survivability test" undertaken on a hard surface with examples chosen at random, a research assistant weighing 110 lbs. could not break even one by hurling, treading heavily, or stamping with the foot. A much larger person could not crush any shell with repeated stamps when the tooth aperture was turned downward, but was able to do so when the aperture was pointed upward. An ordinary footfall will not break them. As Karl Polanyi has said, they can thus be "poured, sacked, shoveled, hoarded in heaps, kept buried in the soil, chuted like gravel" while remaining "clean, dainty, stainless, polished, and milk-white."[8] Unharmed by water, even bilge-water, a ship could use them for ballast; at voyage's end after a washing they would appear as clean as if carefully cared for en route.

The money cowrie is almost impossible to counterfeit. King Gezo of Dahomey told the explorer Richard Burton that he preferred them to gold for that reason. (Shrewdly, the king also pointed out that a hoard of shells is much harder to hide from the tax collector than the equivalent value in gold.) Over 1,800 years earlier, the metal coinage of a Chinese emperor had been so disastrously clipped and counterfeited that in A.D. 10 he decreed a return to the ancient cowrie standard. A related cowrie, the *Cypraea annulus* of the East African coast, Red Sea, and Indian Ocean basin, could often pass for *moneta* in color, shape, and size, but unwitting substitutions between the two shells cannot occur. Every example of *annulus* ("ring" in Latin) has a little tell-tale yellow-orange circle on the crown of the shell.[9]

Adult money cowries are esthetically satisfying to handle, actually easier to lift off a flat surface than a metallic coin, and pleasant to look at. They are thoroughly homogeneous once odd sizes and "dead shells" are culled out (see the discussion in chapter 7 about preparation).[10] Their cost per individual shell was so very low, even thousands of miles from where they were fished, that one unit of the cowrie if used as a currency would be less in value than any metallic coin of copper, bronze, or iron. This very low "natural unit value" was appropriate where incomes and prices were also very low, and where otherwise suitable small change for accurate payment

6

would have been hard to find.[11] But low cost could be disastrous if it meant constant and unlimited supply. We shall see that for hundreds of years supply *was* limited by the royal monopoly in the Maldive Islands, their only major source.

Finally, unlike the world's other commodity currencies – gold, silver, iron, copper, other metals, cloth strips, tobacco, liquor, etc. – there was very little "leakage" into commodity use. Aside from religious ritual, decoration, and playthings, the shells had only the very limited value of their lime content. With lime usually available in the form of limestone in many parts of the world (though less so in West Africa), this aspect of the cowrie became significant only when a residual use had to be found for large demonetized stocks – as eventually happened during the colonial period.[12]

All these attributes – long-lasting, durable, easy to handle, portable, hard to counterfeit, right unit value for market needs, adequate constraints on supply, and little leakage into other uses – are mentioned by money and banking texts as the properties of the ideal commodity money.[13] Cowries were never the perfect ideal. But for a currency in regions of low income, their advantages were great.

THE COWRIE'S RANGE

Cypraea moneta and *Cypraea annulus*, two of the approximately two hundred recognized species of cowrie, occur quite widely where waters are warm and lagoons are shallow in the basins of the Indian and Pacific Oceans. Map 1 shows cowrie habitats ranging from the Red Sea to Mozambique in the west, to Japan, Hawaii, New Zealand, and the Galapagos in the east.[14] *Moneta* and *annulus* often occur together, lending confusion to the identification of large sources of supply. But due to the principle of "competitive exclusion of closely related species," one or the other dominates, frequently by a ratio of 100 to 1. Major concentrations of *moneta* exist in the Sulu Islands southwest of the main Philippine Islands and are a source of exports to the latter and to China and Indochina; in present-day Indonesia (especially from Bima near Makassar, Borneo, and coastal Sumatra) and the Ryukyu Islands, which supplied the shell to both China and Japan.[15] There are mentions of occurrences at two spots on the China coast, where they are otherwise rare, and on various Philippine Islands among the predominant *annulus*.[16]

Over a small part of their range, both the money cowrie and *annulus* are found in great quantity in the same locations. A case in point is the Seychelles. Here *moneta* is classified as "common," with *annulus* "easily the most abundant."[17] Collection of just one of the species thus becomes a time-consuming process of sifting through a mass of shells and rejecting many, with large-scale supply accordingly less practical.

Remarkably, one part of one small chain of islands, the Maldives of the Indian Ocean, was the source of most of the *moneta* entering world trade.

7

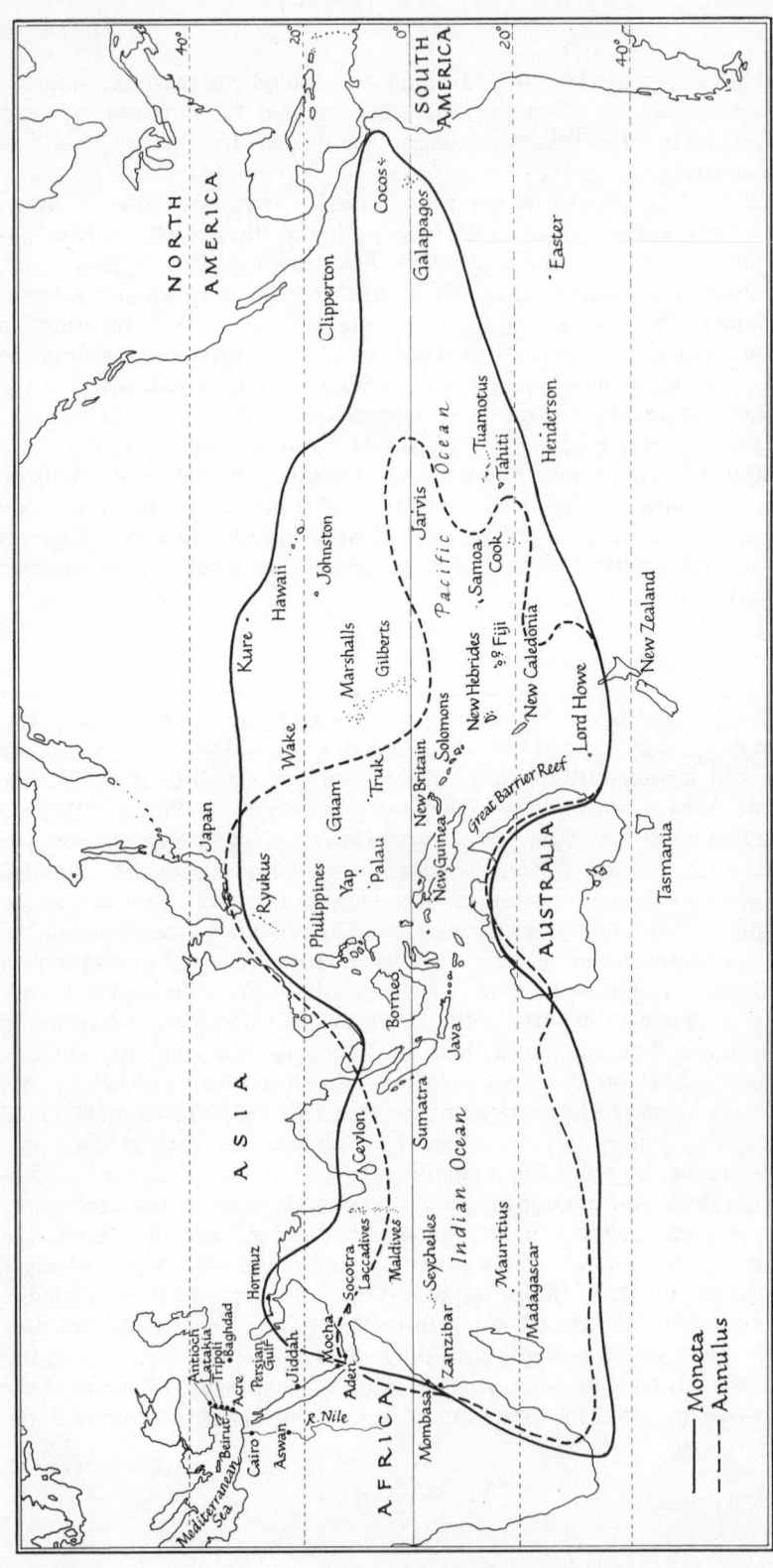

Map 1 Range of *Cypraea moneta* and *Cypraea annulus* (Adapted from Burgess, *Living Cowries*, pp. 342–343)

8

The fact of its unique position as a supplier has long been recognized and is generally agreed upon. Cowries are not found in like quantity "in any part of the world but the Maldive Islands" claimed Tavernier in a volume published in 1684. "Above all from the Maldives," wrote Dr. von Martens in 1871; "in greatest amounts" from there, stated Oskar Schneider in 1905. "Famous from the earliest times for their wealth in cowries, and [with some exaggeration] the sole source of supply of this currency to India and Africa," stated J. Allan in 1912. "The Maldive Islands have been, since time immemorial, the principal finding place of cowries," according to Paul Einzig in 1949, and "primary producer of cowries" and "the major world exporter," in the view of James Heimann in 1980.[18]

Several south-central atolls of the Maldives are especially important sources of supply. These atolls are Haddummati, Huvadu (Suvadiva), Kolumadulu and Ari[19] (see Map 2). Exactly *why* the money cowrie is so abundant in these atolls is not completely clear. Malacologists speculate that the vast quantities may be due to a plentiful supply of foods, a relative absence of predators, or especially favorable reproductive conditions, the latter perhaps influenced by ocean currents. Flat lagoons of vast area and a sizeable tidal range allow good fishing conditions.[20]

Adding to the advantages, in the Maldives *moneta* is not only abundant, but it occurs in relatively "pure stands". *Annulus* is not much present, for example, so that the sorting problem encountered in the Seychelles does not apply.[21]

There is one additional explanation for the unique prominence of the Maldives. It concerns the size of the shells, and is significant for the economics of their export. One individual money cowrie when used as currency always had the same purchasing power as any other, whether that other was slightly larger or slightly smaller. Thus, as we have already noted, the smaller the shell, the greater the number in each pound shipped, the more profitable for the merchants and traders who carried them to their eventual markets, and the more convenient for users in those markets. There is good reason to believe that shells from the main producing atolls of the Maldives are *smaller* than the world average for *Cypraea moneta*.

The size of cowries used as money has been a vexed question, with many differences of opinion. A. H. Quiggin states that *moneta* is often called the large cowrie, M. Hiskett states that *moneta* is normally considered to be larger and *annulus* smaller, and A. G. Hopkins agreed.[22] Others affirm the opposite: Marion Johnson says *annulus* is "somewhat larger;" "*C. annulus* is markedly larger than the *C. moneta*" according to Philip D. Curtin; John Hertz compared "die kleinen Maldive" shells to "die grosseren" cowries from Zanzibar; Paul Einzig says the same.[23] The reason why such a disagreement could come about is hinted at by Quiggin in a sentence also quoted by Hiskett: "Size is an unsafe guide in conchology, and the *Cypraea* are notoriously variable."[24] This is correct. The scientific literature on

9

cowries does indeed emphasize variability in size. More than that, however, we shall see that there was an important *economic* aspect to the size of the shells reaching Africa.

Various studies have determined world-wide maxima and minima for the shell length of adult examples, and have also (somewhat heroically) attempted to establish world-wide averages. The Schilders, lifelong students of the cowrie in nature, in their article "The Size of 95,000 Cowries," found a range for *moneta* from 10 mm. minimum to a maximum of 44 mm., with a median length of 20 mm.[25] Another authority, Dr. C. M. Burgess of Honolulu, quotes a world *moneta* range from 12.2 mm. to 38.5 mm. This range is also given by J. G. Walls in the second edition of his book *Cowries*, along with an average length of 23.6 mm.[26] These scholars have also found the size of *annulus* to be highly variable as well. The range quoted by Dr. Burgess is 12.6 mm. to 29.0 mm., while Walls states it to be 10 mm. to 34 mm., with an average length of 24.2 mm. Virginia Orr's study from Zanzibar gives a slightly smaller *annulus* average of 21 mm.[27] The upshot is that the apparently contradictory claims of the economic historians all have some foundation in fact. The range figures show that some *moneta* are larger than all *annulus*. The studies indicate the average *moneta* is smaller than the average *annulus* (but not by much, 23.6 mm. to 24.2 mm. according to Walls or 20 mm. to 21 mm. using the data of the Schilders and Virginia Orr).

The real reason for the contradictory statements of the economic historians is that the money cowries occurring in the main producing atolls of the Maldive Islands appear to be significantly smaller than *moneta* in many other parts of its habitat. This would of course explain a great deal. Those who have examined *moneta* in the markets where it was used as currency (West Africa, for example) would find the "small Maldives" as they came to be known in the trade. These shells would be distinctly less large than the *annulus* of East Africa. Further, if Maldive shells are indeed undersize, then those atolls would obviously have a comparative advantage based on transport costs that would, predictably, lead them to be preferred as a source of shell money. The economist would find this a satisfying demonstration of one of the major principles of location theory.

Evidence that Maldive *moneta* from the major producing atolls is small in size was obtained during the 1982 fieldwork. Hogendorn brought back from the islands about a thousand shells, most obtained from a commercial supplier, and exactly 220 from the fisher-ladies of Guraidhoo Island in the southerly region of major production. The *largest* shell from the commercial firm measured 23 mm., just under the world-wide *average* quoted by Walls. The three largest given to Hogendorn at Guraidhoo were 19 mm. The mean of the 220 Guraidhoo shells was 16 mm.; numerous shells measured only 12–14 mm. Compare the smallest length in samples of *moneta* measured by Crawford Cate and the Schilders in various issues of *The Veliger* from 1964 to 1969.[28]

Place	Minimum length in sample (mms.)
Hawaii	21.0
West Australia	18.8
Philippines	16.4
Ryukyus	15.0
East Pacific	25.1
Guam	16.8
Thailand	23

Only in the Ryukyus was the *smallest* shell in the sample equal to the average of those brought back from the southern Maldives. We attempted to confirm these findings with various specialists in malacology. Research staff of the Academy of Natural Sciences, Philadelphia, investigated their collection at our request and as a result wrote the following: "*Cypraea moneta* from the Maldives are notably small (as indicated by our collection, which I feel is representative)." The Academy's collection fortunately included examples from one of the atolls identified as a major producer, Ari. The lot (number ANSP 303922), measured 10.5 mm. to 15 mm., with most about 12–13 mm., smaller even than the shells brought back by Hogendorn.[29]

For a time it was quite a puzzle as to *why* the cowries from the Maldives were small. An explanation was provided by Walter Sage of the Invertebrate Department of the American Museum of Natural History, New York City, who described for us the "Rule of Bergmann" which dates from 1847. As it applies to molluscs, Bergmann's Rule states that the warmest waters produce the smallest specimens.[30] It then required only reference to the *Oceanographic Atlas of the Indian Ocean* to discover that the southern atolls of the Maldives are not only in an area of exceptionally warm and shallow ocean water (above 80°F. every month of the year, and usually above 82°) but are also on the equator, their shallow lagoons thus receiving maximum solar radiation. Strikingly, only a very few areas including parts of coastal Sumatra and a portion of the southwestern Pacific Ocean share this year-round very high water temperature plus direct equatorial solar heat.[31] In these very warm waters the cowries do not attain large size as frequently as elsewhere, with higher proportions of the small ecotype "E" (as described by the Schilders) rather than their other ecotypes which are classified as medium, rather large, and large.[32]

Of course, large money cowries do occur in the Maldives, perhaps even more frequently than our limited samples show. But the entrepreneurs of shell-money would be interested not in the outliers, but in the averages. The relatively small mean size in the Maldives would satisfy shippers and customers at every stage by cutting transport costs and reducing the waste and labor if large shells had to be culled out and disposed of. This discussion should clarify both the long-standing debate on the size of the shells, while

11

at the same time casting light on why the Maldive Islands, especially the southern atolls of the group, were for centuries the world's major producer of shell money.

Another debate has long surrounded the question of whether the money cowrie occurs on the coasts of Africa. Some writers, including the careful German scholar Oskar Schneider, have stated flatly that *moneta*'s habitat extends neither to West nor to East Africa. This contention is clearly not correct, with every modern scientific study available to us indicating that *moneta* does indeed occur on the shores of Mozambique, Tanganyika, and Zanzibar. But it is much rarer than *annulus*, which occurs by the many thousand million on these coasts. Fieldwork by Virginia Orr Maes in Zanzibar revealed *moneta* in quantities of 15 or more at only one of 23 localities sampled. *Annulus* was overwhelmingly dominant, a good example of the competitive exclusion of closely related species referred to earlier.[33] It is true, however, that no *moneta* (nor *annulus*) occurs at all in West Africa. Von Martens states that all the early mentions of living money cowries in that area are false,[34] representing perhaps mistaken identification of other species of cowries, or the inferior olive shells ("zimbos" of the genus *Olivella*) of Angola which were used as money in Central Africa and even imported there from Brazil.[35] Shipwrecks are a second source of confusion, since money cowries will be found washed up on the beaches for many years after a wreck.[36] But the mistake of believing that the creature's habitat includes West Africa is still perpetrated, excused perhaps by incredulity that every one of the little shells still encountered in that area had to be shipped such vast distances.[37]

WHERE THE COWRIE FOUND USE

J. Wilfrid Jackson's map of areas where the cowrie was put to use ranges across the world from Western Europe and West Africa out to Oceania and even to North America. It may indeed be safe to say, as do Safer and Gill, that the shells "have circulated as currency in more places in the world than any coin".[38] Earliest references to cowrie use are ancient, and come from China. Paul Einzig dates their circulation as money to an extremely early period, claiming that the Chinese invaders of the twenty-fourth century B.C. found indigenous peoples employing the shells as currency. Einzig and other authorities allude to one of the oldest of Chinese books, of possibly the fourteenth century B.C., and its statement that a hundred thousand dead shell-fish are the equivalent of riches, to show very early Chinese use of cowries.[39] The dating of these and other Chinese literary sources has been seriously challenged,[40] but there seems no reason to doubt that in China by the seventh century B.C., cowries were in circulation, edicts against hoarding them had been issued, shortages of supply had been experienced, and (toward the end of that century) metallic cowries had been manufactured and issued.[41] Various bans on the use of shell-money in the third and fourth

12

centuries B.C., and another ban by Wang Mang in A.D. 14 after the temporary resurrection of four years before, all point to long-continuing cowrie use in China.[42] The literary evidence is buttressed by many early archaeological finds, and by the widespread use of the *pei* character in Chinese (meaning "sea creatures which live in shells") in the early depiction of words such as money, buying, selling, tribute, miserly, expensive, cheap, valuable, hoarding, and many others.[43] When Marco Polo visited China (1271–1291) he found cowries still used in Yunnan, but they were fading and by the nineteenth century had gone out of monetary use though still found as ornaments.[44]

On China's south and southwest borders were areas of large-scale use in Indochina, Thailand, and Burma (Arakan and Pegu). The southeast Asian part of the cowrie zone is of especial interest because supplies of shell flowed there both from the Maldives and from Sulu and Indonesia.[45]

To China's east, in Japan, money cowries have been found in some quantity, apparently mostly imports from the Ryukyu Islands to the south. But there is debate whether they were ever actually used as a currency there, Schneider believing they were, while Quiggin and Jackson are doubtful.[46]

Far away in the Pacific were other peoples employing the cowrie as a means for transactions. Strings of *moneta* could be used to make purchases in the Sandwich Islands (Hawaii) in the nineteenth century.[47] In the South Pacific, *moneta* passed as money in New Caledonia and served for ornamentation and decoration in Tahiti, the Gilbert and Ellice Islands, the New Hebrides, and in New Guinea.[48] The German adventurer P. Wirz found a people along western New Guinea's Dika River whose cowrie money was so scarce that a single shell could command more than one knife or ax. After shipping in three cases from the coast at heavy expense, he was discomfited to find there were special requirements of size, weight, and color – only two dozen shells among his many thousand qualified.[49]

Half a hemisphere away in Europe, money cowries were used for decoration and religious ritual (though not as money) from prehistoric times. Quiggin suggests they found their way along the early trade routes for amber and other high-value products. They have often been found, near the skeletons of women, in burials at English pit-dwellings, in Saxon caves, near Frankfurt, on a Swedish island, in Lithuanian and Latvian graves, along the Caucasus, and elsewhere. Cowries were fabricated in bronze by the Etruscans, and in gold by Cypriots.[50] The shells even reached North America, where they found use as sacred objects among the Ojibwa and Menomini Indians. Though Jackson concluded that this must imply pre-Columbian contacts across the Pacific, the fact appears to be different though hardly less interesting: the shells were imported by the Hudson's Bay Company to barter for furs. Other areas of the Americas received shell imports during the slave trade, no doubt in part due to a demand by transplanted black Africans who had known the cowrie in their homeland.[51]

THE GREAT MARKETS: BENGAL AND WEST AFRICA

Of all their areas of use, money cowries were in greatest demand and of longest-lasting circulation in India (primarily Bengal) and in West Africa. Both regions were supplied from the Maldives.

Moneta has been found repeatedly at prehistoric sites in India, and was in very early use as an amulet to ward off the "evil eye," as adornment for females, and as decoration for domesticated animals.[52] Some authorities believe it was used as money prior to the expedition of Alexander the Great, and there have been finds associated with coins at excavations of sites from the first century A.D.[53] Sushil Chandra De suggests that early trading contacts between India and China would have led to knowledge of the latter's successful cowrie currency; this opinion seems reasonable.[54]

For the first eye-witness accounts of the cowrie in India we are indebted to observant Chinese travellers. Fah-Hian, in about A.D. 400, reported shells in use at Mathura along the Jumna River between Delhi and Agra (see Map 3). "They use shells for money in their traffic."[55] Hsuan-tsang (*c.* A.D. 640) saw cowries employed as currency during his Indian travels.[56] Early stone inscriptions in Orissa record their use.[57] A steady flow of evidence attests to their continuing circulation after that time. Al-Mas'udi the Arab traveller wrote (*c.* 943), "trading affairs are carried on with *cowries* which are the money of the country."[58] A twelfth-century treatise on mathematics written in Hindi illustrates fractions (and heaps scorn on an avaricious miser in so doing) with cowrie shells as the lowest common denominator.[59] Thirteenth-century accounts treat the shells as commonplace. Chau Ju-Kua called cowries the currency of India; Tabakat-i-Nasiri reported on them in Bengal *circa* 1240; Minhaj-us-Siraj said, around 1242–1244, that in Bengal nothing circulated except cowries.[60]

Less than seventy years before the Portuguese arrived in India, the Chinese traveller Ma Huan found the cowrie central in the economic life of Bengal ("Pang-ko-la" he writes); he noted that monetary values were calculated in units of cowrie.[61] When the Portuguese came on the scene after 1498, they found numerous areas using shell money, especially Orissa and Bengal on the bay of that name. This abundance of cowries had great commercial interest for the European newcomers, as we shall see. By the seventeenth century, the cowrie as money was circulating widely in India, in the plains of the north and northwest, along the east coast, and in the high Deccan (though not along the Malabar coast opposite the Maldives nor in Ceylon.)[62] Frank Perlin has recently produced a thorough accounting of their employment in India during this period, based on an extensive search of sources.[63] Though contraction of the cowrie zone took place in the eighteenth century, circulation remained vast in Bengal and Orissa, which became the major trans-shipment point for the shell money of the slave trade.

THE COWRIE IN WEST AFRICA

The cowrie shell first reached its other great market, West Africa, via a route still somewhat shadowy and controversial – although less controversial than it was before Hiskett published his persuasive essay.[64] Archaeological discoveries indicate Egypt as the first area where *moneta* made its appearance, it being found in small quantities (together with *annulus*) in several pre-dynastic burial sites and at Karnak. The main apparent uses were as charms and amulets, although Jackson allows the possibility (incorrectly, we believe) that they may have seen very ancient use as money.[65]

By the Middle Ages, a major market for cowries is said to have existed at Cairo.[66] This is likely, as we discuss in chapter 2, but the case is largely circumstantial and by no means certain. There are some references in the medieval *Geniza* documents explored by S. D. Goitein, and other scattered mentions of Cairo noted later in the text. Ivan Hrbek was moved to say that the evidence is so meagre that it "does not justify the conclusion that the main flow of the cowries to the Sudan in the period before the fifteenth century passed through Egypt."[67] Levantine ports at the end of trade routes from the Persian Gulf, such as Antioch, Latakia, Tripoli, Beirut, and Acre, could also have served as transit points. Venice, too, may have been an eventual entrepôt for Africa, and Philip D. Curtin may be correct in stating that some cowries, having first come to Egypt by way of the Red Sea, were "trans-shipped by way of Venice to the Maghrib and then across the Sahara. . . ."

Certainly they were known there at the time of Marco Polo, called by him *porcellani*, from the diminutive of *porco*, pig. Etymologies attribute the name to the hog-backed shape of the shell, or in what is surely a flight of imagination, the resemblance of its fissured underside to a sow's vulva. The *Oxford English Dictionary* notes the interesting transfer of this word's meaning from sea-shells to China-ware. The term "little pig" survived for centuries in the cowrie trade. A Portuguese pilot wrote about 1540 of the "shells which in Italia are called porcellette – little white ones which we call *buzios*, and which are used for money in Ethiopia [Africa]". They were still known as "porcelains" in eighteenth-century Marseilles, and even in the nineteenth century Germans were calling them "Porzellanschnecken."[68]

Whether arriving through Cairo or other ports on the Mediterranean, cowrie shells first trickled across the Sahara to the African empires along the great bend of the Niger River. Though we cannot know with certainty, it is most likely that a few would have been carried in a trader's pack or on his person as a lucky charm. We can postulate first familiarity and then a demand on a small scale. The familiarity might even have come much earlier, since the shells have been found in Punic graves and the Carthaginians possibly had some over-desert trading contact with black Africa. The Romans, too, had the cowrie, and posts deep in the Sahara.[69]

The first we know from written accounts is early enough as it is. The Arab geographer al-Bakri, in a passage relating to A.D. 1067, wrote of Kougha (probably down river from present-day Gao in Mali and one-time capital of the Songhay Empire), that cowries were among the city's imported goods (see Map 7). Al-Bakri says nothing of their use as money, and he was usually alert to currency forms in areas about which he wrote. But at least the mention indicates quantities large enough to obtain notice.[70] Another traveller, al-Zuhri, in a manuscript dating between 1154 and 1161, simply notes cowrie imports; but the next Arab reference, by Ibn Sa'id who died 1274, is a clear statement of how the shells came across the desert. He wrote of merchants travelling from Sijilmassa (just across the Atlas Range in southern Morocco) to the ancient Ghana Empire carrying cargoes of copper, cowries, figs, and salt.[71] A recent archaeological discovery, near the caravan route from Sijilmassa to the Ghana Empire, confirms that shells were coming along the trans-Saharan routes before they came by sea. At Ma'den Ijafen, in what our maps tell us is a particularly inhospitable stretch of the Mauritanian Sahara, an abandoned caravan has been uncovered, revealing skeletal remains, fragments of cloth, and part of a cargo of cowries.[72]

It is said that one of the Askiyas of Songhay found cowries imported from Cairo were cheaper than those from Morocco, which were henceforth banned. Some years later, in 1591, Askiya Ishaq proposed to end the ban and renew the importation of cowries from Morocco as part of his offer of homage to the Sultan Mawlay Ahmad al-Mansur.[73] (A small caravan traffic in cowries, anachronistic in the era of large maritime shipments, survived to be reported in the eighteenth century. The old caravan route from Morocco to West Africa was still in use during that century [and the next], the shells by this time coming from Asia to European ports and thence to North Africa for the desert crossing. The English and the Dutch are known to have been importing them into Morocco at the end of the eighteenth century,[74] and some shells are known to have been passing through Meknes early in the century.[75] A few may also have made the more easterly desert crossing from Tripoli to Hausaland in the later part of the eighteenth century.)[76] Daumas's account of trade and routes in the "Algerian Sahara" in 1845, based on recent interviews, includes references to the purchase of cowries (*ouda'*) at Tidikelt by caravans bound for Timbuktu and Jenne, "which, having reached Timbuktu, serve as money;" and at Nefta (now in Tunisia) "the shells of Tunis called *el ouda'* which serve as money when they reach the Soudan [i.e. Hausaland]."[77]

To the fourteenth century, there is still no confirmed reference to the use of the shells as money in West Africa. The first report comes in the *Masalik al-absar* of al-'Umari (died 1349) where he states that "all internal business transactions" in the Mali Empire are "in cowries imported by the merchants at a considerable profit."[78] Some twenty years after this, the intrepid traveller Ibn Battuta saw them used as money in the Mali Empire. His account is noteworthy because he is the only known person before the age of European participation in the trade actually to see at first hand the cowries fished in the Maldives (see chapter 2) and their use as money in West Africa.[79] There is a reference, from the fifteenth century (in the *Ta'rikh al-Fattash*), to cowries being used for payment in the Mali Empire, and Leo Africanus saw them used as small change in Timbuktu early in the sixteenth century.[80] By this time, they are being mentioned by European writers. On his first voyage of 1455, Cadamosto heard of their use inland from Arguin, and as a Venetian he recognized them as "those small kinds which are brought to Venice from the Levant."[81]

Concerning the flow of shells to West Africa, there was once current a theory that on the present evidence is highly improbable. This theory suggests that the cowries came from east to west, overland from the Indian Ocean. It seems to have originated by J. Wilfred Jackson's *Shells as Evidence*, and is based on Jackson's scholarly map showing the world-wide distribution of cowrie use.[82] The map shows a band of use right across Africa from the coasts near Zanzibar to West Africa. But the map stands as a warning to archaeologists and economic historians, because distribution need not be (in this case it is not) tantamount to the direction of imports. The mistake has been perpetuated by G. I. Jones, who says, "Cowries, which are shells found in the Maldive Islands, must originally have come overland through the Eastern Sudan and East Africa ... "; by M. D. W. Jeffreys who writes, "This shell, whose origin is the Red Sea and Indian Ocean, ... must have spread from East to West"; and by Sir Hamilton Gibb in his edition of Ibn Battuta, "The existence of a cowry exchange in the Malli empire ... is conclusive evidence of the commercial relations across the African continent ... , as cowries are found in Africa only on the east coast."[83] In our opinion Hiskett has demolished these never very probable arguments by pointing out the lack of evidence for east–west shipment; the impracticability of camel porterage on part of the route; the absence of the cowrie in Bornu and Kanem astride the supposed route of importation; the statement of the *Kano Chronicle* that the cowrie made its first appearance in Hausaland in the eighteenth century (it actually arrived earlier, as we shall show in chapter 8, but still centuries after major use had developed in the west); and the relatively recent importance of the cowrie as currency in East Africa.[84] (Cowries were indeed of little significance in East Africa until quite late in the day. A mention of shell exports in the early Greek *Periplus* is obscure, and probably refers to tortoise shells.[85] Ibn Battuta, who mentioned cowries often on his travels, failed to do so on his visits to Mombasa and Kilwa in the fourteenth century, nor did the early Portuguese visitors record their use as money.[86] Only in the nineteenth century did the shells achieve importance in East Africa. In inland Uganda, they are said to have been introduced during the last quarter of the eighteenth century, and were originally so rare that "two shells would buy a woman."[87])

Hiskett does not exclude the possibility that an occasional specimen might have trickled through from east to west. He does insist, reasonably we believe, "that there is no general pattern of early or consistent cowry use throughout East Africa such as would justify us in believing that East Africa was the *point de départ* for the diffusion of the shells across the continent. . . . Thus the broad band which Jackson shows stretching from east to west across Africa is not necessarily the line of entry, but merely a line of retrieval."[88]

In short, as European navigators and merchants were making their initial contacts with West Africa, they found cowries in wide use as money, and in even wider use as charms for decoration (though, of course, in much smaller quantity). The earliest cowrie currency area that we can trace was, as we have seen, on the upper and middle Niger. It extended by the fourteenth century to the Mali Empire with an eastward protrusion to Gao, capital of Songhay, and finally included Timbuktu, Jenne, and also probably the Bambara country (western part of old Mali) by the early sixteenth century. It is not possible to tell whether, during these early centuries, the imports were a deliberate act of state (for there were elements of strong centralized government in these areas), or a market response by a well-organized group of merchants, or the result of a myriad of individual economic decisions. A combination of all three is perhaps likely. Nor is it clear in the desert-edge cowrie zone whether the trans-Saharan imports were the more acceptable because they replaced an existing shell money procured on the Atlantic coast. Philip D. Curtin has written that the "usual hypothesis is that other, local shells were already in use as currency, which prompted North African merchants who knew of the Indian-Ocean cowrie zone to introduce the exotic shells."[89] It was possible, in the late eighteenth century, for shells other than cowries – such as the various striped Atlantic *Persicula cingulata*, *Marginella amygdala*, and *Columbella rustica* – to be put into circulation temporarily as a substitute for *moneta* at a time when the latter was exceptionally scarce. For the inflation so caused, see chapter 9.[90]

Whatever the motive for introducing the money cowrie, and whether or not it replaced an already-existing shell money, there is no reason to doubt that *moneta* was in continuous use as currency in the major markets of the middle Niger, certainly from the fourteenth century and possibly from the eleventh. That use was spreading, in spite of the tremendous distances involved. In their zone of circulation, they were some 3,000 miles of caravan and sea travel distant from their points of distribution in the Eastern Mediterranean. In turn these points were more than 3,000 miles away via either the Red Sea or the Persian Gulf from their source of supply at the Maldives, and about the same distance from their other great area of monetary use, Bengal. The distances were colossal, but they were to become larger yet when the Europeans entered the trade.

It is another long leap, nearly a thousand miles as the crow flies, from Timbuktu southeast to the beaches of the Gulf of Guinea near Benin. Here when the Portuguese arrived in the late 1480s they found a shell-currency in

18

use, the only one recorded along the West African coast at that early date. It is unlikely, however, that many of these shells were *moneta*. Small olive shells (genus *Olivella*), somewhat similar to cowries but lacking the characteristic lip, were found in quantity on some West African beaches. These *Olivella nana* are abundant at Luanda Island in northern Angola; known locally as "zimbos," these Atlantic shells were the dominant currency in the Kingdom of Kongo and its vicinity.[91] There is no large local supply of *Olivella* near Benin, so the shells in use there may well have been an import of zimbos from more southerly waters. Our major reference, Pacheco Pereira, does not appear to think so, however. He writes that "In the country of Beny . . . they use as money shells which they call Iguou, a little longer than the 'zimbos' of Manicongo. They use them to buy everything, and he that has most of them is the richest."[92] What these shells were is still unsettled; the question awaits treatment by archaeologists. In any case, the Portuguese rapidly (at latest just after 1515) introduced Indian Ocean *moneta*. Their immediate acceptance by the population at Benin and in the Forcados River may suggest that some of the Maldive shells may already have been circulating. They may have seeped through down the River Niger from their main area of use. A few East African shells may have also trickled through, as A. F. C. Ryder suggests, but this is much less likely.[93] Whatever the origins of the pre-Portuguese currency, an outpost of the money cowrie was soon established on what later came to be the Slave Coast; in time this became a major area of circulation.

A quarter of a world apart, in India and West Africa, were regions where a cowrie currency reigned. In both areas, their use as decoration was always geographically wider, but in quantity far smaller, than their use as money.[94] In both areas, the supply was largely from the Maldives. But there were also three major dissimilarities. In Bengal the shells were handled loose, like coins, while in parts of West Africa they often came to be strung like beads. In Bengal, the Maldive market was so near that small coasting vessels could carry any quantity; but a major expansion of seaborne trade to West Africa would require large ocean-going ships capable of sailing to windward that only the Europeans possessed. Finally, in the markets of Bengal the little shells were used only to buy food, clothing, plus all the hundred other humble and harmless items of domestic life; whereas in West Africa the cowrie also became the shell money of the slave trade.

2

The Maldive Islands

A traveller on a night flight from London or Paris to Colombo's Katunayake Airport is still an hour away from the delights and troubles of Sri Lanka when the dark sea below suddenly commands attention. Dozens of little lights wink from horizon to horizon in a rough north–south alignment. They are the kerosene lamps, Coleman lanterns, and occasional electric bulbs run from the generators of the island chiefs of the Republic of Maldives. The greater glow is from Male, the capital. Many travellers backtrack from Sri Lanka for a week at one of the lovely resort islands; many others arrive direct at Male by charter flight. During Europe's winter these tourists find an ideal climate, with warm weather, reasonable humidity, breezes stirring the coconut palms, and breakers crashing over the coral reefs that ring the atolls' shallow lagoons. In the few villages that tourists are permitted to visit (for the government carefully guards its citizens from contact with them), they will find an idyllic setting, exceptional in this part of Asia. The village streets are clean, swept daily with palm-frond brooms. Along them lie houses built with the same palm branches, and boatyards with coconut-wood craft under construction. In the lagoons, fishermen cast their nets by hand. The islands are superb scenery, and it is hard to imagine them as the source of the slave trade's shell money.[1]

The independent republic has an unusual "landscape," if that is the proper term. Just over a thousand islands (less than 200 inhabited) in nineteen atolls lie stretched out for 475 miles on a north–south axis. The northernmost are roughly 400 miles due west of Colombo; while the southernmost extend just south of the equator. The people, about 150,000 in number, are predominantly Indo-European in origin with a mixture of Arab, Dravidian, and African blood, the mixture more pronounced in the northern atolls.[2] They speak a language called Divehi (from *divesi*, "islander") which is similar to the medieval form of the Sinhalese spoken in Ceylon. One single word of Divehi has entered the English language. Altogether fittingly, it is *atolu*, meaning atoll.[3] The name Maldive originated apparently with South Indian traders, who later passed it on to the Portuguese. It is derived from Sanskrit *mala* (garland) and *dvipa* (island),

20

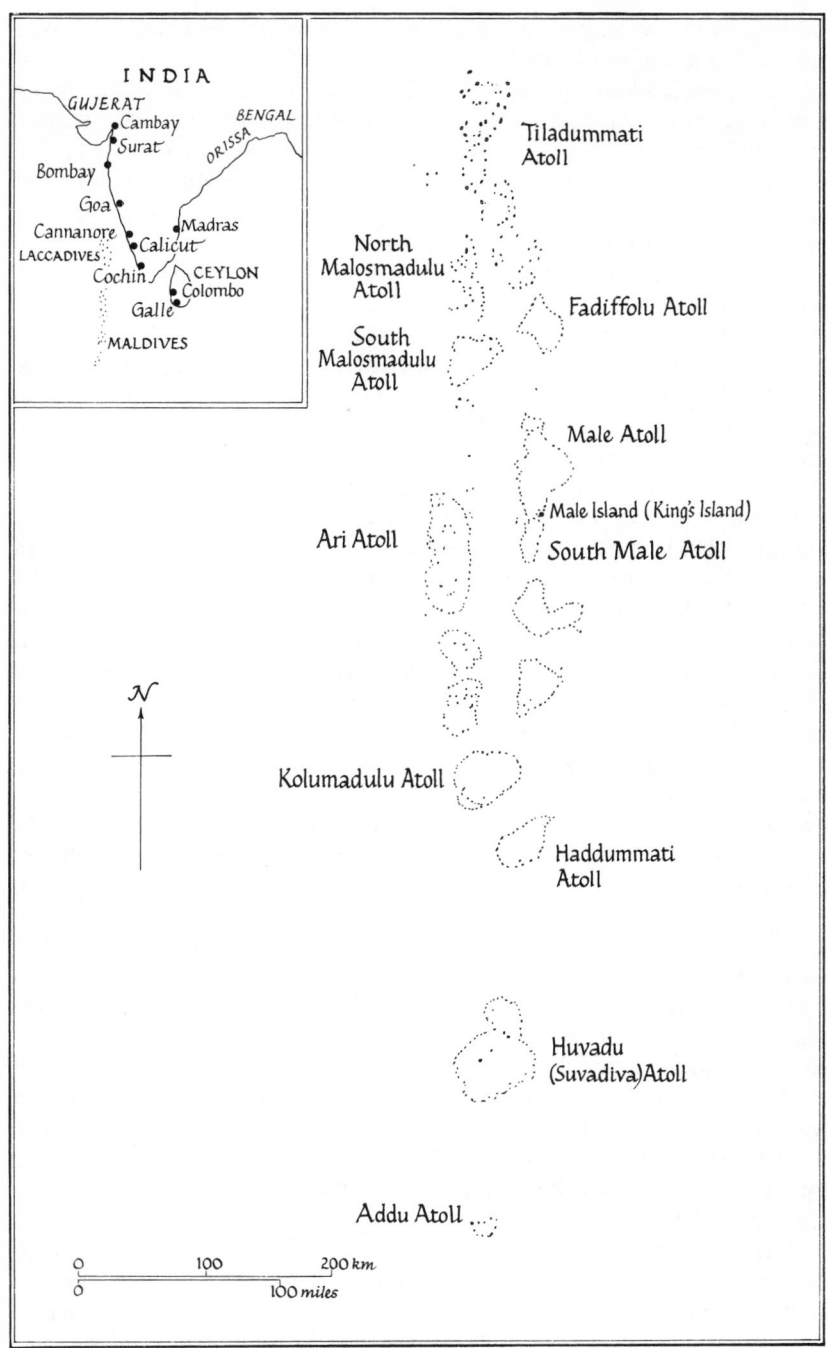

INDIA

GUJERAT
Cambay
Surat
BENGAL
ORISSA
Bombay
Goa
Cannanore
LACCADIVES
Calicut
Madras
Cochin
CEYLON
Colombo
Galle
MALDIVES

Tiladummati
Atoll

North
Malosmadulu
Atoll

Fadiffolu Atoll

South
Malosmadulu
Atoll

Male Atoll

Male Island (King's Island)
South Male Atoll

Ari Atoll

N

Kolumadulu Atoll

Haddummati
Atoll

Huvadu
(Suvadiva)Atoll

Addu Atoll

0   100   200 km
0   100 miles

Map 2 The Maldive Islands

21

and indeed to the seafarer approaching the chain it does resemble a long and green garland of islands.[4]

Most of the land area lies along the coral rims of the atolls, with a lagoon in the center that can be as large as 15 to 40 miles across. Islands are often only four to six feet above sea level, and a height of twelve feet is a Maldive mountain. Many are a quarter to half a mile in length; some reach two or three miles. They are usually much longer than they are wide.[5] A rainy season sets in with the southwest monsoon which prevails from May to August. The rainwater sinks into the porous sandy surface and forms a water table floating on an underlying table of denser ocean water. Wells of six to eight feet in depth provide water that moves with the tide but remains fresh, so making the islands inhabitable. The northeast monsoon succeeds in October to March, and is relatively dry. Settlements tend to cluster in locations protected by a reef but with a passage through it, where bait-fish can be caught, where boats can be beached, and with available fresh water.[6]

Very few scholars are working now, or ever have worked, on Maldivian economic history or any other social science.[7] It is thus doubly fortunate that the islands have over the centuries been visited by a number of extremely perceptive travellers, without whose information we would be virtually helpless in examining the cowrie trade or any other part of Maldivian history. Ibn Battuta, the able Moroccan who saw *moneta* at Timbuktu, was the first of these, in the fourteenth century.[8] The second was the shipwrecked Frenchman, François Pyrard de Laval, who was forcibly detained at Male between 1602 and 1607. Pyrard's *Voyage*, issued in two volumes by the Hakluyt society in 1887 and 1890, is indispensable for the economic historian. Ranking above all as a scholar of the Maldives is the Englishman H. C. P. Bell, who as a civil servant of the Colony of Ceylon first visited the islands in 1879 (four years before they became a British protectorate).[9] He came merely to investigate the wreck of a British ship,[10] but his interest continued until his death in 1937, and his last monograph on the Maldives bears the date 1940. In those sixty years, the results of research on the islands poured from his pen, and the works cited so frequently in our footnotes do not include the many others he wrote on Maldive art, religion, archaeology, linguistics, and geography. His collected papers are in the Sri Lanka National Archives, and show the degree to which, amongst our Victorian forefathers, hobby could grow almost to obsession.[11] For our purposes, these foreigners must be relied upon. The surviving Maldivian chronicles, the *Ta'rikh* and the *Radavali*, are useless as sources of information about the cowrie, and oral traditions are sparse concerning the shell trade.[12]

Working from the *Ta'rikh* and the *Radavali*, Bell brought home to European readers the fact that the Maldives had a continuity of government that in duration rivaled Britain's own. The sultanate was in a succession from Muhammad-ul-adil, who converted to Islam in A.D. 1153, right up to the proclamation of a republic in 1968, barring a brief period of presidential rule in 1953 and a Portuguese occupation of fifteen years in the 1500s.[13]

The very earliest mentions of the Maldives, Buddhist literature from Ceylon, make no reference to the cowrie.[14] Neither do Roman writers, from the unknown author of the *Periplus*, through Ptolemy in the second century A.D., to Ammianus Marcellinus in the fourth.[15] One classical allusion to cowries from the Indian Ocean is suggested by E. H. Warmington, who attributes it to Athenaeos.[16] In Justinian's reign (sixth century A.D.), the Egyptian voyager Cosmas Indikopleustes spoke of Maldive coconuts but not of cowries.[17] (The coir rope made from coconut palms was a valuable product of the islands in a time and place where ship timbers were held together with rope, not nails, and when the rigging was also of coir.)

The first direct mention of *moneta* in the Maldives derives from early contacts with Arab ships, seamen, and merchants. "Sulayman al-Tajir," (Arabic: "The Merchant"), whose actual identity has not been verified, made several journeys in the middle of the ninth century A.D. from the Persian Gulf to India and China. He did not personally visit the Maldives, but from information obtained from other travellers he noted that the islands

> are all inhabited, and they grow the coconut tree in all of them. The wealth of the people is constituted by cowries; their queen amasses large quantities of these cowries in the royal depots, ... The cowries are got by them from the surface of the sea. [The shell] encloses something living. To fish them up, they take a branch of the coconut tree, and put it in the sea, and the cowries attach themselves to it.[18]

Sulayman's description, though short, is fascinating. It points to a royal monopoly from the very first, a monopoly that we shall see lasted a thousand years. It is also the first account of the "tree branch" method of collection, which many subsequent writers alluded to, including some in the 1800s, centuries after the method had died out.[19]

The well travelled Baghdad Arab, al-Mas'udi, who died c. 956, visited Ceylon early in the tenth century and closely follows Sulayman's account.

> The queen has no other money but cowries, which are a kind of mollusc. When she sees her treasure diminishing, she orders her islanders to cut coco-branches with their leaves, and to throw them upon the surface of the water. To these the creatures attach themselves, and are then collected and spread upon the sandy beach, where the sun rots them, and leaves only the empty shells, which are then carried to the treasury.[20]

In discussing the islands, al-Mas'udi adds the important detail that traders from Oman and Siraf (a now-vanished port midway up the northeast side of the Persian Gulf) had made the voyage to the islands, in addition to "many navigators," an initial hint of the trade routes running west toward the Mediterranean.[21]

The scholar and scientist al-Biruni (973–1048), writing about a century

23

after al-Mas'udi (*c.* 1030), is the first to call direct attention to the Maldives as a specialized producer of the cowrie. Contrasting the Maldives with its northerly neighbor, the Laccadive chain, he writes

> These islands are, according to their products, divided into two classes – the *Dîva Kûdha*, the islands of cowries, because there they gather cowries from the branches of the coco-nut palms, which they plant in the sea; and *Dîva Kânbar*, the islands of the cords twisted from coco-nut fibre, and used for fastening together the planks of their ships.[22]

There is no discussion of exports.

In the next century, Moroccan-born al-Idrisi (*c.* 1100–1166) wrote his famous geography which discusses the Maldives, but apparently follows closely the earlier authors.

> They use cowry-shells as a means of exchange. ... The king accumulates [them] in his treasures, and these comprise most of his possessions. .... It is said that these cowries, which their king collects, come to them on the surface of the water while they are alive. So they take branches of the coconut-tree and throw them on the water. Then these cowries cling to them.[23]

Again no discussion of exports, not even a distinction between the Maldives and Laccadives. We do learn, however, that the royal monopoly now belongs to a male. Another century later, Ibn Beitha (died 1248) makes mention of the Maldives as the islands where cowries originated.[24]

Several subsequent Arab and European writers speak of the Maldives (in the years 1292, 1307, 1321) without discussing cowries. But just a little later, in the fourteenth century, we get a clearer indication of how the shell trade was being conducted, and our first definitive information on the direction of exports. A Chinese writer, Wang Ta-yuan, states for the 1330s or 1340s that "every sea-trader takes one shipload of cowries to Wu-tueh [Orissa?] and Peng-ka-la [Bengal], where he is sure to exchange it for a shipload of rice and more."[25]

Now Ibn Battuta comes on the scene. This discerning and energetic Muslim traveller was born at Tangier in 1304, spent thirty years on his expeditions, and died in 1378. He is justly the most important of our early witnesses, because he was first to live in the Maldives and the only published author – possibly the only person in his or any age – to see the cowries fished in the islands and also used as money in the markets of Bengal and in the desert-edge cities of West Africa. After eight years of residence at Delhi, where he served as *qadi* (judge) in the service of Sultan Muhammed bin Tughluq, Ibn Battuta arrived at the Maldives early in A.D. 1343. During a stay of eighteen months, he married four wives with noble connections, was appointed *qadi*, and left us the best account of the Maldive cowrie trade (and indeed everything else about the islands) until Pyrard two and a half centuries later.[26] He departed in August 1344, returned for a short time in 1346, and in the account of his travels (that was not known in Europe until the nineteenth century) he wrote:

The money of the islanders consist of cowries. This is the name of a mollusc, collected in the sea and placed in pits dug out of the beach. Its flesh decays and only the white shell remains. A hundred of them is called *siya*, and 700 *fal*; 12,000 are called *kotta*, and 100,000 *bosta*. Bargains are struck through the medium of these shells, at the rate of four *bosta* to a dinar of gold. Often they are of less value, such as twelve *bosta* to a dinar. The islanders sell them for rice to the people of Bengal, where also they are used for money. They are sold in the same way to the people of Yemen, who use them for ballast in their ships in place of sand.[27]

Notice the first reference to the pit burial method of processing (still practiced today); the eyewitness mention of the Bengal trade; the use of the shells as ballast which became standard; and the existence of a westward flow of shells toward the Red Sea and to North Africa. His next sentences describe his unique experience: "These shells serve also as a medium of exchange with the negroes in their native country. I have seen them sold, at Mali and at Gogo, at the rate of 1,150 to a dinar."[28] This was a decade after his stay in the Maldives, on a trip that required a southward crossing of the Sahara in 1352 and a return north in 1354.[29] Ibn Battuta certainly makes it clear why there was a trade in cowries across such vast distances. The figures he quotes show at the very least a West African cowrie price about 350 times greater than the going price in the Maldives.

The fifteenth century was a time of intense Chinese exploration and trade in the Indian Ocean basin. Ma Huan, who served in the Ming Admiral Cheng-ho's fleet, wrote the *Ying-Yai Sheng-Lan* ("Overall Survey of the Ocean's Shores") in 1433. "As to their cowries: the people [of the Maldives] collect them and pile them into heaps like mountains; they catch them in nets and let the flesh rot; ... they transport them for sale in Hsien Lo [Thailand] and Pang-ko-la [Bengal], and other such countries, where they are used as currency."[30] James Heimann has an interesting discussion of the probability of trade between the Maldives and China in cowries during this period, and political relations as well, since China claimed sovereignty of Ceylon at the time. He notes also that one Chinese name for the Maldives, Pei Liu, uses the *pei* sign that can mean cowrie.[31]

Then began the era of the European trade. In 1497 a Genoese merchant, Hieronimo di Santo Stefano, weathered the southwest monsoon in the islands, and the year after that the Portuguese were in India.[32]

THE EXPORT TRADE TO EAST AND WEST

On the eve of European appearance in the Indian Ocean, the Maldive export trade in cowries was already of very long standing, flowing in two streams to east and west from Male. The eastern branch of the trade fed mainly the Bengal market, though it reached further to Burma, Thailand, and possibly China. This eastern branch was by far the largest source of supply in Bengal, and before the European entry it must have been far larger in volume than the western arm of the trade.[33] Interestingly, the exports to the east did not include the nearby Malabar coast or Ceylon, where the shells were not used as money.[34] They were even falling from favor as the Maldives' own money. From being the sole currency in Ibn Battuta's time, within two centuries it had been supplemented with, and was later supplanted entirely by, metallic monies.[35] The metal currency of the Maldives is an interesting subject in itself. The *larin* was a silver wire of high purity, bent in the shape of a Y or a fishhook, and was at first an import primarily from India. The name *larin* has been traced to the now-much-diminished Iranian town of Lar, which lies inland from the Persian Gulf between Shiraz and Bandar Abbas, on what was an important caravan route. At Lar, this money was first produced probably at the start of the sixteenth century. Within about a hundred years, the *larin* was being minted in the Maldives, stamped with the sign of the sultan. Conveniently for calculation, and a sure signal of an attempt to maintain a fixed exchange rate, at the start of the seventeenth century one silver *larin* at Male was worth 12,000 cowries, the traditional *kotta* mentioned by Ibn Battuta and which we shall meet again. (The importance of 12,000 as a measure of cowrie volume stems from the old Maldivian duodecimal system of counting.)[36] Circular coins came to be minted probably in the later half of the seventeenth century, and both cowrie and *larin* ceased to circulate as money in the Maldives.[37]

The western exports of cowries are harder to trace with accuracy. We have already seen from Ibn Battuta that there was a regular cowrie trade with southern Arabia, with Aden probably its major port of call. There is explicit mention of the Yemeni vessels that conducted this traffic, and navigational references making it likely that southern Arabian ships were frequent visitors to the Maldives.[38] Forbes believes the Arab visitors included shipping attempting a direct crossing from southeast Asia to southern Arabia during the winter monsoon. "There is good reason to believe," he says, that they "called regularly at Male to trade, to take on provisions and fresh water, and possibly for shore leave mid-way on this long voyage." He states, on the basis of archaeological finds of potsherds at Male, that the traffic was almost uniformly westbound.[39]

If the shells were frequent cargoes to Aden, that would certainly explain Cairo as an entrepôt for the early West African trade. Travel up the sheltered Red Sea and the short overland leg to the Nile is not the simple matter it seems from a map, because an adverse north wind blows in the top half of that sea all year round, and northward-bound shipping would face tedious tacking. But cargoes of all sorts, no doubt including cowries, were landed further down the Red Sea. If on the east side at Arabian ports such as Jiddah, the journey was by camel to Cairo or other Levantine ports. If on the west side, then a camel trek to Aswan at the Nile's first cataract would permit a long downstream journey by river-boat.[40]

There was an alternative route to the Mediterranean that led first by sea up the Persian Gulf and then overland by caravan route to the shores of the

Levant. We have seen from al-Ma'sudi that even by the tenth century, traders from Oman and Siraf (the vanished port in present-day Iran) had visited the Maldives. These contacts continued. Abd-ur-Razzaq was a Persian emissary to India, in the service of Tamarlane's fourth son, Shah Rukh. He mentions that, in 1442, Maldivian merchants were to be found in the great Persian market of Hormuz.[41] Hormuz is at one end of the principal land route through Baghdad to Acre on the Mediterranean,[42] and in the era when the price differential between Africa and the Maldives was as high as Ibn Battuta reports, transport costs on the overland route would arguably not be prohibitive. (In any case, part of that journey would be by boat on the Tigris or Euphrates.) Leo Africanus speaks of shells at Timbuktu as coming "from the Kingdom of Persia," and although he may have meant no more than "the East," it is not unlikely that some shipments did indeed come up the Persian Gulf rather than the Red Sea.[43] At the right seasons and in the absence of political barriers, however, the Red Sea route must still have afforded the lowest transport costs because it minimized desert travel.

In short, there were two probable routes, both of them major and carrying a wide variety of Asian goods, by which the cowries could conveniently come to Cairo or other ports of the Levant. Either or both must have seen the cowrie in transit for several centuries, but the sudden irruption of the Portuguese was to slow this traffic to a trickle. The Portuguese arrived in India (at Calicut) on May 17, 1498. Within twenty years Vasco de Gama's little flotilla of four ships had grown into fleets under pugnacious commanders such as Albuquerque; the northern Indian Ocean came for the time being under Portuguese command, with the western Indian coast under blockade. Aden was attacked in 1513, Hormuz captured and occupied in 1515. It is thus no coincidence that the first recorded contract for cowrie shipments by sea to West Africa dates from that same year, 1515, and the ships that were to carry them flew the flag of Portugal.

3

The Portuguese domination

In the first years after Vasco da Gama's arrival at Calicut, the Portuguese must often have seen cowries in use and on sale in Indian markets.[1] They did not make contact with Maldive cowrie-carrying vessels until 1503, and that first contact the unfortunate Maldivians had good reason to rue. Gaspar Correa, in his *Lendas da India*, gives a vivid account of how Vicente Sodre, Chief Captain of the Fleet after da Gama's departure for home in 1502, captured four Maldive ships close off Calicut. That city had resisted the Portuguese *cartaz*, or pass system, and Sodre had forbidden the merchants of Calicut to trade with the islands.[2] The Maldive merchantmen were carrying coir rope, dried fish, fabrics and cowries, which, says Correa, "are small white shells found among the islands in such quantity that ships make their cargoes of them. In these a great trade is carried on with Bengal, where they are current as money."[3] The ships had been chartered by a large number of "Moors of Calicut" who had purchased cargoes in the Maldives and were aboard, accompanying their goods back to Calicut. Vicente Sodre's treatment of this little convoy was quick and violent, presaging future Portuguese efforts to control the cowrie trade by conquest. He threatened to burn both ships and men unless the "Moors" of Calicut were pointed out. This having been done, the unarmed Maldivian captains and crews then had to watch the Moors bound, put in the hold of one ship from which the cargo had been removed, and then burned to death when the ship was fired. About a hundred perished, but some managed to get overboard, swim to shore, and spread the story.[4]

Portuguese interest in the shell trade did not develop all at once. The Maldives attracted them primarily because it was a major source of the coir rope used as rigging in the fleet. In time, the islands did indeed supply much of the cordage in the naval stores of Portuguese India. Another Portuguese interest was to extend their maritime blockade and pass-control system to the Maldives. Lying conveniently athwart the direct route from the East Indies to the Red Sea, the islands were suspected of harbouring Arab merchantmen seeking to avoid the Portuguese patrols off the Malabar coast.[5] However, the Portuguese soon became aware of the substantial

28

scope of the cowrie trade. Duarte Barbosa, who served in the eastern empire between 1501 and 1517, noted the "little shells, in which is great traffic with Cambay [at the head of the Gulf of that name in Gujerat, western India] and Bengal, where they are used for petty cash, being considered better than copper."[6] João de Barros, whose *Decadeas* cover the period from 1497 to 1539, was clearly curious about the trade of the Maldives:

> The commonest and most important merchandise at these islands, indeed, the cause of their being visited, is the coir; without it those seas cannot be navigated. There is also a kind of shellfish, as small as a snail, but differently shaped, with a hard, white, lustrous shell. ... With these shells for ballast many ships are laden for Bengal and Siam, where they are used for money, just as we use small copper money for buying things of little value. ... Now the manner in which the islanders gather these shells is: – they make large bushes of palm leaves tied together so as not to break, which they cast into the sea. To these the shellfish attach themselves in quest of food; and when the bushes are all covered with them, they are hauled ashore and the creatures collected. All are then buried in the earth until the fish within have rotted away. The shells (*buzios* as we, and *Igovos* as the negroes, call them) are then washed in the sea, becoming quite white, and so dirtying the hands less than copper money.[7]

Gaspar Correa, writing about the same period, also showed some fascination with "the little white shells found among the Islands in such abundance that whole vessels are laden with them, and which make a great trade in Bengala, where they are current as money."[8]

Everywhere they touched on the subcontinent, the Portuguese must have heard of (and sometimes seen for themselves) the employment of the cowrie currency. The heartland of their use in Bengal and Orissa was visited and remarked upon. "Valid throughout Bengal" and accepted "for a larger number of commodities as they would gold," remarked Tomé Pires during his trip of 1512–1515.[9] But the cowrie's range in India was wider then than it came to be in the eighteenth century, and Frank Perlin gives persuasive reasons why in many regions the "currency area" was growing.[10] Late in the period of Portuguese trade hegemony, cowries were current money in Bijapur and "all the states of the Great Mughal," at Agra, in Bihar and Burhanpur, in Maharashtra, along the Coromandel coast, in Gujerat, and eastward to Assam and Sylhet.[11]

From the Portuguese point of view, the availability of cowrie supplies over such a wide area must have been commercially advantageous. Bengal was far away from their capital at Cochin on the west coast, even further when the capital was transferred to Goa in 1530. Their commercial presence in Bengal was relatively slight, although they did hold Hooghly as late as 1632, thus for the most part barring competing traders from easy access to the interior of Bengal.[12] Buying in Bengal was thus far less attractive for the Portuguese than it proved to be for the British and Dutch in later centuries. Portuguese efforts to obtain supplies focused instead on the west coast and even on the colonization of the source at the Maldives.

The Portuguese adventurers had every reason to think that shells might profitably be shipped to West Africa. Their pioneers there had noticed the coastal shell currencies, and had heard of the using areas inland. (João de Barros had been captain of the fortress São Jorge da Mina on the Gold Coast before his connection with India began.)[13] Knowing that seaborne trade has large cost advantages over carriage by land, they would have concluded that the profits of this trade could be theirs with little effort and with no foreign competition for many years to come. They knew the shells could be used for ballast, and thus would compete for space not with normal revenue-earning cargo but only with other items that could give stability to their merchantmen on the long passage home around the Cape of Good Hope. Stones, sand, and "any old iron", all fully adequate as ballast, would produce little or no revenue, but cowries could. Thus began the Portuguese efforts to turn the trans-Saharan cowrie trade.

THE PORTUGUESE TRADE TO AFRICA

Cowrie shipments to West Africa were flowing along their centuries-old routes to or near Cairo, westward along the North African coast, and then across the Sahara, when the Portuguese initiated their campaign to turn the trade. Albuquerque himself noted the "snail trade" of the Maldives passing through Cairo in a letter written about 1510. There are very early reports of Portuguese cowrie cargoes loaded at the island of Socotra, on the direct route from the Maldives to Aden and the entrance to the Red Sea.[14] The age-old routes did not decay all at once, even in the face of Portuguese efforts to close them down. H. W. van Santen's work at the University of Leiden has explored how the Red Sea route survived into the seventeenth century. There were trans-shipment points at Surat on India's northwest coast, and at Mocha just inside the Red Sea past Aden, with West Africa apparently the ultimate destination.[15]

The first recorded Portuguese shipments to West Africa are described in a contract for the trade of their new settlement on São Tomé island. This commercial agreement between King Manuel and Senhor Fernão Jorge was signed on March 26, 1515. A clause in the contract permitted Jorge to import 500 quintals of cowries (one quintal = originally 108 and later 112.5 pounds, in turn equal to $4\frac{1}{2}$ *kottas*, the measure used in the Maldives). The shells were to come as ballast in the ships of the Indian return fleet, the *carreira da India*, and there was to be no charge for freight.[16] A. F. C. Ryder says, "almost certainly this contract marks the first important introduction of Maldive cowries into West Africa by the Portuguese."[17] Ryder and Magalhães-Godinho both believe it took some time for these first shipments to arrive; the former suggests 1517 or 1518, the latter some time between May 1517 and October 1519.[18] Quantities were probably small at first, but by 1522 "they had become as important as manillas in Portuguese trade with Benin." The mountainous island of São Tomé seems often to have been used as an off-loading and trans-shipment center in these early years, and presumably thereafter as well.[19]

Cowrie cargoes became more frequent in the 1520s, with two such shiploads described by Ryder in his *Benin and the Europeans*.[20] Like almost all shell shipments by the Europeans until well into the nineteenth century, these cargoes were coming around the Cape of Good Hope and sailing north far out to sea in the Atlantic. Prevailing winds prevented calls along the West African coast, and the shell money was taken to European ports (Lisbon in this era) for eventual re-export to Africa.[21] João de Barros remarked on this traffic about 1540:

> And even to this kingdom of Portugal, in some years as much as two or three thousand quintals are brought by way of ballast; they are then exported to Guinea, and the kingdoms of Benin and Congo, where [as well as in Bengal] they are used as money. . . . In this kingdom a quintal of them is worth from three to ten cruzados, according as the supply from India is large or small.[22]

The 24 tonnes per year of Fernão Jorge's original contract is credible enough, equal to what was shipped to Africa by the Dutch and English in some years of the seventeenth century but far below that century's peak. We do have some doubts about de Barros's figures, believing them possibly to be on the high side. The weight equivalent is 98 to 147 tonnes, somewhat implausibly matching the Dutch/English totals for numerous years of the eighteenth century when the trade was booming. Payment for the shells had to be made by exports, and in these years the foreign trade of Africa, in particular slave-exporting, was in its infancy. But there is no reason to doubt the sudden turn toward cowrie shipments by sea, nor that these shipments were very large in scale.

Unlike the later Dutch and English trade, a substantial share of these supplies was purchased commercially by the Portuguese at the Maldives themselves. A colonial occupation was attempted for a time. Other shells were bought at their Indian coastal stations such as Goa and Cochin; for several years some of these supplies came through a farmed-out trade monopoly. Yet others flowed through the regional tribute system.

Portuguese purchases at the Maldives themselves were usually shipped as ballast to Goa and Cochin, and Nunes writes of such buying in the *Subsidios*. Portuguese ships (with local Indian crews) were still calling for cowrie cargoes in the first decade of the seventeenth century, so the hostility engendered by the armed occupation did not end commercial contact.[23] As well as supplying their African trade, the Portuguese shipped cowries from Cochin to Bengal and other Asian destinations. Bal Krishna says of the start of the seventeenth century, "many ships laden with . . . cowries brought from the Maldives left Cochin every year for Bengal, the Coromandel coast, and the eastern country."[24]

Alone of the European powers, the Portuguese attempted to colonize the Maldives and so monopolize its trade. The first expedition of 1506 was abortive. Viceroy Francisco de Almeida had been "informed that many

The shell money of the slave trade

ships from Pegu [Burma], Siam, and Bengal were passing through the Maldive Islands to Mecca." Orders were issued to a six-ship flotilla under Dom Lourenço de Almeida, the Viceroy's son, to "proceed with the Armada, and see what was going on at these islands, and whether ships could be seized." Lourenço's vessels missed their landfall, however, though they did reach Ceylon and began Portuguese relations with that island.[25]

Some three years later the Portuguese began to hear that a merchant from the city of Cannanore on the Malabar coast had acquired monopoly privileges in both the import and export trade of the Maldives. This merchant, Muhummad Ali, called "Mammali Marakkar" or "Mamalle" by several sources, had an agreement with the Maldive sultan for fixed-price exchange of imported rice, salt, and earthenware against exports of cowries, coir, dried fish, and textiles. Mamalle had agents in charge of his stockpiles of export commodities ashore in the islands, used the title "Lord of the Maldive Islands," and apparently exercised temporary sovereignty over several atolls in return for loans to the sultan.[26] The specifics are unusual, but the monopoly status is not. From start to finish, the cowries at their source were not produced under competitive conditions.

Admiral Albuquerque soon encroached on Mamalle's monopoly, and the latter was forced to give the Portuguese trading rights in the Maldives plus payments in coir ropes (2,000 long and heavy ones) to maintain what was left of his privileges. The agreement stood until Albuquerque's departure, but then, says Gaspar Correa,

> his successors, understanding how to profit themselves by the trade, gave it over to their servants and friends, and violated the contract. The ships and armadas sent by the factor of the King of Portugal reduced his profit to nothing, and did many robberies and mischief at the islands, as they are doing at the present day.[27]

Mamalle's last privileges were rescinded in 1518; his erstwhile Portuguese confederates bore him no love, and he was executed by them after a sea-chase by Vicente Sodre in 1525.[28]

By 1517, Portuguese pirates or quasi-pirates were hunting in Maldive waters, in spite of tribute payments by the sultan to Goa. An official expedition sent there on patrol turned buccaneer itself and seized ships with Portuguese passes. A new treaty in 1518 allowed the Portuguese ashore, and in 1519 they erected a warehouse and small fort at Male. But this garrison also behaved piratically, ordered compulsory delivery of export goods at arbitrary prices, and paid at point of pike. Maldive emissaries got through the blockade to Calicut, where they enlisted the support of a merchant who had suffered losses from Portuguese expropriation. An expedition of small boats surprised the unmanned Portuguese ships and the fort's seaward-side, and the Europeans were massacred to the last man. (Maldivians never did take kindly to colonial rule.)[29]

Trade punctuated with Portuguese piracy and attempts to halt any commerce with the Arabs followed for three decades. Then in 1550, a

32

Maldive sultan (Hasan IX) turned Christian, sought protection under the cannon of Cochin and set the Portuguese in motion for further colonial conquest ensuring their source of supply. Hasan, baptized by Francis Xavier himself and suitably renamed Dom Manuel after the reigning Portuguese sovereign, called for his people to convert to Catholicism. Resistance followed; a Portuguese flotilla was defeated; but a fleet returned the next year, and occupied Male and several other islands. Their new fort at Male frowned over the harbour's seawall, as it was to do for centuries until this reminder of the colonial past was demolished in the 1960s. With its guns, the Portuguese enforced a restrictive commercial policy that permitted trade only with Portuguese India and states under Portuguese influence (a trade, incidentally, which thrived). The Maldive people threw off the colonial yoke in the evening of July 30, 1573, surprising the fort in a night assault, killing most of the defenders and re-establishing the sultanate. This was to be the last colonial occupation of the Maldives carried out by force of arms.[30]

After three years of Portuguese attempts at reoccupation, a treaty was concluded that provided for a fixed annual tribute in cowries, coir, and other goods, payable in part to the Christian ex-sultan who took up residence at Cochin, and to his successors. Thus began a long period of two claimants to the Maldive throne, one in possession at Male, the other a pretender under Portuguese protection, the tribute to whom helped swell the westbound flow of cowries. Exact details of the tribute are not known, but it was carried annually in four ships of 150 tons each; one third of it was paid as a contribution by the Christian claimant to the Portuguese government.[31] Within a few years, merchants from Cannanore had taken over much of the islands' overseas commerce, though they had to cope with the discouragements of Portuguese customs officials on the mainland who by the new treaty were empowered to license the Maldive overseas trade. Traffic declined accordingly.[32]

FRANÇOIS PYRARD DE LAVAL

When the sailing vessel "Corbin" left St. Malo in Normandy in 1601, it carried French adventurers seeking the wealth of the Indies and an English pilot who lost his way sometime after leaving Madagascar. On July 2, 1602, the ship fetched up on the reefs ringing Malosmadulu Atoll to the north of Male; and thus came ashore, with forty other sundry survivors, François Pyrard de Laval, who opens for us a window on the conduct of the cowrie trade. Most of the forty died, got away by small boat, or were executed for making the attempt. Four of the mariners, including Pyrard, were interned in a usually pleasant captivity that lasted five years.[33] Fortunately, he was interested in commerce and so to glimpse at first hand the source of the shell money at the start of the seventeenth century, we can let him speak for himself:

33

There is another kind of wealth at the Maldives [in addition to the products of the coconut palm], viz., certain little shells containing a little animal, large as the tip of the little finger, and quite white, polished, and bright; they are fished twice a month, three days before and three days after the new moon, as well as at the full, and none would be got at any other season. The women gathered them on the sands and in the shallows of the sea, standing in the water up to their waists. They call them *Boly*, and export to all parts an infinite quantity, in such wise that in one year I have seen thirty or forty whole ships loaded with them without other cargo. All go to Bengal, for there only is there a demand for a large quantity at high prices. The people of Bengal use them for ordinary money, although they have gold and silver and plenty of other metals; and what is more strange, kings and great lords have houses built expressly to store these shells, and treat them as part of their treasure. All the merchants from other places in India take a large quantity to carry to Bengal, where they are always in demand; for they serve as petty cash, as I have said. When I came to Male for the first time, there was a vessel at anchor from Cochin, a town of the Portuguese, of 400 tons burthen; the captain and merchants were Mestifs [*mestiço*, half-caste], the other Christianised Indians, all habited in the Portuguese fashion, and they had come solely to load with these shells for the Bengal market. They give 20 coquettes [?kegs] of rice for a parcel of shells: for all these *Bolys* are put in parcels of 12,000, in little baskets of coco leaves of open work, lined inside with cloth of the same coco trees, to prevent the shells falling out. These parcels of baskets between merchants are taken as counted, but not by others: for they are so clever at counting that in less than no time they will take tally of a whole parcel. Also in Cambaye and elsewhere in India they set the prettiest of these shells in articles of furniture, as if they were marbles or precious stones.[34]

This passage, by an observer able to witness all the details for himself, is revealing. Pyrard notes the connection of cowrie fishing with tidal conditions, certainly true now and doubtless a constant over the thousand years of the trade. Women did the collecting, also true today. (Men figured only at the peak of production during the heyday of the slave trade.) The Bengal traffic was still predominant. For all the hatred borne them at the Maldives, Portuguese-flag shipping was still calling for cargoes of cowries. The packets of 12,000 shells (the *kotta*) were standard, as they continued to be for another two hundred years.

Pyrard also calls our attention to other aspects of the trade. It was risky. The death of the captain of a foreign vessel meant confiscation of ship and cargo by the sultan, and Pyrard reports this happening to Bengali and Gujerati merchantmen while he was there.[35] It was a trade primarily in exchange for the rice of Bengal, and the growing production of exportables allowed more of such rice imports. This led in turn to settlement on some islands which would otherwise have been uninhabitable.[36] The cowrie trade was still a royal monopoly, as in the times of the earlier travellers. Pyrard speaks of the routing of trade, both imports and exports, through Male the capital, in a mercantilism sterner than that practiced in Europe. Portuguese sources also agree on the sole selling rights of the sultan. Even wearing cowries on the person needed royal permission.[37] A tax payable in cowries "according to their means" was levied by the sultan, fueling the flow of exports.[38] Finally, in a long passage on the money supply, Pyrard describes how cowries circulated as small change alongside the higher-denomination silver *larin* and slivers of silver.[39] As we have seen, in his time a *kotta* of 12,000 cowries exchanged for one silver *larin*.

THE END OF THE PORTUGUESE DOMINATION

After Pyrard's departure, developments in the cowrie trade become more obscure. A Bengali raiding party sacked Male in 1607 but remained on the scene only briefly. Two further Portuguese expeditions to the islands, the first in 1632 and the second about 1650, were both mounted in the joint interest of the Europeans and the Christian pretenders. Both failed to establish a presence ashore.[40] The second of these attacks led the Maldivians to end their tribute payments, stopping one source of cowries for the African trade.[41] But purchases of shells through commercial channels continued.

On the Portuguese side, grants of monopoly trading privileges marked the first half of the seventeenth century. In 1626, Dom Philippe (or Philipp or Philip – the name taken by the current Christian pretender to the Maldive sultanate) was given a favoured position in the Indian cowrie trade wherever Portuguese writ ran. Shortly thereafter, Dom Philippe's monopoly was limited by the granting of a similar privilege to the Duke of Medina. Dom Philippe's position in this resulting "duopoly" declined steadily to the point where attempts were made to end altogether his cowrie-buying franchise and his authority to grant sea-passes. A succeeding pretender, Dom Luis, as a reward for service to Portugal, was given permission to buy and ship to that country without charge 500 quintals (nearly 25 tonnes) of cowries per year. Dom Luis had the bad judgment during 1653 to participate with some nobles in an unsuccessful coup d'etat, and died on the journey to prison in Portugal. Thus also died the role of the Christian "kings" of the Maldives in providing shells for the African trade.[42]

By this time the Dutch and English were both competing with the Portuguese in India, and the latter's long hegemony in the cowrie trade was on the wane. Hormuz, their lynchpin naval base at the entrance to the Persian Gulf, was lost in 1624, a blow from which they could not recover. They were evicted from Ceylon in 1658 after years of struggle against the Dutch. They lost even Cochin, their first capital, in 1663, leaving only decaying Goa as a major possession. For a period, there was some cooperation (no doubt uncomfortable) between the Portuguese and Dutch, the shells brought under commercial auspices to Goa and Cochin (before its fall), then carried by Dutch vessels to Europe.[43] But by 1645, the Maldives were already seeking contacts with the Dutch in Ceylon, and their annual embassy to that island began in that year.

The century and a half of Portuguese domination in the cowrie trade to

Europe and Africa eventually passed with little trace. A few Portuguese ships continued to call for cowries at the Maldives as late as the 1720s, and for many decades Portuguese remained the main European language spoken by Maldive traders.[44] After that died out, there were only the ruined bastions of the fort at Male, the rusted cannon lying on the ground, and the long-lasting antipathy to foreign traders to serve as a reminder of the attempt to colonize the cowrie supply.[45]

The Portuguese part in cowrie deliveries to West Africa proved equally ephemeral. Their decline in India cut off their source of supply. Buying in England or the Netherlands (which countries took over the trade) meant expensive increases in transport costs, with London and Amsterdam many hundred miles of difficult sailing in the wrong direction from Africa. But they left behind an enduring linguistic monument. All along the coast, over the entire area where the cowrie was strung, including both Benin and Dahomey, the strung units carried Portuguese names down through the centuries. Forty on a string were a *toque*, five *toques* totalling 200 shells were a *galinha* (chicken), while 20 *galinhas* of 4,000 shells were a *cabess* (from *cabeça*, head). A. F. C. Ryder suggests that it is even possible, but unlikely, that not only the designations but the counting system itself was a Portuguese introduction.[46]

In the absence of archival data of the quality available for the later Dutch and English portions of the trade, it is possible only to hazard an estimate of the quantities carried to Europe and Africa by the Portuguese. As an upper limit, Philip D. Curtin's statement, based on that of João de Barros, that as much as 150 tonnes per annum entered the trade, is as good as any. Given the many upsets in Portuguese–Maldive relations, however, as well as the very small number of Portuguese ships sailing for home – less than four per year on average between 1500 and 1634 – we suggest an actual average considerably lower than this.[47] The question is perhaps not insoluble, as data may one day turn up in the archives at Lisbon or elsewhere.

There is a certain amount of information on the prices paid and margins in the Portuguese trade. James Heimann, working with figures given by Nunes, reckons as follows:

> in Bengal a quintal of cowries [112.5 lbs.] ... cost 700 reis in 1554. At the Maldives a quintal cost *c*. 2s. 10d. in 1607, and would probably cost even less in 1554. This makes a 300–400% difference between the Maldives and Bengal and, depending on where the cowries were bought, a difference of up to 500% between the Asian price for cowries and the amount given in Portugal. As shipping costs were often nil [true for the grantees of the official monopolies, as we have seen] great profits could be made in the cowry trade.[48]

If the Portuguese saw profits in the trade, so then could competitors of other nationalities. Indeed they did, and before the mid-point of the seventeenth century, the Dutch and English were on the scene. Together, these countries carried the cowrie commerce through to its heyday during the slave trade of the eighteenth century.

4

The Dutch and English enter the trade (seventeenth century)

The Dutch and English East India Companies, attracted by the fabulous profits of the spice trade, were in the field as competitors to the Portuguese shortly after the start of the seventeenth century. The Vereenigde Oost-Indische Compagnie, V.O.C. for short, was chartered in 1602 with the monopoly grant of Dutch trade east of the Cape of Good Hope and west of Cape Horn. From their eastern headquarters at Batavia, they rapidly expanded their many lines of commerce, and in particular they captured from the Portuguese much of the lucrative importation of pepper and other spices. The English East India Company (E.I.C.) was chartered even earlier, in 1600, but its first years were less successful than those of the V.O.C.; one reason was the severe lack of working capital, only one-tenth of the Dutch company's in the early period. The E.I.C.'s headquarters at Fort St. George, Madras, was built in 1640. Its national monopoly extended over the same vast area as the Dutch grant.[1] Together, the V.O.C. and E.I.C. captured from the Portuguese the cowrie commerce to Africa, and thenceforth were the main suppliers of what was to become the shell money of the slave trade.

THE DUTCH ENTER THE TRADE

The first Dutch vessel to visit the Maldives of which there is record came appropriately in the year the V.O.C. was chartered, 1602. The ship was from Middleburg, and after a stay of five days reported that "business could be done there."[2] But nothing came of it for nearly forty years, when, in 1640, a Dutch ship loaded with rice was sent from Ceylon to study trade possibilities. Cowrie purchases began shortly thereafter.[3] The governing council of the V.O.C., the *Heeren 17* (seventeen gentlemen), made their first request for cowrie cargoes, insofar as can be ascertained, in 1642. Cowries were first recorded on Dutch markets in 1647, some 25 or 26 tonnes as best we can calculate. (V.O.C. records provide only a value figure for the first three years.) This beginning was a big one, to be equalled or surpassed only seven times in the remainder of the seventeenth century.[4] Within two

37

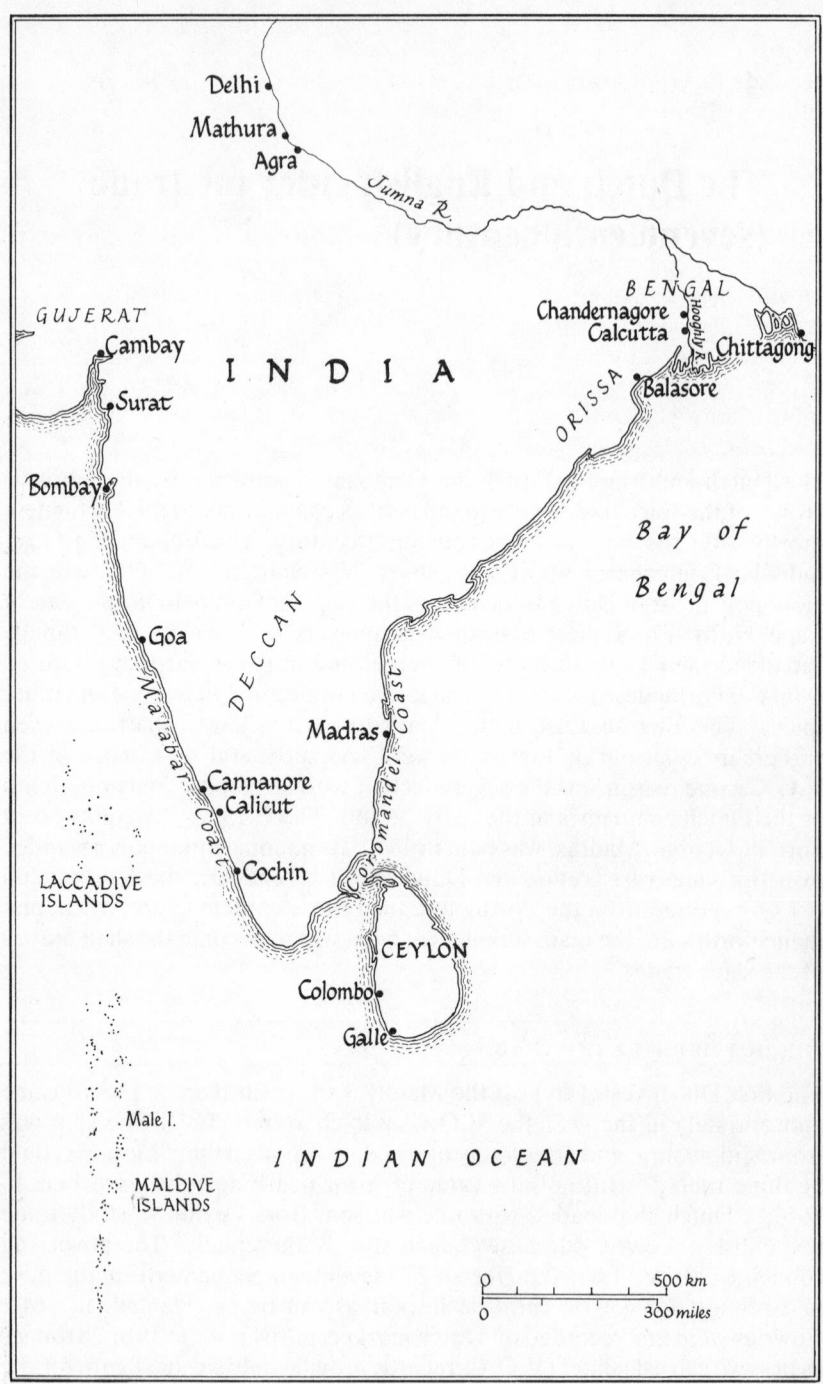

Map 3 India and the surrounding seas

decades, Governor Van Goens in Ceylon was able to write to his successors of the remunerative business to be done in Maldive shell-money.[5] In later years the Dutch acquired much the greater part of their supplies from purchases at their colony of Ceylon. Their first efforts in the trade were most likely purchases from the Portuguese at Goa and Cochin along the Coromandel coast, and in Bengal, as well as at Ceylon. Certainly they were soon on the scene in Bengal, in the midst of that region's cowrie traffic; their Hooghly headquarters had undertaken early investigations.[6] Floris Klinkenberg was unable, however, to find significant archival verification of the provenance of these early purchases.[7] The main Dutch efforts soon concentrated further south, in Ceylon and at the Maldives themselves. Maldive ships had traditionally called at Ceylon with cargoes of dried fish and coconuts. Cowries now came to be included. Almost always these native boats tried to make port at either Colombo or Galle, where they loaded areca nuts, spices, and other commodities for the return trip. Klinkenberg believes these native boat trips to Ceylon accounted for much the greater portion of Dutch supplies.[8]

The Dutch also tried (with little success) to tap the Maldive market directly by sending their own ships to the islands. The Maldive sultan had sent an embassy to Ceylon in 1645, and shortly thereafter requests came from the islands for military assistance against the Portuguese. This led to the dispatch of a small number of vessels, including the *Cockatoo* in 1669 which brought 12½ tons of cowries back to Galle to await the sailing of ships for home. The first Dutch surveying ship to visit the islands, in 1671, also had instructions to "try to traffic in cowries at the chief island of the Maldive king."[9] But Klinkenberg disputes the claim by Bell and Heimann that such voyages were common in this century, and states that they were rare until the 1720s.[10]

Officials in Dutch Ceylon were frequently prodded from Batavia to "incite" the Maldivians, "animate them more and more," and "caress" them for cowries.[11] Efforts to engineer a long-term buying agreement failed in 1688, but by the end of the century a steady and growing supply was flowing to Colombo and Galle on the Maldive boats, which continued to carry away mostly areca nuts and spices.[12] These shells must have been the greatest part of those on the markets of the Netherlands, shown later in this chapter.

The claim has been made by H. C. P. Bell that the Dutch achieved monopoly status in the trade (technically, he means monopsony, "single buyer"). They "were not slow," he says, "to gauge the advantage of complete control over the traffic in cowries. This monopoly they attempted, with much success, to establish throughout the latter part of the seventeenth and eighteenth centuries."[13] Some monopoly power was attained at some times of these centuries, and certainly the Ceylon trade in cowries was pre-empted by the Dutch. But there is no sign of diminution in Maldive shipments to Bengal, and the English were active buyers in the late

The shell money of the slave trade

seventeenth century, as we shall see later in this chapter. In any case, the claim is "late Bell." Earlier (in 1883) he had written only of "fair success" in establishing a monopoly, while in 1925 he confined himself to saying that "they attempted to establish a monopoly."[14] (Bell apparently had some prejudice against the Dutch which may color his views of them as exploiters. "Worthy of the mercenary spirit of the Dutch" and "the proverbial mercenary spirit of the Hollanders" are phrases he was fond of using.[15]) The Maldive sultan, of course, was running a tight royal monopoly of the cowrie trade in his own right.

The available data on prices casts some light on the problem. James Heimann notes that in 1668, a *kotta* of 12,000 cowries cost the Dutch 1.20 rix-dollars (equal to $2\frac{1}{2}$ rupees by his calculation). Meanwhile, the English were writing several letters complaining of a Dutch monopoly, and were having to pay "$4\frac{1}{4}$ rupees a *maund* (at Surat equivalent to about $1\frac{1}{2}$ cottas)." Complain they might, but we fail to see much Dutch monopoly power measured in these figures. The price of $4\frac{1}{2}$ rupees for $1\frac{1}{2}$ *kottas* works out as 2.8 rupees per *kotta*, surely not an exploitative margin when transport costs on a longer route and returns to middlemen are considered.[16] Bell insists that the Dutch "studiously fixed" their buying price "below the fair market value."[17] Temporarily at least, this may be true, since the English found they had to pay 2 rupees per *kotta* at the islands in the early 1680s. But then the Dutch were the steadier customers, no doubt deserving of some economies on this account. They were in something of a protectorate relationship; by Bell's own description, they permitted the Maldivians, "as a kind of set off ... against the low rate" for cowries, to purchase a "certain quantity of areca nuts upon favorable terms. ..." The managed areca price was lowered steadily from the 1680s to the 1740s.[18] As a last argument against much monopoly power, note that the Dutch also raised their cowrie buying price several times during this period; from the original 1.20 rix-dollars to 1.50 in 1697; between that figure and 2.00 up to 1718; and reaching 2.50 in 1740.[19]

What *can* be said with confidence is that the Dutch captured most of the European part of the trade from the Portuguese; they did attempt to establish a monopoly but with limited success; and they presided over a period of steady burgeoning in the traffic.[20] The expanding scope of the African trade, and the increasing connection of the cowrie with slave exports from Africa, meant steadily rising demand. The result: a large advance in the Maldive cowrie price during the seventeenth century, perhaps as much as four to seven times according to Heimann's calculations, which include some depreciation of silver during that century.[21]

THE ENGLISH ENTER THE TRADE

The earliest mentions of cowrie shipments by the English come from the records of the East India Company, and actually antedate the Dutch entry

40

nto the trade. In William Foster's voluminous compilation of documents rom the factors in India, we find orders to obtain the shells for the Guinea rade, attempts by a merchant in the African trade to acquire the shells lirect, and a discussion of sources of supply in India (1630–33); the statement that "they are required for England in good quantetyes" 1634–36); and requests that cowries be sent from Bengal, together with reports of their purchase at southern Indian ports (1655–60).[22] They figure frequently in the E.I.C. court minutes from the 1660s to 1680, including a single order for a hundred tons.[23] At this time the English were buying even further afield, as at Achin on the northwest tip of Sumatra.[24]

But at the Maldives, the English had clearly been forestalled by the Dutch. Their attempts to purchase in the islands were subject to constant frustrations. The first English mariners to make the visit (excepting the pilot of Pyrard's *Corbin*) were, so far as we know, the shipwrecked captain and crew of the *Persia* in 1658. The log of the ship *Recovery*, under the date April 1, 1682, records a visit to Male where she joined in the anchorage two Surat ships, two from Achin, and one from Bengal.[25] The English were well aware that the shell currency of Bengal was coming from these islands, "buried until all their fish is gone out of them, and then sold," in the words of John Marshall.[26] But their efforts to buy at the source of supply were hardly diplomatic, and they even resorted to purchase by force. William Hedges tells the story of an East India Company ship, the *Charles*, attempting to buy cowries in 1683. Her men were pelted with stones and showered with arrows; six of them were wounded. She thereupon opened fire, and "by ye Mouths of [ye] guns forced them to a complyance and permission to load what cowries they would at Markett Price." Assuming that the "60 tunn" of shell they bought equalled some 135,000 lbs., the forced purchase was a large one, more than double the quantities traded by the Dutch in either 1683 or 1684.[27] Two years later, an English vessel calling at the Maldives flew an all-red flag, a piece cut from an English red ensign, "to appear like a Moor's Vessell, not judging it safe to be known to be English, our Nation having lately gott an ill name by abusing ye Inhabitants of these Islands."[28]

Though the E.I.C. had obvious troubles at the Maldives, there were in this period several successful English visits to the islands by company officials working on their own account, and by interlopers (traders illegally infringing the Company's monopoly). Blake, E.I.C. chief factor of Bengal, engaged in several private ventures to the Maldives among other destinations in the 1660s, and ended up with a fortune. Hedges, writing in the very year the E.I.C. took cowries by cannonade, reports private-venture voyages to the Maldives and notes that the sultan has "much countenanced interlopers".[29] The French may also have been competing to some small extent at this time.[30] All this casts further doubt on the validity of the English complaints about a Dutch monopoly, although that was doubtless little consolation to the E.I.C.

Whatever the success of trade at the Maldives, whether Dutch, English or

41

French, it is clear enough that the islanders themselves preferred the Europeans to stay out of their waters. The infrequency of Dutch visits, and the difficulties of the English, certainly suggest this. Maldive preferences are even clearer in a record of an approach by the islanders to Aurangzeb, the Mughal emperor, in the 1660s.

> The King of the Islands of Maldive, fearing aggressive designs on the part of the English and the Dutch Companies sent a representative to the *faujdaar* of Balasore [local ruler of a city long associated with the cowrie trade – see next section] to ask him to request Emperor Aurangzeb to prohibit the English and the Dutch from sending their ships to the said islands. The *faujdaar* replied that there was hardly any point in his bringing the matter to the attention of the Emperor since the latter was master only of land and not of the seas.[31]

Though the Great Mughal could not help, by and large and for a very long time the Europeans took the hint.

BALASORE

The major buying center for the English came to be the little city of Balasore, in Orissa just south of the Bengal border and 60 miles from the mouth of the Hooghly River. Located on the northwest side of the Bay of Bengal, Balasore was the only reasonable seaport on the shores of the bay before Hooghly navigation was improved. Thus it had become the chief point of entry for the Maldive cowries bound for Bengal, and there they were purchased by the European trading companies which had established factories in the city.[32] Balasore's predominance in the shell trade may well have already been centuries-old – we have only the circumstantial evidence that it was the single anchorage of quality over a great distance. We do know that it maintained its position during the European participation in the trade for at least 150 years, and probably longer. A major reason was that Balasore offered not only a suitable anchorage, but immediate access to the surrounding rice-growing area – with rice the main *quid pro quo* in the trade.

Situated on a sandy bay, Balasore was protected by a cape from the southerly winds that blow up from the Indian Ocean. Ships would anchor some distance from the town in the good holding ground of the roadstead.[33] The English established a factory there in 1633, their first settlement in the northerly part of the Bay of Bengal.[34] There were also Dutch and French establishments at the town, and earlier there had been a small Portuguese post. Even the Danes had their chief factory at Balasore before that was moved to Tranquebar.[35] Unfortunately, the English records for Balasore exist only for the years 1679–1687 and are incomplete even for these years; the Dutch records are better, and they extend to a later period.[36]

To Balasore came Maldive boats loaded with cowries to exchange mainly for the rice grown inland from the city. Local Balasore merchants ran the ame route in reverse – rice, cotton cloth, oil, butter, pulses, opium, and other imported goods to Male in the Maldives to exchange for a cargo of cowries. On Balasore's open market, the shells would go either to local buyers as augmentation for the money supply of Bengal and Orissa; or they would be purchased by the Europeans for the African trade. This was the major point of English purchase, complemented by their buying at Surat across the subcontinent.[37]

We are given several good glimpses of this trade in the seventeenth century. Thomas Bowrey, writing in the 1670s, stated that "The Nabob and some Merchants" in the area of Balasore had six or seven vessels regularly employed in going "to the 12,000 Islands called Maldiva to fetch Cowries and Cayre, and most commonly doe make very profitable Voyages."[38] From the Dutch records, we find in the 1680s Balasore and Bengali merchants (Chintaman, Malik Qasem, Nawab Nurallah Khan, Nasib Khan, Shuja Khan, the last four of these members of the ruling class) dispatching ships to the Maldives. Some of these vessels were surprisingly large, 300 to 500 tons, as large as some of the Europeans' own ships. Native vessels from Surat also called at Balasore with cowries loaded at the Maldives. Even the Dutch contributed some supplies, their records showing that some of the Bengali boats had loaded cowries at Galle in Ceylon.[39] At times, therefore, the Dutch must have had supplies exceeding the capacity of their homeward-bound shipping; alternatively, their Indiamen at Balasore may have required ballasting; or perhaps a turn in local demand made the Bengali market specially attractive. By the 1690s, this Ceylon-to-subcontinent branch of the trade was dying out.[40]

Om Prakash has published detailed records kept by the Dutch factors on ship movements in the Bay of Bengal. Among these are departures from Balasore, 1680–81 to 1706–07, and arrivals at that place, 1670–71 to 1704–05. His tables show that, at the close of the seventeenth century, the Maldive trade was much more important than any other for Balasore, that Hooghly (the up-river station that preceded Calcutta) trafficked far less with the Maldives than did its sister port, and that the available data show the trade was largely "on the account of Bengal merchants."[41]

Balasore was the East India Company's main port and trans-shipment center for all the Bengal trade, not just cowries, well into the 1670s. Here the E.I.C. concentrated its cowrie buying, becoming the predominant purchaser of shells among the European companies on the Bay of Bengal.[42] From here sailed at least one, and presumably most, of the E.I.C. ships in the abortive effort to open the Maldive market in the 1680s.[43]

Observers noted the price fluctuations caused by the arrival of the cowrie ships at Balasore, as well as the price differential (handling, transport costs) between that port and points where the Maldive and Bengali merchantmen did not call. Thomas Bowrey wrote that cowries "seldome rise or fall more than 2 Pone in one Rupee (5%), and that onely in Ballasore at the arrival of

Table 4.1 *Available information on the cowrie trade in the seventeenth century (lbs. avoirdupois)*

Year	English (EIC) sales	English (RAC) exports	Dutch (VOC) sales
1650	NA	NA	24,151
1651	NA	NA	18,368
1652	NA	NA	NA
1653	NA	NA	NA
1654	NA	NA	NA
1655	NA	NA	NA
1656	NA	NA	NA
1657	NA	NA	NA
1658	NA	NA	NA
1659	NA	NA	4,066
1660	NA	NA	18,934
1661	NA	NA	NA
1662	NA	NA	NA
1663	NA	NA	1,877
1664	NA	NA	25,440
1665	NA	NA	7,126
1666	NA	NA	5,204
1667	NA	NA	12,828
1668	NA	NA	NA
1669	70,548	NA	NA
1670	216,053	NA	3,732
1671	235,895	NA	43,282
1672	30,865	NA	NA
1673	293,295	NA	NA
1674	326,284	26,768	NA
1675	NA	20,384	NA
1676	NA	14,336	NA
1677	NA	NA	21,228
1678	NA	NA	10,544
1679	NA	NA	32,678
1680	257,941	16,576	43,740
1681	NA	137,200	56,864
1682	174,165	146,608	56,391
1683	456,357	181,888	67,289
1684	376,991	116,032	56,776
1685	306,443	253,120	28,756
1686	209,439	NA	33,801
1687	0	NA	65,956
1688	0	64,176	89,111
1689	NA	36,736	84,077
1690	90,390	36,400	89,705
1691	0	16,576	89,528
1692	0	52,976	92,679
1693	498,245	84,000	84,376
1694	NA	64,288	78,994

Table 4.1 *cont.*

Year	English (EIC) sales	English (RAC) exports	Dutch (VOC) sales
1695	NA	41,664	75,553
1696	NA	48,048	75,868
1697	NA	8,848	217,975
1698	74,957	11,648	147,076
1699	11,023	NA	126,406

NA = not available, either because the figure is missing or the company was not operating.

The 1699 English export quantity from the customs records is 47,864 lbs. See Table 5.1 for the continuation of the series based on customs records.

The E.I.C. sales data are from Curtin, "Wider Monetary World," Table 13. The figures were collected by K. N. Chaudhuri from the India Office Records, Foreign and Commonwealth Office, London, Accountant General's Department, General Commerce Journals and General Ledger Books.

The R.A.C. exports are from Davies, *Royal African Company*, p. 357, and were obtained from the R.A.C. Invoice Books, Outward, PRO T. 70/910–920.

N.B. The totals of columns 2 and 3 should not be added. This would involve double counting.

For Dutch V.O.C. auction sales, see the Klinkenberg thesis, p. 79. The data are from the *Generale Staten* series. See Table 5.1 for more complete citation.

the Ships from Insulae Maldivae."[44] John Marshall wrote in 1677 that at Hooghly the cowrie is 5%, 6%, 7% or sometimes 10% dearer than at Balasore.[45]

Several sources state that the English in India commonly paid a rupee for about 2,500 to 3,200 shells in the later years of the seventeenth century.[46] This works out at 3.75 to 4.16 rupees per *kotta* of 12,000 shells, about double the Maldive price – figures that hint at good but not exorbitant profits in the trade when hard voyages, small ships, risks (or insurance), and handling at either end are taken into account.

From the 1680s to the end of the century, Balasore was gradually abandoned for most purposes by the East India Company.[47] With development of large-ship navigation of the Hooghly River by the Dutch, and the growing availability of pilots, the English took their Indiamen upriver (to Calcutta after its foundation by Job Charnock in 1690) instead of transshipping at Balasore.[48] But the cowries continued to come to this traditional haven, because of the availability of foodstuffs surplus to local needs that Balasore and the rice-bowl of Orissa could provide for the food-short Maldives.

So, in the later half of the seventeenth century, there flowed two distinct streams of cowries toward Africa. The first and presumably larger was from the Maldives to Ceylon to the Netherlands, where the V.O.C. marketed them to traders headed for the West African coast. The second stream was from the Maldives to Balasore and other Indian ports, then to Europe, largely London, where the E.I.C. and private dealers sold them to merchants in the African trade. These two streams far overshadowed the remaining Portuguese trade, which was falling to insignificance; and the nascent French participation which had yet to flower. Both streams were about to grow to a flood as the eighteenth century began.

5

Prosperity for the cowrie commerce (eighteenth century)

When the slave trade prospered in the eighteenth century, the associated cowrie commerce prospered also. In 1732 John Barbot or his editors gave the whole extent of the shell trade a largely accurate overview.

> The boejies or cauris ... are produced and gathered among the shoals and rocks of the Maldivy islands ... and are dispersed to the Dutch and English factories in India; then brought over to Europe, more especially by the Dutch, who make a great advantage of them, according to the occasion the several trading nations of Europe have for this trash, to carry on their traffic at the coast of Guinea, and of Angola; to purchase slaves or other goods of Africa, and are only proper for that trade; no other people in the universe putting such a value on them as the Guineans.... And so, proportionately to the occasion the European Guinea adventurers have for those cauris, and the quantity or scarcity there happens to be of them, either in England or Holland, their price by the hundred weight is higher or lower.... They are commonly brought over from the East-Indies, in packs or bundles, well-wrapped, and put into small barrels in England or Holland, for the better conveniency of the Guinea trade.[1]

In India, the sub-continent's vast internal cowrie market was in many areas giving way to copper coinage and had receded into its heartland of Bengal and Orissa (although Bombay was still purchasing shells well into the nineteenth century).[2] But these two provinces continued to absorb vast quantities in spite of the growing demand for shell money in the slave trade.[3] Cowries were a common means for payment of taxes, for rendering the tribute, and in the setting of ferry rates at river crossings.[4] They continued to have a decorative function.[5] But above all, they were used in market transactions as a medium of exchange. Just after mid-century, a pound of rice exchanged for only 15 cowries in Bengal.[6] Small transactions such as this were impracticable with coins even of the lowest value, and the cowrie thus retained its place as a major money in markets and for wage payments.[7] Especially it was important in the huge, labor-intensive textile industry that was the growth sector of the day.[8] The onerous charges for exchange between cowries and coin are an ongoing theme of Bengali economic history at this time.[9]

Bengal's demand was growing, fueled by prosperity in an export sector that included rice, cotton goods, silks, opium, indigo, and saltpetre.[10] (This last commodity, as we shall see, was a competitor with the cowrie as a profitable item in ballast.) Down to the early 1750s, economic conditions continued to improve. As a result, Bengal's own cowrie demand combined with the increasing demand of the Europeans, with the result that cowrie prices rose, as shown by Heimann's calculations.[11] (Some of the price change was, however, due to the increased silver supplies in India which depreciated the value of the rupee.)

Economic conditions in Bengal declined later in the 1750s, and not long thereafter the English authorities began efforts to replace the cowrie with copper coinage.[12] But the growing cowrie demand from Europe and ultimately from Africa kept prices relatively high right down to the end of the century.[13] Some shells even flowed to Bengal from East Africa during this period (*annulus*, presumably?).[14]

Balasore continued as the main market for the cowrie well into the century, although in other commercial respects it was in decline. It remained "a very great stragling towne but scarce a house in it but dirt and thatcht ones."[15] Captain Alexander Hamilton in his book of 1727 caught the reason why the cowrie commerce was still centered there:

> The Town of *Ballasore* drives a pretty good Trade to the Islands of *Maldiva*. Those Islands . . . have no Rice or other Grain of their own Product, so that *Ballasore* supplies them with what Necessaries they want, and, in Return, bring *Cowries* and *Cayar* [coir] for the Service of Shipping.[16]

And, speaking of the Maldives, he relates how the islanders exchange their cowries "for Rice, Butter and Cloth, which Shipping bring from Ballasore in Orixa near Bengal."[17] Hamilton saw how the cowrie ships had to anchor in the roadstead some distance from the shore because of the shallow depths near the city.[18]

Om Prakash notes that the participation of local titled families in this trade was on the decline from the start of the century, perhaps due to the impoverishment of nobles following the breakup of the Mughal Empire.[19] We can see Balasore as entrepôt from various angles: through the eyes of the Maldive sultan (letter in Portuguese to the Dutch governor of Ceylon, 1734), who describes the sales on credit lasting a year made by the captains carrying the imports;[20] via the Bengali merchants carrying rupees to Balasore "where the cowries were purchased" (1738);[21] from reports of Ostend Company competition said to be raising prices there in 1726;[22] and some similar price-raising competition from the French in 1739.[23] The French had little presence in Bengal after Clive's victory at Plassey in 1757, but part of their trade was still conducted at Balasore. Interestingly, a little plot of 38 acres in that city still flew the French flag in the twentieth century, a remnant of their factory there and governed from the Liechtenstein-size French enclave at Pondicherry.[24]

48

Balasore was still dealing in very large lots well into the century. A surviving letter of the E.I.C.'s Calcutta Council dated 1738 contains an order for 80 tons from Balasore, although by 1746 (and doubtless earlier) cowries were being brought up the Hooghly to Calcutta.[25] As late as 1787–88, the coconut-wood native craft were still bringing cowries to Balasore. In those years the Dutch agent there complained in two official letters to the British authorities concerning the behavior of the city's E.I.C. factory manager. His trade with the Maldivians "who frequented the port of Balasore" was, he claimed, being obstructed.[26] Even in the nineteenth century, according to Thomas Thornton's information, the native boats continued to call:

> ... the trade is carried on in their own boats, some of them of 30 tons burden, which are formed of coco-nut trees. They arrive at Balasore, in fleets of about 20 or 30, in the months of June or July, when the S. W. monsoon is steady in the Bay of Bengal.[27]

At Balasore (and later at Calcutta), no doubt at other Indian ports where and when ships touched from the Maldives, at Ceylon, and sometimes at Male in the islands themselves, the Europeans bought the shells in increasingly vast quantities.

THE DUTCH SUPREMACY

The V.O.C., among the European chartered companies, was still the leader in many lines of trade at the start of the century. Textiles, silks, and beverages were rapidly superseding the old pepper and spice supremacy.[28] Steadily, ground was being lost to the English; but not the supremacy in the cowrie trade. From 1710 to 1750, the Dutch shipped 50% of all the cowries they were ever to carry, with a further 30% of their total coming in their declining years to 1790.[29] (See Tables 5.1 and 5.2 at the end of this chapter for a detailed census of shell movements by the Dutch, 1700–1796, after which date they were ousted from the trade, as they had earlier ousted the Portuguese.)

The V.O.C.'s demand for shells was expressed in their announced buying targets. The target was 500,000 pounds in the 1720s; 400,000 pounds as quoted in a 1740 memoir for Governor Bruininck of Ceylon; dropping to 150,000 to 300,000 pounds in 1764–1766.[30] Actual sales to the African trade were, however, almost always below these figures as is shown in the data in Tables 5.1 and 5.2.

As in the seventeenth century, the shells flowed to the Netherlands along three routes. The first of these, from the Maldives to Ceylon in native vessels and then home on the Indiamen, was much the most important, with some 90% of the traffic according to Klinkenberg.[31] The "Missives" of the Dutch governors of Ceylon to the sultan make constant mention of this route. In the letters of 1712 and 1713, we read of too many shells for Dutch

49

needs brought by the Maldive boats to Colombo and Galle; in 1715, a request that the Maldive shippers come to Galle rather than the capital; in 1716, instructions to ship "as much as Your Highness shall be able to send over hither;" in 1717 an order to "bring hither a great quantity of these shells as we request Your Highness again to do;" and 1718's appeal for "all the cowries which Your Highness may have occasion to send hither in your own or subjects' vessels."[32] The letter of 1720 conveys a long complaint concerning the late arrival at Colombo and Galle of the Maldivian cowrie ships. The governor notes that if the cowries are to go to the Netherlands in ballast, they must obviously be in Ceylon in time to meet the Indiamen on the way home from the Bay of Bengal. Departure from the Bay used to be in December, he writes, but now they weigh anchor in November. Since the rendezvous was missed, the "shells cannot be used for (ballast in the fleet), but must be held up the whole year."[33]

In the letter of 1722 we read:

> I have learned with singular satisfaction that Your Highness is ready to send hither in good time, the vessels with the cowries, as some have already appeared in the capital here. [And] I do not doubt that next autumn, as soon as the north monsoon will allow it, the barges of your vessels will come again in good time to Colombo or Galle with good cargoes of cowries so that here may be no want of cowries as ballast for the ships returning home.[34]

In 1728, the governor entreats the sultan to ship a greater quantity than last year, "for otherwise, one could find no reasons to boast and to be pleased."[35] There are further references to the annual arrival of the Maldive cowrie vessels in Governor van Imhoff's letter of 1740, and in a governor's letter to his successor in 1757 that notes how "the Maldivians still come quite willingly in their little boats to trade with us."[36]

The second direction of traffic in the trade involved visits of Dutch ships to the Maldives themselves, with eventual trans-shipment of cargo at Ceylon for home. These visits were more important in the first half of the 1700s than they were in the preceding century, but they still ranked in importance far behind the voyages to Ceylon. Klinkenberg gives a thorough accounting of these voyages in 1723, 1727, 1728, 1732, 1734, and 1735, which brought nearly half a million pounds of shell to Ceylon.[37] These voyages, for some of which we have the best surviving accounting for trade with the Maldives, had several interesting features. They were the "tip of the iceberg" in the sense that the Dutch frequently used the threat of more such visits (disliked by the sultan and his people) to persuade the Maldivians to increase the supplies they themselves carried to Ceylon. The captains of the Dutch ships were sent off with detailed instructions that show some of the mechanics of cowrie-buying. Orders to the officers of the *Edam* and the *Africa* in 1723 run as follows:

> ... it is found that sand in smaller or greater quantities is hidden in the shells to the amount of 20 or 25 lbs./kotta [about doubling the weight of clean shells]. Taken in thus it can be but a hinderance to the load of the ships which go under

your charge. Yet in the purchase or barter, no rebate may be allowed on the weight but on the number of 12,000 shells which make a kotta.

The captains were instructed to bargain for a deduction covering

> ... dead shells, which means all cowries which can be crushed with a foot and also those that are of different shape than the real cowries. .... We only want to warn you that the Maldivian merchants would easily give you short quantity; spotted and dead shells are found in the consignment, a practice that has never been allowed here and which you should also decline to accept in conformity with our local custom here.[38]

There are thorough instructions covering the cargoes (rice, areca nuts, textiles, spices) carried for exchange.[39] There are details of the credit arrangements (some cowries to be paid in the next year's delivery at Ceylon). The Dutch were not, incidentally, very liberal with their credit. The sultan complained in a letter of 1734 that though the merchants of Balasore frequently extended credit against future delivery of cowries, the Dutch demanded immediate payment for their trade goods, with the effect that the sultan sometimes had to borrow cowries from the merchants of Male.[40]

The Dutch tried to overcome the islanders' palpable dislike of them by using in their contacts with Maldivians, when possible, the Dutch burgher community in Ceylon instead of government and V.O.C. officials. This burgher community was largely made up of discharged soldiers, sailors, and clerks. The policy had some success in increasing the flow of cowries, according to S. Arasaratnam.[41] But the real key to understanding the continued flow of cowries to Ceylon, and the favored position of the Dutch, was foreign policy. The Dutch acted as a kind of protecting power and wanted cowries; the Maldives needed the protection and so ensured the supply. This is illustrated by an incident in 1726 when the Maldives came close to involvement in war with the state of Cannanore on the Malabar Coast. The sultan blamed the war scare for the reduced shipment of cowries to Ceylon; the Dutch at once guaranteed military assistance if needed; Cannanore was in no position to challenge the Dutch navy; supplies resumed.[42]

There was doubtless a third direction of Dutch trade – cowries purchased at their stations in Bengal, Orissa (including Balasore), and elsewhere in India. The Dutch had a post at Pipli in Orissa as early as 1627, and by 1655 they were trading at both Balasore and Hooghly. We have already seen complaints of the Dutch agent at Balasore about obstruction of his cowrie commerce. But the sum total of this third route must have been small. Trade from Ceylon to Bengal declined substantially during the eighteenth century; a handsome saving of handling and distribution costs could be made if shells were shipped home from Ceylon instead of going through the middlemen of Bengal and Orissa; and the distance travelled could be reduced by about 1,500 miles if the shells went to Ceylon and not Balasore.

Thus it is not surprising that Klinkenberg found little archival confirmation of Dutch purchases in India, and that the Dutch encouraged their factors to buy at Ceylon instead of on the subcontinent.[43]

It has been claimed that the Dutch held a monopoly position (actually, a simultaneous monopoly of sales in Europe and monopsony of purchases in Asia) in the trade. H. C. P. Bell said that in much of the eighteenth century the Dutch established such a position "with fair success" or alternatively "with much success;" they did hear arguments that a monopoly might make them "complete masters of the Slave Trade;" in 1740 Governor van Imhoff spoke of encouraging "the Maldive merchants to give us exclusively all they can find." The Dutch did pay low prices, and they did extract in 1740 a decree from the sultan that Maldivian vessels calling at Balasore should consign their cowries to the Dutch factory there. Table 5.1 (p. 58) certainly shows numerous years when shipments to the Netherlands were dominant. An associated statistical series, "English Imports from India," not published here, shows no imports of cowries in 1708–1711, 1717, 1734–1738, 1750–1758 (excepting 1753), and 1761–1769 (excepting 1767). We conclude that there was indeed a central period of effective Dutch monopoly/monopsony extending through the 1750s and the 1760s. Dutch buying prices at Ceylon are sketchy, if known, but the information available tends to corroborate the existence of some temporary market power. The steady rise in price from 1.5 rix-dollars per *kotta* of 12,000 in 1697, to 2.0 at times up to 1718, to 2.5 in 1740, thereafter turned sharply down. In the early 1750s the price had sunk to a low of 1.0 rix-dollar, then rose to 1.5 in 1753. Just before 1767 the price was still very low, at 1.04, but in that year it rose first to 1.42 and then to 1.5. In 1769, the Dutch refused the sultan's request to boost prices to 2.0, but by 1795 the price was about 3.0, thus returning to the trend that had held up to the 1740s. In those central years, 1750–1770, the Dutch apparently were successful in turning part of the cowrie trade from Balasore to Colombo and Galle, and also in limiting English access to the shells brought to Balasore by Maldive merchants.[44]

But it must also be said that the monopoly/monopsony power was both incomplete and temporary. The English still had over 40% of the combined Anglo-Dutch trade in the century, as Table 5.2 (p. 62) shows, and quantities shipped to England in some years surpassed the Dutch figures. Dutch efforts to extract a firm, exclusive, long-term buying contract apparently never succeeded.[45] Low Dutch buying prices encouraged competition about which they frequently complained.[46] The Ceylon governor's letter of 1721 chided the sultan for inadequate supply and notes that the French had sold to the Dutch in Ceylon quantities that they had carried from the islands. He says,

> From this I see that these strangers get a preference in this trade in the dominions of Your Highness, and that the subjects of Your Highness are not pressed by Your Highness to bring early into this island greater quantities of cowries.[47]

52

The letter of 1727 amplifies:

> ... why should our vessels not be favoured as much as those of other European nations that dwell much further from Your Highness' islands and kingdom? For one has much more interest in the friendship of neighbours than in that of them that dwell far away and live outside the range of possibility to bring help in time of need.[48]

The letter of 1735 similarly mentions the competition of other European ships buying at the Maldives.[49] Finally, a memoir of 1743 concerning the administration of factories on the Malabar Coast states:

> I have sounded these [Maldivian] envoys about the cowries and why they did not carry more of them to Ceylon ... I think they got too little for the cowries and take them in their own vessels to Bengal and from there take rice in return. Some time ago ... they sold many cowries to the French, who on this account send many vessels lately to the Maldives ... I think it is not only expedient but even necessary to maintain our friendship with this prince and open a helping hand to his vessels when they come here.[50]

After about 1770, as we shall see, the monopoly power of the Dutch had clearly broken down. H. C. P. Bell characteristically put it in an uncomplimentary way:

> ... the Dutch, with everything originally in their favour, from the illiberality which characterized their commercial policy, saw a trade that, judiciously fostered, would have continued to yield them ample profits, gradually slip through their hands to the enrichment of other nations.[51]

To put another light on it, the Dutch demanded the Maldive cowries, and the Maldives desired imports in return. But the latter craved more than just trade goods. They also wanted a few Dutch men-of-war to interpose themselves if and when necessary in the heavily travelled waters off the Malabar Coast. Anticipating the teachings of Mahan in the next century, the Maldivians appreciated fully the futility of defense without a fleet. The broadsides of a ship-of-the-line were beyond their technology. For such protection, they had to pay. Surely it is this, as much as commercial cupidity, that brought the Dutch to dominance in the eighteenth century cowrie trade.

Table 5.1 (p. 58) shows the total quantity of Dutch cowrie sales at the V.O.C.'s auctions in the Netherlands. Barring the minute amounts purchased for export to other destinations for purposes of ornamentation, all went to West Africa. Assuming further that losses on the voyage thither were also minute, these auction sales data are the complete equivalent of cowrie imports to West Africa from the Netherlands. For the entire period 1700–1790, the Dutch average annual supply was 74 metric tonnes, with a maximum of 276 tonnes in 1749. Thus in an average year over 60 million individual shells entered West Africa via the Netherlands.

The years 1785 to 1790 were great ones for the Dutch, with shipments in four of those years equaled or surpassed only once since the maximum in

53

1749. But the Dutch trade was about to become a thing of the past. Only 39,001 lbs. altogether were shipped in the two years 1791 and 1792, collapsing to a total of only 1,203 lbs. in the four years 1793 to 1796. A note from the governor of Ceylon in 1793, its text imperfect, tells its own story: "now almost two years ... the Maldives ... almost no cowries".[52]

The great European War was stifling the Dutch cowrie trade. By 1795, not just shipments of shell but the whole of Holland's commerce was in ruins. The French Revolutionary General Pichegru captured Amsterdam in that year, the Stadholder fled to an English exile, the Batavian Republic was proclaimed, and the country itself was caught up in the war. Ceylon fell to the British in 1796, a year after the last recorded visit by a Maldive cowrie boat.[53] The V.O.C. was wound up, bankrupt, in 1798. Possibly the otherwise unexplained imports to Great Britain from the continent of Europe about this time are the final liquidation of the V.O.C.'s inventory of shells. The 191,748 lbs. of 1797, 392,312 lbs. of 1798, and 145,464 lbs. in 1801, during the short-lived Peace of Amiens, would thus represent the last Dutch purchases made several years before and finding their way to the British Isles by one route or another.[54]

Thus ended the era in which the V.O.C. "supplied the European nations with the far greater part of this negro money", in the words of the "Dutch Gentleman" quoted in our epigraph. The "chief European market for these shells ... at Amsterdam" was closed down.[55] The mantle passed to the English.

THE ENGLISH COMPETE

Their East India Company rapidly becoming larger and more profitable than the V.O.C., the English were, with the Dutch, the largest interoceanic shippers of the cowrie in the eighteenth century. The imports, largely to London, were sold regularly at the E.I.C.'s auction sales for the African trade and, together with the shells brought to England by interlopers, entered the customs records on their re-export.[56] From the evidence available, the English made most of their purchases in Bengal and Orissa (especially Balasore), and acquired far smaller amounts at ports on India's west coast and in the Maldives themselves. They continued subject to frustrations in trading direct with the islands. Especially frustrating was the failure of two small English expeditions to restore a deposed sultan in 1711. This ex-sultan, Ibraihim, promised the Company "the sole trade of the islands" for its efforts, but all it earned was the enmity of the new government.[57]

The English cowrie business can be traced through various records of the East India Company. Just at the start of the century we see the Board of Directors in London asking their factor at Hooghly to encourage Bengal merchants to send more cowrie ships to the Maldives.[58] We find cowries in the inventories at Fort William (Calcutta) at various times; letters from

Calcutta ordering the purchase of shells at Balasore; careful attention to the merits of buying at Balasore or elsewhere in Bengal; general information about purchases; and repeated instructions from home to buy for return shipment.[59] Near mid-century, this snippet occurs in the Fort William records:

> Our Hon'ble Masters having expressly directed ten tons of couries to be laden in each of their ships homeward bound, we ordered the Secretary to prepare a protest against Captain Cooke for refusing to take any on board the Admiral Vernon.[60]

The powerful competition of the Dutch in Ceylon led to low levels of English trade in the 1750s and 1760s; in no year between 1752 and 1770 did the trade exceed 22 tonnes. This compares to an annual average for the English trade of almost exactly 50 tonnes for the whole of the century.

The greatest proportion of English shipments probably was sold into the African trade at the London auctions of the East India Company, although an accounting of these auctions is not available to us. Interlopers played a major part in the English trade, more so than in the V.O.C., as did shipments by E.I.C. employees on their own personal account. Late in the century the company attempted, with some success, to recover the trade it had partially lost over the previous fifty years to its own "captains and officers," as well as the "country traders" of other nationalities.[61]

Detailed sailing directions exist for one vessel, the *Mary Galley*, which was not a company ship. In 1705 this ship, belonging largely to Thomas Bowrey, was ordered to load "as deep as she will swim with Rice, etc., for Maldiva," where she was to trade for cowries. But the papers leading up to these orders make it clear that the English at this time had little knowledge of navigation in those waters, the normal method of transacting business there, and what sort of imported goods were in demand. In this they were far behind the Dutch.[62]

An English entrepreneur named Price had a contract business with the East India Company from 1772, in which year he sent a ship to Male with presents to the sultan. He was replaced after a time by another contractor named Fergusson. Whether these contracts involved many visits by English vessels to the Maldives is not known to us; some such ships are reported buying cowries at Male in 1777.[63] After the next year, the E.I.C. gradually reasserted itself in the shell trade, as already noted. The Dutch post at Balasore had fallen into English hands in 1781 during the War of American Independence, and its captors did not hand it back until January 1786, years after the peace treaty.[64] Earlier in this chapter we saw the determined actions of the E.I.C. factor at Balasore which effectively stifled Dutch cowrie purchases there for several years. No indication has come to our attention that the connection between the Netherlands and the shell trade at Balasore was ever effectively restored.

With the rapid decline of Dutch exports after 1790, and the capture of

Ceylon in 1796, the English were left alone in the trade. There were some very big years thereafter, as Table 5.1 shows, but little time remained because the abolition of the "legitimate" slave trade in 1807 amputated the African demand. By the last years of the century, the trade had once again become a Maldive/Bengal and Orissa exchange of cowries for rice. Foreign ships ceased to call at the islands, and in fact *no* English ship is known to have visited there until the surveying expeditions of the 1830s.[65]

Though the interest of the English in shell money died away in 1807 for the time being, they had moved a very large quantity in the preceding century. Their annual average between 1700 and 1799 was 50.1 tonnes. Inclusion of the years 1800 to 1807, several of which saw large shipments, raises the annual average to 51.46 tonnes. The biggest English year was 1722, in which fractionally more than 200 tonnes made the voyage to West Africa.

THE FRENCH PARTICIPATION

Our account of the French connection with the shell supply is more impressionistic, there being no long-run series of quantities shipped as there is for the Dutch and the English. In the future, work at the French archives may reveal a total for independent French activity in the trade. So far as we know, no such information has yet come to light, and the available data on French imports from the Maldives and re-exports to West Africa are sketchy. In many years, there was apparently no separate French supply at all, with cowries for African transactions purchased largely at Amsterdam, as well as in England and at Altona (Hamburg).[66] In some scattered years, however, French trade was quite large, and Tables 5.1 and 5.2 must then represent an underestimate of the grand total of shells used as money in West Africa.

J. P. Colbert, the famous Minister of Finance, was responsible for the first French mainland factories, with one at Chandernagore in Bengal established in 1688 (five years after Colbert's death) and one at Balasore some time thereafter. But their early activities were "not in a flourishing condition" according to Sinha, and improvements were not registered until the 1720s, the same years when the French promoted their independent purchases.[67] Until 1717, says Simone Berbain, French shipowners in the African trade had to depend on foreign supplies, largely Dutch. In that year agitation arose at home which led the *Compagnie Française des Indes* to begin importing from the east. A large target of 300,000 lbs. was discussed, and for some years may have been achieved or even exceeded.[68] Importation to France from other European countries fell away for a time, with shells available at the company's sales at Nantes from 1719 to 1733, and at Lorient thereafter until the company was dissolved in 1769. Some shells, apparently independent imports, were also on sale at Marseilles.[69] The French often obtained their supplies at Surat; or even at the Maldives themselves, with French ships expressly mentioned by Dutch governor Rumpf in his letter of 1721 to the Maldive sultan. (The governor says he actually bought shells from the French for a lower price than was current in Ceylon that year.)[70] One of the sultan's letters to the governor (1726) was in French, according to H.C.P. Bell, who says that ships carrying the Bourbon flag frequented Male in this period.[71] (Another letter of the 1720s, this one from the Dutch, complained that some Maldive ship captains were selling off to French shipping cowrie cargoes intended for Dutch Ceylon. This raises the interesting question of whether these captains were operating with the sultan's permission or illegally on their own account.[72]) There was further improvement in the general condition of French Indian trade after 1732, when the energetic Dupleix was appointed governor of Chandernagore. Sinha says, "Chandernagore, which had not a single ship in 1732, possessed fifteen or twenty vessels in daily use by the Company [des Indes] employees when he left in 1742."[73] Reflecting Dupleix's energy, a Dutch letter of 1743 says the French "send many vessels lately to the Maldives".[74]

French power in India was at its height in the early 1750s. Dupleix, who had of course seen cowries and heard much of the Maldives while governor at Chandernagore, was invited to position a small French garrison at Male; a unit commanded by a corporal was put ashore there in 1754. It was no doubt the Franco/Dutch alliance that led the Maldive sultan to permit the unwonted foreign presence. The detachment was supplied from Dutch Ceylon.[75] But whatever advantage this may have gained the French in the cowrie trade was lost by the outbreak of the Seven Years' War in 1756, which the British prosecuted at sea with great success. The French garrison was recalled by Dupleix's successor, Lally, in 1759, and these were the last foreign troops to be quartered at Male.[76] The war virtually halted all French trade in these waters, and even after the Treaty of Paris in 1763 it was slow to revive. When the *Compagnie des Indes* ceased operations in 1769, traders to Africa had once more to depend on the auction sales in the Netherlands.[77] French private merchants were soon competing again, however, and once more moved cowries to Europe, with Marseilles mentioned as a market. Until their embroilment in the War of American Independence, in 1778, the French again had their factory at Balasore, "filled their ships" with the produce of Bengal, says Sinha, and even helped employees of the British E.I.C. to conceal the transport of private cargoes and remission of funds to Europe.[78] At one point, an advantageous arrangement for cowrie supply was negotiated:

> M. Varlie, a Frenchman, an inhabitant of Chandernagore, having rendered the King of the Maldiva islands some essential services, secured a favourable contract from the King for 20,000 cottah of cowries annually. He paid for them in rice valued at a high rate and by this means the French ships from Pondicherry, Chandernagore and Mahe procured a quantity of cowries to ballast home their Europe ships. What more cowries were found in the islands were sold to the Dutch. Some few came in their small boats to Pipli and Balasore.[79]

French vessels are reported at Male in 1777.[80] The war which followed in the next year must have once again made inroads into the French cowrie commerce, and there is no sign of any substantial recovery before the Gallic share of the trade was again lost during the French Revolution and Napoleonic Wars.

MISCELLANEOUS SHIPPERS

During the eighteenth century there were aside from the Dutch, English, and French cowrie trades, also the Danes, the Ostend Company, Altona (Hamburg), still an occasional Portuguese shipment, and no doubt other members of the miscellany as well. There is a report in 1791 of a Danish shipment of nearly 25,000 lbs. The Ostend Company's buying at Balasore has already been mentioned. The independent Altona (Hamburg) trade is known to have attracted French buyers in Europe. Portuguese ships on occasion still called for cowries at the Maldives, as in the 1720s. The total quantities involved are unknown, but probably small by comparison with the major shippers.[81]

The eighteenth century flowering of the cowrie trade brought vast quantities of the shell to West Africa. The data in Tables 5.1 and 5.2 indicate total Dutch plus English shipments 1700–1790 of 25,211,792 lbs. (11,436 metric tonnes), or slightly more than 10,000,000,000 individual shells. In spite of substantial variations in quantity, there was a large-scale base of 100,000 lbs. (about 45 tonnes, or 40 million shells) that was almost always shipped. The only exceptions were the years 1719, 1757, and 1765. These figures were to decline precipitously when the legal slave trade ended in 1807. But there were even bigger boom years still ahead in the nineteenth century.

Table 5.1 *Cowrie imports to West Africa (lbs. avoirdupois) annually, 1700–1799*

Year	English (English exports minus imports from northern Europe)	Dutch (V.O.C. *kamer* sales at Amsterdam, Hoorn, Enkhuizen, Delft, Rotterdam, and Kamer Zeeland)	Total (English plus Dutch)
1700	155,273	47,624	202,897
1701	103,703	68,691	172,394
1702	58,118	66,873	124,991
1703	127,876	166,174	294,050
1704	73,469	145,681	219,150
1705	M	183,436	183,436
1706	27,329	191,342	218,671

Table 5.1 *cont.*

Year	English	Dutch	Total
1707	124,706	147,590	272,296
1708	22,880	141,871	164,751
1709	78,567	172,326	250,893
1710	19,716	169,541	189,257
1711	59,491	237,215	296,706
1712	M	171,029	171,029
1713	85,186	167,597	252,783
1714	104,502	232,286	336,788
1715	43,713	286,149	329,862
1716	83,880	258,248	342,128
1717	162,393	294,382	456,775
1718	34,529	206,326	240,855
1719	33,804	63,087	96,891
1720	158,384	218,526	376,910
1721	360,871	117,612	478,483
1722	441,936	272,612	714,548
1723	346,776	210,479	557,255
1724	285,269	266,466	551,735
1725	340,792	231,691	572,483
1726	295,878	200,739	496,617
1727	239,090	160,416	399,506
1728	287,257	123,639	410,896
1729	264,819	235,792	500,611
1730	283,569	184,814	468,383
1731	104,961	218,950	323,911
1732	156,285	171,668	327,953
1733	102,651	157,370	260,021
1734	72,385	144,103	216,488
1735	39,988	151,041	191,029
1736	139,810	385,252	525,062
1737	60,403	401,790	462,193
1738	144,338	201,491	345,829
1739	95,187	136,025	231,212
1740	173,485	45,853	219,338
1741	101,839	181,577	283,416
1742	123,734	130,428	254,162
1743	203,920	130,294	334,214
1744	69,417	257,729	327,146
1745	63,839	189,863	253,702
1746	18,415	222,405	240,820
1747	199,461	189,895	389,356
1748	166,968	130,458	297,426
1749	66,516	608,477	674,993
1750	102,140	259,834	361,974
1751	150,064	103,799[a]	253,863
1752	44,938	94,147	139,085
1753	38,652	121,981	160,633

Table 5.1 *cont.*

Year	English	Dutch	Total
1754	48,057	133,581	181,638
1755	14,812	113,464[b]	128,276
1756	10,248	142,841[b]	153,089
1757	22,316	44,615	66,931
1758	8,344	116,095	124,439
1759	5,460	147,645	153,105
1760	9,478	151,026	160,504
1761	7,224	195,517	202,741
1762	2,398	133,065	135,463
1763	3,321	152,398	155,719
1764	470	112,038	112,508
1765	224	58,222	58,446
1766	11,234	153,985	165,219
1767	2,731	105,275	108,006
1768	26,784	99,492	126,276
1769	10,500	96,828	107,328
1770	55,351	133,968	189,319
1771	72,292	184,004	256,296
1772	67,852	97,538	165,390
1773	135,147	190,155	325,302
1774	314,464	190,875	505,339
1775	164,052	109,690	273,742
1776	126,091	110,737	236,828
1777	62,269	61,663	123,932
1778	63,806	49,489	113,295
1779	143,583	9,348	152,931
1780	200,688	46,813	247,501
1781	71,750	117,258	189,008
1782	348,055	M	348,055
1783	230,555	37,758	268,313
1784	193,820	93,617	287,437
1785	361,335	217,759	579,094
1786	80,140	221,282	301,422
1787	61,727	419,790	481,517
1788	20,972	91,096	112,068
1789	226,893	92,162	319,055
1790	35,045	210,548	245,593
1791	5,600	39,001[c]	25,101
1792	187,040		206,540
1793	30,688		30,991
1794	63,504	1,203[c]	63,804
1795	35,952		36,252
1796	51,632		51,932
1797	93,184	0	93,184
1798	54,208	0	54,208
1799	158,256	0	158,256

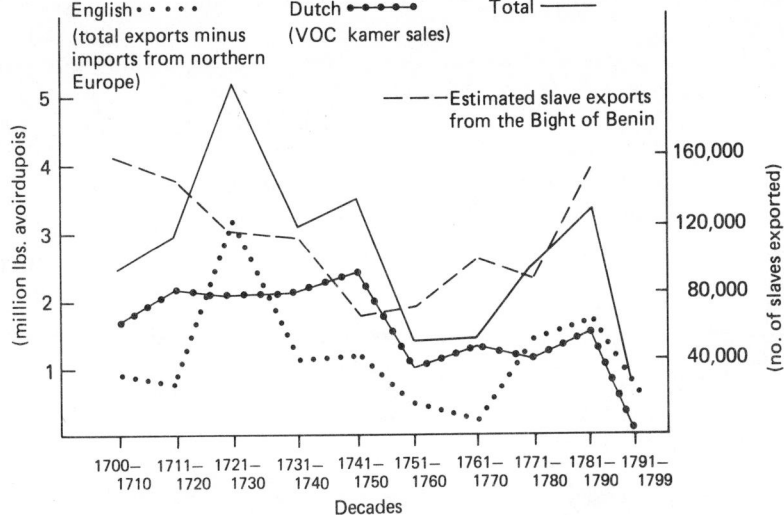

Cowrie shell imports to West Africa by decades, 1700–1799

Notes to Table 5.1

M = missing

[a] The Kamer Amsterdam sales figure for 1751 is missing, but can be reconstructed from the quadrennial returns for auctions at that city.

[b] As for 1751, the Kamer Amsterdam sales figures for 1755 and 1756 are missing. The quadrennial returns allow us to determine sales in the two years together. We have prorated them 50% to 1755 and 50% to 1756. Other Kamer figures available.

The data used in calculating sales in 1751, 1755, and 1756 are in the Klinkenberg thesis, pp. 69, 87.

[c] From the Kamer Amsterdam quadrennial returns. The total in the fourth column includes the Dutch figures prorated for each of the two years 1791–92, and each of the four years 1793–96.

Table 5.2 *Cowrie imports to West Africa (lbs. avoirdupois) by decades, 1700–1799*

Year	English (English exports minus imports from northern Europe)	Dutch (V.O.C. *kamer* sales at Amsterdam, Hoorn, Enkhuizen, Delft, Rotterdam, and Kamer Zeeland)	Total (English plus Dutch)
1700–10	791,637[a]	1,501,149	2,292,786
1711–20	765,882[a]	2,134,845	2,900,727
1721–30	3,146,257	2,004,260	5,150,517
1731–40	1,089,493	2,013,543	3,103,036
1741–50	1,116,249	2,300,960	3,417,209
1751–60	352,369	1,101,605	1,453,974
1761–70	120,237	1,240,788	1,361,025
1771–80	1,350,244	1,050,312	2,400,556
1781–90	1,630,292	1,501,270[a]	3,131,562
1791–99	680,064	40,204	720,268
Grand total	11,042,724	14,888,936	25,931,660

[a] Imports for one year missing in total.

Note on method: No explicit cowrie export series is available for the Netherlands. We have utilized instead the records of the auction sales at the *kamers* of the V.O.C., as obtained by Hogendorn's research assistant, Floris Klinkenberg, at the Rijksarchief, Den Haag. The archive numbers for the data are as follows: KA10.238, VOC4587; KA10.239, VOC4588; KA10.240, VOC4589; KA10.241, VOC4590; KA10.242, VOC4591; KA10,242A, VOC4592; KA10.242B, VOC4593; KA10.242C, VOC4594; KA10.242D, VOC4595; KA10.242E, VOC4596; KA10.242F, VOC4597. There is a minor complication in interpreting the Dutch figures, which are for a type of fiscal year, "boekjaar," usually running May to May and sometimes June to June. (The English data considered below are for the approximate calendar year Christmas to Christmas.) There is no apparent way to convert the Dutch figures to the English basis. Thus the Dutch sales data for the year 1720 actually cover the period May 1719 to May 1720. This is fortunately of little moment, and will not distort the statistics to any significant degree. By far the greatest part of the auction sales of cowries took place in the autumn, especially in October and sometimes well into November. As is discussed in chapter 7, the preparation and shipment of these shells by the purchaser could take weeks, and the shells sold in 1719 would thus frequently not be exported from the Netherlands until after the start of 1720. For this reason, the auction sales of a given year (say Autumn 1719) are listed in our tables under the following year (1720), this appearing the best way to use the data as a proxy for Dutch exports. Even where this is not accurate, it will be erroneous by a matter of only a few weeks.

All Dutch figures are converted from Amsterdams ponds to pounds avoirdupois by multiplying the former by a factor of 1.09. Dutch sales figures are after sorting. As noted in the text, barring a minute quantity purchased for export to other destinations for purposes of ornamentation, all Dutch cowries went eventually to West Africa. Assuming losses on the voyage were also minute, V.O.C. *kamer* sales are thus equivalent to cowries originating in the Netherlands and imported to West Africa.

Notes to Table 5.2 *cont.*

The English data are derived from Marion Johnson's research on the customs records housed at the Public Record Office, London. The main file is PRO CUST/3 to 1780 and CUST/17 from 1781. The data were originally in hundredweights, and have been converted by us to pounds avoirdupois. Two series are available covering 1700–99. The first is "English imports," subdivided by us into imports from India, Northern Europe, and "other." The second series is "English exports," subdivided by us into exports to Africa, Northern Europe, Southern Europe, and "other." "English imports" would appear to be the less appropriate measure because they include unknown quantities of cowries discarded in the sorting process before export to Africa, and also include some imports of Dutch cowries eventually re-exported from England and hence double-counted if English imports are considered tantamount to imports into West Africa.

"English exports" are much more directly comparable to the Dutch "V.O.C. *kamer* sales," since they would not include shells discarded in the sorting process. There is still the problem of double-counting Dutch shells among British re-exports. To take account of this problem, we have subtracted "English imports from Northern Europe" from "English exports to Africa." The double-counting of Dutch shells is thus eliminated, and the only resulting inaccuracy from this step is the exclusion of some small quantity of Ostend Company and Altona (Hamburg) shells imported from Asia independently, and then re-exported first to England and then to West Africa. From all indications available to us this does little to affect accuracy. English exports to all destinations are included in the total. We consider this a reasonable procedure, since non-African buyers would be purchasing for their own eventual re-export in the African trade. These secondary markets for English exports included the Netherlands, Flanders, Germany, France, Portugal, Madeira, and Spain. Inclusion of the Netherlands in this list means the *possibility* that some shell was purchased from England by the V.O.C. and then resold at the Dutch auctions, with resultant double-counting. There is no evidence of this however.

6

Boom and slump for the cowrie trade (nineteenth century)

The cowrie trade went through a cycle of boom and slump, boom and slump, in the nineteenth century. In 1800 the British had achieved almost complete ascendancy in shipments to West Africa, with the Dutch and French now entirely out of the running. This led to a surge in British shell exports in the first eight years of the century, to an annual average of over 68 tonnes compared to the 24-tonne average for the eight years 1791–1798. These figures are substantially above the British annual average for the eighteenth century to 1790 (though only some 55% of the 125-tonne annual mean for 1700–1790 when Dutch sales are included). As before, the auctions of the East India Company remained the major mart for putting the shells in the hands of merchants trading to Africa.[1]

Depression loomed, however, with a twofold cause. After decades of anti-slavery agitation, the British banned the slave trade in 1807. Slaves had been, of course, the major means of paying for shell imports to Africa. Simultaneously, British monetary policy in India was causing a rapid slackening in the demand for cowries in its remaining markets, Bengal and Orissa. Together, these events wrought temporary ruin for the shell trade, and presumably brought an economic slump to the Maldives, mitigated only by the maintenance of its coir exports.[2]

The first cause of the great cowrie depression, abolition of the slave trade, demonstrated vividly the direct link between the export of blacks and shell imports to West Africa. In 1808, the first full year after Britain's law prohibiting slaving, cowrie shipments to West Africa collapsed to only 1.2 tonnes, with an annual average of about $4\frac{1}{2}$ tonnes in the years 1808–1818.[3] Cowries as an imported commodity had to be paid for. Ruin for Africa's major export (most justifiable ruin, we hasten to add) meant equivalent ruin for major imports such as the cowrie and for the producer of those imported goods, in this case the Maldives. Africa and the Maldives, with sudden monetary constriction in the former and a sharp decline of exports in the latter, must both have suffered serious consequences for internal exchange, though there is little evidence pointing to the predictable severity beyond the foreign trade statistics.[4]

Meanwhile, declining demand in Bengal and Orissa was also contributing to the depression. At the start of the century, cowries retained their monetary significance. Taxes and tribute were still payable in shells and they served as small change as before. New imports of cowries continued to flow in large numbers from the Maldives, though the quantity estimates are poor; estimates by British officials, early in the century, of imports to Orissa (via Balasore) mostly be ranged from approximately 23 tonnes to 70 tonnes. One official said two-thirds of these shells were shipped onward to Bengal.[5] But change was coming. Parallel to later events in Africa, the British implemented legislation requiring the government revenues to be collected in silver coin (in Orissa after 1807), and they stepped up efforts to introduce a copper coinage to replace cowries. There had been no copper coins used in Bengal prior to 1781–82, but in that year Warren Hastings ordered the minting of copper *pice*, apparently to save from bankruptcy a friend, Johannes Matthias Ross of the E.I.C., who on his own private account had become heavily overstocked with copper. The low-value *pice* had little success at first; but English merchants were given further contracts, and soon the famous Boulton works at Soho, Birmingham, were turning out the coins. The E.I.C. purchased £4,000 worth of these coins in 1790, a figure which had doubled to £8,000 in 1793.[6] It would take a long time to replace the shell money of Bengal and Orissa, but the tide had turned. Holden Furber writes, "Thereafter the cowrie was in retreat. The millions of cowries slowly gave way to the millions of copper pice cut out by the machines of Messrs. Boulton and Watt."[7] The combined effect of this new British monetary policy, which cut the cowrie demand, and the virtual end of shipments to West Africa, which increased supply in India, was a sharp decline in the cowrie price, fully apparent by 1812. The heavy depreciation (a figure of 70% to 80% is mentioned) of course eroded the value of the existing stock of shells, and was said to be one cause of the rebellion in Orissa during the year 1817.[8]

REVIVAL

The British had always had little luck in trading at the Maldives, and at the start of the century they were not buying there. The last European ship to visit the islands, in 1803, sailed four years *before* the cowrie trade collapsed, and no ship is known to have called again until the 1830s.[9] The sultan continued to export to Bengal and Orissa in return for rice imports, but the decline in the terms of trade must have caused hardship of which there is no record. The bad times lasted for what must have seemed a long decade, but then came a stroke of fortune. Slowly at first, then rapidly, the West African demand for shell money revived. This resuscitation must have been as unexpected as the collapse had been to the islanders on their remote atolls. The cause of the revival was a resurgence of African exports that once again was paid for partly in Maldives shell money. The new African export was that exemplary substitute for slaving, palm oil. Palm oil greased the wheels of the industrial revolution. It lit the lamps of homes and factories. As the chief ingredient of soap, it cleaned the bodies and clothes dirtied in the smoke and grit of that polluted age. And it was a major input in tinplate manufacture. By 1820 West Africa's palm oil exports were already 887 tonnes, but that figure had risen to over 22,000 tonnes in 1850.[10] (Wood, groundnut, and gum exports also grew very substantially in those years, but these originated mostly in areas that did not use the cowrie currency.)[11] There was also, alas, a continuing traffic in slaves from the Slave Coast eastwards to boost income.

Great quantities of cowries were needed to buy these exports. As seen in Table 6.1, there was a great revival during the 22-year period to 1840, with the annual average of exports from Britain to West Africa soaring to 100 tonnes, close to the Anglo-Dutch figures of 125 tonnes during the eighteenth century to 1790. The table shows a steady rise for the most part, with the average pulled up by years of 230 tonnes in 1836 and 209 tonnes in 1840. The years 1823–1828 were, however, relatively poor ones, all with under 35 tonnes. Even so, their average of 21 tonnes exceeds the $4\frac{1}{2}$ tonnes average of 1808–1818 by a wide margin.

These shells were still coming from the Maldives, but we have no first-hand reports from there until the 1830s. Not until 1834 did a British surveying expedition, led by Captain Moresby on the surveying ship *Benares*, arrive at Male to renew contacts with the islands. The Europeans were not initially welcomed, but two members of the ship's complement, Lieutenant Young and Mr. Christopher, got permission to stay ashore for a time, and landed at Male in June of 1835. During their stay of a few months, they saw the newly resurgent cowrie commerce at the source and were the first Europeans to write about it.[12] Calcutta and Chittagong are noted as major destinations, but Balasore is not. That age-old cowrie port must have been losing importance; it was still mentioned prominently by Thomas Thornton in 1825, who says "cowries imported at Calcutta, Chittagong, or Balasore only," but not by subsequent visitors.[13] Young and Christopher found the shells on sale in the bazaars of Male at one rupee per *kotta* of 12,000, but some were available for export only at a price of two rupees, the difference representing "charges for godown rent and anchorage." The cowries were exchanged largely for imports of rice, and also areca nuts, goods of cotton and silk, and other commodities.[14]

The two visitors noted carefully the port charges (40 rupees paid by every trading vessel) and duties in the form of fixed quantities of each merchandise import distributed to the sultan, "to the officers of the Government, the Sultan's relatives &c.," and to the official "whose duty it is to superintend the division and distribution of the presents" – he got one-sixth of the whole, the "principal emolument of his office." But the captains of visiting merchantmen could select for payment articles in least demand, say Young and Christopher, thus lessening the impact of the duties.[15] H. C. P. Bell

Table 6.1 *British cowrie exports to West Africa, 1800–1850 (lbs. avoir-dupois)*

Year	Amount	Year	Amount
1800	164,864	1826	8,176
1801	99,008	1827	51,184
1802	259,728	1828	40,432
1803	35,504	1829	121,184
1804	184,240	1830	80,304
1805	202,272	1831	160,832
1806	123,872	1832	171,584
1807	136,976	1833	42,896
1808	2,576	1834	200,144
1809	5,488	1835	387,408
1810	12,880	1836	506,016
1811	10,192	1837	310,016
1812	9,632	1838	370,048
1813	M	1839	301,504
1814	2,128	1840	460,656
1815	32,592	1841	645,456
1816	7,728	1842	614,880
1817	1,232	1843	844,144
1818	9,968	1844	613,648
1819	138,096	1845	1,255,632
1820	52,640	1846	1,043,280
1821	46,256	1847	1,130,640
1822	169,344	1848	699,888
1823	40,544	1849	1,061,200
1824	64,848	1850	821,296
1825	74,256		

Total: 13,829,312 lbs. = 6,273 tonnes
Annual average: 271,163 lbs. = 123 tonnes

M = missing
Source: PRO CUST/17 and CUST/4

wrote in 1883 that "there is reason to believe that these [port dues and charges] have varied but slightly since."[16]

The British mariners also noted how the annual taxes paid by the sultan's subjects helped to swell the flow of exports. The "public treasurer" at Male was in charge of collecting the tax revenues, which were paid in produce. This produce was then sent "in the Government boats, on account of the Government, to Bengal, and to the different trading ports." The boat captains were paid by being permitted to trade on their own account (similar to E.I.C. practice in the preceding century). On each atoll, an atoll-chief was in charge of collecting the tax revenue, and responsible to him on each major island was an island-chief seeing to tax collection at the local level.[17]

This account does not explicitly single out cowries as the main means of tax payment, but subsequent authors certainly do so. H. C. P. Bell wrote later in the century of a fixed poll tax, variable as between different islands, and collected in double amount on each male between the ages of 15 and 60 (the doubling thus covering the female population). He suggests 1½ *kottas* as a representative figure for the doubled tax. W. T. Taylor, Ceylon Controller of Revenue, stated that in 1899 the direct tax per couple between 15 and 60 was 28 lbs. of cowries, 25 fish, and 25 coconuts. Later work by Bell (1917–1922) also notes cowrie taxes. During Hogendorn's fieldwork, informants frequently stated that tax payments had many years before been made in part with cowries. The practice only died out between the two world wars. The tax revenue was used in part to recompense the atoll-chiefs and island-chiefs, most of whom (says C. W. Rosset) were assigned for life, with vacancies filled by the reigning sultan's appointment.[18]

We suspect that these descriptions of the tax system, the first dating from 1835, are also accurate for a much earlier period as well, and are important in understanding how government fostered a large steady supply of cowries when these were demanded during the slave trade.

To this point, the nineteenth-century revival seems identical in almost all aspects to the condition of the trade in the decade leading up to Abolition in 1807. There was one substantial difference, however, in the shipment of shells. When the cowries were purchased in Bengal, Orissa, or Ceylon, the British buyers were now private commercial concerns without official status. The East India Company, after years of sharing supremacy with the Dutch, had come under attack in London. "John Company" lost its monopoly of the Indian trade with Lord Liverpool's bill of 1813. After Earl Grey's Act of 1833, the E.I.C. "ceased to be a trading concern and exercised only administrative functions."[19] The numerous house flags of the private companies thereafter replaced the red-and-white striped banner of the E.I.C. on the masts of the ships carrying the cowries to Britain. Presumably, the shells still rode as ballast, as they had for centuries before.

NEW RECORDS IN THE COWRIE TRADE

For nearly a decade, there were no further first-hand reports of production at the Maldives, but from Table 6.1 it can be seen that around the 1840s the cowrie trade entered an unprecedented period of expansion. The year 1836 was a 200-tonne year (230 to be exact), only the second time the British had ever achieved that figure – the old record of 200 tonnes had been set over a century before, in 1722. The decade after 1840 saw quite remarkable growth, records repeatedly broken, and production levels so high that they lead inevitably to conjectures of over-fishing. During the decade 1841–1850, the annual average rose to an extraordinary 396 tonnes. Four of these years were over 470 tonnes, and one of these, 1845, hit a new high for the Maldives trade of almost 570 tonnes (the peak years of the eighteenth century, Dutch and British together, did not exceed 327 tonnes).[20] Ever greater West African prosperity, primed by palm oil exports, was obviously exerting a substantial effect on that area's demand for money. The effect on the Maldives must, however, have been somewhat less pronounced than the figures indicate. A proportion of the shells exported to Africa must have represented a progressive run-down of stocks held in Bengal and Orissa, a topic to which we shall return.

Right in the middle of the boom, in 1844, a little German sailing vessel anchored at Male and attempted to buy cowries.[21] The ship belonged to Adolph Jacob Hertz of Hamburg, who had been in the shipping business since 1836, and was to become the pioneer of *annulus* exports to West Africa. Knowing that the cowries were coming from Calcutta (some via Chittagong) and Ceylon, he thought he would buy at the source, as the Dutch had done in earlier centuries. Hertz's son John left a valuable account of the visit, which did not appear until 1881.[22]

At "King's Island," the only spot where foreign trade was allowed, the expedition was told that no European merchantmen had visited in living memory. Difficulties were encountered almost at once. The intention was to buy cowries with cash, unlike the voyagers of previous centuries who had brought cargoes of imported goods to make the exchange. But the Maldivian officials were not comfortable with the idea. Clearly they hesitated to take any steps that might interfere with the essential flow of rice imports from Bengal and Orissa. The arrangements were of long standing, and to interrupt them for profit that might prove impermanent seemed too hazardous.[23] Despite its best efforts, the Hertz expedition had to content itself with the purchase of only a limited number of cowries, and even that required the sacrifice of a wheeled cart ("Rollwagen") on board the ship which had caught the fancy of the sultan.[24]

It was in 1845, on the way back from this unsuccessful effort at the Maldives, that the Hertz ship stopped at Zanzibar, saw *Cypraea annulus*, and took along the small quantity that started a revolution in the world's cowrie markets.[25]

Hertz was no doubt persuaded to make this trip to the Maldives because the cowrie boom, led by demand from West Africa, was causing prices to increase. Back in 1835, Young and Christopher reported that a *kotta* of 12,000 cowries could be purchased at Male for two rupees including port charges and fees. A *kotta* at this time would weigh about 30 lbs.; the average size of shells shipped having risen slightly since the eighteenth century. Converting at 2 British shillings to the rupee, this gives a price of just under £15 per tonne. (With British prices at the time around £20, this implies transport costs plus profits equal to about one-third of the purchase price in transactions with London. This is not, we suggest, a very high margin.)[26] The Hertz expedition, however, found prices at Male to be $8 to $9 per hundredweight, which comes to $157 to $176 per tonne. Assuming these were Maria Theresa dollars, as implied by Ernst Hieke – Hertz did not say

Table 6.2 *Cowrie imports to Britain, 1851—1870 (lbs. avoirdupois)*

Year	British India	Ceylon	Singapore	Philippines	Europe	East and South Africa	Miscellaneous
1851	2,198,560	217,392	112,896	153,328	10,416	10,752	3,920
1852	995,792	130,592	—	1,680	203,616	—	8,288
1853	830,592	744,016	125,440	23,520	—	—	3,808
1854	423,584	464,016	—	—	15,680	—	—
1855	361,200	285,712	336	252,672	—	112	896
1856	855,120	1,093,344	—	147,952	8,176	21,728	5,600
1857	924,896	545,440	—	421,344	560	—	784
1858	1,129,408	517,552	1,232	365,680	30,128	22,176	—
1859	620,816	474,544	—	468,048	7,280	—	1,008
1860	771,008	219,296	—	113,568	71,456	56,224	112
1861	222,656	374,080	2,240	221,200	20,944	—	—
1862	273,168	345,968	—	5,600	82,656	—	—
1863	508,032	538,048	—	267,456	—	323,232	9,408
1864	341,152	471,520	—	29,120	—	92,400	1,680
1865	211,792	238,336	—	412,608	—	—	9,632
1866	407,456	—	—	129,472	—	33,376	—
1867	256,816	—	—	182,336	—	31,024	112
1868	122,416	116,480	—	229,712	—	—	—
1869	335,712	15,680	2,800	347,312	62,272	—	55,440
1870	258,832	72,240	—	340,256	9,520	—	4,368

Total: 24,509,856 lbs. = 11,118 tonnes   Annual average: 1,225,493 lbs. = 555.88 tonnes

The European shipments came from the Hanse towns, France, Sweden, Portugal, and the Netherlands. East and South Africa includes Mauritius. Miscellaneous includes China, New South Wales, Morocco, Egypt, Chile, the U.S., Puerto Rico, Japan, the Gold Coast, and West Africa (mainly Nigeria in the later years).

Source: PRO CUST/5

what dollars they were – they would thus be equivalent to about 4s. 2d. each.[27] A metric tonne of cowries at the Maldives would therefore be worth £30 to £34 in 1844, about double the figures based on the Young and Christopher information. According to Hertz, at this time (1844) the sale price on the West African coast was $18 per cwt., or £75 per tonne.[28] Between Male, Bengal, London, and the African West Coast there was thus a margin of 100%, or a little more, over the original purchase price to recompense for transport, handling, sorting, insurance, and profit. This may well represent a decent return for those engaged in the trade, but it is certainly not a bonanza and appears to have involved no major foreign exploitation of the Maldives royal monopoly.

ANNULUS

There were still a few great years left for the Maldives. (See Table 6.2 for cowries entering Britain, 1851–70. The imports from British India and Ceylon must have been predominantly Maldive shells, but the rundown of Bengal/Orissa monetary stocks means that the published import figures must be greater than current Maldives exports). But that Hertz sailing ship from Hamburg had done more damage than anyone could have expected, and within twenty years of its visit the cowrie trade from the islands was practically dead. How this happened in such a short space of time is an astounding aspect of monetary history, still somewhat difficult to explain. In the harbour of Zanzibar, Hertz examined with interest the East African *Cypraea annulus*, orange-ringed and larger than the *moneta* of the Maldives but otherwise so similar. These *annulus* were present in enormous numbers on the East African coast and Zanzibar. Hertz thought the major concentration was in the shallows of Mafia Island, between the town of Chole and Juani Island; other traders spoke of large quantities further to the south in the Ibo Islands. (Mafia Island is south of Zanzibar and north of Kilwa, a few miles off the coast of present-day Tanzania; the Ibo Islands are even closer to the coast, a little to the south of the present border between Tanzania and Mozambique.)[29]

The economic incentive for suppliers to ship *annulus* is clear enough. Hertz noted that even though a hundredweight of the Zanzibar species contained slightly less than half the number of individual shells contained in a hundredweight of Maldives *moneta* (18,000 to 20,000 against 45,000 to 48,000 by his calculation), it was still very much more profitable to ship *annulus* if these shells were acceptable. The ring-cowries could be purchased in East Africa for only $0.75 per cwt., as against 10 to 12 times that price for Maldive shells, but they could be sold on the West Coast for $8 or $9 per cwt., just about the going sale price for Maldives *moneta*.[30] (Table 6.3 sums up Hertz's figures). Obviously the profits were there if only West African consumers would be willing to absorb *annulus* along with their traditional *moneta*.

71

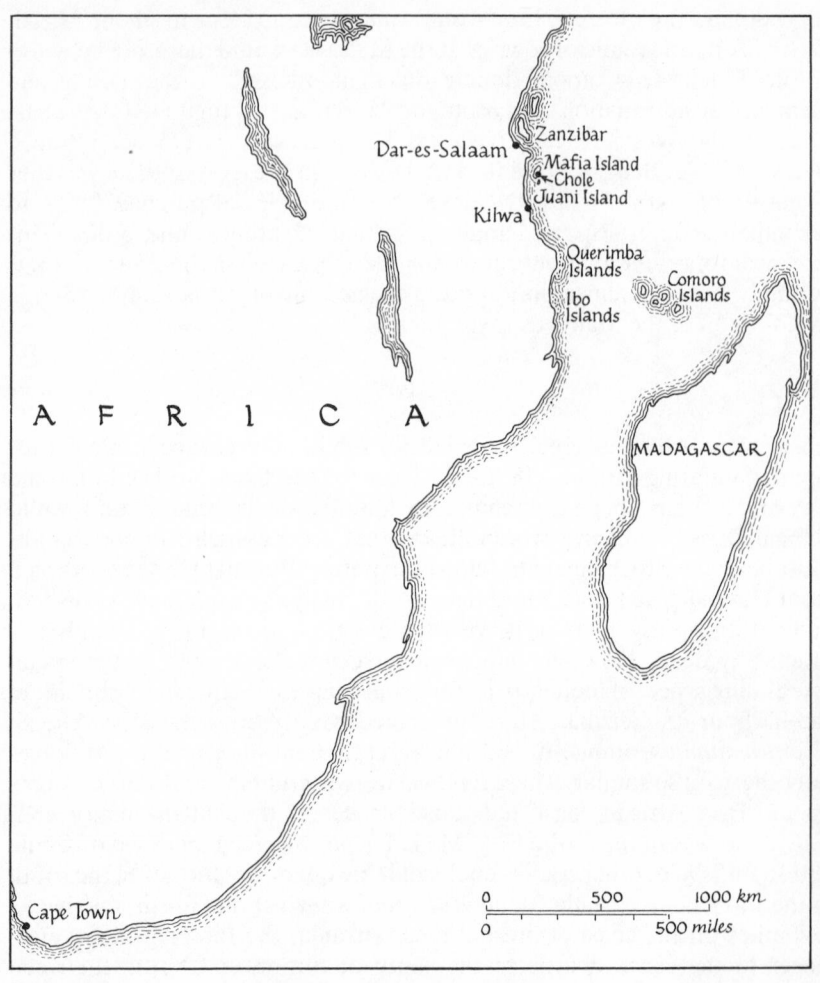

Map 4 East Africa: *Cypraea annulus*

The prejudice against *annulus* had if anything grown stronger from the start of the eighteenth century. By the end of that century they went at a substantial discount if they could be disposed of at all. The Frenchman Morice, testifying before a British commission in 1777 as an expert on the East African coast, stated that the East African cowrie "can only be sold in Bengal. It is worthless for the Guinea coast." He added that such a small number were suitable (perhaps the local *moneta*, perhaps young or under-sized *annulus*) that "they are not worth the trouble of collecting them."[31] There *were* some exports of *annulus* to Bengal, from Pate by the British

Table 6.3 *Prices of Maldive and Zanzibar cowries, 1844, following Hertz*

	Number of shells per cwt.	Buying price per cwt. $	Selling price per cwt. $
Maldive cowries (*C. moneta*)	45,000–48,000	8–9	18
Zanzibar cowries (*C. annulus*)	18,000–20,000	0.75	8–9

where "some small ships take on cowries," said M. Morice, and from other points as well, as indicated by Thomas Thornton. These exports were conducted by the French, by the Portuguese (mentioned as shipping sometimes substantial quantities of shell to Bengal from the Querimba Islands off Mozambique in the 1750s and 1760s) and doubtless by other nationalities including Arab and Indian seafarers as well. (There was also some reverse flow of *moneta* to East Africa, conducted by local shipping in the nineteenth century.)[32]

Hertz was certainly not the first merchant to see the possibilities of importing the East Africa shells in quantity to West Africa. Fowell Buxton, quoting "the captain of a merchant vessel who was long on the East Coast of Africa," wrote in 1836: "A most profitable trade might also be carried on in cowries, which abound on the coast, where he has purchased them at 4d. a bushel; on the West Coast they are current coin, and are told out by the 100."[33] Somehow, though, Hertz was lucky enough to be there when the resistance to *annulus* began to break down. The question is why was the traditional barrier pierced at this time, and why so quickly. We already know of the importers' potential for profit, but that had been there for a very long time. We know too that merchants in the palm oil trade, which thrived during the Crimean War, could also profit by using cheap *annulus* if palm oil producers could be persuaded to take them. But this, too, had long been the case. The answer must necessarily lie in the determinants of the demand for and supply of money. The palm oil boom and the resulting increase in *moneta* prices must have increased the attractiveness of "monetary innovation;" as a result some individuals must have been willing to try a small quantity of "substitute money." Other individuals took some of it in market exchange – not everyone, not everywhere, and often at some discount – but the results were obviously successful enough to encourage further imports. There was no particular act of state leading to the *annulus* imports. It seems entirely a phenomenon of the market, perhaps akin to the early adoptions of paper money in western Europe and the United States. When the "orthodox" money became more expensive, even obvious prejudice against the unorthodox Continentals, assignats, Pitt's paper currency, state bank notes, and Greenback Dollars did not greatly hinder their acceptability until over-supply eroded their value.

At first the ring-cowries were sold for Spanish and South American gold doubloons, originally acquired by African and Portuguese-African coastal traders in their dealings with Brazilian slave traders. (These doubloons had no currency inland from Whydah and Lagos). Within a few years, with the slave trade in decline and these gold coins becoming scarce, the cowries were used to buy palm oil at the rate of 3 gallons of oil for a silver dollar's worth of shells. With the palm oil trade more clearly seasonal than slave exports, cowrie sales too thus came to be seasonal.[34]

From the first experimental introduction of *annulus* at Whydah in 1845 (used, incidentally, to finance a war and thus augment the supply of slaves for the Brazilian market), the trade in East African shells was more direct than was the importation of *moneta*. Distances were much shorter, and the ships carrying the ring-cowrie, smaller than the East Indiamen and better suited for the creeks and anchorages, had no valuable cargoes to hurry home to Europe. Some vessels were thus able to shuttle back and forth from Zanzibar and elsewhere on Indian Ocean shores to the West Coast. (This direct trade declined greatly from about 1852 when payment came to be made in palm oil, as mentioned in the last paragraph – the cowrie ships had to carry the oil to Europe). Even in the earlier years, there were other ships coming from Europe carrying manufactured goods (firearms, powder, spirits, cottons, other manufactures) when outward bound to Zanzibar, then loading cowries for West Africa, then sailing homeward with ivory, palm oil, and other African products.[35]

The high profits brought fierce competition in the imports of *annulus*, though still within the family of Hamburg firms; as late as 1853 Campbell, the British consul at Lagos, spoke of the Zanzibar shell trade being "entirely monopolized by the Hamburgers." One such Hamburg firm, Wm. O'Swald and Co., showed much ingenuity and notably little scruple in the battle, during which it succeeded in pushing the pioneer Hertz out of the business. A second casualty was Diedrichsen, the Flensburg merchant later naturalized as a citizen of Hamburg, who did much of the work of selling cowries on the west coast. One of O'Swald's enterprising ship captains, Hans A. Rodatz, had penetrated Hertz's trade secret within a year; O'Swald made a trial shipment (150 tons) in 1848, and by 1849 had established an agency at Zanzibar. By 1851 the firm had such a stranglehold on the Zanzibar supply that a Hertz ship took from October to March to acquire even a small cargo. At this time O'Swald ships were loading in full with cowries in twelve days. Eventually the Hertz company was put to the indignity of depending on its tormentor to obtain supplies. Monopsony tactics were also used by O'Swald on the West African coast; one Hertz ship had to return to Hamburg with its cowrie cargo unsold. Before its monopoly was broken by the French, 40% of O'Swald's shipping was engaged in the transport of shells. (The reader who thinks the name of the firm does not sound German is quite right. The founder, a Silesian German, J. C. H. Wilhelm Oswald, was an admirer of Sir Walter Scott's novels, and he changed his name to give what he apparently thought would be a Highland flavor; the flavor was Celtic, at any rate.)

Outsiders, including Americans, attempted to obtain information on the new trade in *annulus*, and the German merchants reacted by surrounding their activities with considerable secrecy. Ring-cowries were referred to as "Kaffee" (coffee); other names were used also, but coffee was retained as a code word for the longest period. "Coffee is a good item that doesn't go out of fashion here," said one dispatch. Or, as in a letter to the O'Swald office in Zanzibar, a joking remark that poor Hertz on the west coast did not know what to do with his "coffee supply." Some French visitors in Zanzibar were told that the shells they saw being loaded there were raw material for the porcelain industry at Dresden (thus reflecting the very old linguistic usage referred to in chapter 1, wherein the shells had been known in the medieval Mediterranean as "porcelains" or some related word with the meaning "little pigs"). Some shells came, via middlemen, to O'Swald's Zanzibar agency from as far away as the Comoro Islands and Madagascar. (Some *moneta* cowries were also purchased in India, for in these early years of the *annulus* trade the shipments were mixed to cover the risk that a cargo of ring-cowries might not sell.)[36]

The direct import of *annulus* rapidly achieved hugh proportions, with new French competition, especially from the house of Victor Régis commencing 1855–1857, adding to the total.[37] Between 1851 and 1869, when the trade was at its height, just five German and French companies supplied something over 35,000 tonnes of *annulus* (some 14,000,000,000 shells), all reaching West Africa from Zanzibar and other parts of the East African coast and islands (see Table 6.4). Some 70% of this was shipped by O'Swald and Hertz, with the remainder coming mostly from Régis, Hansing & Cie., and (after 1866) Roux de Fraissinet & Cie.[38] This total, averaging about 1,870 tonnes per year during a two-decade span, was far larger in weight and almost equal in number to *all* the shipments of Maldive *moneta* by the Dutch and British in the eighteenth century and by the British between 1800 and 1850. (These together comprised something less than 18,200 tonnes in total, some 16,000,000,000 shells.)

Annulus did not displace *moneta* as money. The two were often strung together on the same cord in areas where strung cowries were the rule, and everywhere the old Maldive stocks were as useful as ever.[39] But new production in the Maldives fell off precipitously, as discussed below, and *annulus* spread rapidly. By the 1860s the large Zanzibar shells had displaced the small Maldive shells at Lagos and as far inland as Abeokuta. They were carried northwards, probably in diminishing proportions (because of their weight) as they went inland. In 1889 large cowries were reported at Walewale, in what is now northern Ghana, selling at a discount of only 10%. By the 1890s most of the cowries in use in Togo and in Yoruba country

Table 6.4 *German and French ascendancy in the annulus trade: cowries shipped, 1851–1869 (lbs. avoirdupois)*

	O'Swald	Hertz	Régis	Roux de Fraissinet	Hansing
1851	549,920	274,400			
1852	975,520	672,000			
1853	1,384,320	476,000			
1854	1,433,600	1,428,000			252,000
1855	2,199,680	1,832,320			
1856	3,500,000	2,178,400	2,419,200		274,400
1857	3,255,600	2,029,440	4,692,800		
1858	3,147,200	2,206,400	1,644,160		1,232,000
1859	2,671,200	293,440			
1860	3,584,000		2,178,400		537,600
1861	504,000		3,218,880		537,600
1862	2,732,800		492,800		
1863					
1864	1,431,920				324,800
1865	3,214,400				
1866	4,093,600				
1867	3,505,600			1,601,600	
1868	2,486,400			3,151,680	
1869	2,772,000			1,685,600	
Totals:	43,411,760	11,390,400	14,646,240	6,438,880	3,158,440

Grand Total, five companies, 1851–1869: 79,045,680 lbs. = 35,854.9 tonnes.

Source: Hieke, *Deutschen Handels*, Vol. 1, p. 283.

were East African *annulus*.[40] They were not, however, accepted every-where in the cowrie zone. They were never in use at Accra or anywhere else on the Gold Coast west of the Volta River (probably because the govern-ment refused to accept them in payment of taxes – one trader recalled a shipment being thrown into the sea).[41] They did not penetrate into Igbo country east of the Niger, apart from the town of Onitsha itself.[42] In these areas of non-acceptance, Maldive *moneta* typically carried a value double that of the larger variety elsewhere. Resistance to the introduction of *annulus* was also reported from Adamawa.[43] Anywhere far away from the coast, *moneta* was obviously cheaper to transport than was *annulus*. A bag of 20,000 *moneta*, a common unit and at about 50 lbs., was a reasonable load for a man over long distances; the bag would have weighed upwards of 100 lbs. if filled exclusively with large *annulus*. Bags moving north were indeed mixed by the late nineteenth century, but the further the distance to be travelled, the greater the cost barrier for the larger shells. (That did not protect northerly areas from monetary inflation, however. When inflation hit coastal areas, it became more profitable to ship the now-depreciated *moneta* to areas where its purchasing power had not yet been eroded. Thus the currency crisis could spread to regions where *annulus* was little seen.)

THE GREAT INFLATION

A currency crisis did indeed ensue. In Lagos where the impact of *annulus* was great, cowries in 1895 had only a little more than a tenth of the value that they had had in 1850, measured in cowries per pound sterling. (If 1850 = 100, the price index for cowries was 13 in 1895). At Whydah, where the reported rates are various and fluctuating, the 1895 index ranges from 10 to 18. At Accra, where *annulus* had less effect, the index during the same period went from 1850 = 100 to 1895 = 24.[44] By the end of the nineteenth century, the inflation had caused the long-distance inland transport system for cowries to break down. Any trader attempting to headload a cargo of shells had to face the fact that his human carriers would consume the entire value of their burden in subsistence costs alone within two to three weeks. There is a detailed account of the great inflation in chapter 9.

Unlike a paper currency, a badly-depreciated commodity money such as cowries is difficult if not impossible to reform. The shells could not be withdrawn, and there was no easy substitute. Thus the inflation served to ruin the usefulness of the cowrie currency for transactions of any size. The tedium of dealing with vast numbers of the shells greatly increased the attractiveness of the new colonial coinage, the introduction of which was much easier because of the collapse in cowrie values.

END OF THE COWRIE TRADE

Overborne by the East African competition, the Maldive shell industry withered away. Our statistics on this are imperfect, since our "British import and export" series in Tables 6.1 and 6.2 are compromised by three problems. First, some *moneta* was now coming in large quantities from other sources of supply in Asia (see the shipments from the Philippines and Singapore in Table 6.2). Second, with *annulus* having become acceptable in West Africa, from the mid-1840s some unknown proportion of imports to Britain and exports to Africa must certainly have consisted of these ring-cowries. Third, and perhaps most important, is the already-mentioned run-down of shell-money stocks in Bengal and Orissa, where minted coins, in particular copper *pice*, were replacing Maldive *moneta*.

All three reasons presumably explain why shell imports into Britain from "British India and Ceylon" could stay very high after 1850 (Table 6.2), while from available indications Maldive Islands cowrie exports went into a steep decline. Evidence for this is not comprehensive. However, we do know, from H. C. P. Bell, some Maldive export figures for 1853 to 1881.[45]

77

These figures were apparently found by searching the Indian and Ceylonese import records to find the Maldives when mentioned. Bell warns that "the figures for British India are very incomplete owing to want of details in the annual returns." For what they are worth, however, they show a steep drop through the 1850s to rock-bottom in 1866. The statistics are in pounds sterling, converted from rupees, and there is no volume data. In 1856, nearly £18,000 of cowries went from the Maldives to India and Ceylon, much of which would have been eventually shipped to Africa. By 1860, that figure had dropped to only £4,143, while by 1864 there had been a further decline to £2,501. In 1866 the figure was £89. These data are only indicative but, even with a wide margin for error, it looks as if the collapse were nearly complete. As late as 1880, old stocks of *moneta* ("common Maldive") were still listed as available in London at a small fraction of the prices being paid in India (at least £8 per tonne at Bombay and double that at Calcutta). The existence of old stocks presumably reflected a price so low in West Africa due to the competition of *annulus* that transporting them was now uneconomic.[46]

The bubble of the East African *annulus* trade burst only a few years thereafter. The intense competition between Wm. O'Swald & Co. and Victor Régis in the direct trade led to a renewed surge in imports, especially

Table 6.5 *Imports of cowries into Lagos, 1865–1904 (in tons)*

Year	Amount	Year	Amount
1865	1,636	1885	615
1866	3,237	1886	323
1867	3,404	1887	191
1868	3,275	1888	10
1869	2,802	1889	83
1870	2,517	1890	47
1871	2,182	1891	201
1872	1,741	1892	—
1873	1,059	1893	46
1874	1,078	1894	—
1875	1,094	1895	149
1876	2,327	1896	1,025
1877	3,030	1897	4
1878	4,472	1898	1
1879	2,878	1899	1
1880	1,347	1900	5
1881	494	1901	—
1882	391	1902	1
1883	796	1903	—
1884	421	1904	3

Source: A. G. Hopkins, "Currency Revolution," p. 475.

at Lagos where the movements have been documented by A. G. Hopkins.[47] Shipments were very high through the 1860s (see table 6.5), followed by a downward trend with a temporary revival in 1876–1879. For Lagos, 1878 was the record year, with a huge total of over 4,500 tonnes of shell imported. But after 1880, the ruinous inflation destroyed demand, and the inflow of *annulus* rapidly died away. Only in 1896 was there a temporary resurgence, coming almost wholly from Germany and no doubt representing a final clearing out of now unwanted stocks. The firm of G. L. Gaiser, which had bought out O'Swald's interests in the trade in 1869, itself ceased shipments from East Africa in 1882, and Régis followed suit soon thereafter.[48] G. W. Neville said he saw a sailing ship arriving at Lagos from Zanzibar in the 1880s, carrying 300 tons that he believed was the last direct importation.[49] (He was wrong – the last significant direct shipment was in 1891).[50] After the final dumping of stocks in 1896, only a few thousand pounds more trickled through from European sources, last examples of the billions that had come before. Their further importation was soon prohibited by the colonial governments. Southern Nigeria, for example, in its "Importation of Cowries Prohibition Proclamation No. 6 of 1904," made imports a criminal offense subject to a £50 fine or three months' imprisonment. (This proclamation was simultaneously enforced in Lagos and Northern Nigeria as well).[51] At about the same time requirements were established that taxes be paid in coin. In Northern Nigeria, all taxes were collected in coin in most areas for the first time in the year 1911.[52] In French territories, the story was much the same. Cowrie imports were first forbidden, and then eventually public treasuries were prohibited by a law of January 18, 1907, from accepting cowries.[53] Thus within the space of a few decades the shell-money trade with West Africa died away completely, 600 or more years after its birth and only a quarter-century from the time of its frenzied climax.

7

Collection, transport and distribution

The collection, transport, and distribution of the shells was an unique exercise quite unlike any other export of Asia or import to Africa. The mechanism that was firmly in place at the start of the eighteenth century worked smoothly for the most part, even though the "invisible hand" of Adam Smith shared its grip with monopoly and monopsony at several stages.

"PRODUCTION" OF THE SHELLS

It might be assumed that the shells could simply be plucked off Maldive beaches and loaded into ships for export. Such a view would be wholly wrong on two accounts. First, if the inhabitant of the shell were already dead and the cowrie had been rolled along the sand by waves and tides, its enamel would be worn and its lustre much diminished. Shells in this condition were fragile, useless for ornamentation, and were often rejected for money use, or commanded a lower price.[1] Second, if the animal was still alive when put into a ship's hold, it would not long remain so and there would soon be an overpowering stench. "Dead Maldives," a sales category at the European auctions, were of the first type – collected after the mollusc had died. "Live Maldives," the major category, were not however shells shipped with a live mollusc inside. Such a practice was rare, although one nineteenth-century writer does describe the "stinking and very unhealthy" condition of cargoes shipped with the living creature still resident at the start of the voyage.[2] Instead, "live Maldives" were shells that had been processed, and even the word "manufacture" is perhaps appropriate.[3]

These considerations led to methods of collecting the shells with their inhabitants alive, and processing them to rot out the animal matter. There are three traditions of methods for collecting, but only one for processing.

Collection methods on the atolls of the Maldives included the well attested wood floats and wading, and the (dubious) employment of hooks.[4] The early travellers were unanimous in their description of coconut branches placed in the shallows, then hauled ashore a few months later after

80

cowries had attached themselves to the wood and palm leaves.[5] This method of collection appears to have become obsolete, to be succeeded by the "wading" method that we suspect had probably always been in use. The wading method was apparently first observed by Pyrard, who noted how the cowries were fished twice a month, three days on either side of the new and full moon, by women wading waist-deep in the shallows.[6]

In 1883, H. C. P. Bell wrote that "twice a month, when the tides suit, men and women wade into the sea waist-deep and detach them from the stones under which they cling. One man will sometimes gather as many as 12,000 in a day," this comprising the traditional Maldives measure called the *kotta* of cowries.[7] The indication is that female labor was the rule in the seventeenth century, with the sexes mingling by the nineteenth.

In Bell's "Small Notebook A" in the Sri Lanka National Archives is the best contemporary description of collection, probably written long after 1883.

> At present day, the fishing takes place from 3 p.m. – 6 p.m. and 6 a.m. – 8 a.m. (low water) on the *poya* days each fortnight. Done only by women and boys. They carry a small woven coir bag (*Mohi*) over the shoulder and knock the cowries off the coral stones they cling to by a short stick. When cowries get on to seaweed places they can easily be collected by hand.[8]

Declining demand must have been the main reason why at this time men were no longer involved in the collection. Each month, says Bell, the fishing takes place on the 13th, 14th, and 15th, and the 27th, 28th, 29th, and 30th because of the great tidal range on those dates. (Lunar months do not of course have a 29th or 30th. Bell must have been working from one month's observation plus oral information about "months.") He notes that every four months, when the constellation *Keti* is near the moon, a time called *Haju Faru Foia*, the water is especially low and then the greatest catch is made with the least labor.

In field work during 1982, Hogendorn investigated how closely cowrie collection today resembles the traditional pattern. Fishing is still governed by the tides, with the best catches expected at the times reported by Bell. In a typical village, fifty or more women and girls from the age of about ten will turn out for the fishing, with a good day's production totalling something over 50 kilograms. The ladies work in small groups, ankle to knee-deep in the water, bending down to pick up any kind of debris on the floor of the lagoon. To this debris – usually pieces of coral, old palm leaves, marine plants, fishbones, or (in 1982) fragments of old tin cans – are attached by suction one, two, six or eight, or sometimes dozens, of *moneta*. By hand or stick, the shells are knocked into half a green or ripe coconut shell (and also plastic bowls), all apparently replacing the *Mohi* coir bags mentioned by Bell. There was no sign of the ancient coconut-branch technique.

The third method of collection, by "bait and line," is far less frequently mentioned, and engenders a considerable degree of scepticism. Captain W. F. W. Owen wrote in 1832 that coconut branches and leaves

81

are laid together and lashed up into bundles about the size of a wheat-sheaf, two of which constitute what is called a balsa. ... On these balsas they then take a number of trot lines, baited as we bob for eels, viz. with short threads attached to them at every five or six inches distance, and each with a bit of offal meat for bait, tied by a knot to prevent its slipping off. The shell-fish swallows this, knot and all, and is hauled up with the trot line.[9]

The scepticism arises because, by comparison to the two other methods, the costs in time and handling would be exceptionally large. The thought of millions of little cowries caught on their own individual little fishhooks verges on the ludicrous. Owen perhaps saw a fishing rig designed for far larger denizens. There was no recollection of any such method for catching cowries among informants during the fieldwork of 1982.

PROCESSING

Processing the shells after their collection was an important part of the "production," and here the tradition is clearer. Al-Mas'udi, in the tenth century, said they were sun-dried on beaches, during which time the bodies rotted, leaving behind the empty shells.[10] After that, however, the sources refer to the burial method, said to be superior because it keeps the shine on the shells. Ibn Battuta said the cowries were placed in pits dug in the sand of the beach, where the mollusc was allowed to decay.[11] João de Barros said "buried in the earth;" John Marshall in 1677 said "buried until all their fish is gon out of them;" Captain Hamilton stated (1727) that pits were dug in the sand, where the shells were placed, covered, and left, "two or three years in the Pit, that the Fish may putrify, and then they take them out of the Pit, and barter them for Rice, Butter and Cloth. ... "[12] Burial was the method of processing in the nineteenth century as well. H. C. P. Bell reported in 1883 that the shells were kept below ground "until all traces of putrefaction have disappeared."[13]

In the fieldwork of 1982, particular attention was paid to processing. The fisherladies of Guraidhoo, a cowrie-fishing village in South Male Atoll, were asked to demonstrate the modern method of processing from start to finish. They obliged by digging small pits with half of a coconut shell. The pits were dug inside the compound walls of a village house, next to other pits where cowries had been buried earlier. The light sand was easily removed. The molluscs were alive as they were placed in the hole and buried. The fisherladies here and elsewhere did not know whether in former times to accommodate greater production, the pits were larger; but they did say the larger the collection the bigger the pit. After some months (two weeks minimum said the informants) the shells are dug up. When the ladies dug out a pit filled some weeks before, there was no trace of offensive odor. The cowries were then put into half a coconut shell, carried to the beach, and washed by thrashing them around in the half-shell. The water became quite dirty in the process. They were then transferred to another coconut shell, returned to the compound where they had just been exhumed, and washed again in fresh water from the well. The ladies adopted a squatting posture to do this. From this second washing the shells emerged clean and bright, money fresh from the mint or so it seemed.[14] On a coir mat they were then laid out to dry in the sun. The shells had already been pre-sorted to some extent. Small cowries predominated, and only a few large ones were present. (This was the day when the sample of several hundred, mentioned in chapter 1, was given to Hogendorn.) When asked whether we had a *kotta* before us, it became apparent that the fisherladies did not know the word, but an old man on the fringes of the group enthusiastically volunteered its meaning. (There was far less than a *kotta*.) After drying, the shells were packed in a bag (plastic!), tied with twine and ready for shipment to the still-existing market at Male.

The conclusion is that collection and processing were labor-intensive, time-consuming tasks that together took some weeks at a minimum, usually months, even if "two or three years" must have referred to storage into inventory and not processing. There was thus always a capital aspect to the production of shells, and an accompanying need for work long before reward. With such a delay before shells were ready for market, any ship calling for a cargo at the Maldives would have found the short-run elasticity of supply (apart from any processed shells held in store) necessarily low. This aspect of cowrie production has heretofore been little noticed. On a year-to-year basis, however, supply elasticity would have been much higher, limited only by the constraints of labor supply, transport, and the admittedly huge reproductive capacity of the shellfish themselves.

SHIPMENT TO MALE AND EXPORT

Male, the "King's Island" of the early European writers, is located on the south side of Male Atoll. It is to the north of the main cowrie-producing islands, and was the first destination of the freshly-processed shells. They were shipped late in the year and put into storage at Male, some in warehouses, some underground as a cheaper way to hold stocks.

> *Cowries* are to be had at any time of the year, but in Novbr. and Decmr. most, by reason they are brought to ye *King's Island* to Lade ye Bengall Shipping [according to a letter probably written by the captain of the *Britannia* arriving at Hooghly on 1 July 1683]. They have Thousds. of Tuns buried in ye ground for Store (and for want of Ware-houses) in this Island wch. is not above 4 English miles in Circuit.[15]

William Hedges wrote of a visit in March 1685, "I saw the Houses, which were Magazines for ye cowries that were taken for ye King."[16] The captain of the *Britannia* (?) thought that over 90% of the processed cowries were actually kept on another island to guard against raids by pirates. If his arithmetic is correct this would mean at least 50,000 tons in inventory, not an impossible figure given the scope of the trade.[17] Before export the cowries were packaged. The usual practice was to put them in three-cornered bundles of material woven from the fibre of coconut leaves. Called *kottas*, these bundles weighed approximately 25–30 lbs. each and were intended to contain 12,000 shells. The packages were stitched tightly at their base or mouth with coir. The shells might alternatively be thrown loose into the hold of a ship, but this seems to have been done far less frequently.[18]

At Male the *kotta* packets were taken aboard merchantmen, whether Maldive, Bengali, or other Indian provenance, bound for Balasore, Bengal, Ceylon (in the eighteenth century), and less frequently for other ports. Or they were loaded on the European ships that called from time to time. The local Maldive boats were thought by Captain Hamilton in 1727 to average 20 to 30 tons, but Bell reported in the nineteenth century large 100 to 200-tonners capable of sailing to Balasore or Calcutta, and smaller 50–60-ton craft as the chief carriers in the Ceylon trade.[19] The Maldive vessels were made of coconut wood, with rigging and sails of coconut fibre. Hamilton said, "their Hulls, Masts, Sails, Rigging, Anchors, Cables, Provisions, and Firing are all from this useful tree."[20] Lieutenant Young and Mr. Christopher in the nineteenth century were unimpressed with the large boats, which, "from their build and rig, are totally unfit to work to windward, or to make moderate progress unless the wind is even abaft the beam."[21] (They do note that 50-tonners with much superior sailing capabilities also formed part of the Calcutta convoys.) They were much more impressed by the seafarers themselves.

> The navigators of these vessels evidence a degree of confidence in making the passage, which is not very common among natives; for, after leaving the Maldives, they sight no land, until nearing the shore on which stands the pagoda of Juggurnath, sailing right up the middle of the Bay of Bengal.[22]

Bishop Reginald Heber, far from "Greenland's icy mountains" (which well-known hymn he composed), described a portion of the annual cowrie flotilla in his book of 1828. Passing upriver near Calcutta,

> he was again greatly struck by the Maldivian vessels, close to some of which our boat passed. Their size appeared to me from 150 to near 200 tons, raised to an immense height above the water by upper works of split bamboo, with very lofty heads and sterns, immense sails, and crowded with a wild and energetic looking race of mariners, who Captain Manning told me, were really bold and expert fellows, and the vessels better sea-boats than their clumsy forms would lead one to anticipate.[23]

The visitor to the Maldives today can – if he dares – experience for himself the dead-reckoning skills of the "bold and expert" Maldive navigators, the queasiness as the sturdy boats rise and fall on the Indian Ocean's steady swells, the usually successful attempts to cope with engine failure or major leaks as a seam gives way.[24]

Typically, the Maldive vessels would sail with favorable monsoon winds.

Departures for Bengal took place "late in August or early in September, annually, having the South-West monsoon in their favour, and return in December and January with the North-East monsoon."[25]

THE ROYAL MONOPOLY

Cowrie exporting was largely a Maldive royal monopoly for a thousand years from the earliest mention of the trade well into the nineteenth century. The first Arab travellers had reported a royal monopoly.[26] The Portuguese in their earliest contacts found the island-king had farmed the trade monopoly in cowries (and coir) to Muhammad Ali, the merchant of Cannanore, and the instructions to the seventeenth-century Dutch expeditions clearly indicate a royal monopoly over the shell trade. In 1683, the captain of the *Britannia* (?) referred to the complete royal control of the trade, while in 1685 William Hedges spoke of the shells "taken for ye King."[27]

A passenger on the *Boscawen* in 1749 wrote that cowries are "the King's sole property," while the Abbé Prévôt's compilation (published 1780) also explicitly mentions royal and noble control of the trade.[28] The situation was the same in the nineteenth century once shipments sprang up again; "the whole of the export and import trade of the Islands is conducted at Male, whither the produce of each Atol is brought to be exchanged for that of other groups."[29] The cowries in particular were used as exchange for rice (and salt), a circumstance carefully noted many years later in 1844, when the Hamburg firm of Hertz sent its ship to the Maldives. The captain recorded that cowrie exports were carried out exclusively from Male, under tight royal control. The Hertz ship had great difficulty in buying any cowries at all for cash, as the sultan feared to interrupt the essential rice trade with Bengal for so temporary a gain.[30] The two British officers, Young and Christopher, spoke of the centralization of trade at Male after their visit of 1835.[31] Fifty years later, C. W. Rosset wrote that "no other part of the group is allowed to traffic with foreigners, all the produce having to be brought to Male." Goods sent from other atolls would arrive at the capital, "where they are purchased by the Sultan, who gives rice, cloth, etc., in exchange."[32]

Enforcement of the royal monopoly seems always to have been the province of noble "fief-holders" in their respective atolls, responsible for the receipt of tribute and taxes and also for the application of the restrictive trade laws. The shells figured even in the port dues and charges collected at Male. In the nineteenth century these were payable in cowries, even though the shells were not a circulating currency in the islands. (Rice had been the preferred medium for collecting customs duties in the seventeenth century.)[33]

Few monopolies are ever completely air-tight. Reports of Maldive ship captains trading with the Dutch, possibly on their own account, have been

The shell money of the slave trade

noted in chapter 5. The sultan is also observed as borrowing some shells from local merchants to meet his commitments to the Dutch in 1734, which must also signal some private trade, or possibly a royal farming of the monopoly. But the general impression is one of exceptionally strong royal control, made possible by the system of fiefs which put a (usually) loyal royal representative in charge of every important atoll. Smuggling is notoriously easy when the goods involved are small, light, and simple to conceal. One cowrie shell fully fits this description, but not a fifty-ton shipload.

SHIPMENT TO EUROPE: THE COWRIE AS BALLAST

Whether in native boats sailing to Bengal and Ceylon, or in the Indiamen of the V.O.C. and E.I.C., certain distinct principles of long-distance ocean transport governed the lading of the cowries. Any ship, large or small, requires ballast for stability. Without something heavy low in the vessel, rolling even in light seas becomes uncomfortable, and in stormy seas is dangerous. Any heavy material such as stones, sand, or old anchors would serve. But, from a commercial point of view, a ballast that was also a commodity that could generate sales revenue was obviously superior to a waste material. Sometimes it is said that materials shipped in ballast carry no transport costs.[34] This is not correct. The cost is an opportunity cost, forgone revenue from whatever other commodity that could have served as ballast. Cowries were transported free only when stones and sand were the sole alternatives.

On all the shipping routes, only those traversed by the native boats had no good revenue-producing alternative to shells in ballast. Here indeed transport costs can be considered very low. There is an explicit statement of cowries preferable to sand as early as Ibn Battuta. Both Barbot and Perlin noted the shells as ballast on the local craft.[35] The smallest of these vessels had an open bilge, with the cargo stacked layer by layer right from the top of the keel. The *kotta* packets serving as ballast would have other cargo (including more cowries if desired) piled directly on top of them.

For the Indiamen of the European chartered companies, there were several alternatives. Coarse commodities such as saltpetre, copper, tin, spelter, and even sugar could be used. Porcelain would serve as well. The Heeren 17 (directors) of the V.O.C. considered saltpetre the ideal ballast, commanding as it did high prices in the munitions industry of Europe.[36] Produced mainly in Bihar and brought down the Ganges, it was much wanted to service the homeward shipping, with keen competition between the V.O.C. and E.I.C. for the available supplies.[37] In years when the European saltpetre price was low, copper imports to Europe rose – the clear implication being a substitution of ballast material.[38]

Cowries had two special advantages, however, that made the shells a desirable ballast commodity as well. They could be loaded right into the

86

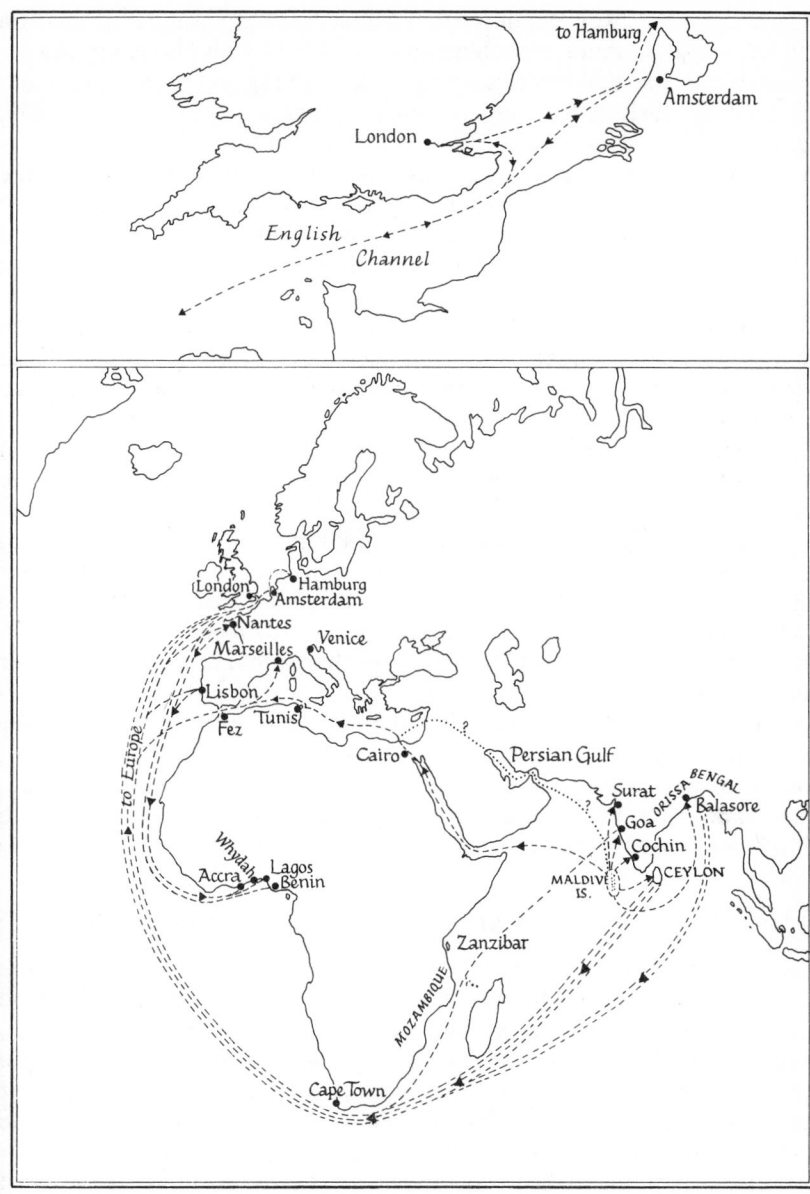

Map 5 The main cowrie routes

bilge because they were not harmed by contact with bilgewater.[39] (Porcelain had the same attribute. Another attribute shared with porcelain to a far lesser degree was that cowries could be damaged by being shot loose into the hold; an early E.I.C. minute claims damages from the ship *African* because of this practice.[40]) The second advantage possessed by cowries was that they were easily available in Ceylon to service the return ships of the V.O.C. from that island. When departure occurred in November or December, sometimes no other suitable ballast material was available, and there was understandable consternation whenever a ship had to sail with a worthless stone ballast. The Dutch labored hard to make this infrequent.[41] The layered character of the cargo, with cowries the lowest, has been described by Don Weyers.[42] All during the seventeenth and eighteenth centuries, the shells appear to have been shipped to Europe in their original *kotta* parcels of 12,000, little baskets of coconut leaf lined with cloth made from the same material. These *kottas* with their triangular horns, stowed at the lowest level of the ship, were still the method of packing as the slave trade ended.[43]

The economics of cowries as ballast are interesting. Delivered supply in Europe was determined in part by the total tonnage of other products shipped home in the Indiamen. The larger the entirety of the Indian Ocean trade, the larger the supply of cowries in Amsterdam and London. To the extent that this resulted in greater supplies than would be justified by profit maximization, it would then presumably explain why the Dutch in particular continually complained that the cowrie commerce was not very profitable for them. The competing possibilities for substitution in ballast, and the resulting effect on the aggregate supply of the commodity so used, show plainly that the "simple" economic decisions of an earlier era were more complicated than they sometimes seem.

ARRIVAL IN EUROPE AND DISTRIBUTION TO THE AFRICAN TRADE

The shells then sailed on their longest voyage, over 15,000 miles from Bengal and some 14,000 from Ceylon in the holds of the Dutch and British East Indiamen. The route was southwest around the Cape of Good Hope, then the long haul northwest and then northeast through the South and North Atlantic. The question naturally arises, why did not the ships deliver their cowries direct to their West African markets, rather than wasting the transport to Europe and then eventually back again? There are four answers, all pointing to the rarity of such direct delivery. First, we have just explored the use of cowries as ballast. When so used, their off-loading along the Guinea Coast would involve a difficult transfer of the lowest level of stacked cargo into canoes or surfboats under conditions of inadequate anchorage. Second, the prevailing winds and currents along the coast and past Cape Verde (near Dakar) meant hard sailing, close-hauled against the northeast tradewinds and breasting first the strong Guinea Current and then the even stronger Canary Current. The preferred route from Asia to Europe was far out to sea in the Atlantic, away from the winds and currents that made a northerly voyage from West Africa so difficult.[44] Given that the really valuable Asian cargoes such as spices were not demanded on the Guinea Coast (far too high in price for one thing), a long delay in the arrival of these cargoes in Europe was economically not sensible. Finally, the Indiamen of the V.O.C. and E.I.C. were typically much larger vessels than the ships in the West African trade. For example, the E.I.C.'s two classes of vessels trading with India were 500-tonners and 800-tonners, smaller than the 1,200-ton class in the China trade but still two to four times the usual size of a slaver. Heavily loaded and deep in draught, these Indiamen were wholly unsuited to the shallow creeks and anchorages of the coast.[45]

Thus avoiding the West African coast, the ships generally arrived in Europe during the summer, July or August usually, safely avoiding the storms of autumn and allowing auctions of their cargoes before frozen canals halted trans-shipment.[46] They dropped their last anchor either at de Vlieter across the bar of the Zuyder Zee, or just below the City of London.[47] Their cargoes were then cleaned, sorted, and auctioned to West African traders (more cosmopolitan in the Dutch case than the British), loaded in casks – for shipment in sacks was far less common on the sailing to Africa – and exported, more than a year after they had been taken from the lagoons of the Maldives. Earlier in the trade, the cleaning and sorting was done more carefully in the Netherlands than in Britain. The Dutch cowries were almost always "garbled" (*gegarbuleerd* in the antique Dutch) with the larger sizes carefully culled out and thus more acceptable in the African markets.[48] There were numerous complaints about the dirty and unsorted condition of E.I.C. stocks, leading to comments on the "much better" and "more esteemed" quality of V.O.C. supplies.[49] Even the V.O.C. was not immune, however. In 1722, the Royal African Company wrote to them saying that the cowries sold at the last auction were very foul and a great deal of dirt was taken from them when they were shifted into other packages before they were sent abroad. The R.A.C. thought an allowance should be made, and, as they had heard that some of those to be sold at the next sale were fouler, they wanted to know "whether you intend to garble them before you sell them or to sell them as they are and declare what allowance you will please to make for their foulness."[50]

Over the years Dutch shells retained their reputation for cleanliness and careful sorting, but the British labored to close the gap. By the 1740s, garbling appears in British account books, and this may have become standard practice; Thomas Hall was told by Mr. Pinnell in the 1750s that "the English cowries are very fine."[51] There was more than just aesthetic significance to the cleanliness of the shells. Sand in dirty shells could raise weight to almost double the total of clean examples, with deleterious effects on transport costs.

From the decline of Lisbon in the seventeenth century, the principal

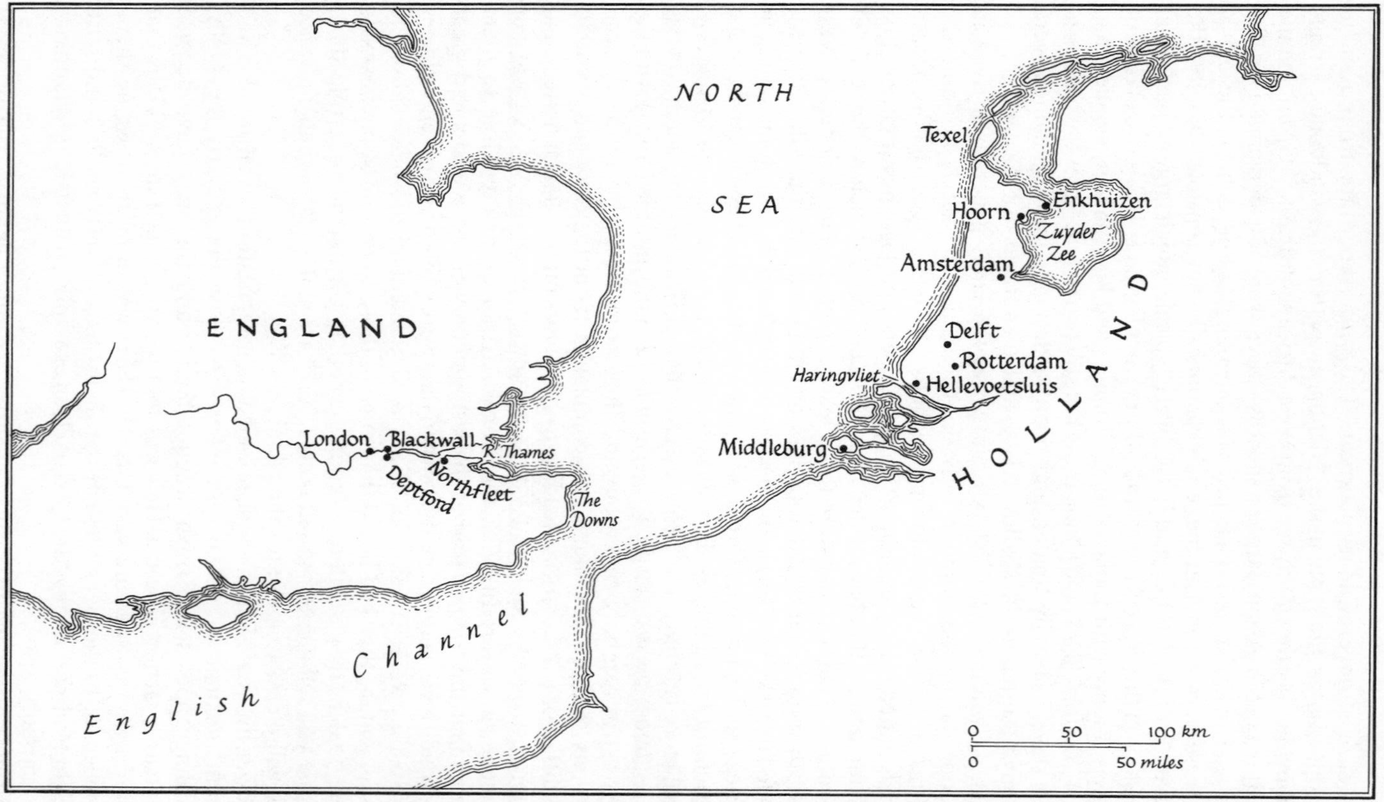

Map 6 The Netherlands and the Thames

European cowrie markets remained Amsterdam and London, though the federal structure of the Dutch V.O.C. ensured that sales were also held in other provinces of the Netherlands. The ships carrying the Dutch supplies usually arrived at Texel, the island at the entrance to the Zuyder Zee, crossed the bar at that point, and anchored at de Vlieter. There the shells were off-loaded into shallow-draught lighters, which carried them and the other V.O.C. cargoes along the excellent system of inland waterways and canals.[52] Following its federal charter, the V.O.C. distributed its freight in fixed proportions to the six cities prescribed as *kamers* (chambers or markets). Amsterdam received half, one quarter went to Middleburg in Zeeland, and one sixteenth went to each of the remaining four: Rotterdam, Delft, Hoorn, and Enkhuizen.[53] The Heeren 17 made the decisions as to what would be offered at the biannual auction sales; the autumn one was always more important than the spring one since ships from the east generally arrived in summer.[54] Some goods were not always sold at every *kamer*, and Klinkenberg's careful attention to the geographical distribution of Dutch auction sales of shell shows many years in which the smaller *kamers* did not receive their legal share.[55] "Dutch Gentleman" in his pamphlet of 1754 stated that the "chief European Market for these Shells is at *Amsterdam*, where are spacious Warehouses of them, the *French* and *English* Merchants buying them up to send to Africa."[56]

The English Company's returning ships were moored opposite Deptford, Blackwall, or Northfleet, not far from the Company's headquarters, the India House in Leadenhall Street, London. Cargo was unloaded into decked barges ("hoys") for transfer ashore, until the opening of the East India Dock in 1806 gave quayside accommodation. The merchandise was moved to the E.I.C.'s own warehouses in the East End of London in wagon-loads called "caravans."[57] The Company conducted auction sales of shells from the stores held at these London warehouses. Though there is a resemblance to the Dutch auctions, the transactions were simpler because there was less internal transport involved, no distribution to a federal membership, and (for some years at any rate) no time and money spent on cleaning and sorting. Interlopers sold privately, and there were brokers in this trade. Some shipments, presumably not those of the E.I.C., came from time to time to other ports such as Bristol and Liverpool, but London was the main entrepôt.

As centers of the commerce, Amsterdam and London became the source of supply for other nations wanting cowries for the African markets. This developed into a healthy intra-European traffic. French buyers frequented the Dutch auctions, and acquired substantial amounts in the many years when independent French imports from Asia by the Compagnie des Indes and private traders were small or nonexistent. Portugal and Denmark also bought there. The English market saw customers from Portugal, Madeira, Flanders, Denmark, and even France. Finally, the Dutch and English rather frequently purchased cowries at each other's auctions.[58]

The reason for an intra-European trade lay largely in the supply variations which in turn caused European prices to vary substantially both over time and between markets. In chapter 5 we assessed the yearly supply variability in Holland and England, one cause of which was the partially successful effort by the Dutch to achieve monopoly status. Even within a given year the method of sale by auction and its direct reflection of current supply and demand led prices to fluctuate widely. Lack of stability is reflected in the English data. Between 1674 and 1695, prices taken from the Royal African Company's books varied from £3.35 to £5.40 per cwt. In 1696, the price was £7, and in 1697 £7.50. By 1698 there had been a rise to over £14. The next available R.A.C. prices are £9 in 1701 and £11 in 1702; after that, prices dropped to £6.75 in 1703 and a little over £5 in 1704. In the next decade, figures from the accounts of trading voyages varied from £5 to £8. In 1720, cowries were being invoiced at £10.10s. per cwt.; but later in the same year the price fell to £3. In 1723 they were invoiced at £7.10s., and £8, and similarly in 1724. The price then fell to £6.15s. in 1726, reaching as low as £4.12s. at the end of 1727 (though this latter price must be in part a demand phenomenon, since in that year the affairs of the Royal African Company were at a low ebb and the conquest of Whydah had temporarily put a stop to slave trading there). Invoice prices were higher, but below £7, for several years thereafter. Toward the end of the century, prices were lower but still variable. The *Dahomet* was paying the equivalent of £4.75 in 1772. John Adams, who was on the West African coast between 1786 and 1800 (but who did not write until 1823) gives European values of £2–£4 per cwt., while prices were in the range of £4 to over £6 in 1789. "Declared" values from the English customs records are almost always higher. There is a long and detailed price series for the Netherlands in the Klinkenberg thesis that exhibits similar wide variability.[59]

In years when supplies were short in London, and when the Dutch were successful in obtaining relatively large quantities, the Dutch price would fall noticeably lower than the English, and vice versa when English supplies were the more ample. One result was that the "have-not" countries (France, Portugal, Denmark) would transfer part or all of their cowrie-purchasing activities from one main market to the other, depending on whether the price advantage lay with the Netherlands or England. This caused a shift in an already existing intra-European trade. A further result of a price differential opening between the Netherlands and England was a temporary surge of trade in cowries from one entrepôt to the other, a trade additional to that between the "haves" and the "have-nots." Sometimes shells were exported from England to the Netherlands, as in the early 1720s and again from time to time until the beginning of the war in 1739, when they became a regular feature. Such exports were usually under 15 tonnes, but they did reach a maximum of over 70 tonnes in 1747. (Table 7.1 shows English shipments to all European destinations, 1700–1790.) At other times, the flow was in the opposite direction, with the English buying in

Table 7.1 *English cowrie exports to northern and southern Europe, 1700–1790 (cwts.)*

Year	Amount	Year	Amount	Year	Amount
1700	413	1727	50	1754	7
1701	386	1728	237	1755	0
1702	2	1729	45	1756	70
1703	326	1730	297	1757–1769	0
1704	121	1731	218	1770	77
1705	M	1732	834	1771	864
1706	0	1733	184	1772	9
1707	21	1734	278	1773	498
1708	12	1735	144	1774	0
1709	61	1736	754	1775	348
1710	12	1737	174	1776	149
1711	0	1738	128	1777	414
1712	M	1739	567	1778	329
1713	570	1740	1,257	1779	849
1714	401	1741	729	1780	1,014
1715	159	1742	1,014	1781	2,068
1716	284	1743	1,693	1782	1,936
1717	696	1744	491	1783	998
1718	115	1745	547	1784	1,552
1719	33	1746	85	1785	2,231
1720	543	1747	1,515	1786	65
1721	1,844	1748	1,403	1787	36
1722	1,833	1749	512	1788	51
1723	1,728	1750	869	1789	1,425
1724	171	1751	1,202	1790	0
1725	1,415	1752	118		
1726	519	1753	86		

M = missing

Table 7.2 *English cowrie imports from northern Europe, 1700–1790 (cwts.)*

Year	Amount	Year	Amount
1700	8	1771	812
1701	125	1772	565
1702–04	0	1773	0
1705	M	1774	62
1706–11	0	1775	435
1712	M	1776	407
1713–66	0	1777–85	0
1767	74	1786	205
1768	0	1787	290
1769	229	1788–90	0
1770	154		

M = missing

Holland (and small amounts elsewhere as well). The quantities recorded in the English customs data are modest (see Table 7.2), but this is because it was convenient for ships bound from London to call at Dutch ports, load there, and sail direct for West Africa. Only a minority of Dutch shells purchased by their neighbor across the North Sea were actually landed in the British Isles. Numerous archival survivals attest to English ships purchasing in Holland after the start of the voyage to Africa. The agents of the Royal African Company were ordered to buy cowries there, for example, in 1716–1717, when 38 barrels of shell were taken aboard at Rotterdam by a southbound ship.[60] Another example is a report of 1734 from James Pearce to Thomas Hall, one of the leading Guinea merchants,

> Yesterday I employed a person to buy what cowries I could [in London] – but upon enquiry find them mostly large and out of time [that is, imported too long previously to be able to claim a drawback from customs on re-export] so that we cannot depend on having any more here than . . . about three tons and a half. The sooner you write to Holland the better.[61]

Elizabeth Donnan's documents from the slave trade frequently mention the long-standing English practice of taking on cargo in Holland before final departure for West Africa.[62]

Though frequently mentioned, little detail has been available on the size of these transactions, how they were conducted, and under whose auspices they were made. A discovery in the Public Record Office, London (Kew), in 1980 by Marion Johnson now allows us to trace one of these cowrie transactions in the Netherlands in great detail. Since the transaction also included information on cleaning, sorting, packing for shipment to Africa, and costs of these operations, and since it stands alone as the single most complete discussion of a cowrie purchase we have seen in any archive, we describe it here in detail.[63]

There had been a significant decline in supply on the London market during the year 1723, its cause unexplained. This led to a large cowrie purchase in that year by the Royal African Company (R.A.C.), whose commission agent in the Netherlands took two months to accumulate the 63 tonnes involved and eight months more to prepare the shells and ship them on three different sailings of R.A.C. vessels. Almost every step of these events was painstakingly recorded by the company's agent, Mr. Thomas Wilkieson, a "Merchant of Amsterdam." Through Wilkieson's meticulous reports, we are able to trace a process that led from the arrival of the cowries in the Netherlands, their sharing out to the internal markets of that country, their purchase by the English R.A.C., their shipment to Hellevoetsluis on the Haringvliet arm of the Rhine, and their eventual dispatch to West Africa in ships of the R.A.C.

At Amsterdam in 1723, Thomas Wilkieson was working for the R.A.C. as their agent on a commission basis, in frequent contact through correspondence with the R.A.C.'s Clerk to the Committee of Buying in London, William Hagar.[64] On August 22 of that year, a minute from London

94

directed Wilkieson to purchase 140,000 pounds of cowries for the R.A.C.'s African trade.[65] There was some initial misunderstanding concerning the packing of the cowries. The R.A.C.'s original instructions were to prepare them for shipment in 200-lb. casks, but this was countermanded with an order to use 136-lb. casks. The size of the containers might appear unimportant, but this is good corroboration that cowrie cargoes came in casks to the African coast. Repacking was necessary, because the Dutch typically put the newly arrived shells in barrels more than twice the 136-lb. size requested by the R.A.C.[66] On reflection, the reasons for shipping in small casks to the African coast are obvious. Small lots were convenient for the limited demands at each individual port of call. The risk of pilfering was too great for shipment in unprotected sacks. The soft *kotta* parcels from the Maldives might be safe enough in an Indiaman or the warehouses of Europe – value was low and cowries were just another commodity. But on the beaches of Africa, a knife-slit in a sack was all too simple, and a shell stolen was a shell soon spent. Even the wooden casks were not always secure. William Bosman writes that

> In my time the English sewed up their small barrels of boesies [cowries] (the money of this country) in sacks, thinking thereby to have secured them from the pilfering fingers of the Negroes: but they were mistaken; for as they were carrying them, on the way they cut the sacks of the barrels, and dug out their boesies at the chinks of the barrel with an iron chisel.[67]

Wilkieson now turned to the task of accumulating a cargo of about 70 tonnes, an amount by no means small since little more than 170 tonnes was available in all of the Netherlands. The prospective purchase was easily the equivalent of all Dutch sales in many years of the eighteenth century. Wilkieson sensibly set about buying in different locations, his aim to conceal the magnitude of the purchase.

Wilkieson began in Amsterdam by buying 14,000 lbs. at $11\frac{1}{8}$ stuivers per lb., and soon followed that (October 12) with a report of 25,000 lbs. more purchased in that city for $11\frac{1}{2}$ stuivers per lb.[68] Acquisitions now promised to become more difficult, however, as the news from London portended heavier competition in Amsterdam. London prices at the East India Company auctions were at the high level ("yet dearer than ordinary") of £7 per cwt., due to reduced imports to England during this period. Even including "drawback . . . in the buyer's favour" this London price was high. Wilkieson feared such a price would shift demand of other buyers to Amsterdam. "There's scarce 255,000 lbs. in all" coming up for auction at the V.O.C.'s Amsterdam sale on October 25, he complained; "to my knowledge there are already large commissions coming both from England and Portugal for said merchandise." Furthermore, as he reminded his principal, the Dutch cowries were sorted and cleaned.[69]

His warning proved accurate. At the Kamer Amsterdam auction on October 25, there were "unlimited" orders from Lisbon for 40,000 lbs. and for 50,000 lbs. from the Dutch West India Company. Wilkieson dared not bid for the full 100,000 lbs. he wanted – he estimated that would have pushed prices to 15 stuivers.[70] Thus he settled for a far smaller quantity, 55,000 lbs., at an average of about 11⅞ st.[71]

What to do now? Wilkieson's next decision was to bid at the Kamer Middleburg auction sale scheduled to take place on November 8. He understood that 78,955 lbs. would be on sale.[72] Note here and henceforth how the auction sales at the various *kamers* allowed plenty of time for buyers who had not filled their needs to make the journey in comfort. "The cowrie there is as good and small" as at Amsterdam, he wrote, "but not altogether so clean." Given the prevailing shortage, though, he expected "little or no difference in the price on that account."[73]

At the Middleburg sale, he was a successful bidder for 27,000 lbs. more, at the advanced price of about 12¼ st.[74] He wanted to have at least 25% more, and at lower prices too. But this time it was the French company (Compagnie des Indes) providing the competition. Its order for 50,000 lbs. came just the night before the sale and ran prices up to a height "contrary to everyone's expectation." Fortunately, he says, all the buyers conducted their negotiations with "moderation and privacy," so limiting the damage.[75]

Now there were over 60 tonnes in hand – 123,000 lbs. of the required 140,000. Next he decided to try the auction at Hoorn, on November 23, and he also approached merchants in Amsterdam who had purchased at the Kamer Amsterdam's big sale in October, through whom he might succeed in "picking up quietly what can find here at reasonable prices." Only some 17,000 lbs. more were needed to complete the order.[76] Back came a letter from London. The price was already too high, said the R.A.C. "Decline buying" at Hoorn; give yourself no "further trouble," was the instruction. "In less than a fortnights time a ship will be ordered" to the Netherlands for the cargo. Remember to have them packed in 136-lb. iron-bound casks, it said, and attach the company's identifying mark.[77]

Meanwhile, in Amsterdam Wilkieson purchased on the private market 3,700 lbs. more at 11⅞ st. I "shall go on picking up quietly what can find" until the remaining 13,000 or 14,000 lbs. are acquired.[78] Within ten days he bought privately in the same market 24 more barrels (7,300 lbs.) at 12¾ st., the price reflecting increasing tightness in the market. Now he awaited news from the V.O.C. auction at Hoorn to see if the cargo was complete.[79] Alas, the Hoorn auction's results were unfavorable. His agents there sent news that the cowrie price had been "run up so high" (12¾ st.) that he purchased only two lots. There were still some cowries available privately in Amsterdam at the same price, and Wilkieson completed his purchase there with three final lots.[80] As Hoorn is further than Amsterdam from the R.A.C.'s embarkation point at Hellevoetsluis, there was no doubt a saving in transport cost in so doing.

With the 70 tonnes now in hand, attention turned to preparing them for shipment. First he had to apologize to the home office for not suspending purchases as required. "Your favour of the 8th current O.S. which as it came only yesterday to hand arrived too late to prevent my proceeding to compleat the aforesaid orders." He would sell off the excess, at no loss and possibly a gain to the R.A.C. No matter, replied the company by return post. Ship all you have, we are "well satisfied."[81]

Next came the details of sorting and packing. The "garbling" was done by the V.O.C., and the service was included in the purchase price. This process of cleaning and sorting for size was not rapid, and by November 26 only one-third of his large initial purchase at Kamer Amsterdam's October 27 sale had been garbled.

> It will still be six weeks or two months before the rest are gott ready. Theyve dayley people at work. I press them as much as possible. However, this is no uncommon thing seeing the same happens here almost every year.[82]

The shells were delivered to warehousing which Wilkieson had arranged in Amsterdam, and here they were transferred from the large barrels used by the V.O.C. to the 136-lb. casks of the R.A.C., which held slightly less than half the weight of the standard Dutch containers. Clearly, the entire 70 tonnes would not be ready for the next R.A.C. ship, the *Sherbro Galley*, sailing under Captain William Powis from Gravesend on November 22, 1723 (O.S.), touching briefly at Hellevoetsluis for cargo, and then bound for West Africa.[83] Shipping arrangements were rapidly completed. The shells were invoiced at £7 sterling per 100 lbs. Dutch weight and consigned to Jeremiah Tinker, the R.A.C.'s agent at Whydah on the coast of Dahomey.[84]

Wilkieson now had to attend to all those little details encompassed by the term "free on board." He worked "with all dispatch imaginable" as he put it, and his account books show where he directed his efforts.[85] There were broker's charges on the cowries bought in private sales (116.11 in guilders and stuivers). There were freight charges on the shells shipped from the Zeeland Kamer at Middleburg (48.0). Once the shells were all together, it was decided that the contents of 226 Dutch barrels (about 34 tonnes) should go on the *Sherbro Galley*. There was then the weighing fee (one-half of 210.12, the V.O.C. presumably responsible for the other half), wages to the weigh-house laborers for receiving (75.4) and "bringing home" the shells, plus the costs of warehousing them (100.0), and charges for filling 470 small casks at 28 st. each (658.0), less a rebate for the 226 barrels now left over (100.8). All that remained was boat hire to ship the shells along the inland waterways system to the wharves of Hellevoetsluis (60.0),[86] and payment of a heavy customs duty "with passport and seals" (probably reflecting the internal tariff barrier at Gouda) of 1,460.0.[87] Total charges were thus 1,900.8, added to an original cost of 41,505.10, at which point Wilkison took his 2% commission (868.2).[88] The cost of 470 small casks (35.5) and four iron hoops for each (423.0) was invoiced separately.

Wilkison wrote on December 21 advising that the *Sherbro Galley* had arrived safely at Hellevoetsluis. There was a long delay; more than two weeks later the ship was still "waiting with many others for a fair wind."[89] Eventually she got away, as we find her anchored in the Downs a few days later. (R.A.C. ships bound for West Africa via the Netherlands frequently paused in the Downs for a short time to receive last minute instructions and to take on passengers.[90]) Thence she was bound for Sierra Leone, trading from that point to Cape Coast Castle, and finally unloading her cowries at Whydah, the furthest point on the West African coast she was scheduled to touch.[91]

There remained about 36 tonnes of shell to ship from the 1723 purchases in the Netherlands. The tale is more briefly told, as the accounts are similar in their arrangement to those of the *Sherbro Galley*. The *Clarendon* (commanded by Captain William Gower) was dispatched to pick up the largest part of the remainder, again consigned to Jeremiah Tinker at Whydah.[92] On her were loaded almost 28 tonnes (56,304 lbs.) invoiced at £8 per cwt., contained in 414 of the R.A.C.'s 136-lb. casks, transfer having been made from 174 original V.O.C. barrels.[93]

Six tonnes still remained to be shipped in June of 1724, ten months after the first orders had arrived from London. They were finally got away on the *Hamilton* (Captain Ford Kirke commanding), again packed in the standard R.A.C. casks, loaded at Hellevoetsluis, and consigned to Tinker. Once more the invoice survives, and once more the arrangements were the same as for the *Sherbro Galley* and the *Clarendon*.[94]

Thus was completed a very large intra-European redistribution of cowries, each step of which would have been repeated hundreds of times for hundreds of voyages during the heyday of the slave trade. Cowries were a staple of that trade; without them slave buying was difficult or even impossible at certain times and places. That a mechanism would spring up to allocate shells between the major Anglo-Dutch markets, and among the other buyers with no first-hand access to the Maldivian sources of supply, is thus not really very surprising. The only cause for wonderment is that (in the archives) one single operation of the mechanism is described in such unique detail.

SHIPMENT TO AFRICA

From Europe, the shells flowed south to coastal West Africa aboard the slavers and carriers of general merchandise, mainly flying the flag of Portugal well into the seventeenth century. Thereafter the English and Dutch dominated, Portugal also maintaining a presence along with the French, Danes and others yet more minor. Slavers from the Americas seldom had easy access to cowries except on the coast itself, where the Brazilians especially often bought shells on the spot from the English ships for easier commerce ashore.

There were two major differences that distinguished the shipment from the Maldives to Europe from the remainder of the journey. First, on the Europe–West Africa route the cowries were far less frequently put in ballast. Second, rather than being landed all at once, they were often parcelled out in small quantities wherever in the cowrie zone a ship called to traffic in slaves or other commodities. The first difference stems from the second. When ships needed cowries to make purchases, bringing them up in small quantities from the bottom layer of ballast would have posed great inconvenience. Thus the practice of packing in casks as part of the general cargo. (When all cargo was consigned to one West African port from one European point of shipment, then it was possible to use the cowries as ballast, which was just as desirable in the West African trade as it had been on the East Indiamen.)[95] Reflecting the preponderant influence of Amsterdam in the commerce, it was very common over many years to find cowrie weights expressed in Dutch pounds by traders of many different nationalities.

If shipped by one of the chartered companies with posts ashore, such as the Royal African Company or the Dutch West India Company, it was common to consign the shells to a resident agent who would pay them out against purchases of slaves and commodities, and for local expenditures. This, the "fort-trade" so-called, gave storage capacity ashore both for export and import items, and was usually the more stable side of the commerce. The most imposing of these trading castles, on the Gold Coast, were just on the edge of the cowrie currency zone; apart from the Accra forts, only the Danish posts of the eastern Gold Coast and the various forts at Whydah, a primary point of import, lay within the cowrie zone. The "ship-trade" was managed by private merchants to a far greater degree than the fort trade. It was carried on in African coastal towns along the creeks, rivers, and lagoons, and must also have been the venue for introducing a share of the cowrie currency into domestic circulation. (Many of the creeks of the Niger Delta, and the "Rivers of the South" of Guinea/Senegal, were, however, outside the cowrie zone.)

The export data given in chapter 5 is not sufficiently refined to reveal what cowrie quantities were carried by individual shippers or merchants. In the English data, we can follow the decline of the fortunes of the Royal African Company in the years before 1720; its active revival in the earlier 1720s, and the growing competition of the separate traders. That the death of the most important of these, Humphrey Morice, occurred in 1731 with a simultaneous sharp decline in cowrie exports to Africa is probably no coincidence.[96]

The cowrie shells in their casks were landed by surfboat or creek canoe, for in West Africa it was almost never possible to unload direct on to a dock. They came to shore packed low in the boat, "au fond des pirogues," says Berbain, just as they had left the Maldives.[97] The lightweight casks were no doubt appreciated by those who manhandled them ashore and rolled them into storage. By this time the shells had been empty of their mollusc for about two years and had travelled vast distances. But travel was not to cease, for the cowrie was a circulating money, and its zone of circulation in West Africa continued to expand well into the nineteenth century.

8

Cowries in Africa

When the slave trade to the New World reached large proportions in the seventeenth century, the imported cowrie currency was already in use over a large zone of circulation in West Africa. The zone itself was expanding, and the eighteenth-century peak in the slave trade was without question a major reason why cowrie imports also reached record levels in the same century. After quiescence early in the nineteenth century, the zone of circulation continued its expansion until the time of the great inflation. In this chapter, we shall view this large currency area and trace its growth and decline.

In Africa, as on other continents, cowries were used as ornaments, charms, ritual objects, or for magical purposes more widely, but of course in very much smaller numbers, than they were as money. As this aspect of their use is of little relevance to the shell money of the slave trade, it will not be discussed here. Nor shall we more than mention the circulation of cowries beyond the bounds of their main zone. We have already noted in chapter 1 that this currency found some substantial use apart from its West African heartland. Far to the south in the Kingdom of Kongo, for example, imported cowries at one period devalued the traditional zimbo (*nzimbu*) shell money from the island of Luanda. David Birmingham interprets the use of *nzimbu* shells as currency in the Kongo Kingdom as a result of Portuguese influence, whereas previously they had only been "part of the royal treasure."[1] Whatever the truth of this, there is no doubt that the zimbo shells suffered considerable devaluation as a result of the importation of cowries, which were eventually accepted as substitutes in commercial transactions. Thus in the thirty years between 1619 and 1649, the *cofo* of 20,000 shells (corresponding to the bag or sack in West Africa) fell from 7.5 to 4 cruzados, or approximately £1.50 to £0.80. Thereafter they did not lose much further value, but the Kingdom of Kongo ceased to be of major political or economic significance after its great defeat by the Portuguese in 1665. Cowries were still in use in the later part of the nineteenth century, but only as one of a variety of goods used in payment for ivory and other items.

101

No detailed study has yet been made of the Kongo cowries, but it seems that they were of minimal importance in the African slave trade, as compared with the cowries of West Africa. Their value in Kongo was much lower than it was in West Africa, and increasingly so as the shell currency depreciated, so that it must have become less and less worthwhile to import shells to Kongo rather than to their major circulating area. Shells may however have been dumped there in the shock years after British abolition of the slave trade, and again after imports of *annulus* from Zanzibar had so inflated the West African cowrie currency that its value fell even lower than was the case in Kongo.

We have also already noted, in chapter 1, that a cowrie currency seems to have been established in Uganda. It has also been suggested that there was a cowrie money area on the Swahili coast, but this is quite unlikely since the shells could literally be picked up on the beaches, and thus could not have retained their value anywhere near the coast. (By contrast, the zimbo supply of the Kongo Kingdom was located 240 km. south of the capital, facilitating the maintenance of a royal monopoly.)

For all practical purposes, then, the cowrie currency of the slave trade consisted of imports either across the desert to the West African savanna from North Africa (mainly Morocco), or by sea to the Guinea coast, for the most part between Accra and the western portion of the Niger Delta. There are several difficulties in analyzing the spread of its use in West Africa before the nineteenth century. Production of the cowrie in Asia was centralized and attracted attention in the written accounts of merchants and traders; by contrast, cowrie use in Africa was diffuse and more difficult to detail. There was a perception (no doubt correct) that journeys were both more arduous and more dangerous than they usually were in India, and memoirs of European travellers in inland regions only begin to be more articulate from the 1790s. Information on the West African interior became much more abundant in the nineteenth century, as is fully reflected in the note references for this and the following chapter.

THE WEST AFRICAN COWRIE ZONE

The early cowrie currency zone, as we saw in chapter 1, included the middle Niger and a coastal enclave around Benin. There was an extension into Hausaland by the sixteenth century, if not before. The zone expanded geographically during the seventeenth and eighteenth-century slave trade, and even further extensions took place in the nineteenth century, by which time the northern and southern regions of circulation had been joined. Vast areas did, however, stay outside the zone. The shells did not serve as money in what is modern Senegal, the Gambia, Guinea-Bissau, Sierra Leone, or Liberia. In the modern Republic of Guinea, they circulated only in the most northerly part, and in the Republic of the Ivory Coast, only in the north and northeast. But their conquests were impressive, and most major West

102

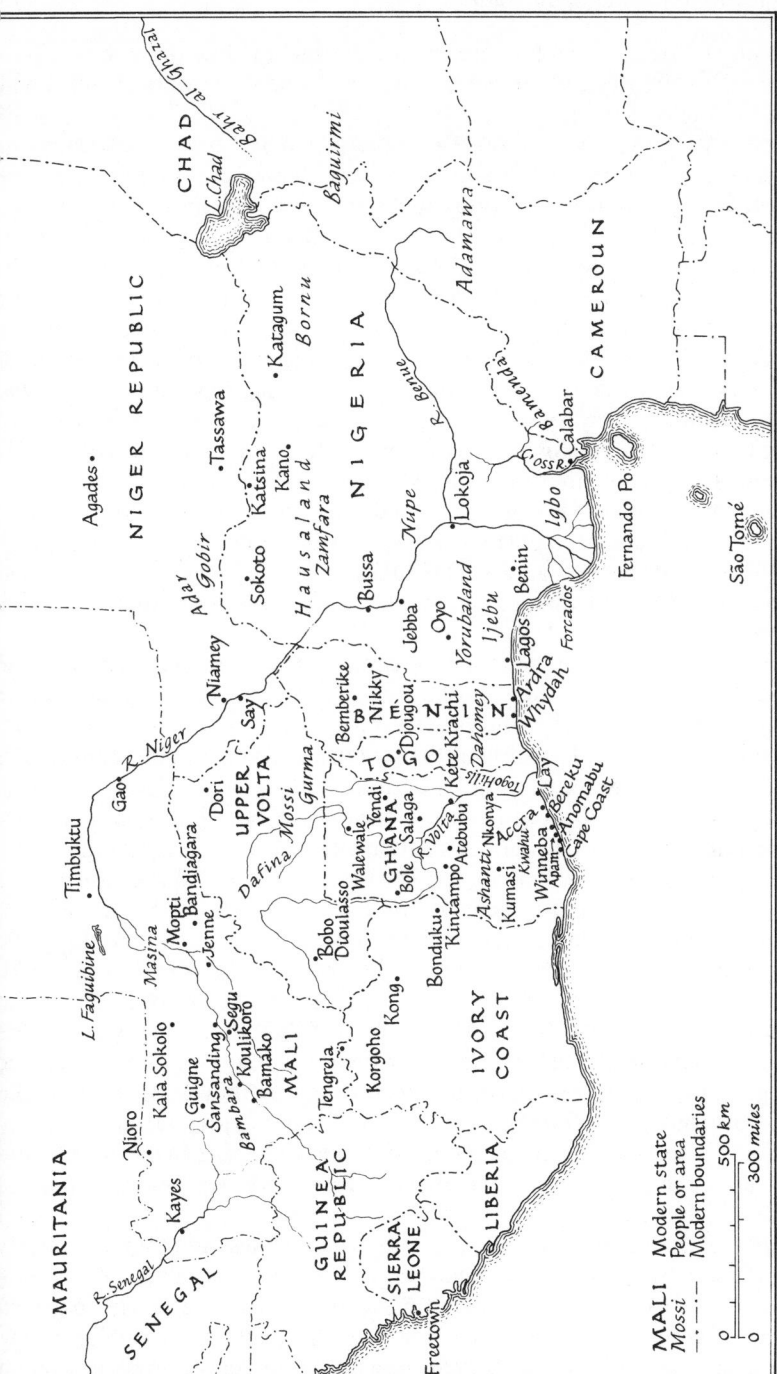

Map 7 West Africa

African shippers of slaves were eventually included in the zone.[2] There came to be almost as many words for cowries as there were peoples who used the shells as money.[3]

The export of slaves across the Sahara had for centuries formed an important part of the trans-Saharan trade, and cowries played their part in this trade, as well as in the internal commerce of much of northern West Africa to the south of the desert-edge. The shells were certainly in use in the Mali Empire in the fourteenth century.[4] Timbuktu seems to have been the northern limit of the use of the shells in the nineteenth century; they were then at a discount because they were not accepted by the desert traders. Caillié was definite that they did not circulate at El Arouan. Further east, they have been found in the ruins of Azalik, near Agades, which was destroyed in the early fourteenth century and had commercial ties with the Songhay economy. In Agades itself, cowries had been in use when the gold trade was flourishing there, and an Agades chronicle tells of an eighteenth-century chief making a gift of a horse and a million cowries. At the middle of the nineteenth century, prices there were still quoted in cowries, though Barth reported that very few were actually available in the market. Even as late as the 1860s a Ghadames merchant paid customs duties there of 10,000 shells.[5]

West of Timbuktu, in the mid-nineteenth century, cowries were found in the region of Nioro, but they may have been a relatively recent introduction there since Mungo Park, who passed through the area in 1799, made no mention of their use. Lenz found them in use at Kala Sokolo as late as the 1880s. By the beginning of the twentieth century, apart from Timbuktu itself they had disappeared from the area north of a line running a little south of the present Mauritanian frontier with western Mali, through Mopti (in the interior delta of the Niger), Dori (in northern Bukina Faso Upper Volta) to Sansanne Hausa (near Say on the Niger south of Niamey).[6]

Southwards from the Niger, cowries appear to have spread along the trade routes, particularly those from Tengrela through Kong to Bonduku (in modern Ivory Coast) and from Dori through the Mossi towns and Bobo Dioulasso (in modern Bukina Faso), Walewale, Yendi, and Salaga/Kete Krachi or Kintampo (all in northern Ghana) to the west, and Sansanne Mango to the east.[7] Early in the nineteenth century they were in use on the west–east route from Bonduku and Salaga through Djougou and Nikky (in the north of what is now the Republic of Bénin) to Bussa (on the Niger), and later along the alternative routes through Bemberike (in Bénin) or Gurma (in Bukina Faso).[8]

Cowries were apparently an earlier arrival in Hausaland than previously believed. There is a recently unearthed reference (Anania's *La Universale Fabrica del Mondo*) to their use in Kano and/or Katsina in the sixteenth century.[9] According to the *Kano Chronicle*, which almost all scholars of the cowrie have depended upon, they arrived in quantity only during the time of Emir Sharifa in the first half of the eighteenth century. The original

104

assumption was that these shells were of trans-Saharan provenance, and the new evidence of their sixteenth-century use in Hausaland does indicate introduction from the west and importation from across the desert. Hiskett argued that they reached Hausaland from the south rather than the north and west, and indeed the reference in the *Kano Chronicle* may mean that Sharifa's raiding and conquests caused a shift in the source of supply to the Guinea coast.[10]

They were current in Zamfara by the 1760s, and in Gobir at about the same time. By 1790 it was known as far away as North Africa that they were circulating in Katsina, and there is no suggestion that they were a recent introduction there. By this time and no doubt earlier, the source of supply had shifted to the Guinea coast. Lovejoy estimates that at least 500 donkey loads (some 25 tonnes) were brought from Nupe to Gobir in the last two decades of the eighteenth century; the merchants who furnished the Katsina supply were thought to procure them "from the southern nations who border on the coast." Adar was using them by 1800. For all these savanna regions, cowries figured in a flow to the north that also included textiles and European manufactured goods, exchanged for exports to the south of slaves, livestock, several varieties of salt, locally-made textiles, leather goods, and agricultural commodities. With most of the region under the sway of the Sokoto Caliphate from the first decade of the nineteenth century, cowries soon came to figure in the nexus of tribute payments, in particular from the more southerly emirates. Soon several sorts of taxation were both calculated and payable in shell money, which, as the taxpayer had to earn the cowries in the first place, served to encourage the spread of a cash economy decades before the colonial authorities were said to have introduced taxes to speed monetization.[11]

By the 1820s the shells had reached as far west as Katagum, but not Bornu where they were deliberately introduced a few years before Barth's visit in 1851. A high government official, Beschir, made the hajj to Mecca in 1845 and was impressed by the monetary systems he encountered on his journey. Bornu's ruler, Sheikh Omar (after failing in an attempt to have his own coins minted in Europe), adopted the suggestion that the Maria Theresa dollar be made the standard large denomination, with cowries the small change. The resulting new demand from Bornu, starting in 1848–49, is said to have sucked in cowries from Hausaland, and to have caused Egba palm oil traders far to the south to insist on payment in shells instead of manufactured goods, which then found their way north to the source of the new demand. Beyond Bornu's borders, in Barth's time cowries had not yet reached Adamawa (which was part of the Sokoto Caliphate), but had done so by the 1890s. To the east of Lake Chad, they had a limited circulation in some of the marketplaces of Bagirmi in mid-century, but in this region they never really established themselves.[12]

In between the northern cowrie zone, supplied from across the desert, and the later southern zone supplied from the coast, was an intermediate area where tenuous links were maintained between the two main zones along the major trade routes. There is little information about this inter-mediate area, concerning cowries or anything else, before the late eighteenth century. Mungo Park found cowries at Sansanding (Sinsani) on the upper Niger above the interior delta in 1805, and some of the towns mentioned by Caillié and Dupuis as cowrie users were in this in-between area.[13] The northward spread of the great inflation toward the end of the nineteenth century makes it clear that by then the northern zone was everywhere in touch with the south, though partially insulated from the worst effects of the inflation by the high and growing cost of moving the heavy shells northward.

It is still an open question how far the northern cowries from the Mediterranean penetrated southwards before the second decade of the sixteenth century, when the Portuguese first brought shells by sea, imported initially to Portugal and trans-shipped thence to the West African coast. Archaeological investigations have revealed cowries at pre-contact sites in Benin, though not in the quantities justifying an assumption of currency use.[14] We quoted Pacheco Pereira in chapter 1 to the effect that a shell money was being used at Benin just before Portuguese shipments began, but this did not necessarily consist of cowries. If the dating of the earlier Benin "bronzes" is anything like correct, however, then other northern imports such as brass and perhaps beads were also reaching Benin before the arrival of the Portuguese. Cowries could have come just as easily.

Cowries were being imported and used by the Portuguese to buy slaves in the Forcados area as soon as their first seaborne arrival in the second decade of the sixteenth century.[15] They may have spread to Whydah, which later became the main center of cowrie imports for the slave trade, and Ardra in the sixteenth century. They were certainly in use there and as far west as Lay (west of the mouth of the Volta, a few miles beyond modern Ada) by the seventeenth century. They were clearly spreading westward, and had arrived at Accra and Christiansborg by the early eighteenth century, if not earlier. Further in that direction, they had reached the Dutch posts at Bereku and Apam by the late eighteenth century, and the English post at Winneba (which lies between them) by the early nineteenth century, if not before, while by 1850 they were at Anomabu. The shell currency apparently never quite reached Cape Coast and Elmina on the central Gold Coast.[16]

Though cowries were used early in the Benin kingdom, they do not seem to have spread to the eastern Niger delta, except to a limited extent in the late nineteenth century. G. A. Robertson, however, stated specifically in his book of 1819 that the shells were formerly current at Calabar. It is true that ships trading there sometimes kept their accounts in cowries, but they seem to have been trading other goods and using the shells only as a unit of account; the cowries imported to the Cross River were apparently for the express purpose of re-exporting them north. Otherwise, there is no independent support for Robertson's assertion of their use as money at Calabar.[17]

Cowries spread from the coast inland along the main arteries of trade, though it is not possible to date their arrival at any particular point. By the nineteenth century they were in use on the lower Niger, throughout Yoruba country and in northern Igbo country, and in all these areas they may have circulated long before this.[18] They seem to have spread up the Benue River only during the nineteenth century; in the middle of that century they were reported as acceptable only if Hausa traders (from the north) were met with.[19] If Hiskett's suggestion is correct, that the cowries of Hausaland were coming from Nupe in the early eighteenth century, then they must presumably have already been established there. There are clear reports of the shells in Nupe about the year 1800, and they were certainly circulating in that area in the 1840s. They could have reached both there and Yoruba country from Dahomey, where they were current throughout the eighteenth century and very probably earlier, and also up the Niger from Igbo country, with upriver movements possible from the 1750s. Shell trans-shipments north from both Nupe and the Yoruba Oyo Empire came to be an integral feature of slave movements to the coast, and of other northern exports as well. The palm oil exports from the Yoruba and Igbo regions expanded rapidly in the 1840s, stimulating slave imports thither from the Sokoto Caliphate; the part payment in cowries for these slaves must have represented a surge in shell imports into the central savanna.[20] Finally, further east, cowries had reached the Bamenda grassfields by the nineteenth century, but it is not known when they were first used there.[21]

Far to the west, behind the Volta Delta and in the Togo Hills, cowries were in use at least as far north as Nkonya in the later nineteenth century. There is an early eighteenth-century reference to the 35-cowrie string of the Togo Hills. They seem to have been in general circulation in the peripheral markets of the Ashanti Empire, of which Salaga on the northeast was the most important. In 1817 Bowdich appears to refer to their use in metropolitan Ashanti, but cowries were clearly forbidden there in later years. The prohibition may well have reflected a change in Ashanti policy associated with the exclusion of muslim traders in the 1820s and 1830s, when Kumasi lost control over Salaga and the northeast, and possibly over the northwest as well.[22]

Though the northern cowrie zone and the zone of the coastal cowries had met during the first half of the eighteenth century, evidence of their meeting becomes conclusive only at a later date. John Adams, writing in the 1820s from experience gained on the West African coast in the last decades of the eighteenth century, but after Park's travels revealed the use of shells in the Senegal–Niger region, stated that cowries were always in great demand at Whydah, Ardra, and Lagos, where they were the medium of exchange and 'whence they are also sent to Dahomey, Hio [Oyo], Hausa, Jaboo [Ijebu],

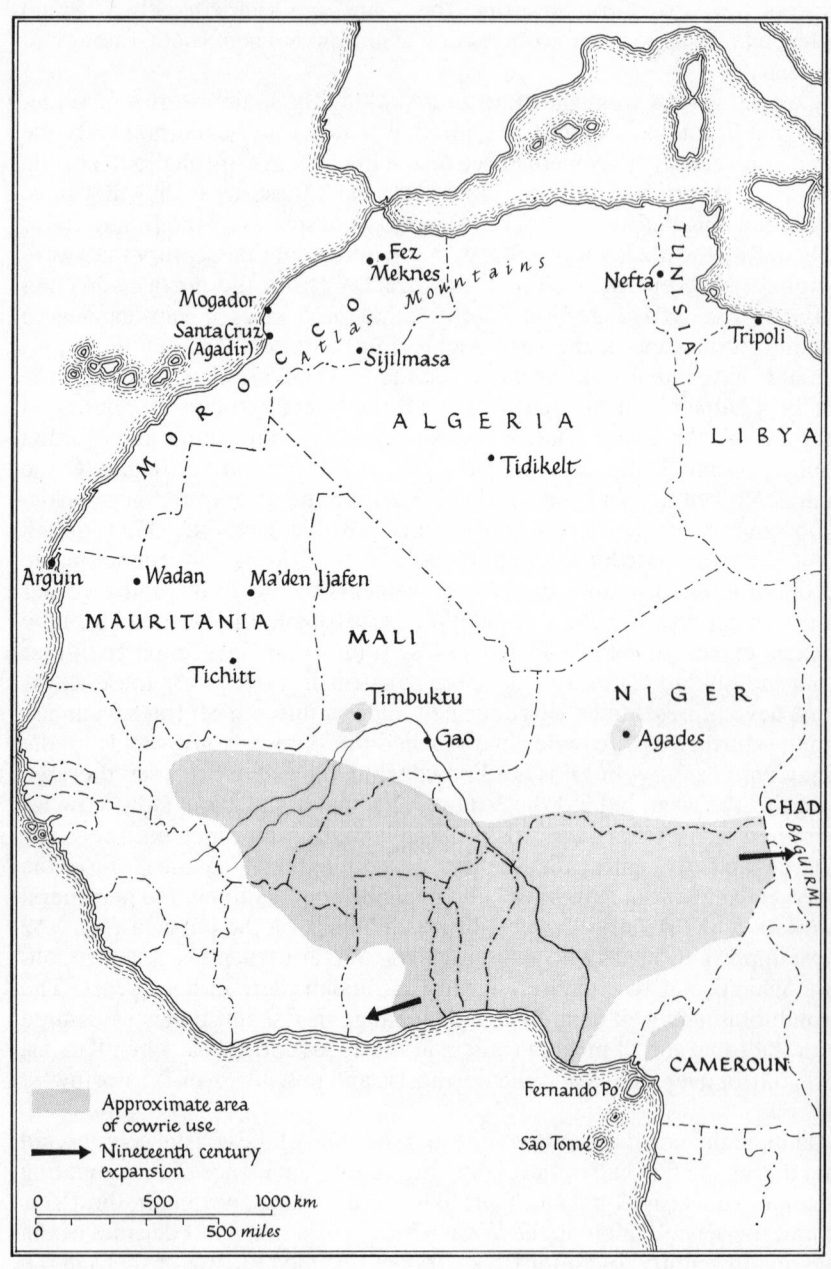

Map 8 West and North Africa and the approximate cowrie zone

nd into the very heart of North Africa, where it is known they are the irculating medium."[23] Joseph Dupuis, writing in 1824 from information btained in 1820, gives exchange rates for cowries and gold along the route rom Salaga to Hausaland via Nikky and other towns in what is now the 10rthern part of the Republic of Bénin, thus indicating their spread in that .rea as well.[24]

The arrival of *annulus* in the 1840s led to another diffusion that had many imilarities with the dispersion of *moneta*. The extent of that diffusion of *nnulus*, and the limitations imposed by the higher transport costs due to 1eavier weight, have already been discussed in chapter 6 and will be eturned to in chapter 9.

OWRIES AND THE PURCHASE OF SLAVES

Cowries played an important part in the sea-borne slave trade of West Africa from the time the initial shipments arrived, shortly after the first ecorded contract for the bringing of the shells to Lisbon in 1515. They were it first exported from Lisbon by weight, but, necessarily, paid out by 1umber. To minimize the possibilities of fraud, it was ordered that when a 1arrel of cowries was broached, the shells should immediately be transfer- ed to chests, double-locked, the two keys being entrusted to the pilot and he clerk respectively. "The said cowries are to be counted before the said :lerk when it is necessary to pay them out, and as soon as this is finished hey are to be locked up again in such a manner that all is done before the :lerk who will record how they are expended."[25]

One of the earliest accounts of the actual purchase of slaves with cowries n West Africa relates to a trading voyage to the Forcados River early in 1520. One unusual feature of this voyage, not matched in the seventeenth and eighteenth-century cowrie trade, was the sale of small quantities of the hip's cargo (red caps) for the shells; they were evidently not a completely nconvertible currency at this date, though the numbers recorded are very small indeed.

At this time, slaves were being bought in the Forcados River for cowries ılone. The standard price for an adult was seven *cabres* ("goats") which a ew years later were apparently units of 910 shells. This would put the price >f an adult slave at 6,370 cowries, approximately 16 pounds weight, if the neasurement is correct. (We have some doubts about this, as will be discussed in chapter 9.) The unfortunates purchased during this voyage were destined for Portuguese São Tomé, not for the New World; the Forcados voyage was doubtless only one of the earliest of such slave-trading ventures that provided the island with labor for its sugar industry.[26]

By the second half of the seventeenth century, sugar production had argely shifted to the Americas. The Portuguese were obtaining most of their slaves from Angola, or illicitly for the most part from other European suppliers. Slaves were being purchased in increasing numbers by the

The shell money of the slave trade

English, French, and Dutch for the new sugar plantations of the West Indies. Many of these purchases were made along the coast to the east of the Volta River. This stretch, where cowries were current money, came to be known as the Slave Coast.

While a number of ships' papers have survived from the era of the slave trade, few of them include the crucial accounts covering the actual transactions on the African coast. There are, however, a number of descriptions of the cargoes needed to purchase a given number of slaves, and correspondence from the resident traders at the European forts often gives information about the going rates for slaves.

In the later seventeenth and earlier eighteenth centuries, valuations on the Slave Coast were normally expressed in terms of the quantities of cowries, or cloth, or guns, etc., that would buy one slave. Estimates for slave cargoes were frequently set out in the form: so many pounds of shells at so many pounds per slave – so many slaves; so many pieces of cloth at so many pieces per slave – so many slaves; so many guns at so many per slave – so many slaves; and so on.[27]

At ports in the cowrie zone where slaves were purchased for export, and particularly on the Whydah coast, shells were accounted an essential item for their acquisition. Thomas Phillips said of the Slave Coast in the 1690s, "the best goods to purchase slaves here are cowries;" both John Barbot and José de Najera said the same.[28] In his *Description of Guinea*, 1705, William Bosman wrote that "The disputes which we generally have with the owners of these slaves are, that we will not give them such goods as they ask for them, especially the boesies [cowries] ... of which they are very fond."[29] The Royal African Company found the shells "almost a *sine qua non*" for trading at Whydah, Ardra, and in the Bight of Benin.[30] At various times, the proportion of cowries involved in an individual transaction was quite large, even surprisingly so given the many desirable imports carried by the European slavers. Barbot stated that the proportion of payment in cowries at Ardra was one-half, falling sometimes to one-quarter or one-third if the supply from Europe was short and if the European slave-buyers bargained successfully.[31] In the 1720s the proportion was about one-third, but must have been lower for most of the eighteenth century. Patrick Manning, in his study of trade in the Bight of Benin, suggests that "cowries continued to represent 20% to 35% of the value of imports, which implies an average value of £50,000 to £75,000 per year in cowrie imports to the Bight of Benin throughout the eighteenth century."[32] When the shells were expensive in Europe, merchants naturally tried to substitute other goods; as the European cowrie price rose, so their proportion to the African trade fell, to a level considerably below the figure earlier in the century. Even this reduced proportion required the import of the very large and undiminished quantities, however, since the slaves were both more expensive, and were being supplied in greater numbers.

Some imported shells were also exchanged for the other export items that

West Africa sent to Europe, but observers consistently point to the direct cowries/slave exchange. Once ashore on the coast, the shells were normally *not* again accepted by the European traders in return for their imported goods, though at Accra small items might on occasion be sold for cowries, which would then be used for local purchases of supplies, or in the slave trade. The cowrie currency was thus a non-convertible one, contrary to the first experiences of the Portuguese, and unlike the shillings and francs of the later nineteenth century. From an early time, therefore, all shells entering West Africa must have been retained there, evidence in itself that the cowrie-using economies of the region must have been expanding and the cowrie zone extending. The ramifications of the eighteenth-century slave trade carried cowries into an enlarging area. There was a major rise in slave prices in the eighteenth century, in terms of shells. "Dutch Gentleman" noted during his *Voyage to Ceylon* (pp. 21–22) that

> Formerly Twelve Thousand Weight of these Cowries would purchase a cargo of five or six Hundred Negroes; but those lucrative times are now no more; and the Negroes now set such a Value on their Countrymen, that there is no such thing as having a Cargo under twelve or fourteen Tuns of Cowries.

The factor at Whydah in 1716 was complaining that a few years earlier he had been able to buy a slave for 100 pounds of cowries, or 12 guns, or one anker of French brandy, or five rolls of Brazilian tobacco, or 25 pieces of Silesian linen, or 15 pounds of gunpowder; whereas currently he had to pay 136 pounds of cowries, or 16 guns, or one and a half ankers of brandy, or seven rolls of tobacco, or 36 pieces of Silesian linen, or 150 pounds of gunpowder.[33]

More generally, the rise in the usual slave price of about 100 lbs. weight of cowries at the end of the seventeenth century to about four times that figure by the 1770s, as shown by the sampling in our table, must in part have represented growing costs as slaves were brought from further away and by more expensive means. Part of this increased cost must have been paid in shells to sellers of local produce along the routes, and spent in other ways as well.

In terms of cowries per slave, prices in the 1680s ranged from about 10,000 to just over 31,000; by the 1710s the price had risen to something like 40–50,000 cowries. (This rise was attributed by the Royal African Company to the increased competition encouraged by throwing open the English trade to all comers, subject at first to a 10% levy. Certainly the price rise was accompanied by a considerable increase in the number of slaves purchased.) By the 1760s, slave prices were equivalent to about 80,000 cowries, and in the 1770s to a range of 160,000 to 176,000 per slave, or even more.

Since the nearer and more easily captured slaves would always be taken first, a slave-trading economy tends to suffer, like Marx's capitalist system, from "inherent contradictions" which make it necessary to expand continuously, often in an "imperialist" manner. This expansion provided the exports to fund the increasing imports of cowries, and maintained their

Table 8.1 *Approximate price of a slave in pounds (lbs.) of cowries*

1667	100 lbs.
1668 (before)	100 lbs.
1680	25 lbs.
1681	72 lbs.
1681	78 lbs.
1682	50–60–70 lbs.
1693	100 lbs.
1694	100 lbs.
1704	200 lbs.
1716	130–136 lbs.
1724	300 lbs.
1726 (?)	180 lbs.
1744	320 lbs.
1767	200 lbs.
1772	400–440 lbs.

Sources: See Marion Johnson, "The Ounce," pp. 207, 212–213; and Richard Nelson Bean, *The British Trans-Atlantic Slave Trade 1650–1775*, New York, 1975, Table A-6, pp. 137–157. When measures are other than in pounds, we have converted at the rate of 400 cowries to the pound. Note that slaves were differently priced at different places even at the same time. (The 1726 (?) figure, from Des Marchais, probably refers to early in the eighteenth century.)

value.[34] The expansion was eventually halted, not by internal strains reaching the breaking-point (though arguably some of the cowrie-using states had reached this point by the late eighteenth century), but by the abolition of the slave trade by the very European nations that were bringing the cowries. After 1807, though an export slave trade did survive and even flourish on the Slave Coast and beyond, the direct link with cowrie imports was broken. When the shipment of shells again reached substantial proportions in the third decade of the nineteenth century, they were generally used to purchase palm oil and other "legitimate" trade goods rather than slaves.

Since few figures are available, it is not possible to say which European firms were the largest individual shippers of shells during the slave trade. One very important shipper up to the 1720s was the British Royal African Company. In the 1680s, when its monopoly was fairly effective, the R.A.C. usually exported well over 50 tonnes a year, and though its shipments in many later years were much lower, they were very high again in the period of the company's resurgence in the 1720s.[35] (These shipments are shown in Table 4.1.) The chartered companies of the other European participants also must have played predominant parts. But the ships of every private merchant firm in the trade, large or small, could and often did carry cowries, and it is not possible to establish a breakdown between them and shipments by the chartered companies.

The very active slaving port at Whydah must be singled out as what may well have been the greatest eighteenth-century importer of cowries, though this must remain impressionistic rather than proven. "Each ship brings 30–60 or even 80 thousand weight," wrote Pruneau de Pommegorge who had been governor of the French fort there in the later half of the eighteenth century. His figures are borne out by the accounts of the French ships trading there.[36] It was by then usual at Whydah to pay for slaves with an assortment of goods always including shells, valued in terms of the "trade ounce." Whydah at any rate was certainly a major point of diffusion, and the Muslim ("Malay") traders who reached that coast in the early eighteenth century are known to have carried cowries inland.[37]

Since cowries were so closely associated with the slave trade, it might be thought that Abolition would have put an end to their use. So for a time it seemed. But while Abolition was effective on the Gold Coast, at least from the 1820s by which time cowrie imports were beginning to revive for the purchase of palm oil, it was less successful elsewhere. The commerce in slaves continued for a generation on the Dahomey coast and at Lagos, in the heart of the cowrie zone. Even the eventual end of the external slave trade did not break the connection between the shells and servitude. Throughout the entire cowrie zone, internal trade in slaves continued and probably increased with the growing demand for tropical produce, until effective European occupation put a stop to it. For example, at the great slave market at Salaga in what is now central Ghana, slaves continued to be sold for shells (70,000 to 80,000 for one individual in the 1870s; 120,000 to 140,000 in the 1880s) until the town was destroyed in the 1890s. In Hausaland, slaves were valued in shells right through the 1890s and up to the British conquest. Almost to the end, cowries remained the shell money of the slave trade.

HEAVY COWRIES

Observers frequently mention that the quality of shipments could vary. The cowries observed at Ardra by John Barbot in 1682 were evidently a very mixed lot.

> These cauris are of many different sizes, the smallest hardly larger than a common pea, and the largest as an ordinary walnut, longish like an olive; but of such great ones there is no considerable quantity in proportion to the inferior sizes, and all are intermixt, great and small.[38]

Barbot gave a detailed account of the cowrie currency which might have allowed the calculation of the average weight of his cowrie cargo. Unfortunately he is both confusing and contradictory, even in the original French version of 1688. At one point he appears to be saying that 10,000 shells weighed 60 lbs., giving, improbably, only 166 to the pound. He may, however, have intended the weight to apply to 20,000 (giving 332 to the pound) or perhaps to 12,000 (giving 200 to the pound, about the same as for nineteenth-century Zanzibar cowries).[39]

Certainly by the early eighteenth century, any large cowries were recognized as lower in value than the smaller sort, and though some large ones were still being taken to West Africa, their quantity was small and the discount high. There were large cowries in the cargo of the French ship *Dahomet* in 1772, valued at four-fifths the price per shell of the small ones, and used mainly in purchases from Portuguese ships. The discount was even greater on a consignment of large shells sent by the English in 1770: "being . . . therefore not so valuable, an order of the Committee was sent with them permitting the Governor and Council to issue them at half the usual price."[40] The Dutch are known to have been importing cowries from Mozambique in 1769 and in the 1780s, at half the value of Maldives cowries.[41] Such shipments were exceptional: both John Atkins and des Marchais give weights for the shells that correspond approximately to the standard figure of 400 that clearly identifies "small Maldives."[42]

COWRIE ARITHMETIC

However cowries may have been transported from the Maldives to Europe, loose in ballast or still in their *kotta* containers, by the time they reached West Africa they were generally in barrels or casks measured by weight. The various users in West Africa devised different ways of counting the shells, adapted to their various needs.

In the northern zone it seems that they were originally used as "small change" for a gold currency. Gold cannot be subdivided beyond a certain point, and very small purchases such as the day's needs of vegetables had to be made in a different medium. The use of cowries in this way presents no particular technical difficulties: five or ten shells for a handful of grain or for a ferry-ride across a river could be quickly counted. Only when cowries were used for large transactions was there a need for a rapid system of counting them. For some two centuries or longer there was a "normal" exchange rate at Timbuktu between cowries and the gold *mithqal*, so that sums larger than a *mithqal*, over 3,000 shells, would probably have been paid in gold in ordinary trade. Similar conditions very likely prevailed in the other merchant towns of the Niger Bend, and may account for the fact that the north never adopted the custom of having cowries ready-strung in larger units.

In this area of the northern zone, they were generally counted in groups of five, pulled out of a heap by the fingers of one hand. These groups were then put together in piles which consisted of 60, 80, or 100 shells, according to the region and the affinities of the merchants. As a rule, the pile was known by the local word signifying one hundred. In Bambara country,

114

southwest of the interior delta of the Niger, the "hundred" was usually 80, at least when cowries were being counted. How old this system was is anybody's guess. It was certainly already in existence at the end of the eighteenth century, when Mungo Park noted: "It is curious that in counting the cowries they call 80 a hundred; whilst in all other things they calculate by the common hundred."[43] René Caillié, some thirty years later, encountered cowries in his first Bambara village and noted: "The price of a fowl is 80 cowries, a number which is called *keme*. To describe our 100, they say 80 and 20, or *keme nimonga*."[44] A little later, Caillié refers to a transaction in which a Bambara man "counted [him] down 100 cowries, adding to this 20 of his own, which were equivalent to 100 of our country." Caillié was unusually tolerant. Most French travellers had something negative to say about this system, which clearly offended the logical French mind.

The fullest account of the Bambara counting scheme was given by the French officer Mage, who travelled through the area almost as far as Segu in 1866. Cowries, he wrote, "are counted by 10s and at first sight it seems that the system of numeration is decimal." But they were actually counted according to the following equation:

$$8 \times 10 = \text{``100''}$$
$$10 \times 100 = \text{``1,000''}$$
$$10 \times 1,000 = \text{``10,000''}$$
$$8 \times 10,000 = \text{``100,000''}$$

This meant that 100,000 was in reality only 64,000 actual shells, that 10,000 was only 8,000, that 1,000 was only 800, and 100 only 80,

> but with practice one learns to count fairly rapidly, even with this system. As to the people of the country, their mode of operation is quite simple. They count by five cowries at a time, which they pick up with dexterity and a speed only acquired by long practice; when, taking them in this way, they have counted sixteen times five, they make a pile of them, that is 100. When they have five of these piles they put them together, make five more, join them all together, and that is 1000. Traders and women, to avoid mistakes, usually begin by making a lot of little piles of five cowries and put them together in eights to make a half-hundred . . . .[45]

By Mage's time all payments were being made in cowries, the gold currency having gone completely out of use. A larger unit of account of "20,000" shells, known here as a "*captif*" (i.e., a slave), had been added to the system. Prices of actual slaves ranged from 4,000 to 40,000 cowries; the conventional *captif* (16,000 shells) corresponded approximately to a man's load. Fractions of the *captif* were, of course, paid in cowries. A slightly larger unit containing 20,000 shells and known as a bag or sack, but with many other local names, was found in other areas.

Oskar Lenz, who passed through the region in 1880, wrote: "In Segou, Massina, and to the north as far as Timbouctou, the number of 16×5 shells forms a sort of unit which is called not 80 but 100."[46] Timbuktu itself, however, was probably never included in the area of Bambara arithmetic, and Barth in the 1850s and Caron in the 1880s both remarked upon the use of the true hundred there.[47] Possibly in that most cosmopolitan city, other counting systems could be found depending on who was in power or on the nationality of one's host. Lenz, like others, remarked on the speed with which sums of 40,000 or 50,000 shells could be counted, but added that the method was only possible in countries where the value of time was unknown.

Two theories have been held as to the origin of this Bambara system of counting. Ch. Monteil and Solange de Ganay, pointing to the existence of a "Mandingo hundred" of 60, as well as the "Bambara hundred" of 80 and the "Muslim hundred" of 100, suggest that the entire counting system of these territories was originally on a base 6, 8, or 10, with a primary unit of 5 or 10, due to the use of the fingers in withdrawing cowries from the heap. Monteil suggested that the Bambara system had been expanding at the expense of others, and thought the *ba* had become 100×8 in place of an earlier 80×8.[48]

Other writers imply that the reckoning of 80 as 100 was a form of discount designed to favor petty trade. Paul Einzig held this view explicitly, basing his theory on Emile Baillaud, who is not quite so explicit.[49]

On this theory, five bars of salt bought in a single transaction for "100,000" would cost the buyer only 64,000 cowries, but could be resold in small quantities for the full 100,000. Similarly, a petty trader might buy goods for 80 cowries, which he could resell for 100. Paul Soleillet, who was in Bambara country 15 years after Mage, put it that there was a 20% reduction for 100 and above: "for 99 cowries one pays 99, for 100 one pays 80, and for 1000 only 800."[50] If this theory is correct, on the basis of Mage's table there should have been, in addition to petty traders buying in quantities of a few hundred cowries, a class of traders who bought in units of "a hundred thousand" shells for which they paid 64,000. In Mage's time 100,000 would buy perhaps two horses, five to ten cows, about five slaves, or five bars of salt. (The same hundred thousand cowries would have been worth about £20 sterling.) Livestock dealers, slave traders, and salt merchants might therefore all be buying in units over 100,000 shells and selling in units below this amount. A system of this sort would have allowed a profit for the dealer within a nominal fixed-price arrangement. Such adjustment in the arithmetic of cowries (and other currencies used by non-literate traders) was not uncommon in precolonial West Africa.

The existence of the "Mandingo hundred" of 60 cowries attested by Mungo Park and later writers,[51] and of the coastal "string" of 40 cowries (which was probably unknown to most of the theorists on this subject) might perhaps strengthen the case for the former existence of counting systems to different bases. It may also suggest an alternative explanation which we will discuss in connection with the value of cowries. In the early twentieth century, when an exchange rate had been established by the French administration at 1,000 shells to the franc, fluctuations in the exchange were achieved by paying the cowries at the Mandingo rate (600), the Bambara rate (800), or the Muslim rate (1,000), regardless of the area where the transaction took place or the origins of the merchants concerned. Maurice Delafosse, writing in 1912, was quite explicit:

> in most of the countries the usual exchange is the . . . Bambara exchange, i.e. 800 cowries for a franc; in some areas there is the Malinke exchange, i.e. 600 cowries to a franc; and in a certain number of towns inhabited by Dioula [Dyula], the Muslim exchange, 1,000 cowries for a franc. In addition, it must be noted that, in a single country, the price of cowries may vary according to the abundance or shortage of this money, and change from the Malinke exchange to the Muslim exchange.[52]

He refers also to the cornering of cowries to raise the exchange rate so that stocks could be disposed of at advantageous rates. The cowrie currency, so it seems, could give rise to quite sophisticated finance. It is not impossible that similar manipulation of the exchange rates may have occurred in the period when the gold–cowries exchange had been "stabilized."

If the Bambara system of counting had been in fact the normal counting method of the country, then everything would surely have been enumerated in this fashion, but Park stated flatly that everything *but* cowries was counted by the normal hundred. There are occasional references to the use of the Bambara hundred for kola, but the "kola hundred" was normally 100. This suggests that the Bambara hundred belonged to the cowrie system, and must be explained in terms of the cowrie currency. Whatever the explanation, it could also be applicable to the kola trade in areas where kola was virtually a currency.

Binger rather confusingly referred to the Bambara system as the "Dioula" hundred, by which name it was known in Dafina, by contrast with the "Mossi" hundred of 100.[53] Dafina, to the west of the Mossi country, was the boundary area between the systems, where it was necessary to specify which one was to be used in any transaction. East of Timbuktu and Dafina, cowries were normally counted in true hundreds.

Further south, other oddities of enumeration could be found. At Kong in the Ivory Coast, the system was based not on 10 and 100, but on 20 and 200, though other multiples of 10 were also used. Binger, who gave a full account of the Kong practice, wrote that credit was granted from one great market to the next. The seller of goods had to come to the buyer, count the proffered cowries, and take them away – "the seller, having the profit, must also have the trouble."[54] Curiously, the Yoruba system was similar to that of Kong. Twenty cowries were called *ogun*, 200 *igba*, 2,000 *egba*, and 20,000 *okekan*, "one bag." At Lagos, however, the shells were counted in the usual coastal "strings" of 40, *ogoji*, heads of 2,000, *egba*, and the same bags of 20,000, *okekan*, as elsewhere in Yorubaland. There was recognition of a unit of 200 at Lagos, in that a discount of two cowries was allowed on every five strings.[55]

In Hausaland, cowries were counted in tens or twenties and hundreds.

117

Barth wrote of a merchant at Tasawa, north of Katsina in the present-day Niger Republic,

> ... occupied in that most tedious of all commercial transactions in these countries, namely the counting of shells; for in all these inland countries of Central Africa the cowries or kurdi (*Cypraea moneta*) are not, as is customary in some regions near the coast, fastened together in strings of 100 each, but are separate, and must be counted one by one. Even those ... sacks made of rushes containing 20,000 kurdi each, as the governors of the towns are in the habit of packing them up, no private individual will receive without counting them out. The general custom in so doing is to count them by fives, in which operation some are very expert, and ten, according to the amount of the sum, to form heaps of two hundred ... or a thousand each. Having at length succeeded, with the help of some five or six other people, in the really heroic work of counting 500,000 shells, our friend went with us.[56]

Barth remarked on the unit, *hawiya*, 20, "which seems originally to have been the highest sum reached by the indigenous arithmetic" – or perhaps the base of a counting system.

Baba of Karo, in the Zaria area of today's northern Nigeria, gave a particularly vivid account of counting cowries from the point of view of the women:

> To count cowrie shells they spread them out on the floor; they counted in groups of five. Ten groups of five were 50. They collected the groups of 50 into groups of 200. Ten compounds of 200 were 2000. When they were arranged in compounds you started to sew up matting and put in the cowries. One mat, 20,000 cowries; that was a man's load, and a strong man would soon get tired of carrying it.... Counting money was the work of a chief's retainers – you can imagine there were a lot of them.[57]

The unit, 20,000 cowries or one bag, would have weighed about 50 lbs. when the Maldive shells were used exclusively – a not unreasonable load for a man to carry over long distances. As the larger Zanzibar *annulus* entered the trade, however, the bag became heavier and heavier. Filled with Zanzibar shells, it could easily weigh upwards of 100 lbs. By the late nineteenth century bags were mixed, and the northward movement of *annulus* thus to some extent was checked by the difficulties of carrying them. Indeed cowries became so low in value by the 1890s that it was scarcely worth while to transport them at all.

As noted earlier, by the eighteenth century the Hausa shell money probably came not by way of Timbuktu, but from Nupe and ultimately from the Guinea coast.[58] There is certainly evidence that considerable quantities of cowries, in the form of tribute, moved northwards to the Fulani states in the nineteenth century.[59] Hiskett conjectured that it was either as booty or in payment for captured slaves that cowries came to Hausaland in Sharifa's time "because he was zealous in raiding" (Hiskett's amended translation of the relevant passage in the *Kano Chronicle*). Methods of cowrie counting might be expected to throw light on this subject. Unfortunately, while Hausa cowrie arithmetic has much in common with that of the Niger Bend, it also has much in common with Yoruba arithmetic except actually on the coast. One piece of evidence stands out, however. In the interior, the strung cowries of the lower Niger and the coastal areas were apparently unknown. Had the shells in fact spread inland from the coast, it seems very likely that the convenient method of counting them in strings would have spread with them. This might suggest that, at an early date and until relatively late in the trade, Nupe and the (Yoruba) Oyo Empire obtained their cowries from the north and not from the coast.

In Bornu, cowries as money were introduced as an act of state in the 1840s, where they served alongside the Maria Theresa dollar. Here the unit for counting the shells was the *rotl*, an Arabic word meaning a pound weight. The *rotl* is believed to have related originally to a copper coinage which circulated in Bornu in the late eighteenth century and early part of the nineteenth century. A pound weight of copper could never have been a coin, though it might have been a copper bar or rod. The cowrie *rotl* consisted of 32 shells, equivalent to four strips of cloth (*gabaga*) at eight cowries each, the *gabaga* having replaced the copper currency in the early nineteenth century. Various writers state that the nominal value of the *rotl* was 33 cowries, the odd shell being set aside as a sort of tally to help in the counting, or as a discount for the labor involved. Three *rotl* would thus make an approximate hundred. This has the appearance of an attempt to reconcile a system based on units which could be physically divided into halves and quarters, usual when currencies are based on weight, with the cowrie system in use on the lower Niger where strings of 66 and 100 were known.

The relation between the *rotl* and the Maria Theresa dollar was never fixed. In Barth's time it was subject to manipulation by politically powerful speculators, and ranged between 45 and 100 to the dollar. Later the range was much narrower; Gustav Nachtigal in the late 1860s put it at 120–130, and P. L. Monteil in the 1890s at 135–160.[60] The actual counting of cowries in Bornu was done in groups of four, not in fives as elsewhere in the unstrung cowrie zone. Presumably this tradition dates back to small copper coins that were subdivisions of the *rotl*.

Counting in unstrung cowries, generally by thousands, extended south to the traditional limits of the northern trade. This method was employed as far as Salaga, in modern Ghana, where (at least after coastal traders began to penetrate the market) 1,000 shells came to be known as a "head"; at Kete Krachi, Atebubu, and Kintampo, all offshoots of Salaga where late nineteenth-century traders were concerned; at Bonduku, where the shells, gold *mithqals*, and gold-dust weighed by Akan gold weights were all in use; and finally all along the Yendi–Nikky–Niger River route, counted in round hundreds, if we may judge from the figures given by Dupuis in the first quarter of the nineteenth century.

THE ZONE OF COWRIES STRUNG

It is not known whether cowries were strung – threaded on a string or stalk of grass – in the Niger Delta at the time of the early Portuguese shell trade in that region. They were certainly counted in units of 40, corresponding to the commonest value for the later "string," but named *galinhas* (hens), a name later used on the Guinea Coast for the larger unit of five strings or a "bunch."[61] The Bubi of Fernando Po used a quite different system of shell money, but counted in strings, right up to the later nineteenth century.[62] It is perhaps likely that the coastal traders may have been using some such system before the arrival of the Portuguese. Ryder remarks on the use in Portuguese trading accounts of a local word for cowries in monetary units, which would make more sense if these shells were either strung or at least pre-counted in units corresponding to strings.

The next larger unit at the time of the early Portuguese trade in the Forcados River, about 1520, was the rather puzzling *cabres*, meaning "goats." Ryder gives the value of one such as 910 cowries. This unit is unusual in not being a multiple of the smaller unit, the *galinha* of 40. An easy multiple was the usual practice, not only for cowries, but also for the conventional "animal" units of exchange, a goat generally being counted as equivalent to a round number of hens. It is possible that the maximum price in *cabres* known to have been imposed on the Portuguese was evaded by enlarging the cowrie content of the unit; or possibly a retailer's profit had been built into the system.[63]

The unit of 40 shells long remained the basic measure of the Guinea Coast cowrie arithmetic, with the name *galinha* attached to the "bunch" of five strings (200 cowries). Twenty *galinhas* in turn made a *cabess*, or grand *cabess*, while half that, ten *galinhas*, made a small *cabess*. The word *cabess* is evidently derived from the Portuguese *cabeça*, a "head." With the change from Portuguese to English as the language of trade on the Guinea Coast in the late eighteenth century, this unit indeed came to be known as a "head." The nineteenth-century "head" was the small *cabess* of 2,000 cowries, which was conveniently equated with the silver dollar in the first half of that century. (It seems just possible that the original name for this larger unit was *cabres* rather than *cabess*. If so, this would perhaps suggest an original value of 800, i.e. 40 × 20, for the Forcados *cabres*.)

The usual eighteenth-century cowrie conversion table runs as follows:
40 cowries = 1 toque or tokky
5 toques = 1 galinha = 200 cowries
20 galinhas = 1 grand cabess = 4,000 cowries
In the early eighteenth century, the grand *cabess* at Whydah was valued at about 25 shillings (= £1.25). By 1726 it was worth about a quarter of a gold ounce, or £1. It would have weighed about 10 lbs.[64] The Danes used the small *cabess* of 2,000 cowries in the eighteenth century, and this became the nineteenth century "head." By the late eighteenth century, the Danish

120

rigsdaler was normally considered equal to 1,000 cowries. European coastal traders always tried to equate cowries with their own currency units; at a period when gold was temporarily high in value, one Danish writer introduced a new unit, a small *cabess* of 40 strings (1,600 shells), a usage that apparently did not survive the gold value to which it was related.[65] English writers in the mid-nineteenth century were valuing the string at one penny, and one of them went so far as to write of a head of 48 strings, its value of 48 pence equivalent to four shillings – a valiant attempt to reconcile English currency and West African cowrie arithmetic. (The 50-string head was equivalent to one dollar at the official dollar value of four shillings, two pence.)[66]

The usual nineteenth-century table runs thus:[67]

40 cowries = 1 string
(5 strings = 1 bunch)
50 strings = 1 head

The bunch was frequently omitted. In the later part of the century came reference to a larger unit, 10 heads or 1 bag. This is the same as the Hausa bag or grass mat already mentioned. (Though the commercial connection between the Hausa country and the Dahomey and Lagos coast was well-developed, the similarity in measures may be coincidence, arrived at independently because the measure was equivalent to a man's headload [of the smaller Maldive shells].) The bag may also have had some connection with the hundredweight sack, containing 10 to 12 heads of cowries, in which the East Coast *annulus* was imported from the 1850s.[68]

On the lower Niger, strings of different numbers were in use during the nineteenth century, and probably earlier. In 1832 Laird and Oldfield found cowries "strung together in portions of one or two hundreds, each portion being on a separate string." According to the Rev. Samuel Johnson, in Yorubaland (by which he probably meant Oyo) cowries were "usually strung by 200 in five strings of 40 each, three of 66 or 2 of 100 each, with a discount of 1 per cent." In the 1880s, when cowries had lost much of their value, they were strung at Lokoja on the Niger in bunches of 1,000, representing one shilling at that date. A woman was employed at the trading station there at ten shillings (£0.50) a month in goods to count the shells.[69]

An attempt was made by the disastrous Niger Expedition of 1841 to reform the system:

> The natives generally drill a hole, and string them in 100s, 10 of which are tied together, thus facilitating the operation of settling, which is a very tedious affair when detached, as both the buyer and seller insists on counting them; when they differ, it has to be done again. As ours were loose, it would have been an endless trouble to have counted them [they had 160,000]. Captain Trotter therefore substituted measure for number, and it was easy to make the natives see, by giving a fair quantity, that it was to their profit.[70]

Like so much of the work of this unfortunate expedition, this apparently sensible step did not endure.

121

The use of measures instead of numbers, with mention of special containers, is also reported in eighteenth-century Whydah and elsewhere along the coast. The "Dutch Gentleman" quoted in our epigraph (the same who believed in the antediluvian origin of cowries) noted copper containers used for counting by weight: "as payments in this Kind of Specie are attended with some Intricacy, the Negroes, though so simple as to sell one another for Shells, have contrived a Kind of Copper Vessell, holding exactly a hundred and eight Pound, which is a great dispatch to business."[71] Measurement also figured in the eastern Gold Coast in the late nineteenth century, but it never became a generally established practice. Possibly there was too much scope for ingenious dishonesty.

In the Igbo country on the lower Niger a quite different system of cowrie counting was in use, one not found elsewhere. The shells do not seem to have been strung, and were counted in sixes, the group of six confusingly called a "head."

> In the counting of cowries the number six is the standard. The one counting squats on the ground before a heap of shells and starts by separating groups of six, and then sweeps ten such piles into one heap to form an *ukwu*.[72]

As the basic unit of six was without parallel in West Africa, it can hardly be used as the basis of any general theory of the provenance of cowries, as Jeffreys attempted to do.[73]

The counting of cowries in strings and heads was subject to many adjustments. In eighteenth-century Dahomey, strung shells were regularly one cowrie short of the nominal 40, the reward to the stringer for the work of piercing and stringing them. But cowries strung at the palace by the king's womenfolk showed a deficiency of three to six shells per string; thus the palace, while nominally making purchases at fixed market prices, was able to obtain goods at a discount of up to 15%.[74] This "royal" string may be compared to the royal gold-weights of the king of Ashanti, as described by Bowdich, heavier than those of ordinary people, and thus a form of taxation. Both were means of obtaining revenue without complex arithmetical processes, and within the framework of a fixed-price system. In the later stages of the nineteenth-century cowrie inflation, part of the loss of the shells' value in Dahomey was taken up by increasing the number of cowries in a string, with the head remaining at 50 strings. At Whydah the string was increased to 50; at Allada and Abomey, 46; while the "royal" string had increased to about 40.[75]

In the later nineteenth century, when cowries were worth one shilling a head of 2,000 on the coast, shillings were selling for half that number, 1,000, at Salaga in the interior. In Kwahu, Nkonya, and the inland Ewe country an intermediate value was achieved by the use of a string of 35 instead of 40 shells, thus giving a head of 1,750 instead of 2,000. The string of 35 cowries was mentioned as early as 1709 for the "upland countries" adjacent to Accra. This quantity, seven-eighths of the coastal measure, may have had some relation to the Portuguese ounce used in the gold trade, which was approximately seven-eighths of a troy ounce.[76] Later, the "head" was equated to the shilling or mark, 2,000 cowries in the south, 800 to 1,000 in Sokode and Fasugu in Togoland, and only 600 to 700 in Salaga.[77]

Very curious arithmetic could result from attempting to equate round numbers of cowries to European coins. At Whydah in 1849, 120 shells were equivalent to three pence, but 25,000 cowries were reckoned as £2, not £2.60.[78] Similar curious relationships were noted by Richard Burton when he was consul for the Bights of Benin and Biafra in the 1860s.[79] He stated that the rates were "extremely various," and gave the following:

40 cowries = 1 string = $\frac{3}{4}$d. to 1d.
5 strings = 1 bunch = 3d. to 6d.
10 bunches = 1 head = 1s. $9\frac{1}{2}$d. to 2s. 0d.
10 heads = 1 bag = 14s. 0d. to $4.

It is clearly very dangerous to base any conclusions about the value of cowries on equivalents given for small numbers. This type of equation could be complicated by the fact that copper coin was at a discount, particularly in Lagos. There, by the 1870s, the bunch was worth $1\frac{1}{2}$ pence in silver, two pence in copper; a mark or shilling in silver was equivalent to 40 strings, while a shilling in copper was equivalent to only 30 strings. By the end of the century, when rates had dropped even lower, 1,000 cowries were valued at 3 pence in silver, but a penny was worth only 300.[80]

Of all West African transactions, the shell money most often brought the need to count in really large numbers, particularly in the later stages of the inflation. Thus it is not surprising that cowrie units came to be applied to the enumeration of large numbers of other things as well. Two thousand men, or yams, could be spoken of as a "head." In Yorubaland, the process went one stage further, and the number could be expressed by its equivalent in English money, at a final and utterly debased rate of exchange. Thus 300 could be expressed as 1 penny, and 1,000 as 3 pence. A man might have a yam farm with "3 pence of yams," while casualties in battle might be recollected as "two sacks of men."[81]

THE COWRIE AS A UNIT OF ACCOUNT

Cowries were always cumbersome to carry, the costs of transporting them by land relatively high compared to their value. Furthermore, the cost of carriage rose in proportion to their value in the nineteenth-century inflation. Their most important use may always have been as a currency within a given market area, rather than as a currency carried from one market to another. For this latter purpose, gold dust with high value for weight and bulk, and other high-value merchandise – kola, salt, and the livestock and slaves that Polly Hill has called "ambulatory purchases" – were always in terms of transport costs alone more profitable for the merchant.[82]

Even within markets, literate merchants did not always handle actual cowries, but kept detailed accounts in terms of the shells. One such case is reported for the early nineteenth century by Daumas and Chancel, from information obtained from a North African merchant who had traded with Katsina many years earlier:

> You understand that we did not load up with these cowries [in which prices had just been quoted], which were actually only a representative value of the goods sold, of which each of us kept an exact record, where the names of the buyers were written, with their purchase and their debt ... later we were re-imbursed by the exchange of objects equivalent to those which we had bought.[83]

Even later, toward the end of the nineteenth century, the Royal Niger Company invented a similar system. All the company's accounts in Africa were kept in cowries, but these were given the value of 15 pence per head of 2,000 – a fairly realistic value when the company started operations, but increasingly unreal as time went on; one traveller reported purchasing shells at half this figure.[84] The same writer described the operation of the system: barter, he says, is simplified

> by using a head of cowries (value fixed as 1s. 3d.) as the base. The price to be paid for native produce is fixed for the district from time to time; thus, supposing that a native brings in 5s. worth of palm oil, the agent allows him to select Manchester goods, salt, or whatever he wants, to the value of 4 "heads" of cowries, the value of all the articles on sale in the store of course being fixed in English money.[85]

The real cowries, which could be obtained much more cheaply, were not allowed into the transaction at all. At about the same time, the porters of Lugard's 1894 expedition were enlisted at 40 heads a month, nominally £2.50; but he calculated that they actually got the equivalent of about £1 a month in actual purchasing power.[86] Thus the cowrie near the end of its working life on the lower Niger had been transmuted for Niger Company transactions into simply a unit of account – a unit of value without being a medium of exchange – a fate that had long since overtaken the Senegambian "bar" (originally a bar of iron) and the trade ounce (originally an ounce of gold).

The use of the cowrie in some areas as a unit of account but not as a medium of exchange may well have long antedated the evidence quoted here. To the extent that it did, the shell standard would thus have played a more important part in economic life than even the large import statistics imply.[87]

Though the many millions of cowrie shells circulating in West Africa were virtually identical, the currency area was in several fundamental respects not a homogeneous one. Local custom, the cost of carrying the shells, and variations in purchasing power split the zone into numerous subdivisions of usage, counting systems, and value. The nineteenth-century inflation would still further reduce the homogeneity of the once-stable cowrie currency.

9

The cowrie as money: transport costs, values, and inflation

How transport costs affected the cowrie's suitability as a circulating medium of exchange under West African conditions, and how well it held its value over time – such questions are an important test of any money.

TRANSPORT

Unlike the transport of cowries by sea, where as ballast the opportunity cost of shipping them might be low, on land their carriage could be so expensive as to affect their relative values from place to place. Since the movement of the shells in West Africa was always accomplished by private enterprise, their value when put into circulation had to be sufficiently high to cover the cost of transport and provide their carriers with a reasonable profit margin.

Canoe. The very cheapest form of transport within West Africa, whenever it was available, was by canoe. A rough estimate of the proportional increase in costs with distance travelled can be made with data for canoe transport on the Volta River and thence to Salaga in 1876.

On the Volta, M.-J. Bonnat purchased a canoe carrying probably about a ton of freight for 25 heads of cowries. The head at that time and place was 50 strings of 35 shells each, i.e. 1,750 cowries, which he valued at "10 dollars and one shilling." He hired five or six men to a canoe at $3 a month each, and took on additional men at each of the many rapids, at one shilling per person plus three pence for subsistence. For a normal journey of something under a month, wages would thus work out at some $15 to $18 per canoe plus perhaps as much again for additional labor at the various rapids. Bonnat reckoned that transport from Krachi to Salaga (headloading over-land) cost $25 per ton, which he considered extortionate.[1] The cost of trans-porting a ton of cowries from Ada to Salaga would be in the region of $55 to $60, plus part of the cost of the canoe, which could be resold or reused. In addition there was an unavoidable toll or present at Krachi, and sometimes at other places on the river, and also the very real risk of loss or damage to canoes, loss of goods by overturning, and risk of loss through plundering.

125

The value of a ton of the smaller Maldive cowries on the coast was at that time some £22.50, or about $100. At Salaga they were worth nearly double this. A merchant could thus expect to make a reasonable profit after all expenses were paid, unless he was exceptionally unlucky. The larger and heavier Zanzibar cowries, however, were worth only some £12 (about $50) a ton at the coast, and double that at Salaga. It could thus scarcely have paid to transport the Zanzibar shells inland. When the Krachi tolls were abolished in 1876, and it was possible to use the upper reaches of the Volta between Krachi and Yeji, the overland cost component was reduced; even so, it would not have paid to transport more than a small proportion of the heavier cowries. Actual costs may have been somewhat higher than stated here, since the charges for canoes and boatmen noted above are for middle reaches of the river, and both charges were higher at the two ends of the journey. Even if it paid to carry cowries, salt was probably always a more profitable cargo. Cowries were carried none the less, though probably only as part of a load consisting mainly of salt. The quoted exchange rates between Salaga and the Niger in 1820 (see below, p. 129) make sense only on the assumption that shells were entering the system at Salaga.[2] The Zanzibar cowries that reached Walewale by 1888, carried apparently by Mossi traders from Salaga, may have come overland from Dahomey. Burton believed that the Dahomey shells were going as far as Segu on the upper Niger in the 1860s, but this may have been guesswork.[3]

The main means of land transport for the shells were by camel, by donkey, and by headload. The camel was restricted to the far north of West Africa, and to the desert trade. Transport by donkey was limited mostly to the northern zone because of high mortality from tsetse-borne trypanosomiasis in the south. (Hausa traders did, however, take their donkeys right to the coast if the value of their cargoes was large enough to offset the high mortality.) Headloading was universal.

Camels. In the northern part of the West African savanna, and in the desert, the best method of transport was the camel. The load of a camel depends to some extent on the distance to be covered, and the nature of the cargo. Nineteenth-century estimates of weight carried range from three to upwards of four English hundredweight.[4] Barth said that a camel would carry 100,000 cowries, a very good camel 150,000.[5] Unless some of the heavier Zanzibar cowries had already found their way north in his day, this should represent 250 to 375 lbs. (The introduction of cowries into Bornu is known to have caused a shortage of shells in neighboring areas, and in fact might have stimulated the movement northwards of the recently introduced Zanzibar *annulus*.)

Shabeeny, referring to an area further west, probably in the 1750s and 1760s, reckoned that a camel carried 4 to 5 quintals, some 190,000 to 240,000 cowries.[6] At the standard rate of exchange, this would be some 64 to 80 *mithqal* of gold (probably a large 75 grain *mithqal*), so that a camel-load of cowries would be the equivalent of some £40–£50 in gold at Timbuktu. It cost £8–£9 to hire a camel for the desert journey, about a fifth of the value of its load. J. Grey Jackson tells us that cowries could be bought in southern Morocco at 20 Mexican dollars a quintal – about £5 – so that in southern Morocco the load would have cost some £20–£25. Add to this the cost of hiring the camel, and the cost price in Timbuktu would be about £28–£35, as against a gold equivalent of £40–£50. But Jackson also tells us that merchants expected at least 30% profit, and often 50%–60%, to cover the very real dangers of the desert trade. Thus commercial importation by camel would have been just possible, but not highly profitable, at the end of the eighteenth century. When the value of cowries began to decline south of the desert, their import largely ceased, except in times of famine or food shortage in Timbuktu when the shells would have been sent out of the town to buy food further afield. If the exchange rate remained high for any considerable length of time, the rise would have been redressed by imports across the desert, following much the same original route by which cowries first came to West Africa. It is possible that Jackson's figures relate to such a period of currency shortage in the 1790s, when cowries were so scarce at Timbuktu that shells of another species were temporarily brought into use, imported probably from Arguin, causing in train a dramatic inflation. This precursor of the great nineteenth-century inflation is examined later in this chapter.

Donkeys. A donkey's load in the Kano area in the 1890s was 50,000 cowries, often carried in wide-mouth bags of dressed goatskin that retained the shape of the original goat. At much the same time, Lugard was using donkey loads of two bags of 84 lbs. each, for animals making the journey between Jebba on the Niger and Nikky.[7] Lugard's cowries were originally packed in 53 donkey-loads of 84 lbs. each. In Borgu, with most of his donkeys now dead, he found it worth while to sort out his remaining shells. The small ones, presumably Maldive *moneta*, he was able to pack 16 heads to the sack (32,000 shells), making a very heavy headload of 76 lbs. each. This was somewhat below the standard weight of 400 cowries to the pound, presumably because he was able to reject the heaviest of the Maldive shells. Some small specimens of Zanzibar *annulus*, which were often more variable in size than the better-sorted *moneta*, may also have been included. Lugard noted that the small cowries alone were worth transporting, as so many more went into the load. After the sorting, the remaining heavier shells were made up into donkey-loads of 80 lbs. or more, each containing only $7\frac{1}{2}$ heads (15,000 cowries). On this journey, therefore, the larger shells were more than double the weight of the smaller.

There was evidently some variation in the quantity that could be carried by a donkey. In Togo, 100 lbs. was a "fairly heavy donkey-load."[8] Mossi donkeys bred for the long-distance trade were probably larger and stronger than the Hausaland animals, some of which were bred on the farm by farmer-traders.[9] In mid-century, Mossi donkeys were reported to cost 15,000 cowries, less than a third of their load. Hausa donkeys were said at the same time to be worth only 5,000 cowries, but they were not often brought to Salaga because of the tolls payable en route. With inflation, the price of donkeys at Salaga had risen by the late 1880s to 40,000–45,000 shells, the greater part of their load. In Nikky during Lugard's time the price was 60,000 cowries "payable in cloth." Originally, each animal had carried some 40,000 shells; after Lugard's grand re-sorting, each was carrying only 30,000 large cowries, or about half its own value. Transport by donkey could thus only be economic if the animal had a good chance of surviving in a condition to be sold or used again at the end of the route. Lugard's donkeys nearly all died; seven, in a dying condition, were sold for only 63,000 shells altogether.[10]

Human carriers. The economics of human porterage, when the porter was a slave, were similar to the economics of animal transport, there being no wages, and subsistence the only cost. There was, however, one main difference: donkeys and camels (outside the desert) could feed themselves en route, while human porters had to be fed by their master. The porters had either to carry food for the journey or the means to purchase it, so reducing the effective payload.

The best estimate of the cost of transport by slave carrier can be derived from the exchange rates between cowries and gold given by Joseph Dupuis, from information provided by Muslim merchants in Kumasi in 1820.[11] (Some of the carrying in the caravans to be discussed was by donkey, but with little perceivable effect on our estimates.) Comparison between Dupuis' exchange rates and the number of days' journey between towns, as given in the itineraries in the same source, is given in Table 9.1. Apart from the last alternative figure, which may in fact apply to a town on the Hausa side of the river, and so involve ferry costs, the figures are about as consistent as is compatible with an exchange rate expressed in round numbers of shells. If a man's load is taken as the sack of 20,000 shells, the usual convention, then the cost of a day's journey ranges from 80 to 120 cowries. This is in line with Henry Meredith's statement that on the coast a man could live well in the plentiful season on two strings (80 shells) a day; Mungo Park, a few years earlier in Bambara where the value of the shell money was higher, stated that he could feed himself and buy corn for his horse on 100 cowries a day.[12]

By the end of the nineteenth century cowries had fallen in value to about one-tenth of their worth at the beginning of the century. On this basis, a carrier would need something like 1,000 shells a day to subsist, and would consume his whole load in under three weeks even if otherwise unpaid. But by this date carriers were indeed usually paid; Lugard's men, for example, receiving a nominal 40 heads per month. Even with his grand re-sorting and

Table 9.1 *Change in cowrie value of gold mithqal during a journey of 37 days*

Journey	Days	Value of mithqal in cowries at start and end	Percentage change	% per day
Salaga–Yendi	6	4,300–4,200	2.3	0.4
Yendi–Zogho	8	4,200–4,000	4.8	0.6
Zogho–Nikky	10	4,000–3,800	5.0	0.5
Nikky–Niger	13	3,800–3,500	7.9	0.6
		or 3,400	10.5	0.8

unusually heavy loads, his men could each carry only 16 heads. Thus if a man were actually paid the 40 heads, he would have earned in just a fortnight more than he could possibly carry.[13] In practice, as we have seen, men were paid off at the end of the journey, and Lugard's "40 heads" were a money of account no longer bearing any relation to real cowries or real prices. Traders and others took increasingly to carrying trade goods rather than money; the cowrie as a long-distance currency had largely broken down.

The final *reductio ad absurdum* inflicted on transport costs by the great inflation was related by C. H. Robinson, who would have liked to sell a sick horse.

> The trouble is that we cannot sell it, as its value in cowries would require 15 porters to carry, to whom we should have to pay all the money they carried, and a great deal more besides.[14]

COWRIE VALUES

From the accounts of travellers, merchants, missionaries, and, near the end of the shell money's history, from colonial government officials, insights can be obtained into the value of cowries in terms of other currencies or commodities. Since the estimates cover a span of centuries, they give something of an overview of developments in the otherwise little-known "petty economy" of West Africa.

Northern values. The earliest values we have for cowries in West Africa come from Arab travellers visiting the southern edge of the Sahara, and they are in terms of gold. Ibn Battuta in the fourteenth century reported that 1,150 shells exchanged for a gold *dinar* at Mali and Gao.[15] If his *dinar* was the standard *mithqal* of 72 grains (which he as a learned Muslim was probably using), this meant that the 75-grain *mithqal* of the gold-traders would have been worth a convenient round number of 1,200 cowries (and 100 troy grains would be 1,600 shells, possibly already called "2,000" following the logic of the Bambara "hundred"). At that exchange rate with

129

gold, eight cowrie shells had the approximate gold value of a pre–1914 British penny.

Leo Africanus in the second decade of the sixteenth century gave what appears to be a very different value, 400 shells to a "ducat." Elsewhere he seems to equate his ducat with the *mithqal* of $\frac{3}{20}$ oz.[16] This is a value about three times that stated by Ibn Battuta. Possibly this was a famine or emergency value (he wrote of a serious fire in Timbuktu). It is also possible that his ducat was not the gold *mithqal* at all. We know that in the nineteenth century a silver *"mithqal"* existed in El Arouan, north of Timbuktu. If Leo's coin was of similar value, not only would his exchange rate be the same as Ibn Battuta's, but his salt prices (see section on commodity values later in this chapter) would also be similar.

It is unfortunate that Leo's valuation is either ambiguous or an anomaly, as it would be interesting to compare Niger Bend values with those at the coast at the very time when the Portuguese were beginning to ship cowries in quantity by sea.

Figures for shell money exchange rates seem to be lacking until after the Moroccan invasion of the 1590s. Thereafter, writers seem agreed that both at Timbuktu and Jenne, the normal exchange rate was 3,000 to the *mithqal* (20,000 to the troy ounce) until about the year 1830.[17] Evidently, during this time cowries served as "small change" to the gold *mithqal*. This did not prevent cowrie values from soaring in time of famine, and indeed chroniclers seem to have used the shell money exchange rate as a measure of the severity of famine conditions. Presumably only cowries, and not gold, could be used to make purchases of food in the countryside, and thus they acquired a scarcity value.

There is at present no information as to when or under what circumstances the shells depreciated from their fourteenth-century (and perhaps early sixteenth-century) value to their lower value in the late seventeenth century. Three obvious possibilities present themselves: a "first cowrie inflation," resulting from Portuguese shell imports at the coast; a breakdown of the gold trade, such as seems to have occurred in the sixteenth or early seventeenth century, and which might account both for the Songhay attempt to control the source of their salt supplies, normally paid for in gold, and the Moroccan invasion of 1591; and finally the Moroccan invasion itself. It seems unlikely that there was any major change in the cost of bringing cowries to the Niger Bend, the greater part of which certainly must have been the cost of transport across the desert.

During the late eighteenth century there was a temporary cowrie inflation at Timbuktu, referred to earlier, that gives interesting insights into economic behavior when a shell money is in use. Substitute shells, called *koroni* – apparently the West African coastal *Marginella* – were put into circulation in vast quantity at Timbuktu. Indeed *Marginella* shells found at Timbuktu and elsewhere once gave rise to a theory of marine incursion to the area of the Niger Bend in geologically recent times. More convincing was a surviving oral tradition of the use of these shells as currency in the town; it was remembered that when true cowries reappeared, the town chief ordered the *Marginella* shells to be buried. M. D. W. Jeffreys believed this tradition went back to a period before the introduction of Maldive cowries into Timbuktu.[18] Raymond Mauny, influenced by the survival of the oral tradition, was inclined to favor a date in the nineteenth century, or perhaps the eighteenth or seventeenth. He traced a number of other finds of *Marginella* shell, and showed from an analysis of the species involved that they must have come from the Mauritanian coast, probably via Arguin.[19] (Certainly the whole episode implies relatively easy connection with the coast via Wadan, Tichitt, and Lake Faguibine, where *Marginella* shells have been found.)

The importation of these substitute shells in the 1780s and 1790s may have been provoked partly by the loss of over a million cowries to the Timbuktu economy in 1787, when a very large shipment sent secretly to Jenne by Bubakr, son of Pasha Ahmad, was either accepted or seized; the beginning of the French Revolutionary Wars may have disrupted the supply of replacements across the desert. The *koroni* (*Marginella*) substitutes passed at a much depreciated 100,000 to the gold *mithqal*, instead of the traditional 3,000:1 rate for Maldive *moneta*. Then, in September 1795, the newly installed Pasha Bubakr (the same who had sent the cowries to Jenne) reportedly removed the *koroni* shells from circulation, with cowries henceforth the only circulating shell. The exchange rate against the *mithqal* immediately appreciated to the "normal" 3,000 shells. Other prices were also affected at once: the bar of salt, which had likewise been 100,000 shells, fell to 4,000, while the *nafqa* or handful of grain fell from 1,500 to 100. The withdrawal of *Marginella* from circulation was apparently not a response to increasing supplies of money cowries, because the shell money exchange rate continued to appreciate yet further, to 1,500 to the *mithqal*. Timbuktu merchants in 1795 were actively seeking imports of *moneta* from Jenne.[20]

The steady normal rate of 3,000 to the gold *mithqal* was already being eroded in the first half of the nineteenth century, thus antedating the arrival at the coast of the Zanzibar *annulus* that was to spark off the second and general great inflation. The decline in value was rather small, and must have taken place in the second quarter of the century. Mungo Park found the rate to be still 3,000 at Sansanding at the beginning of the century, and René Caillié found it still the same at Jenne and Timbuktu in 1828.[21] Charles Monteil, studying Jenne in 1902, thought that 3,000 remained the rate until the time of Sheikh Ahmadu, *c.* 1827–1842, when it depreciated to 4,000. At Timbuktu, Barth found a rate of 3,800 to the *mithqal* in the 1850s. By the end of the nineteenth century, cowries had depreciated much more seriously. There were about 6,200 to the *mithqal* at Jenne, and something like double that at Timbuktu. These figures reflect the spread of the great coastal inflation, and, where Timbuktu was concerned, the accumulation of

131

Table 9.2 *Cowries to one ounce of gold*

Time	Niger Bend	Coast
14th century	8,000	—
c. 1520	(2,667) (Leo Africanus)	?8,000
c. 1700–1750	20,000 (?16,000)	15,360–16,000
c. 1780	20,000	32,000
c. 1810–1816	20,000	25,600
c. 1820	20,000	32,000
c. 1850	25,000	38,400

shells there because they could not be used in the desert trade, and perhaps the effects of French colonial policy. (When the French were attempting to replace the cowrie currency with francs, they at first accepted them for tax payments but did not pay them out. Some 20 million shells were eventually in store at Segu.[22])

Table 9.2 summarizes the cowrie exchange rates with one ounce of gold, and compares these rates to what is known about coastal rates at the same time. (Coastal rates are discussed below.)

Few figures for exchange rates are available for Hausaland. The recently uncovered information (in Anania's *L'Universale Fabrica del Mondo*, see our chapter 8) that Kano and/or Katsina were using cowries in the sixteenth century unfortunately gives no exchange values. The first information comes in the late eighteenth century from a rather unreliable informant, who gave a figure for Katsina of 2,500 cowries to the *mithqal*.[23] If this was the small *mithqal* of 60 grains, then the figure would correspond to the normal rate of 3,000 for the large *mithqal* of 72 grains. Most later values for Hausaland are given as a cowrie/silver-dollar exchange rate. The Hausa country seems to have followed the Islamic convention of equating the dollar with the silver *dirhem* at two-thirds of a *mithqal*, one-tenth of an ounce of gold. The Katsina rate of 2,000 to the silver dollar c. 1820 thus corresponds to the normal northern 3,000 to the *mithqal*. By the 1850s, the rate had eroded somewhat, but by convention was still rounded off to easily-managed figures, 2,500 to the dollar or 4,000 to the *mithqal*.[24]

Some check on northern cowrie values can be obtained from the prices given for salt, as shown in Table 9.3. Salt from the great Saharan mines at Teghaza and Taodeni was imported for centuries in slabs of a more or less standard size which could be carried by camels. Up to the end of the sixteenth century, salt prices stated in cowries are rare, and when expressed in gold suggest either very large fluctuations or inaccurate information. (These gold prices are for Teghaza salt, which may have been in larger slabs.) After the Moroccan invasion of the sixteenth century, there is rather more information, though we do not know exactly when the prices begin to

Table 9.3 *Cowries per bar of Taodeni salt, 1595–1902.*[25]

Year	Timbuktu	Jenne	Sansanding
1595	20,000 (approx. 1 oz gold)	—	—
1759	(3,000) (approx. 1 mithqal gold)	—	—
		—	—
1805	—	—	8,000
1828	—	10,000 15,000, 20,000	—
1855	3,000–6,000 (approx. 1 mithqal)	—	(7,500) 2 mithqal
c. 1870	—	—	20,000
1880	8,000–9,000 1 mithqal	—	—
1889	—	20,000–25,"000"[a] 3 mithqal	40,000 (uneconomic)
1894	—	—	50 francs (overland)
1895	30–40 francs (15,000–18,000)	60 francs (36,000)	70–80 francs (42,000–48,000)
1901	16–20 francs (16,000–20,000)	25–28 francs (32,500–36,400)	—
1902	—	36,000	—

[a] These are Bambara "thousands," i.e. units of 800.

refer to Taodeni, rather than Teghaza, salt. It seems that a value corresponding to one gold *mithqal* existed from the mid-eighteenth to the mid-nineteenth century, and still obtained as late as 1880 when the value of the gold *mithqal* was 8,000 to 9,000 shells. Prices at Jenne were much higher, three times or more the price at Timbuktu, but taxes as well as transport were included. Prices were higher still at Segu and Sansanding; river communications between Segu and Timbuktu were cut after 1860. By the end of the nineteenth century, the bar of salt was worth some five to six times as many cowries as it had been a century earlier, but the costs of moving the shells through the interior delta of the Niger had relatively diminished, partly owing to the disappearance of the Masina tax system. (The anomalous franc rates for 1895 shown in the table are due to the import of silver coin to pay French forces; cowrie values for salt were evidently not affected.)

Coastal values. Values at the coast are more difficult to interpret, since it was only at Accra and Christiansborg on the Gold Coast that cowries and gold were regularly found together. References to gold elsewhere are either in terms of the "trade ounce" or are merchants' estimates, sometimes based on the invoice value of the shells; this led Karl Polanyi into thinking that an

133

exchange rate of 32,000 cowries for one troy ounce of gold went back to the beginning of the eighteenth century.[26] Several valuations of cowries based on their invoice cost, or "prime cost" so-called, are provided by early authors. Bosman wrote of the shells as 1,000 for 2s. 6d. John Atkins, writing of 1721, referred to cowries at Whydah as "bought at 1s. and sold at 2s. 6d. per pound." (A pound consisted of about 400 shells.) Atkins also mentioned a "grand quibess" (4,000 cowries) "which answers to 25s." Houstoun echoes this value: "cowries which were always formerly current money at five ackies of gold [25s.] for a grand cabess." A little later, the value of the grand *cabess* settled at 20s. (£1) sterling, but had not yet been related to the trade ounce.[27]

At Danish Christiansborg, the *cabess* was normally 2,000 cowries, with a *stor cabess* of 4,000. Rask, the Danish chaplain there in the early eighteenth century, gave the value of the (small) *cabess* as two *rigsdaler*, or one-eighth of a gold ounce, so that the rate was 16,000 shells to an ounce of gold. Rømer, giving a list of prices current in Christiansborg in 1747, referred to 20 lbs. of cowries (about 8,000 shells) as equal to half an ounce of gold, thus repeating Rask's exchange rate of 16,000 to the gold ounce.[28]

Rask tells us that the "string" of 40 cowries was known as a *damba*, and 80 shells was a *taku*; these are the names of the smaller Akan gold-weights. A similar account dated 1709 comes from the English fort at Accra. In the eighteenth century, 24 *damba* or 12 *taku* in gold made one gold ackie; 16 ackies made one gold ounce.[29] (See the summary list below.)

Cowries		*Gold*	
40 cowries	= 1 damba		
2 damba	= 1 taku	2 damba	= 1 taku
25 damba	= 1 rigsdaler	24 damba	
	(= 1 ackie)	or 12 taku	= 1 ackie
50 damba or			
2 rigsdaler	= 1 cabess		
8 cabess	= 1 gold ounce	16 ackies	= 1 gold ounce

As can be seen, the cowrie system had been slightly rounded off, to simplify counting by hundreds instead of by multiples of twelve. The small discrepancy may possibly be accounted for by the customary 4% brokerage charged on the exchange of gold for cowries.

This opens up an interesting area of speculation. In Coast Portuguese, the trade language of the Guinea Coast up to the eighteenth century, a string of cowries was a *toque* or *tokky*. The word means "touch" in Portuguese, and makes absolutely no sense as applied to shell money. It is just possible that *toque* was originally *taku* (which Thomas Bowdich spelled *tokoo*).[30] If one *toque* of 40 cowries was equivalent in the early sixteenth century to one *taku* of gold, then the exchange rate for one standard *mithqal* ($\frac{3}{20}$ of an ounce, or of 16 ackies) works out to be 1,152 shells, since

$$1 \text{ ackie} = 12 \times 40 = 480$$
$$1 \text{ oz. troy} = 480 \times 16 = 7{,}680$$
$$1 \text{ mithqal} = 7{,}680 \times \tfrac{3}{20} = 1{,}152$$

Ibn Battuta's figure in the fourteenth century was 1,150. This seems almost too good to be true.

If it is anything more than a rather remarkable coincidence, we would have to assume not only the survival of the fourteenth-century rate into the early sixteenth century, but also a long-distance trade connection between the coast and the Niger Bend using a constant exchange rate between cowries and gold. There is plenty of evidence for the trade connection, but none for the use of cowries alongside gold on the Guinea Coast at this period.

The hypothesis of a constant gold–cowrie rate in the early sixteenth century might explain some of the oddities of cowrie arithmetic, and also some of the various gold units in use. The 75-grain *mithqal* would be 12 "Muslim hundreds" or 1,200 shells. The small *mithqal* or *gros* would be 12 "Bambara hundreds" or 960 cowries. The *soa*, basic weight of the Ashanti system, but probably originating north of the forest, would be 12 "Mandingo hundreds" or 720 shells; and the coastal ackie would be 12 strings or 480 shells. An ackie of goods at the coast would sell for a *soa* at the first great market, for a *gros* at the second, and for the large *mithqal* at the Niger Bend. Such a system would imply a northward flow of goods in exchange for a southward flow of gold. It would therefore seem to date from after the arrival of the Portuguese on the coast with trade goods, and before the importation of Maldive *moneta* had become sufficiently large to depreciate coastal cowrie values. It could, however, relate to the northward movement of salt from the coastal lagoons. (There is evidence of the existence of a unit rather close to the *soa* in the hinterland behind Accra early in the eighteenth century, based on a 35-cowrie string and a *damba* one-third larger than the coastal *damba*. European merchants were well aware of the profit that could be made by Africans engaging in arbitrage by purchasing cowries at the coast at the standard rate of 40 to the coastal *damba*, then using them to buy gold at 35 cowries for $1\tfrac{1}{3}$ of a coastal *damba*, worth 60 cowries at the coast. The resulting increase in cowrie value corresponds closely to the difference between the coastal string of 40 and the Mandingo "hundred" of 60.)[31]

Large imports of cowries in the sixteenth century certainly did lead to their depreciation, as also happened in the Congo. A system linked to gold would be much more stable, but only so long as gold continued to flow. If the gold trade were interrupted, the whole system would have had to "go off the gold standard." Something of the sort did happen on the coast in the second half of the eighteenth century. At that time, through the medium of the trade ounce, the gold-values of cowries halved during a period of

135

interruption in the normal gold trade, and when gold was actually being imported into the Gold Coast in place of the normal export.[32] There may have been a similar interruption of the normal gold trade in the sixteenth or earlier seventeenth centuries. A breakdown of the northward trade through Begho seems to have occurred in the sixteenth century, when a punitive expedition appears to have been sent because of a cessation of the flow of gold to Mali.[33] It is possible that this was part of a much more general derangement of the gold trade which also affected the southward flow of gold.

The exchange rate on the coast in the early eighteenth century was, as we have already seen, 15,360 to 16,000 cowries to the gold ounce. On the Niger Bend it was 20,000 to the ounce, 3,000 to the *mithqal*. This might suggest that, despite the much higher cost of bringing the shells across the desert, cowries were actually lower in value on the Niger Bend than on the Guinea Coast. (This assumes, of course, that gold was everywhere of the same value, an assumption that makes nonsense of the entire gold trade, but is nevertheless usually made because of the relatively low transport cost of gold.) The suggestion may be an illusion. As we saw in chapter 8, the Bambara country west of the interior delta of the Niger counted by "Bambara hundreds" of 80 shells, and we know that this method of counting extended as far east as Jenne in the nineteenth century; thus "20,000" shells may have been only 16,000, and relatively small changes in the value of cowries could have been taken up by changing from the Bambara hundred to the Muslim hundred, or vice versa, as in the early twentieth century.

During the Napoleonic Wars, it was England that went off the gold standard. The value of gold on the Guinea Coast rose in terms of cowries; at Accra, the value of a gold ackie was only 1,600 cowries, though by 1820 it had recovered to the earlier level of 2,000.[34]

By the 1840s, the coastal exchange rate had depreciated to 2,400 cowries to the ackie (38,400 to the gold ounce). This seems to have been a part of the general decline in the value of shells which also affected the Niger Bend, where by the 1850s the gold ounce was 25,000 shells – well before the massive influx of Zanzibar *annulus* that later fueled the great inflation.[35] By this time, there was a large and permanent difference between the coast and the Niger Bend in the cowrie exchange rate against gold. From about the beginning of the nineteenth century, the only practical common standard was the silver dollar, not the gold ounce.

Cowries and dollars. The various silver dollars which circulated in West Africa were of nearly the same weight, namely that of a Spanish ounce of gold, or about $\frac{7}{8}$ of a troy ounce. With the gold ounce valued at £4 sterling, the silver dollar was valued at 4s. 6d. But in West Africa it was usual in the eighteenth and earlier nineteenth centuries to equate the dollar with the ackie, one-sixteenth of a troy ounce, or 5 shillings.[36] In the north, however, the Islamic ratio of 10:1 still prevailed.

136

Silver dollars seem to have been introduced in any quantity during the eighteenth or early nineteenth century, both in the north and on the coast. They did not circulate everywhere as currency – there were large areas where they were simply raw material for the jewellers to turn into rings and other ornaments. During what appears to be their first introduction, anomalous values are reported from various areas: thus a Danish source valued the dollar at Christiansborg in 1750 at 1,600 cowries, one-tenth of the value of the gold ounce of the time. Thirty years later, dollars stood at 2,000 shells, a sixteenth of the then current gold value of 32,000 cowries an ounce.[37]

By the beginning of the nineteenth century, the dollar was for the most part valued at 2,000 cowries all the way from the coast to Hausaland, where in the 1820s Lyon heard of this value at Katsina; Clapperton found the same rate at Kano.[38] Since the gold/silver ratios were different, however, this necessarily implied a varying gold/cowrie exchange rate. Some indication of such a variation can be obtained from Joseph Dupuis' figures quoted earlier, though there are also indications of a higher rate, 3,000 cowries to the dollar, at both Timbuktu and Kano in the 1820s. If correct, this suggests instability in the exchange rate.[39] One thing is clear: from being "small change" for gold, cowries in the nineteenth century had become "small change" for dollars, at least along the coast-to-Hausaland route.

By 1850, the Accra rate for the dollar was 2,400 shells, though it could be as high as 2,600 at Whydah where the slave trade continued. In Kano, the figure was 2,500 in the early 1850s. The small depreciation of shell money is evident here, while the rate remained nearly constant from the coast to Hausaland. In Timbuktu, however, the rate was 3,000 to the silver dollar.[40]

Later figures for the cowrie exchange rate at the coast are complicated by the curious systems of reckoning on the Gold Coast. By an Order in Council, the troy ounce of gold was valued at £3 12s. in West Africa, by contrast to the mint value of nearly £4. The difference, some 10%, was officially supposed to cover freight, insurance, and other transport costs.[41] (The disparity cannot represent, as Timothy Garrard suggests, the difference between coined gold and pure gold, as a corresponding difference was applied to silver dollars.[42]) The value of £3 12s. was known as the "sterling" value, and was used by the Gold Coast Government. The merchants, who were actually engaged in the gold trade and were buying gold by the grain, continued to use the much more convenient system of valuing gold at £4 an ounce, or two pence a troy grain, a value which was called "currency." They naturally accounted their transport costs separately.

Under the same Order in Council, dollars were valued at 4s. 2d.; for a time the merchants continued to reckon the dollar at five shillings "currency," but by the 1850s they usually calculated it at 4s. 6d. "currency." The *Gold Coast Blue Book* for 1855 says: "The dollar is reckoned at 5s. currency, but is paid by Order of Council at 4s. 2d.; but in fact passes at 4s. 6d. sterling, so that in practice the denomination in currency exceeds that in sterling by one tenth."[43] The arithmetic is hard to understand (5 shillings are 60 pence, 4s. 2d. make 50 pence, while 4s. 6d. make 54 pence). Non-literates, or the barely literate, working in cowries, must have found it even harder.

It is ironic that the official value of 4s. 2d. continued long after the dollar had lost bullion value after 1870, so that it actually paid merchants to ship dollars from Europe and use them for payments to the government, which not only had to accept them at the 4s. 2d. value, but also had to pay to ship them back to Europe – a merry-go-round fully described by A. G. Hopkins. They were not demonetized until 1880 in Nigeria and the Gold Coast, and remained current elsewhere until the 1920s.[44]

THE GREAT COWRIE INFLATION

The decline in cowrie values in the second quarter of the nineteenth century, though slight compared with the great inflation to follow, suggests that more cowries were already being imported than could be absorbed at prevailing rates. The quantity was increasing greatly on the Gold Coast in 1850 and 1851, to the point where Brodie Cruikshank wondered how long it could be before a depreciation commenced.[45] His query was certainly justified: before his book appeared in print in 1853, shell money values on the Gold Coast had begun to collapse.

The immediate cause of the collapse was almost certainly the new poll tax, and had nothing to do with Zanzibar *annulus*. The first year's tax, though somewhat disappointing to officials, yielded nearly 20,000 heads of cowries, all told some 40 million shells.[46] Off hand, it might be thought that the collection of 40 million shells would have an obvious deflationary effect. But most of these shells almost certainly came from hoards, these hoards being the reason why the large recent importation had not already caused serious depreciation of the cowrie. Moreover, the cowries collected in the eastern districts could not be sent to Cape Coast, where the shells were not used as currency; even if it had been attempted, the accumulated revenue at some 45 tons would have been hard to move. They must have been "realized" on the open market at Accra. The sudden deluge of 40 million shells on this market had the effect that economic theory would anticipate: their value sank rapidly to three-quarters of the old level. Continuing large imports – some 300 tons are reported to have been brought to the Gold Coast in 1853 – did nothing to stem the depreciation.[47]

Serious political troubles followed the introduction of the poll tax in the area of Accra, culminating in riots and the shelling of the town of Christiansborg from the sea. Loss of confidence in the cowrie currency, and the very real loss of accumulated savings both to taxation and to inflation, must surely have been one cause of the disturbances.

The value of cowries never recovered. The official value had fallen to 2s. 6d. per head in 1859 and 1861; by the end of the 1860s it had fallen

138

urther to 2s. 3d., but was unstable, and reached as low as 1s. 6d.[48] Further
depreciation followed rapidly, perhaps partly a result of the 1869 war,
involving large payments in cowries to African allies in 1873, which brought
the value to 1s. per head. The Accra inflation, at least in its earlier stages,
owed nothing to the introduction of Zanzibar *annulus*, which were never
accepted by the British government there in payment of taxes and dues.
There are reports of a cargo of Zanzibar shells thrown into the sea.)[49] It
was due, as we have seen, to the over-importation of Maldive *moneta* and
the unanticipated effects of the collection of the new poll tax. East of the
Volta, and possibly at Ada at its mouth, things were very different. By the
middle of the nineteenth century, cowries were already suffering some loss
of value, and the first experimental shipments of the Zanzibar shells had
already been accepted at Whydah in 1845. Though slaving did figure in the
first *annulus* imports, most of the many thousand millions eventually
brought into the West African economy were paid out in return for exports
of palm oil, not slaves. By the 1850s, the influx that would bring some 35,000
tons (= some 14,000,000,000 shells) to the coast between 1851 and 1869 was
in full swing.

From a value of 2,400 to 2,600 cowries to the silver dollar, they rapidly
depreciated to 6,000 in 1857 and 10,000 by 1871. Nor was the slide halted
here; by 1889, 2,000 shells were equivalent on the coast to six pence, and in
the 1890s a value as low as 2,000 for half a French franc ($4\frac{1}{2}$–5 pence) was
recorded, the lowest in West Africa. The coast of Togo had a similar story to
tell. By the 1890s, cowries were 4,000 to the mark (equivalent to one British
shilling). The inflation spread to the interior of this part of the coast, though
not quite to the same devastating extent.[50]

In Lagos, where cowries were also used to pay for palm oil, events ran a
similar course. From 4s. a head in the early 1850s, values per head of
cowries fell to 2s. 6d. by 1855, to 1s. 6d. by 1859, then down to 1s. by 1876
and finally to 6d. by 1895.[51] Hopkins attributes the final fall in values to
monetary changes, including the demonetization of the dollar and the
increasing use of British silver. It would seem that the circulation of
Zanzibar *annulus* was also an important causal factor, since the final fall in
values did not take place on the Gold Coast, affected by similar monetary
changes, but did occur in Dahomey, which had Zanzibar shells but no direct
effect from British monetary changes. The extent of the coastal inflation is
summarized in Table 9.4.

The great inflation inland. Not many figures are available for the changing
values of cowries inland as the great inflation spread, but we can be sure that
merchants everywhere seized the opportunity, whenever they were able, to
take shells to areas where they remained more valuable. Thus did the
inflation affect an ever-wider area.

On the lower Niger, until the arrival of the European traders and their
steamers in the nineteenth century, cowries had circulated alone without

Table 9.4 *Value of one head (2,000 cowries) in terms of shillings and pence, 1850–1895, at Accra, Whydah, and Lagos*

	Accra	Whydah	Lagos
1850	4s. 2d.	3s. 8d. to 4s. 2d.	4s.
1853	2s. 9d. to 3s.	—	4s.
1855	3s. 4d. variable	—	2s. 6d.
1857	—	1s. 6d.	—
1859	2s. 6d.	—	1s. 6d. to 1s. 9½d.
1863	—	1s. 4½d. to 1s. 9½d.	1s. 4d.
1870	2s. 3d.	1s. 3½d.	1s. 3d.
1874	1s. 3d.	—	—
1876	1s.	—	1s.
1881	1s. .	—	9¾d. to 1s. 1d.
1882	1s.	—	6½d.
1889	—	6d.	—
1895	1s.	4½d. to 9d.	6d.

any other currency, and the same was true of many areas between the coast and the east–west routes of savanna country. There are thus no meaningful exchange rates for such areas until the penetration of European currency which did not begin on any scale until the 1870s. On the lower Niger, rates were quoted by the expeditions of 1831 and 1842, but these were based on the "prime" cost of shells in Europe, and were therefore much lower than coastal exchange values at this time. As late as 1857, there are estimates of exchange rates at 2,000 to the dollar – a value already long out of date on the coast.[52]

In the 1870s, we hear of a widespread rate of 1,000 cowries to the British shilling, half the coastal rate at that date. The 1,000:1s. value was reported at Salaga and Kete Krachi and throughout much of what is now the northern part of Ghana. It obtained in parts of northern Togo and on the Niger at Lokoja and Onitsha.[53] By about 1890, when rates at Lagos and Whydah had depreciated still further, the rate at Lokoja on the Niger, Loko on the Benue, and Djougou in inland Dahomey was 2,000 to the shilling and mark. At Ilorin the rate was about 3,000. The official rate of the Royal Niger Company was still 1s. 3d. per head of 2,000, about 1,600 to the shilling (actual rates were often below this, though 1,600:1s. did prevail in Nupe). By 1902, the rate at Ilorin was 4,000 to the shilling, about the same as on the coast, and a similar value was remembered at Kiama near the Dahomean frontier. At Lokoja it had only fallen to 2,500:1, and at Bida to 3,000:1. In Igbo country the rate was still relatively high at 1,500 to the shilling.[54]

Farther north, even fewer figures are available. In Hausaland, the *mithqal* rate at Kano was 4,000:1 at mid-century, falling to 5,000 by 1862 while a gold rate at Zaria in 1861 implies a *mithqal* value of 6,000. By the

1890s, in Hausaland, the *mithqal* was worth about 15,000 cowries. Silver-dollar values of 2,500 to 3,000 in the 1850s and 1860s had by the 1890s reached 5,000, which seems to have been fairly standard over a wide area of the north from Yola to Kano and as far south as Zaria and Lokoja. By 1902, shillings were coming into use, with a rate of 2,000 to 1 at Zaria, 1,200 at Kano, and 1,000 at Illo on the Niger, which was still the rate at Salaga and Kete Krachi. Reported exchange rates in Bornu in these years do not differ much from those of Kano, though it seems certain that the absorption of cowries in that area after its mid-century adoption of shell money restrained inflation elsewhere (for example, to the south in Egba-land).[55]

In Timbuktu, the 1855 figure of 3,800 to the gold *mithqal* had given place by 1880 to a figure of 8,000 or 9,000, while the dollar in that time moved only from 3,000 to 4,500. By 1891 the *mithqal* was 10,000 to 15,000 cowries, and the dollar had disappeared, its place taken by the French 5-franc piece at 5,000 shells. Timbuktu cowrie values were lower than else-where in the north in the later nineteenth century, because the shells were not acceptable in the desert trade; that very early user of the shell money eventually became an isolated outpost of the cowrie currency zone.[56]

In Jenne, the value of 4,000 cowries to the *mithqal* dating from Sheikh Ahmadu's time had declined only to some 6,000–8,000 shells by the 1890s, though these rates may refer to a rather smaller *mithqal*. In 1895, silver 5-franc pieces had been imported as pay for French soldiers in such quan-tity that the exchange rate of 2,500–3,000 shells was substantially higher than the rate at Timbuktu; by 1902 the rate against the 5-franc piece had depreciated to 4,000–5,600.[57]

Cowries and the 5-franc piece. On the upper Niger and in the country to the west, the place of the dollar was taken by the silver 5-franc piece. Though this coin was nearly 10% smaller than the silver dollar, until the late nine-teenth century this was more than compensated for by the great premium on silver. A standard rate near the goldfields west of the Niger was one 5-franc piece to one *gros* ($\frac{1}{8}$ oz.) of gold. At 20,000 cowries to the ounce, the value of the 5-franc piece should have been 2,500 cowries; this was the rate at which Raffanel actually sold his coins in Kaarta in 1848.[58]

On the upper Niger, Mage quoted an approximate value of 3 francs for a Bambara thousand (800) in the early 1860s, but it does not seem that 5-franc pieces were yet current there, and the basis for his calculation is uncertain.[59] Not until after 1870 did real exchange rates between cowries and French silver become established in this area. By that time the coins no longer contained even approximately their face value in silver, so that it becomes very difficult to interpret their values. As the French advanced, shell-money exchange rates became increasingly related to the value of the (gold-based) French franc; and at the same time the high premium on silver declined as the French brought in more coin. Meanwhile, the world

141

value of silver was still falling. To add to the confusion, in the area west of Timbuktu all values are quoted in Bambara hundreds of 80.

In 1878 the 5-franc piece was worth "3,500 to 4,000" (2,800–3,200 actual shells) at Guigné (north of Bamako), and "5,000" (4,000 shells) near the river. In 1880, under very disturbed political conditions, the value at Segu and in the adjacent area ranged from "2,500" to "5,000" (2,000–4,000 cowries). The lower figure, "2,500," was still current at Koulikoro, Yamina, and Sansanding in about 1890, though to the south of Timbuktu, at Bandiagara, the rate was 5,000 to the 5-franc piece. This was also the figure at Timbuktu, and probably also at Jenne. After the French conquest this became the official French rate, and continued to be the ruling rate at Timbuktu, on the upper Niger, and in the inland Niger delta. By 1902, however, the actual rate was 6,500 (though these were possibly Bambara "hundreds" of 80). Further east, in the region between Dori and Say, the cowrie was higher, 3,500 to the 5-franc piece, a rate similar to the 1s. per thousand quoted at Illo.[60]

The Middle Zone about 1890. In the area that is now the southern part of the Republic of Guinea, 5-franc pieces were found by Binger in 1889. If not in circulation, the coins at least had recognized rates of exchange with cowries. At Oulosebougou the rate was 1,600 shells; further east at Tenetou, Tiong-i, Fourou, and Benkhobougoula it was 2,000. Still further east, no silver was in circulation, though it was occasionally sold in the markets as a commodity bought by jewellers. Binger had to express his prices in francs through the medium of gold dust at the current (European) rate of exchange.[61]

Binger also gave a number of exchange rates between cowries and gold. He spoke in terms of the *"barifiri,"* which he equated to four *mithqal*. In Salaga at least, the *"mithqal"* of this date must have been about nine-tenths of the Nikky *mithqal* of seventy years earlier. It was now worth some 10,000 cowries, as against Dupuis' value of 4,300 shells. This is the only figure from Binger's series which is directly comparable with Dupuis' values. Binger's rates range from 24,000 to the *barifiri* at Kong, and a little above that at Bobo Dioulasso, to 30,000 at Bonduku market (though gold could be obtained more cheaply in the nearby gold-mining villages), 40,000 at Salaga, 55,000–60,000 at Kintampo, and "nearly 80,000" at the "posts on the coast."[62] This last would correspond to half a gold ounce at the Gold Coast rate of 2,000 cowries to a shilling; but this was a silver rate, and the rates for gold may have been different. Kintampo, between Bonduku and Salaga, was at this date cut off from Ashanti trade, which would account for the high value of gold there.

Further east, at Djougou, cowries were 2,000 to the silver mark, compared with 1,000 to the shilling at Salaga, thus reflecting the low value on the Dahomey coast. At Nikky, where the gold ounce had been about 25,000 shells in 1820, Lugard gave a "local value" in 1894 which would correspond to just double that figure.[63] This was apparently an island of higher cowrie values, as might be expected in an area where European penetration was so late.

The value of cowries in any particular place was of course dependent on the uses to which they were put. Where they were purely a commodity with no monetary significance, as in areas of production and trans-shipment, and also in "consumption" areas where they were used in small quantities solely for decoration or ritual, value was determined by the standard mechanism of supply and demand. Local prices at any particular spot not using the shells as money would, however, be pulled up by demand from areas of monetary use, since the market for cowries was about as close to world-wide as for any other commodity of the sixteenth to eighteenth century, and was still extensive in the nineteenth century. The open auction markets of the Netherlands and England virtually guaranteed rapid reflection of demand and supply changes.

On the supply side, "costs of production" included not only the cost of gathering and processing in the Maldives (or later, Zanzibar), but also the subsequent costs of cleaning and sorting, ocean transport in or out of ballast, and the much higher cost of transport overland in Africa. At each stage of the journey from their original lagoon or beach to their final destination in West Africa, merchants would expect to cover cost price plus cost of transport plus insurance (or an allowance for risk) plus a profit. These components would normally put a floor under the price at which merchants would be willing to sell cowries. But it must also be remembered that, as with the case of almost every other item imported into West Africa during much of the span of our story, merchants had to engage in "assortment bargaining." This practice often required them to include in the bargain for slaves or other purchases, an assortment of goods which included some items they considered to be going at a loss. Without these, no trade at all could be done; the loss was compensated for by more profitable items.

Where cowries circulated as money, two different situations are recognizable: conventional "fixed" rates, and floating rates. We have seen them circulating very commonly as small change for either gold or silver, at a conventional rate which was sometimes above their intrinsic value, i.e. the market price at which they had been imported. In the case where cowries circulated at a value above their import price, a seigniorage yield was gleaned either by merchants, by government officials, or with a share taken by both. Whenever this was the case, it would require some methods for restricting free importation (customs houses, licensing, and the like) without which the conventional value could not have been maintained. The only example of such government intervention known to us before the twentieth-century prohibition on imports by the colonial authorities is that reported many years later by General Daumas' informant at Katsina in the early nineteenth century.)[64] More frequently, however, the value of the shells as small change was most probably at about the level where the profits on importation were similar to those on other goods. That would have made it possible to maintain the rate of exchange with gold or silver for long periods, without seigniorage above the normal rates of profit and thus with no need officially to restrict imports.

In the West African zone of cowrie currency, it would seem that serious inflations were uniformly due to two main causes: first when there was a major change in the cost of transport, as when the Portuguese began to bring shells by sea, or when some direct trade in Zanzibar *annulus* sprang up in the mid-nineteenth century; secondly, when a substitute shell cheaper at its source was brought into use, temporarily as with the Timbuktu *Marginella* of the late eighteenth century, or permanently, as with the Zanzibar cowries. Appreciation in value of the cowrie could also occur. Typically this would take place during long periods of otherwise stable exchange rates (3,000 to the *mithqal* for example), when emergencies such as famines led to temporary shortages of shell. Since they flowed out of towns to buy grain at higher prices in rural markets, and not all flowed back in the short run, their scarcity would then command a premium. In the longer run, however, many more would eventually return to the town, and further, any prolonged rise in value would encourage merchants to import additional supplies.

There were other places and times in West Africa where the cowrie currency existed without any precious metal alongside. This might be transitory, a result of some disturbance to the gold trade, as when the Gold Coast took to importing gold in the later eighteenth century. Or it might be long enduring, as in the case of the lower Niger or the Dahomean coast. If the conventional cowrie/gold rate overvalued cowries, then going temporarily "off gold" – and in the absence of any enforced restrictions on import – could lead to a rapid depreciation in cowrie values. This seems to have been the case in the later eighteenth century on the Gold Coast.

A cowrie currency with no fixed rate (i.e. no backing by gold or silver) would necessarily float. Its value could only be meaningfully expressed, as with any other sort of money, in terms of the things it would buy. Travellers sometimes made elaborate calculations, translating cowries into gold or silver, or shillings or francs or dollars, apparently believing in some intrinsic permanence for their calculations. Like any other floating rate of the 1980s this simply was not so.

The value of the shells when the cowrie currency was floating would depend largely on normal monetary factors. If no new shells were entering the system, their value would depend on the quantity of goods they were chasing, and if the local economy were expanding, their value would tend to rise. In practice, until the twentieth century, new cowries were normally always entering the system faster than they were being lost or otherwise

144

Table 9.5 *Prices of hens and gold 'Taku' expressed in cowries, c. 1520–1850*[65]

	live hen	gold taku	galinha
early 16th century	(?)40	(?)40	40
early 17th century	—	—	(?)80
late 17th century,			
early 18th century	240–280 (Accra)	80	200
late 18th century	266–333 (Whydah)	160	200
mid 19th century	200–280 (Allada)	200	—

taken out of circulation. If they were coming in faster than the economic system was expanding, their value would tend to fall. Both the rises and the falls tended to be self-limiting. An appreciation would cause merchants to expand their shell imports, so impeding the rise. A local depreciation would erode the profit margins of the merchants doing the importing, and so constrict shell imports. This seems to have been the normal condition over most of the history of the cowrie currency.

The cowrie currency in the eastern Gold Coast, and to a lesser extent on the Popo and Whydah coast, was partially underpinned by the overlap between gold dust and cowries in the Accra area, and less directly by the extension of the trade ounce system to Dahomey in the later eighteenth century. It is informative to contrast the changing shell prices for a common commodity purchased on the coast (live hens, for which there is surprisingly good information) with the cowrie price of the gold *taku* (approximately 2.5 troy grains) of gold dust. In Table 9.5 we also show the number of cowries in the conventional measure known as the *galinha*, or "hen." It is probable that the currency unit known as the *galinha* or "hen" represented the cowrie value of a real live hen in the Forcados River in the early sixteenth century, and that the transfer of the name to a larger unit by the seventeenth century represents a rise in the cowrie price of live hens – the "first" cowrie inflation caused by the new Portuguese imports. By the later eighteenth century, the *galinha* unit had become conventionalized, and probably no longer bore any relation to live hens, which appear to have been dear at this date.

In terms of the hens they would buy, cowries seem to have depreciated only to about half their gold value between the early eighteenth and the mid-nineteenth century. This was a time when very considerable quantities of cowries were imported, these years encompassing the most important period of the slave trade. These shells must have remained in Africa, since the importing merchants would not accept them in payment for other trade goods. How then was hyperinflation avoided during this period?

There are only two possible explanations: either the velocity of circulation (the V in the $MV = PQ$ of conventional monetary economics) was falling, or the economy serviced by the cowrie (PQ) was expanding. A fall in velocity could have occurred in any special circumstance where extraordinary hoarding was taking place, but aside from the already-discussed events in the Gold Coast at the time of the poll tax, there is no reason to expect this as a major explanation. A much more likely interpretation is that the cowrie economy was expanding, both in its geographical spread and in its internal economic activity. The slave trade carried shells into an enlarging area in the eighteenth century, both for purchases of the slaves themselves and in payment for the costs of transport. By the early eighteenth century, shell money was certainly being carried inland by the Muslim ("Malay") traders who frequented the coast around Whydah; this inland movement may already have been a flow from the southern zone to the northern, such as was unquestionably taking place by the end of the eighteenth century. Not only slave exports, but any other conceivable product, could be paid for by cowries in place of some less convenient money, or, looked at in another way, could be used by non-monetized areas, or by areas with a less desirable money to pay for imports of the more convenient cowrie. This accounts for a geographical spread; but there was a deepening as well as a widening of the cowrie economy. Expansion of the internal monetized exchange economy of an area already using the cowrie would just as effectively provide the new monetary demand that would serve to limit inflationary tendencies. More cowries were clearly chasing more goods, so long as the slave trade continued. In fact, the absence of hyperinflation during a long period of huge money imports is convincing evidence that growth in the scale of monetary transactions was taking place in West Africa during the era of the Atlantic slave trade.

How long the system could have continued expanding before the breaking point (i.e. hyperinflation) was reached can never be known. The abolition of the slave trade in 1807 by Britain, the major buyer of the time, caused the collapse of shell imports discussed in chapter 6. Relative monetary tightness must have succeeded relative ease; the reduction in money imports must have been far greater than the reduction in West Africa's internal monetary transactions at this time. Only when palm oil began to emerge as a substitute "legitimate" export, did imports of shell money resume on a large scale. By this time, the Maldive cowries were not only rapidly losing their role as the shell money of the slave trade, and becoming the "shell money of the palm oil trade," but they were about to lose their centuries-long pre-eminence to the Zanzibar *annulus*.

For many years, until the 1850s, cowries lost little in value. Imports of the shell money were financed by exports, largely of palm oil, with a non-inflationary result as long as the domestic economies of the cowrie zone grew at a sufficiently rapid rate to absorb the increased quantity of money. By the early 1850s, economic expansion had slowed down throughout most of coastal West Africa; combined with burgeoning shipments of both *moneta* and *annulus*, limits to importation were soon reached beyond which inflation and exchange-rate depreciation took place. Some idea of these limits emerges from a comparison between the annual value of cowrie imports and exchange rates expressed in European currencies. At Lagos, for example, from 1856 increases in imports by German firms much beyond an annual local value of £250,000 sterling were quickly offset by a further decline in the exchange rate. Imports from Britain to the Gold Coast, though on a smaller scale, show a similar pattern, with some sort of ceiling beyond which the economy could not absorb much currency without affecting prices and exchange rates. Renewed economic expansion in the later 1860s raised this ceiling for Lagos and its hinterland to at least half a million sterling by 1869.[66] (There was no corresponding increase on the Gold Coast, presumably because of the impact of the Ashanti Wars.)

The end of the story, as we have seen, was one of galloping inflation, with the limits to monetary expansion beyond which inflation/depreciation would occur clearly exceeded.[67] In no part of West Africa was the collapse as complete as it was for the Revolutionary Continentals, or Confederate States Dollars, or the German mark in 1923, or the Hungarian *pengö* after World War Two. Even enormous imports of a commodity money cannot keep pace with a modern printing press, or even an old one. But their gross inconvenience at the values finally reached soon spelled *finis* for any kind of major transaction with the shell money.

10

The last of the cowrie

The death of the cowrie currency brought painful economic change in the areas where the shells circulated and where they were produced. In West Africa, shell money might yet have had a long and important life as a subsidiary currency for very small purchases. But because of a combination of opposition by the colonial authorities and continuing twentieth-century inflation, that was not to be. The sad end of the shell money, and the unlucky result for the final holders of the now-useless stocks, are surveyed in the first part of this chapter.

Imports to West Africa came to an end several years before the shells actually ceased to be an important currency. Around 1900 the shell money was still circulating vigorously in much of its old zone, though certainly in decline. British silver coin had long since replaced cowries on the Gold Coast for all but the smallest market transactions, and in southern Nigeria, at least along the coast, the shells were being replaced, again by British silver. Francs were ousting cowries on the upper Niger and to the west of the river; in French territory by 1914 prices nearly everywhere were being quoted in francs even though the shells survived in many markets.[1]

The attitude of the colonial governments was variably hostile. Doubtless influenced by the strong and almost universal belief in the rightness of fixed exchange rates, colonial officials attempted to fix rates between the cowrie and the metropolitan currency during the period just before the First World War. The French in particular did so avidly (the rate being typically 1,000 to the franc). This was widely evaded in the western part of French territory by counting in Bambara "hundreds" of 80, while in Mossi a rate of 800 to the franc was established after 1906. (Fixed rates were always very difficult for the French to manage, because throughout their territory there was much seasonal fluctuation, due partly to the seasonal demand for coin to pay taxes.) The Germans in Togo also attempted to fix rates, which then had to be adjusted to keep up with changing market conditions.[2]

Governor Lugard in Northern Nigeria (some of whose earlier experiences with cowries have already been recounted in chapter 9) considered the stabilization of shell values to be of the greatest importance. In his

148

official *Political Memoranda* dated 1905, a long note on shell money begins:

> *Cowries.* The cowrie will always remain (as it does in India to this day) a medium of exchange for very small values, but it is most eminently desirable that it should be replaced for higher values by metal coins on account of (a) the bulk and weight and the great time taken in counting, (b) the wastage involved by breakage, leakage of bags, etc.; and (c) its fluctuating value.[3]

In the meantime, Lugard intended to concentrate on the problem of stabilizing the value of cowries, the exchange rate for which in the southerly provinces of Northern Nigeria was double the rate in the more remote northern areas. With importation already prohibited (see below), he made provision for every Resident to maintain a reserve of shells.

> The fluctuations, of coinage are controlled and credit maintained in every country by the principle of a reserve, which enables a State to redeem its tokens (whether they consist of paper money, or of coins whose face value is less [*sic* – greater] than their bullion value) at the nominal value which the State has placed upon them.

Residents in the more northerly areas were to defend the standard rate (which Lugard hoped he could stabilize at 1,200 shells to the shilling) at all times, whatever the market rate. They could buy cowries if the market fell below the standard rate (taking care not to overstock themselves), or sell stocks requisitioned from the Residents of the southern provinces, where they were always cheaper. Lugard's memorandum is of interest as one of the very few attempts by a government officer to treat the cowries as a genuine, if now inconvenient, currency subject to the normal laws of economics. Things did not work out quite as expected – British coin was accepted sooner than he thought possible, and the cowrie/shilling exchange rate remained, in Zaria at least, double the rate Lugard had hoped to establish.[4]

As late as 1908, Assistant Residents in Nigeria were still being required to pass an examination on how to enter cowries in the official accounts,[5] but it was not long until the colonial governments ceased to recognize the shells as a valid money. We have already seen that the Royal Niger Company (and its successor, the Niger Company, Ltd.) continued for a long period to use cowrie shells as a unit of account; that company refused in spite of government urging to conduct a cash trade until after about 1905. (A. G. Hopkins argues, reasonably we believe, that the advent of European coinage probably did increase the competition for firms like the Niger Company. As long as shell money was the standard, then competitors had to master its complexity and also be prepared both to import goods and to export produce, since the shells were not acceptable in Europe. Even when cowries were used as a unit of account only, they were still centerpiece to a barter trade in which both imports and exports would be necessary. Potential competitors could not therefore specialize as much as they might have wished.)[6]

The great nineteenth-century inflation that depreciated the cowrie so badly ended its efficacy for large transactions. But it would not have been a sufficiently strong cause to end its usefulness for the smaller everyday purchases in the market place. The gross reduction in their value did not utterly rule out their employment there, because they remained much lower in value than any coin which might have been used as a substitute.[7] C. A. Birtwistle, the Commercial Intelligence Officer for Southern Nigeria, visited the north in 1907 and recorded his experience at a large market near Sokoto. He saw items on sale that no existing coin would serve to buy. Among them were small bowls of drinking water priced at 1 cowrie (= one hundredth of a penny); sweets for 2 cowries; pieces of boiled cassava or a boiled sweet potato or a small bundle of firewood for 5 cowries.[8] Thus, for these and many other commodities, the shells still changed hands by the millions in local markets.

However, an assault against the shell money was about to be mounted by the colonial authorities, who mostly considered the cowrie currency a primitive survival. The assault took the form of several official government acts aimed at the cowrie, in a generally successful attempt to discourage its monetary role.

These acts were, first, decrees against their importation; secondly, refusal to accept them for tax payment; and finally, the provision of large supplies of low-denomination coins. We have already discussed, in chapter 6, the decrees against imports (which affected the greater part of British colonial territory in 1904) followed by non-acceptance for taxes, not enforced everywhere at the same time but fully binding in major areas of Northern Nigeria by about 1911. In French territories, decrees against import preceding orders to local treasuries not to accept the shells were in force in 1907. The last tax payments made in cowries in French Niger were in 1910. Imports of cowries into German Kamerun were prohibited in 1911. Meanwhile, huge inflows of new coin were entering West Africa – shillings and francs and marks to pay the government labor force, the military and police, and the suppliers of every sort of item purchased locally by the colonial administration. Trading firms also moved rapidly toward paying coin for produce. The result was that in the five years from 1906 to 1910, imports of British silver to West Africa at £666,190 per year were almost as large as the coinage issued for use in Britain itself during those years.[9] Simultaneously came the introduction of new denominations to help the process, the penny and more particularly the one-tenth penny ("anini") authorized by the Nigeria Coinage Ordinance of 1906. Until that time the silver three-penny piece was simply too large a unit to compete with the shells in many transactions. The very low-value tenth-penny coin, meant to "supersede cowries," was extremely light 15-grain aluminium, even lighter than a single Maldive cowrie – too light, in fact. There was consumer resistance; new nickel-bronze coins of 35 grains weight were issued in the later part of 1908. Incidentally, these coins and the pennies were made with

150

holes in the center to facilitate stringing in the manner of cowries in their southern zone. The one-tenth penny was unable by itself to eliminate the cowrie; there were still an enormous number of purchases that could be made below that value. But it helped.[10]

Somewhat ironically, given the colonial antipathy for the shell money, there was no drastic fall in value after the official actions were implemented. In many areas values in 1914 showed little change from those at the turn of the century – 1,200 to the shilling in the far north of British territory, 1,000 to the shilling over wide areas of the middle north, rising to 2,000:1 on the Gold Coast and 4,000:1, or even more, east of the River Volta and over parts of southern Nigeria. There were even areas where the value of the cowrie *rose* after the actions taken against it. In parts of Nigerian Igbo country its value doubled from 1,500 to the shilling at the time of the import ban, to 720 in 1915. Einzig reports even greater appreciation in some spots, to as high at 620:1. At Timbuktu, between 1902 and 1928, cowries expressed in francs appreciated by a multiple of seven, due mainly to the over-issue of the French colonial currency and the fall of the franc.[11] The reasons for the shell-money's stability or even appreciation are fairly obvious: a rapidly increasing supply of European currencies but a fixed supply of still-useful cowries, since imports were banned; declining numbers of cowries in some markets because African traders found other imported goods more profitable to carry and European firms chose not to handle them (thus even after appreciation, transport costs were still a major or even an insurmountable problem); distrust of paper currency notes, with their soon-confirmed inflationary potential, when they were introduced by the French about the time of World War One; and finally for the 1915 figures, fears perhaps that the money of the allies might not survive the war with intact values. Even after the end of the war, cowries were still hoarded, in part because of a perception that a hoard bought security.[12]

THE LAST OF THE SHELL MONEY

Each of the imported shells, thousands upon thousands of millions of them, must at some point in some up-country market have been used for its very last transaction. They had "entirely vanished" from the markets of Kano and Zaria by 1922–23, according to Lord Lugard, though they were still encountered in the more remote markets in the 1930s.[13] They remained in use longer in the more northerly French territories, having proved in the 1920s and 1930s more stable than franc notes. But by 1940, even at Timbuktu near the ancient center of their zone, they were gone, replaced by French currency.[14] Cowries went out of use in Togo in the 1920s, and mostly so in Dahomey during the same period.[15]

The cowrie money showed perhaps its greatest residual strength in the Igbo country of southern Nigeria, where the shells were still circulating widely in the 1920s. Basden saw them stored in number "literally as sand on the seashore." He spoke of visiting treasure houses where the cowries "reminded me of heaps of newly threshed corn."[16] This was an area of very low income, and the shell money was still useful for purchases below the value of the one-tenth penny "anini." Cowrie counters still plied their trade in village markets, just as they had in the nineteenth century and presumably from Portuguese times; Basden saw the deft grasp with the toes that women used to pick up fallen shells along the roadside. In the late 1930s, values were still being quoted for cowries (6 pence per thousand), but demand was declining, and the figure was down from nearly three times that in 1924. A number of ceremonial expenditures, however, remained fixed in cowries.[17]

To the north, in the Nupe country of Nigeria's Middle Belt, there was a remarkable resurrection of cowrie use during the depths of the Great Depression. The reappearance came about because of the deflationary effect on prices taking place on a world-wide basis in the early 1930s. As prices fell, the one-tenth penny's value appeared larger and larger, and as export markets for produce contracted, coin became scarcer as well. Thus the old shell money became more and more appropriate for small transactions. The Depression had similar effects in some parts of southern and northern Nigeria, in Dahomey, and no doubt over much of the old cowrie currency area in many instances that went unrecorded. But the reappearance is most convincingly described for Nupe, in the works of S. F. Nadel. In Nupe country, cowries had stayed in circulation quite late, but by the late 1920s, though still used for the payment of bride wealth and for certain traditional gifts, they had for the most part gone out of use. With the trough of the Depression, in 1932, they began again to appear. Their price of 250 to the penny in the Nupe markets of Bida and Agaie was sufficiently high to attract shells out of hoards in the neighboring Gbari country around Abuja, where traders purchased them for 500 to the penny. The Gbari of Abuja had hoarded large stocks of shells in the hope of an eventual revival. In 1924 they had requested permission from their emir that cowries again be considered legal tender; the colonial authorities made it clear that this would never happen. Whether originating in Gbari country or Nupe itself, many shells had obviously been buried, as they had traces of earth clinging to them. Even slight economic recovery halted the cowrie comeback, however. By October 1933 the shells had once again disappeared. When Nadel asked if he could be shown any, he was told that they were no longer in use and not available.

> I said that I was prepared to pay money for them, whereupon large baskets full of cowries suddenly turned up, and . . . I had to do my best not to be inundated with the suddenly rediscovered currency.

In the Nupe countryside, they remained in some use for very small transactions for a long time.[18]

In a very few areas cowries survived as a circulating currency after World

War Two. With the immediate postwar inflation, the rising prices of goods seriously eroded the usefulness of the shell money, since even very small transactions could now be carried out with coin. The end was to come rapidly.

The best-documented area of their survival, thanks to Ofonagoro, was in the Igbo area of southeast Nigeria. There in parts of Umuahia and Owerri divisions some transactions-demand for cowries still existed as late as 1950, by which time the one-tenth penny was going out of circulation, and even the $\frac{1}{4}$ penny coin was becoming scarce. The storerooms housing heaps of shells were still there, as in Basden's day. Elsewhere in Nigeria, they still circulated in some remoter portions of the north, and, remarkably, even on a small scale at the capital, Lagos.[19]

Continuing postwar inflation, eventually fueled by the worldwide Korean War commodity boom, meant however that any moderately large purchase with shells was now becoming out of the question. Ofonagoro notes that

> between 1939 and 1945/46, bride prices in southeast Nigeria increased from 30 bags of cowries [36,000 shells] to £15 [432,000]; they rose to £20 [576,000] in 1948 and to £25 [720,000] in 1949. Those who continued to use cowries in the payment of a bride price now required the services of fifteen porters to carry £25 worth of cowries to the prospective in-laws.[20]

With the customary unpaid labor of kinsmen no longer so easily available, says Ofonagoro, the tradition of paying the bride price in cowries rapidly died away. Soon thereafter, even the tiniest purchase could no longer be made with them:

> In 1952 it was still possible to use cowries for a snack of peanuts in village markets. . . . But by 1955 one could not use them even for a peanut snack.[21]

They lasted a little longer in some remote areas, still used as a medium of exchange in local markets for very small transactions. They continued to be found in the mid to late 1950s circulating in some parts of northeast and northwest Ghana, in some Bambara markets, in the Dogon country, among the Mossi of Upper Volta and the Senufo of the Ivory Coast, and no doubt in other areas as well.[22] In northwestern Ghana by the 1960s they had become somewhat scarce, however, and their value varied between 10 and 20 to the Ghanaian equivalent of the British penny. In some markets, in spite of hints that currency controls had caused an illicit inflow of smuggled cowries across the northern frontier, they could even rise to 5 to the penny, by contrast to the turn-of-the-century value of 100:1.[23] (The wheel in this one region had come very nearly full circle. Ibn Battuta's fourteenth-century value was about eight to the [gold-standard] penny.) Long obsolete at Whydah (Ouidah), their old port of entry in what is now the Republic of Bénin, they were still remembered at the end of the 1960s for buying a handful of groundnuts, according to a personal communication from Dr. Josette Rivallain.

The gastropod money was finally all but dead, the coup-de-grace delivered at last by inflation of the colonial coinage. Its demise was perhaps even welcomed by the numerous Africans who had come to view cowries not as a memorial to ancient commercial enterprise, but with disdain as a shameful relic of a primitive past and a reminder that in the days of the slave trade their forefathers had been willing to exchange people for shells.[24] For their last holders, the sad task of stacking them in a heap in a back alley, or a hoard buried underground, signalled a now-total loss of value. The loss was not only in a personal sense for the last holder (who indeed may have acquired them quite cheaply), but for the economy as a whole, in that centuries' worth of export value sold in exchange for cowries was now gone completely. Some shells were crushed for their lime content, but the recoupment of commodity value was very low. Mostly the loss was total, and Walter Ofonagoro has written eloquently of

> the bitter decision to abandon them as junk. Stocks of . . . cowries hoarded by being buried in the ground, a testimony to centuries of accumulation, have since been abandoned in their permanent graves, mute witness to the loss incurred by the Southern Nigerian population, their fee for the entry of their country into the sterling trading area.[25]

There was a remarkable contrast between the unsung disposal of the now-valueless shell money and the treatment by the colonial authorities of the indigenous copper currency of the extreme southeast of Nigeria that existed contemporaneously with the cowrie. The horseshoe-shaped manillas had a history much like that of cowries in some respects. A nineteenth-century inflation eroded their value (it was due to technical advance in Europe that allowed for cheaper manufacture of the manillas and so increased supply); their importation was prohibited in 1902; a 1911 ordinance unsuccessfully forbade their use as a currency, and was replaced by a 1919 ordinance making it illegal for non-Africans to deal in them. But the manillas had very significant metal content, which could be realized by sale for scrap. The Nigerian government therefore mounted a large campaign, "Operation Manilla," in 1948–49, during which the coins were purchased at one-half penny each – less than their current purchasing power but more than their value as copper metal. The operation cost the government £248,000; the metal when exported brought £153,000 on the open market.[26]

There certainly seemed little resemblance between the coins and paper currency of the colonial governments, and West Africa's shell money. Interestingly, however, the modern moneys for many years did share one similarity with the cowrie. The similarity held whether the notes and coins were issues of the West African Currency Board (W.A.C.B.), established for the British territories in 1912, or of the Banque de l'Afrique Occidentale (B.A.O.), founded 1901 as the sole bank of issue for French West Africa. In both cases the currencies were full-bodied in the sense that they had to be acquired by exporting, just as the cowrie was. Pound for pound, franc for franc, the colonial authorities issued new currency notes and coins only on deposit of cash balances ("reserves") held in London or Paris. Thus the colonial systems were fully comparable to any other full-bodied money such as one supported by 100% reserves of gold, or a cowrie currency which had to be imported.[27] In British territories the reserves against the W.A.C.B. issues even (from 1926) exceeded 100%, with the figure usually being on the order of 110%.[28] By the 1980s, however, the "full-bodied" nature of currency in former British territories had disappeared, and the Ghanaian cedi had undergone a long-drawn-out hyperinflation of its own, even worse than the nineteenth century shell money inflation.[29]

Little now remains of the great cowrie currency. Some shells on sale in markets as knick-knacks or for adornment, mouldering heaps here and there where they were finally discarded, cowries built into the walls or floors of old rooms as a sign of (former) wealth.[30] Yet in two areas of West Africa, in Ghana and the vast region where Hausa is spoken, day-in-day-out even children who know nothing of the slave trade's shell money still unwittingly speak of it – for the name of the modern currency of Ghana, the *cedi*, is the word for cowrie in the Akan group of languages (Fante, Twi, etc.) of Ashanti and further south; and the Hausa name for money itself, *kudi*, literally means cowrie.[31]

In a few local areas, West Africans can even see for themselves the shell money still circulating, according to the occasional report. Daniel McCall (in a personal communication) has told us that the cowrie is presently spent with some regularity in the vicinity of the Black Volta in northwestern Ghana. There, in the Lobi area and among the Dagari and Birifor, the river forms the border with Upper Volta and the Ivory Coast. The shells are used to avoid the problems of currency exchange across the frontier by peoples who have the same language and intermarry, but find exchanging the modern small coins an inconvenience, especially with the Ghanaian *cedi* as unstable as it has been in recent years. The cowries are favoured by some women beer-sellers, who much prefer them to coin, but not by all, perhaps reflecting some supplies of beer coming from across the borders. Professor McCall also encountered a German agronomist who, to the north of Bole near where Ghana, Upper Volta, and the Ivory Coast all meet, found a price fixed in cowries when he attempted to purchase a bullock from a local farmer. McCall thinks this unusual quotation in cowries for a large item may just have been a more polite way of saying "no sale."

We also have a report that in the early 1980s one could only buy groundnuts in small quantities with cowries near Korhogo in the Senufo country of the northern Ivory Coast. In other parts of West Africa there may well be some further survivals on a small scale.

Here and there are still encountered oral traditions that attempt to explain whence had come these vast supplies of former money. In a Borgu tradition communicated to us by the late Musa Baba Idris, West African rivers are said to have been the source of the shells. In Upper Volta, there is an explanation that the shells were produced by a "mother of cowries," who

155

lived deep underground in the bush. The person who could find her would gain a fortune, but somehow no one ever did.[32] To the south, along the old Slave Coast in the Bénin Republic, another and much more gloomy tradition survives. The shells, so it is said, came from the off-lying waters, where they fed on the cadavers of less desirable slaves thrown into the sea as their food. The bodies, or sometimes dismembered limbs, when pulled ashore were covered with attached cowries. Though macabre, this tradition as allegory is right on the mark – slaves certainly did in an economic sense "feed" the shell trade.[33]

(Across the continent, the evanescent Zanzibar industry – its heyday had lasted less than forty years – vanished with virtually no trace. There was a very late and very short period of exporting to Uganda from coastal German East Africa, but the British put a stop to that in 1901.[34] Accumulated and now unwanted stocks were sometimes burned to recover their lime content.)

CHANGES IN THE MALDIVES

In the Maldive Islands, one result of the collapse of shell exports was a decision by the Maldive sultanate to allow a community of Gujerati Muslim merchants from Bombay to settle in the islands. These "Borah" merchants, with their already established trading relations in the Arabian Sea and their existing community in Ceylon, were expected to help build other lines of commerce, and they did so with a vengeance. The Borahs, with seven firms by 1887, before the end of the nineteenth century had acquired a monopoly over Maldive foreign trade. A tightly knit community of Shia Muslims with the only non-Sunni mosque in the islands, they gave the commercial area of Male its present appearance. They also excited animosity among the islanders (all their stores were burned down in riots of 1886), but their monopoly continued well into the twentieth century and they became a major source of finance for the government. The Urdu-speaking Borahs, who for many years made Urdu the favored second language of the islands, were finally ousted from the Maldives in the 1950s. But they left their mark by transforming an economy based on the cowrie and coir into an economy based on fish.[35]

It seems somehow fitting that in the Maldives, unnoticed, the thousand-year history of the cowrie commerce still continues, outlasting the virtual end of their circulation in West Africa and long-surviving the demise of East African *annulus* production. The obituaries of the 1870s were premature; the trade in Maldive *moneta* sprang up again, and endures today. But these more recent shell exports were not intended to serve as money. There was a growing demand from the Indian subcontinent for cowries as decoration, as a raw material in ceramics manufacture, and, surprisingly, as medicine. There were again substantial exports from the Maldives in the 1860s. By 1881–82, exports to India had reached 135 tonnes worth nearly £2,000; the average between 1881–82 and 1892–93 was 97 tonnes. In the period 1890–91 to 1892–93, the value of these exports averaged only £680, but in the year 1900 the figure once more exceeded £2,000. These exports do not include large quantities shipped from Ceylon to India during this period, which must presumably be Maldive shells.[36] No official Maldive customs records dating before 1915 appear to be available, but from that time on there is an annual accounting of cowrie exports. The 36 tonnes of 1915 is modest, but that figure was normally far surpassed in the years thereafter. The annual average of exports, 1915–1970, was 61.6 tonnes, with very low points in the Great Depression and the early years of World War Two, but reaching 160 tonnes in 1945 and 173 tonnes in 1951.[37]

The trade has since declined, to an annual average for 1971–1980 of 25.5 tonnes – but there are still more than enough shells being produced and shipped for a visitor to see at first-hand the traditional methods of an age-old enterprise. The women and girls still wade in the lagoons at the time of lowest tides, twice daily, when the moon is new and when it is full. Tin cups and bowls are used now for the collection, along with the traditional half-coconut shells, and the cowries today cling not only to coral lumps and fallen palm leaves, but also to discarded tin cans and other modern detritus. Processing is still by the burial method. The traditional *kotta* packages survived for a long time,[38] but nowadays the shells ride to market at Male in anything from small plastic bags to burlap gunny sacks, and the wooden boat that carries them often has a small Japanese diesel engine.

At Male, the buying season starts in September, picks up in January, and lasts until May. Approximately five firms buy and sort the shells, discarding the "dead" ones that have lost their luster just as was done for the Dutch and English buyers of two centuries past. In the largest warehouse, we came upon about 250 burlap bags of 50 kilos each stored alongside piles of today's much more important export of the Maldives, dried fish. The shells go now mostly to Bombay and Calcutta, some to Madras, and Cochin, a few even to Pakistan. Their fate at these destinations is very different from the days when they served as currency. Some are still sold for ornament and decoration around the house or on the harnesses of draft animals. Others are crushed, their powder employed in the manufacture of plates and saucers. Most dramatically, large quantities are made into medicine for internal consumption. Powdered cowrie being extremely high in calcium content, it is used as a dietary supplement and general physic, especially recommended by practitioners of the Hindi Ayurvedic medicine which is popular among non-Hindus as well.[39]

The fisher-ladies of the southern atolls looked sceptical when they heard that their seashells were ending up in Indian homes as a medicine. They were even more unbelieving when told that the produce of their day's fishing had for centuries been exported in giant shipments, first to Europe and then to West Africa, as the shell money of the slave trade.

Notes

Preface

1 Marion Johnson, "The Cowrie Currencies of West Africa," *Journal of African History*, Vol. 11, 1970, (Part 1) No. 1, pp. 17–49, and (Part 2) No. 3, pp. 331–353.

2 Marion Johnson, "The Nineteenth-Century Gold 'Mithqal' in West and North Africa," *Journal of African History*, Vol. 9, No. 4, 1968, pp. 547–570; and "The Ounce in Eighteenth-Century West African Trade," *Journal of African History*, Vol. 7, No. 2, 1966, pp. 197–214.

3 H. A. Gemery and J. S. Hogendorn, "The Atlantic Slave Trade: a Tentative Economic Model," *Journal of African History*, Vol. 15, No. 2, 1974, pp. 223–246. The same authors expanded their treatment of money in their "Technological Change, Slavery, and the Slave Trade," in Clive Dewey and A. G. Hopkins, eds., *The Imperial Impact: Studies in the Economic History of Africa and India*, London, 1978.

4 Floris M. Klinkenberg, "De Kaurihandel van de VOC," unpublished University of Leiden M. A. thesis, 1982.

5 Marion Johnson, Jan Hogendorn, and Joanne Lynch, "The European Cowrie Trade," *Slavery and Abolition*, Vol. 2, No. 3, 1981, pp. 263–275.

6 The world value of silver declined rapidly after 1870, but the silver dollar was not demonetized until 1880 on the Gold Coast and at Lagos, and not until the 1920s in the Gambia.

7 K. N. Chaudhuri, *The Trading World of Asia and the English East India Company 1660–1760*, Cambridge, 1978, p. 471. *Encyclopaedia Britannica*, 13th ed., Vol. 23, p. 855.

Introduction

1 The term "primitive money" has somewhat fallen from favor since the well-known works by A. H. Quiggin and Paul Einzig were published with the term in their titles. See James L. A. Webb, Jr, "Toward the Comparative Study of Money: a Reconsideration of West African Currencies and Neoclassical Monetary Concepts," *International Journal of African Historical Studies*, Vol. 15, No. 3, 1982, pp. 455–456.

2 For the very low figure see Walter I. Ofonagoro, "From Traditional to British Currency in Southern Nigeria: Analysis of a Currency Revolution, 1880–1948," *Journal of Economic History*, Vol. 39, No. 3, 1979, p. 635. The substantivist school of anthropologists has sometimes written of the cowrie as a "special purpose money," governed by principles of reciprocity, redistribution, and ritual. It is true that very late in the life of the cowrie currency it did survive for yet a few more years as a means for making ritual payments (see chapter 10). For most of its life, however, any argument that the shells were a traditional special

158

purpose money is untenable, as the portions of this book dealing with its use in West Africa will demonstrate conclusively. Representative works from the substantivist school of anthropologists include Karl Polanyi, *Dahomey and the Slave Trade*, Seattle and London, 1966, espec. pp. 173–194; George Dalton, "Primitive Money," *American Anthropologist*, Vol. 67, 1965, pp. 44–65; and Paul Bohannan, "The Impact of Money on an African Subsistence Economy," *Journal of Economic History*, Vol. 19, No. 4, 1959, pp. 491–503. There is a persuasive critique of the substantivist position in A. G. Hopkins, *An Economic History of West Africa*, New York, 1973, pp. 68–70. Other anthropologists who have contributed to the subject of "primitive moneys" include Marshall Sahlins (especially his discussion of reciprocity in *Stone Age Economics*, London, 1972); Thomas Crump, *The Phenomenon of Money*, London, 1981; Raymond Firth, ed., *Themes in Economic Anthropology*, New York, 1967; Edward E. LeClair and Harold K. Schneider, eds., *Economic Anthropology*, New York, 1968; and C. A. Gregory, *Gifts and Commodities*, London, 1982. A recent discussion of cowries and slavery by an anthropologist is Françoise Heritier's, "Des Cauris et des hommes: production d'esclaves et accumulation de cauris chez les Samo (Haute-Volta)," in Claude Meillassoux, ed., *L'Esclavage en Afrique précoloniale*, Paris, 1975.

3 General works that consider slavery in Africa include Suzanne Miers and Igor Kopytoff, eds., *Slavery in Africa: Historical and Anthropological Perspectives*, Madison, 1977; Claude Meillassoux, ed., *L'Esclavage en Afrique précoloniale*, Paris, 1975; Paul E. Lovejoy, ed., *The Ideology of Slavery in Africa*, Beverly Hills, 1981; and H. A. Gemery and J. S. Hogendorn, eds., *The Uncommon Market: Essays in the Economic History of the Atlantic Slave Trade*, New York, 1979. Some important monographs are Frederick Cooper, *Plantation Slavery on the East African Coast*, New Haven, 1977; Allan G. B. Fisher and Humphrey J. Fisher, *Slavery and Muslim Society in Africa*, London, 1970; John Grace, *Domestic Slavery in West Africa*, New York, 1977; and Patrick Manning, *Slavery, Colonialism and Economic Growth in Dahomey, 1640–1960*, Cambridge, 1982. Paul E. Lovejoy, *Transformations in Slavery: a History of Slavery in Africa*, Cambridge, 1983, is a wide-ranging examination of the topic. The period of European abolition of the African overseas trade can be studied in Roger Anstey, *The Atlantic Slave Trade and British Abolition, 1760–1810*, London, 1975; Seymour Drescher, *Econocide: British Slavery in the Era of Abolition*, Pittsburgh, 1977; and Suzanne Miers, *Britain and the Ending of the Slave Trade*, New York, 1975. For the number of slaves exported, the pioneering work is Philip D. Curtin, *The Atlantic Slave Trade: a Census*, Madison, 1969. The statistics have been revised and updated by Paul E. Lovejoy, "The Volume of the Atlantic Slave Trade: a Synthesis," *Journal of African History*, Vol. 22, No. 4, 1982, pp. 473–501. Finally, the large bibliographies compiled by Joseph C. Miller, which have appeared in various journal articles and books, are thorough. There is also an excellent bibliography in Lovejoy, *Transformations in Slavery*.

4 Lars Sundström, *The Exchange Economy of Pre-Colonial Tropical Africa*, New York, 1974, pp. 107–108, names many African areas where such multiple currency use was reported.

5 The unexpectedly successful introduction of the larger East African shells was a monetary innovation of magnitude. For other such episodes of monetary change see Richard Sylla, "Monetary Innovation in Economic History," in Paul Wachtel, ed., *Crisis in the Economic and Financial Structure*, Lexington, Mass., 1982.

6 Hopkins, *Economic History*, p. 149; Jacques Melitz, *Primitive and Modern Money*, Reading, Mass., 1974, p. 123.

1 The cowrie

1 *Kaparda* in Sanskrit. See A. H. Quiggin, *A Survey of Primitive Money*, New York, 1970, p. 26. F. A. Schilder examines the etymology in "Die Ethnologische Bedeutung der Porzellanschnecken," *Zeitschrift für Ethnologie*, 1926, pp. 313–327. The word is also spelled "cowry" in English. The plural "cowries" is universal.

2 Quoted by A. S. Kenyon in "The Cowrie Shell in Primitive Currency," *The Numismatist*
  May, 1941, pp. 341–342. What the cowrie actually resembles was discussed at length in
  various issues of *Man*, the journal of the Royal Anthropological Institute of Great Britain,
  from 1939 to 1943. If its underside can be imagined as a half-closed eye, that might explain
  its use as a charm against the evil eye. Indeed it was frequently used to represent the eye in,
  for example, Ivory Coast carvings. The Ashanti word for a single cowrie, *niwa*, is said to
  mean "eye." If the underside was thought to be a female vulva, then its use as a cure for
  infertility might be understood. E. G. Gobert summarized the discussion in his "Le
  pudendum magique et le problème des cauris," *Revue Africaine*, Vol. 95, 1951, pp. 5–62.
  Our attention was brought to Gobert's work by M. Hiskett's statement that Gobert's
  "notable scholarship . . . demonstrates convincingly that behind the magical and life-giving
  properties attributed to the cowry lies an age-old concept of *le pudendum magique*." Some
  of the larger species of *Cypraea* are actually much more "suggestive" than is *moneta*. A
  recent and general anthropological survey of shells from the American Museum of Natural
  History is J. F. Safer and F. M. Gill, *Spirals from the Sea: an Anthropological Look at
  Shells*, New York, 1982.
3 The information in this paragraph is based on L. H. Hyman, *The Invertebrates*, Vol. 6,
  Mollusca I, New York, 1967, especially pp. 159, 334, and on discussions of *Cypraea moneta*
  with W. F. Holmstrom of the Department of Zoology, University of Birmingham, and with
  Walter Sage of the Invertebrate Department, American Museum of Natural History, New
  York City. Mr. Holmstrom prepared an informative memo for Hogendorn's use entitled
  Cypraea moneta, and Mr. Sage made a special trip to Maine to provide assistance. Their aid
  is gratefully acknowledged. The striped appearance of *C. moneta* when alive is striking. See
  Scott Johnson, *Living Seashells*, Honolulu, n.d., p. 34.
4 Mr. Holmstrom's speculation. See also Jerry G. Walls, *Cowries*, Neptune, N.J., 1979, p. 14.
5 Hyman, *Mollusca I*, p. 159. It is "rather mysterious" says Hyman (p. 334) that the colorful
  shell is so completely concealed in life.
6 See Quiggin, *Primitive Money*, pp. 25–26; and Melitz, *Money*, p. 109.
7 Quiggin, *Primitive Money*, p. 25.
8 Karl Polanyi, *Dahomey*, p. 178; and Melitz, *Money*, p. 109. The slow fading is noted by
  C. M. Burgess, *The Living Cowries*, New York, 1970, p. 344.
9 The Chinese emperor was the usurper Wang Mang who reigned from A.D. 9 to 23. See Paul
  Einzig, *Primitive Money*, London, 1949, p. 254; Kenyon, "Cowrie," p. 342; and Col. Henry
  Yule and A. C. Burnell, *Hobson-Jobson*, London, 1968, p. 269. For King Gezo, see
  Polanyi, *Dahomey*, p. 178. A rare story of forgery with this virtually unforgeable currency
  is told by H. C. Monrad, *Gemälde der Küste von Guinea*, Copenhagen, 1822, Weimar
  1824, p. 162: "They are sometimes forged with a similar kind of smaller and yellower shell,
  which is found on the shore" (probably an olive shell, see below).
10 Melitz, *Money*, p. 118.
11 *Ibid.*, pp. 109, 118–119.
12 Various peoples did use the lime from pulverized and burned shells for building material,
  fertilizer, for tempering pottery, etc. See Safer and Gill, *Spirals*, pp. 29–30.
13 Compare the list in Quiggin, *Primitive Money*, p. 25.
14 Burgess, *Living Cowries*, pp. 342–343; R. Tucker Abbot, *Kingdom of the Seashell*, New
  York, 1982, p. 150; Quiggin, *Primitive Money*, p. 26; J. Wilfred Jackson, *Shells as Evidence
  of the Migrations of Early Culture*, Manchester and London, 1917, pp. 123–124. Hawaiian
  occurrence is discussed by Jackson in another article, "The Money Cowrie (*Cypraea
  Moneta*, L.) as a Sacred Object among North American Indians," *Manchester Memoirs*,
  Vol. 60, No. 4, 1916, p. 1
15 The principle of competitive exclusion of closely related species is stated in Eugene P.
  Odum, *Fundamentals of Ecology*, Philadelphia, 1971, p. 213. Our thanks to Virginia Orr
  Maes of the Academy of Natural Sciences, Philadelphia, for explaining to us how this

principle applies specifically to *moneta* and *annulus* (personal communication of June 1, 1983). See also her article, "A Bionomic Shell Study of *Monetaria Annulus* (Gastropoda: Cypraeidae) from Zanzibar," *Notulae Naturae*, No. 313, 1959, pp. 1–11 plus plates. For the occurrence of *moneta*, see Abbot, *Kingdom of the Seashell*, pp. 152, 178; Burgess, *Living Cowries*, pp. 341–344; Oskar Schneider, *Muschelgeld-Studien*, Dresden, 1905, p. 102; E. von Martens, "Ueber verschiedene Verwendungen von Conchylien," *Zeitschrift für Ethnologie*, Berlin, 1872, p. 65; Henri Labouret, "L'Échange et le commerce dans les archipels du Pacifique et en Afrique tropicale," in Jacques Lacour-Gayet, ed., *Histoire du commerce*, Paris, 1953, Tome 3, *Le Commerce extra-Européan jusqu'aux temps modernes*, p. 108; William Hedges, *The Diary of William Hedges, Esq. 1681–1687*, London, 1887, Vol. 3, p. viii; Schneider, *Muschelgeld-Studien*, pp. 103, 110–112; von Martens, "Conchylien," p. 65.

16 Schneider, *Muschelgeld-Studien*, pp. 103, 109; Yule and Burnell, *Hobson-Jobson*, p. 270; Dutch Gentleman, *Voyage to Ceylon*, p. 21; Kenyon, "Cowrie," p. 341.

17 David Slimming and Alan Jarrett, *The Cowries of Seychelles*, London, 1971.

18 Jean-Baptiste Tavernier, *Travels in India*, London, 1684, p. 22; von Martens, "Conchylien," p. 65; Schneider, *Muschelgeld-Studien*, p. 102; J. Allan, "The Coinage of the Maldive Islands with some Notes on the Cowrie and Larin," *Numismatic Chronicle*, Vol. 12, 4th series, 1912, p. 315; Einzig, *Primitive Money*, p. 118; James Heimann, "Small Change and Ballast: Cowry Trade and Usage as an Example of Indian Ocean Economic History," *South Asia*, Vol. 3, No. 1, 1980, pp. 48–49. *Cf.* Edouard Foà, *Le Dahomey*, Paris, 1895, p. 147, "c'est dans les îles Maldives qu'on pêchait le cauris en plus grande quantité;" Labouret, "L'Échange," p. 108, "recoltées en grande quantité" in the Maldives; and Mr. Holmstrom's memo, "common in the Indo-Pacific" but "abundant in the Maldives." Compare its much more limited abundance in the Laccadive Islands just to the north, as discussed in the next chapter. The Laccadives did produce significant quantities, but their role has been less studied. See Safer and Gill, *Spirals*, p. 51.

19 Three major producing atolls were identified by H. C. P. Bell. See "Excerpta Maldiviana: No. 4, A Description of the Maldive Island *circa* A.C. 1683," *Journal of the Royal Asiatic Society (Ceylon)*, Vol. 30, No. 78, 1925, p. 139. Another atoll, Kolumadulu, was identified by Hogendorn's informants during field work in 1982. This seems reasonable as Kolumadulu lies just next to Haddummati. Ari now produces only a small number of cowries. Bell notes that few cowries are gathered in the furthest northern atoll, Tiladummati, nor in the extreme southern atoll, Addu (once a British military base).

20 According to Mr. Holmstrom and Ms. Maes – see footnotes 3 and 15. The data are not conclusive as to which of these conditions is most important.

21 *Annulus* is "scarce from the Maldives. . . ." Personal letter from Virginia Orr Maes of the Academy of Natural Sciences, Philadelphia, July 27, 1983.

22 Quiggin, *Primitive Money*, p. 36; M. Hiskett, "Materials Relating to the Cowry Currency of the Western Sudan – II: Reflections on the Provenance and Diffusion of the Cowry in the Sahara and the Sudan," *SOAS Bulletin*, Vol. 29, No. 2, 1966, p. 339; A. G. Hopkins, "The Currency Revolution in South-West Nigeria in the Late Nineteenth Century," *Journal of the Historical Society of Nigeria*, Vol. 3, No. 3, 1966, p. 274.

23 M. Johnson, "Cowrie Currencies," Part I, p. 23; Philip D. Curtin, "Africa and the Wider Monetary World, 1250–1850 A.D.," in John F. Richards, ed., *Precious Metals in the Later Medieval and Early Modern Worlds*, Durham, N.C., 1983, typescript of the Curtin paper p. 31 (all citations of this useful essay are to pages in the typescript copy); John E. Hertz, "Ueber Verwendung und Verbreitung der Kauriemuschel," *Mitteilung der Geographische Gesellschaft in Hamburg*, Hamburg, 1881, p. 16; Einzig, *Primitive Money*, p. 136.

24 Quiggin, *Primitive Money*, p. 36; Hiskett, "Cowry," p. 339.

25 F. A. Schilder and Maria Schilder, "The Size of 95,000 Cowries," *The Veliger*, Vol. 8, No. 4, 1966, p. 211.

26 Burgess, *Living Cowries*, p. 343; Walls, *Cowries*, pp. 149, 268.
27 Burgess, *Living Cowries*, p. 341; Walls, *Cowries*, pp. 136, 259; Orr, *"Monetaria Annulus,"* p. 4.
28 See the series of measurements by Crawford Cate in *The Veliger*, Vol. 8, No. 2, 1965, p. 54; Vol. 7, No. 1, 1964, p. 15; Vol. 8, No. 4, 1966, p. 247; Vol. 10, No. 1, 1967, p. 30; Vol. 12, No. 1, 1969, p. 117; Vol. 12, No. 1, 1969, p. 129; and by the Schilders for Thailand in Vol. 8, No. 1, 1965, p. 27.
29 Personal letter from Virginia Orr Maes of the Academy of Natural Sciences, Philadelphia, July 27, 1983. No *moneta* over 21.5 mm. in length were present in four other lots from different atolls. A measurement as large as 27.5 mm. was recorded at Imma Island, Male Atoll, and 26 mm. was registered at Fadiffolu Atoll. The shells were collected in the 1960s by Dr. Robert Robertson, presently Curator of Malacology at the Academy, whose assistance is gratefully acknowledged. The lot numbers in the ANSP are 303922, 304228, 305333, 304972, 304905, 304857, and 305611.
30 Maria Schilder and F. A. Schilder, "Revision of the Genus *Monetaria (Cypraeidae),*" *Proceedings of the Zoological Society of London*, Part 4, 1936, p. 1129. The exact reasons underlying Bergmann's Rule are not entirely clear. Malacologists speculate that in colder waters, growth is slower but longevity is greater, so the creatures attain larger average size; that in relation to volume, surface area is relatively smaller when the creature is larger in size, which is advantageous in cooler waters in that heat-loss is minimized (microeconomists use a similar volume-to-surface area principle as one explanation for economies of scale in industry); and the possible greater vulnerability of large-size molluscs to predators under tropical warm-water conditions. Our thanks to Dr. Robertson (see footnote 29) and Clyde Goulden, of the Ecology Department, Academy of Natural Sciences, Philadelphia, for the speculations.
31 Klaus Wyrtki, ed., *Oceanographic Atlas of the International Indian Ocean Expedition*, Washington, D.C., 1971, Chapter 1. (Our thanks to William Dunkle, Data Librarian of the Woods Hole Oceanographic Institute, for bringing this atlas to our attention). *The Times Atlas of the World*, London, 1980, Plate 3, shows similar information.
32 M. Schilder and F. A. Schilder, "Revision," p. 1122. The Schilders showed how Bergmann's Rule applies to east coastal Australia with the smaller shells in the warmer north. See "Latitudinal Differences in Size of East Australian Cowries," *The Cowry*, Vol. 1, No. 7, 1964, pp. 100–101. A more wide-ranging application of the rule is made by F. A. Schilder in "Die BERGMANNsche Regel bei Porzellanschnecken," *Verhandl Deutsche Zoologische Gesellschaft Hamburg*, 1956, pp. 410–414.
33 Schneider, *Muschelgeld-Studien*, p. 102; Burgess, *Living Cowries*, p. 343; J. F. Spry, *The Sea Shells of Dar-es-Salaam*, Dar-es-Salaam, Tanganyika Society, n.d., p. 15; personal communication from Ms. Maes, June 1, 1983.
34 Von Martens, "Conchylien," p. 66.
35 Polanyi, *Dahomey*, p. 183. For a full account see Edmond Dartevelle, *Les "N'zimbu," monnaie du Royaume de Congo*, Brussels, *Mémories de la Société belge d'anthropologie et de pré-histoire*, 1953, p. 124; and Carlos Couto, *O Zimbo na Historiografia Angolana*, Luanda, 1973.
36 Shipwrecks have led to the erroneous conclusion that the money cowrie is indigenous to the Netherlands and Britain. Quantities were found during the construction of the Zuider Zee's Northeast Polder, and there have been finds along the coast of Zeeland. See P. van Emst, "De Weg van de Kauri," *Tijdschrift voor Economische en Sociale Geografie*, Vol. 49, No. 12, 1958, p. 271, and referring to W. S. S. van Bentham Jutting, "Vondsten van Tropische Kauri's in Nederland," *Basteria*, Vol. 19, No. 1, 1955, pp. 1–20. There *are* British species of cowries, even at John O'Groats, but they are smaller (their specific name is *trivia*) and quite unlike *moneta*.
37 See, for example, G. J. A. Ojo, *Yoruba Culture: a Geographical Analysis*, Ife and London,

1966, p. 100: "The point that emerges ... is that money cowry along West African coasts were derived either by direct introduction or by the exploitation of probable local deposits." Some local West African traditions refer even more improbably to West African rivers as the source. Another suggests that an underground "mother of cowries" produced them locally. See chapter 10 for details.

38 Jackson, *Shells as Evidence*, p. 125. There is a long and detailed survey of using areas in von Martens, "Conchylien," *passim*; the large German literature on the subject is cited by F. A. Schilder, "Porzellanschnecken." The quote is from Safer and Gill, *Spirals*, p. 50. See the similar statement by Bennet Bronson, "Cash, Cannon, and Cowrie Shells: the Nonmodern Moneys of the World," *Field Museum of Natural History Bulletin*, Vol. 47, No. 10, 1976, p. 12: "It is said to have the widest circulation of any single kind of money that has ever existed. No modern currency circulates in nearly as many places as did the cowry during the past."

39 Quiggin, *Primitive Money*, p. 224; Einzig, *Primitive Money*, p. 253; Yule and Burnell, *Hobson-Jobson*, p. 269. Terrien de Lacouperie also claims great antiquity for the Chinese shell money (23rd century B.C.). See "The Metallic Cowries of Ancient China (600 B.C.)," *Journal of the Royal Asiatic Society*, Vol. 20, 1888, p. 438. Vitorino Magalhães-Godinho states that cowries had a very large circulation in China between the 16th and 8th centuries B.C. See *L'économie de l'empire portugais aux XVe et XVIe siècles*, Paris, 1969, p. 398.

40 Especially by Wang Yu-Chuan, *Early Chinese Coinage*, New York, 1951, pp. 56–57. See also Jackson, *Shells as Evidence*, p. 177; Safer and Gill, *Spirals*, p. 50.

41 For a full account of the cowrie in China see Namio Egami, "Migration of Cowrie-Shell Culture in East Asia," *Acta Asiatica*, No. 26, 1974, pp. 1–52; Einzig, *Primitive Money*, p. 254; Kenyon, "Cowrie," p. 342. C. G. F. Simkin believes the early Chinese use of cowries is evidence of ancient contacts between the Maldives and China; see *The Traditional Trade of Asia*, London, 1968, pp. 3–4. But there are other, nearer sources of *moneta* to China and it would be extremely difficult to tell a Maldive shell from any other of similar size. The authors are therefore doubtful. Other sources on cowrie use in China are Lien-Sheng Yang, *Money and Credit in China*, Cambridge, Mass., 1952; Alexandre Del Mar, *Monograph on the History of Money in China from the Earliest Times to the Present*, San Francisco, 1881; J. Gunnar Anderson, *Children of the Yellow Earth: Studies in Prehistoric China*, New York, 1934; Harry Gibson, "The Use of Cowries as Money during the Shang and Chou Periods," *Journal of the North China Branch of the Royal Asiatic Society*, No. 71, 1940, pp. 33–45; Lacouperie, "Metallic Cowries;" and Wang Yu-Chuan, *Early Chinese Coinage*.

42 Einzig, *Primitive Money*; Yule and Burnell, *Hobson-Jobson*, p. 269; Jackson, *Shells as Evidence*, p. 178; Quiggin, *Primitive Money*, p. 227; Kenyon, "Cowrie," p. 342.

43 Quiggin, *Primitive Money*, pp. 224–225; Kenyon, "Cowrie," p. 341. The *pei* sign is discussed thoroughly by Gibson, "Cowries as Money," pp. 33–45.

44 Marco Polo, *The Book of Ser Marco Polo the Venetian Concerning the Kingdoms and Marvels of the East*, ed. and trans. Col. Sir Henry Yule, p. 183; Quiggin, *Primitive Money*, pp. 29, 227.

45 Magalhães-Godinho, *Empire portugais*, p. 391; Schneider, *Muschelgeld-Studien*, pp. 110–112; Jackson, *Shells as Evidence*, pp. 168–169.

46 Schneider, *Muschelgeld-Studien*, p. 103; Quiggin, *Primitive Money*, p. 224; Jackson, *Shells as Evidence*, p. 183.

47 Schneider, *Muschelgeld-Studien*, p. 2; Jackson, *Shells as Evidence*, p. 174.

48 Jackson, *Shells as Evidence*, pp. 174–175.

49 P. Wirz, *Im Lande des Schneckengeldes*, Stuttgart, 1931, p. 70, quoted by Einzig, *Primitive Money*, pp. 88–89.

50 Quiggin, *Primitive Money*, p. 29; memo by Mr. Holmstrom; Jackson, *Shells as Evidence*, p. 130.

Notes to pages 13–15

51 Jackson, *Shells as Evidence*, pp. 184–190; see also his "North American Indians;" Quiggin, *Primitive Money*, p. 36.
52 Jackson, *Shells as Evidence*, p. 140; Sushil Chandra De, "The Cowry Currency in India," *The Orissa Historical Research Journal*, Vol. 1, No. 1, 1952, pp. 3–5.
53 The earliest dating is doubtful since an Indian cowrie currency is not mentioned by any Greek or Latin author. See Yule and Burnell, *Hobson-Jobson*, p. 269. For notice of archaeological finds see Allan, "Coinage," p. 317; Jackson, *Shells as Evidence*; Safer and Gill, *Spirals*, p. 50; and De, "Cowry Currency in India," pp. 4–5.
54 De, "Cowry Currency in India," p. 3.
55 Fah-Hian, *Travels of Fah-Hian*, trans. Samuel Beal, New York, 1969, p. 55.
56 Chau Ju-Kua, *On the Chinese and Arab Trade in the Twelfth and Thirteenth Centuries*, trans. F. Hirth and W. Rockhill, St. Petersburg, 1911, p. 113; and Simkin, *Trade of Asia*, p. 70.
57 Sushil Chandra De, "Cowry Currency in Orissa," *The Orissa Historical Research Journal*, Vol. 1, No. 1, 1952, p. 10.
58 Yule and Burnell, *Hobson-Jobson*, p. 270, quoting Maçoudi, *Les Prairies d'Or*, ed. and trans. by Barbier de Meynard and Pavet de Courteille, Paris, 9 vols., 1861–1877, Vol. 1, p. 385.
59 Robert E. C. Stearns, "Ethno-Conchology, A Study of Primitive Money," in Smithsonian Institution, *Report of National Museum, 1887*, Washington, 1887, p. 301, quoting the *Lilivati of Bhaskara Acharya*. See also Quiggin, *Primitive Money*, p. 193. Other Hindi references are given by De, "Cowry Currency in India," p. 5.
60 Chau Ju-Kua, *Chinese and Arab Trade*, pp. 35, 111; Yule and Burnell, *Hobson-Jobson*, p. 270, quoting Major H. G. Raverty, *Tabakat-i-Nasiri*, London, 1881, p. 555 ff.; and Magalhães-Godinho, *Empire portugais*, p. 390.
61 Ma-Huan, *Ying-yai Sheng-Lan, "The Overall Survey of the Ocean's Shores,"* [1433], trans. J. V. G. Mills, Cambridge, 1970, p. 161. It is worth noting Frank Perlin's apt warning that the evidence is thin and exaggeration of long-term continuity a strong possibility. See his paper, "Money-Use in Late Pre-Colonial India and the International Trade in Currency Media," presented at the Mughal Monetary Conference, Duke University, June 1981, footnote 33. (All our references to this paper are to the typescript copy.)
62 Schneider, *Muschelgeld-Studien*, pp. 110–112; Quiggin, *Primitive Money*, p. 29.
63 Perlin, "Money-Use," especially footnotes 31–33. For descriptions of Indian monies see also John F. Richards, "The Early Islamic Monetary Realm in India," paper presented at the Comparative World History Workshop in Pre-Modern Monetary History 1200–1750 A.D., University of Wisconsin, 1977; also the essays contained in Richards' *Precious Metals*, a volume of conference papers given at Duke University in 1981.
64 Hiskett, "Cowry," pp. 339–366.
65 Jackson, *Shells as Evidence*, pp. 128–130. Imitation cowries made of gold have been found in Egypt. See Quiggin, *Primitive Money*, p. 29. The shells were still used in the nineteenth century as protection against the evil eye, according to E. W. Lane, *Modern Egyptians*, London, 1860, p. 251, quoted by Hiskett, "Cowry," p. 343.
66 E. W. Bovill, *The Golden Trade of the Moors*, London, 2nd ed., 1968, p. 148; also editorial comment on Laing's letters in *Missions to the Niger*, Cambridge, 1964, p. 245: "Cowries were imported into Africa from Asia, mostly through Cairo."
67 S. D. Goitein, *A Mediterranean Society*, Vol. 1, *Economic Foundations*, Berkeley, 1967, pp. 153–154, 275; Ivan Hrbek, "Egypt, Nubia and the Eastern Deserts," in *The Cambridge History of Africa*, Vol. 3, ed. Roland Oliver, London, 1977, p. 92. Cairo is so strategically placed at the meeting of trade routes up the Red Sea and along the Mediterranean that it is hard to imagine any alternatives as equally acceptable, in spite of the weak evidence. It should be noted that the transit trade in cowries attracted little attention even in eighteenth and nineteenth-century Europe.

68 Curtin, "Wider Monetary World," p. 2 (Karl Polanyi also posits Venice as a major market, *Dahomey*, pp. 179–180); Marco Polo, *Book*, Vol. 2, p. 74; C. T. Onions, ed., *The Oxford Dictionary of English Etymology*, Oxford, 1966, p. 697; *Oxford English Dictionary*, Vol. 7, part 3, p. 1127; John W. Blake, ed., *Europeans in West Africa, 1450–1560*, London, 1942, Vol. 1, p. 157. Magalhães-Godinho, *Empire portugais*, p. 380, concludes that "selon toute probabilité," the shells seen at Venice are "venus des Maldives par l'Égypte." Later Venetian interest in these movements is indicated by a map made there in 1457–59 that terms the islands and ocean near Ceylon "mar nel qual nasce porcelate [cowries] e spendese per moneda." Schneider, *Muschelgeld-Studien*, p. 110; Heimann, "Small Change," p. 51. For the French and German linguistic usage, see Simone Berbain, *Le Comptoir français de Juda (Ouidah) au XVIIIe siècle*, Paris, 1942, p. 82; Gerh. Rohlfs, "Geld in Afrika," *Petermanns Mitteilungen*, 1889, p. 189; and above all F. A. Schilder, "Porzellanschnecken," pp. 322–326.

69 Hiskett, "Cowry," pp. 340, 344. He discounts the possibility that tin objects resembling cowries found at an early Nok site in Nigeria actually do signify knowledge of the shells at an ancient date. *Ibid.*, p. 344.

70 *Ibid.*, p. 345, quoting al-Bakri, *Description de l'Afrique septentrionale*, trans. de Slane, Paris, 1913, p. 335. Most of the early Arabic references to the cowrie can be found in a recent French translation by Joseph M. Cuoq, *Recueil des sources arabes concernant l'Afrique occidentale du VIIIe au XVIe siècle*, Paris, 1975. For al-Bakri's text, see p. 104. There is a new English translation by N. Levtzion and J. F. P. Hopkins, eds., *Corpus of Early Arabic Sources for West African History*, Cambridge, 1981. The text by al-Bakri is at p. 83.

71 Hiskett, "Cowry," p. 344, quoting H. L. Fleischer, ed., *Abulfedae historia anteislamica*, Leipzig, 1831, pp. 175–176; and Cuoq, *Sources arabes*, p. 122 (Ibn Sa'id says there was a stretch on this route with no water for twelve days' travel). It might appear that Morocco lies too far west for economical transport costs where goods coming from the Indian Ocean are concerned. But sea transport would be cheaper than desert travel, and the route from Sijilmassa to Ghana, Timbuktu, or Gao is in mileage the shortest desert crossing.

72 Geoffrey Barrclough, ed., *The Times Atlas of World History*, London, 1979, Maps 1 and 2, pp. 136–137.

73 The information concerning the askiyas is from Nehemia Levtzion, "The Western Maghrib and Sudan," *Cambridge History of Africa*, Vol. 3, ed. Roland Oliver, London, 1977, p. 448. Other references to trans-Saharan cowrie traffic are in Sundström, *Exchange*, p. 94.

74 Ch.-A. Julien, *Histoire de l'Afrique du nord*, Paris, 1961, p. 234. The English were importing to Morocco in *c.* 1800: "Guinea cowries, which are shells serving as money in that country." J. Grey Jackson, *An Account of the Empire of Marocco*, 3rd ed., London, 1814, p. 24.

75 Commodore Stewart, quoted by Thomas Winterbottom, *An Account of the Native Africans in Sierra Leone*, London, 1803, p. 221: "The goods they [the Moroccans] bring to Guinea are salt, cowries, etc."

76 As suggested by M. Johnson, "Cowrie Currency, Part I," p. 27.

77 M. J. E. Daumas, *Le Sahara Algérien*, Algiers, 1845, pp. 298 and 199.

78 Hiskett, "Cowry," p. 346, quoting al-'Umari, *Masalik al-absar*, trans. Gaudefroy-Demombynes, Paris, 1927, Vol. 1, pp. 75–76.

79 Ibn Battuta, *Travels in Asia and Africa, 1325–1354*, trans. H. A. R. Gibb, London, 1963, p. 334.

80 Hiskett, "Cowry," p. 346, quoting Mahmud al-Kati, *Tarikh al-fattash*, Paris, 1913, pp. 107–108; Leo Africanus, *The History and Description of Africa . . . of Leo Africanus*, trans. Pory, ed. Robert Brown, London, 1896, Vol. 3, p. 825.

81 A. Cadamosto, *Voyages*, ed. G. R. Crone, London, 1937, p. 29. The account is from Cadamosto's "Prima Navigazione," as he called it.

82 Jackson, *Shells as Evidence*, p. 125.
83 G. I. Jones, "Native and Trade Currencies in Southern Nigeria during the 18th and 19th Centuries," *Africa*, Vol. 28, 1958, p. 48; M. D. W. Jeffreys, "The Diffusion of Cowries and Egyptian Culture in Africa," *American Anthropologist*, Vol. 50, 1948, p. 47; Ibn Battuta, *Travels*, note 33, chapter 14, p. 382. This controversy is reviewed by Hiskett, "Cowry," pp. 347–349.
84 Hiskett, "Cowry," pp. 350–351.
85 Jackson, *Shells as Evidence*, p. 143; Hiskett, "Cowry," p. 350.
86 Hiskett, "Cowry."
87 John Roscoe, *The Baganda*, London, 1911, p. 456; Hiskett, "Cowry." Franz Stuhlmann, *Mit Emin Pasha ins Herz von Afrika*, Berlin, 1894, says they were originally used in high-value transactions such as the purchase of slaves and boats, p. 82, quoted by Einzig, *Primitive Money*, p. 133. Some Maldive *moneta* figured in East African cowrie use, but east coast *annulus* predominated. See Andrew Forbes and Fawzia Ali, "The Maldive Islands and their Historical Links with the Coast of Eastern Africa," *Kenya Past and Present*, Vol. 11, 1981, p. 18. See also Einzig, p. 136.
88 Hiskett, "Cowry," pp. 349–350.
89 Curtin, "Wider Monetary World," typescript p. 17. Sundström, *Exchange*, p. 95, says "it seems likely that the cowrie shell was preceded as an ornament in Africa by other shells." See also J. Deutsch, *Die Zahlungsmittel der Naturvölker in Afrika*, Marburg, 1957, especially pp. 45, 48.
90 There was a minor fifteenth-century Spanish export trade of unspecified shells (probably not used as currency) from the Canary Islands to coastal West Africa via Seville. The Portuguese in time put a stop to it. Sundström, *Exchange*, and sources quoted there.
91 Archaeological work at Benin has uncovered only a tiny number of Indian Ocean cowries (four plus a fragment) at levels dating from before contact with the Europeans. See Graham Connah, *Archaeology of Benin*, Oxford, 1975, pp. 218–219. For zimbos see Dartevelle, *Les N'zimbu*; Couto, *O Zimbo*; Quiggin, *Primitive Money*, pp. 46–47; Magalhães-Godinho, *Empire portugais*, p. 383; Curtin, "Wider Monetary World," typescript pp. 17–18; Polanyi, *Dahomey*, p. 183. The Congo shell-currency was contiguous neither to the West nor East African area of circulation. Zimbos were inferior in that they were not brilliant, but they could be polished. The color of female shells was preferred to that of males, as was the color of examples from Luanda by comparison to those from other beaches in Angola and Benguela. Dartevelle warns that politics may have "colored" the preference for Luanda shells. Sundström, *Exchange*, p. 95, calls them *nsimbi*, a word apparently meaning "God's children." Their collection at Luanda Island was a royal monopoly which eventually passed to the Portuguese. There are seventeenth-century reports of similar shell exports from Porto Seguro, Brazil, and São Tomé, to both the Congo Kingdom and Angola (*ibid.*, and many sources quoted therein). There was a quite different type of shell currency in use on the island of Fernando Po. It survived until the later nineteenth century, and was described by T. J. Hutchinson, *Impressions of West Africa*, London, 1858; Mary Kingsley, *Travels in West Africa*, London, 1891, p. 59; and Oskar Baumann, *Fernando Póo und die Bube*, Vienna, 1888, pp. 83–84.
92 Pacheco Pereira, *Esmeraldo de situ orbis*, ed. and trans. G. T. Kimble, London, 1936, p. 145. In the Edo language of Benin, *igos* later came to mean money in general. A. F. C. Ryder, *Benin and the Europeans 1485–1897*, London, 1969, p. 60. It was just as well for monetary stability that shells acceptable as money were not freely available on West African beaches, for that would seem a high road to hyperinflation. The results of an uncontrolled supply of some item serving as money, M in Fisher's equation $MV = PQ$, is discussed by Crump, *Phenomenon of Money*, pp. 85–86.
93 Ryder, *Benin*, pp. 60–61, and his "An Early Portuguese Trading Voyage to the Forcados River," *Journal of the Historical Society of Nigeria*, Vol. 1, No. 4, 1959, p. 301.

94 Jackson, *Shells as Evidence*, pp. 152 ff., has a section on areas of Africa where the cowrie was used in non-monetary ways. Sundström, *Exchange*, p. 112, quotes many sources, and notes that if the shells were pierced for ornamental use they lost monetary value. This loss of value must relate to areas where they were not normally strung. We find no suggestion that the shells once strung had to remain so. The cost for the labor of stringing would of course be lost if the shells came unstrung, which must have happened often enough if only by accident, and they were certainly used in loose condition even in areas where it was standard to find them strung.

2 The Maldive Islands

1 This introduction is taken from Jan S. Hogendorn, "A Research-Trip to the Maldive Islands, 1982," *Itinerario*, Vol. 6, No. 2, 1982, pp. 59–67.
2 Clarence Maloney, *People of the Maldive Islands*, Madras, 1980, p. 1; Andrew D. W. Forbes, "Archives and Resources for Maldivian History," *South Asia*, Vol. 3, No. 1, 1980. p. 71. Maloney says 1,009 islands while Forbes says 1,196, nicely illustrating the numbers problem discussed by Maloney, pp. 5–6, wherein travellers could never seem to agree on how many islands there actually are. Maloney is an anthropologist, and his book, published by Orient Longman in 1980, gives useful background information on the Maldives.
3 Maloney, *People*, pp. 1–2, and J. Stanley Gardiner, "The Maldive and Laccadive Archipelagoes" in A. J. Herbertson and O. J. R. Howarth, eds., *Asia*, Vol. 2 of *The Oxford Survey of the British Empire*, Oxford, 1914, p. 314. Divehi is written in an indigenous script called *Tana* that is based on both Arabic and South Asian writing systems. Forbes, "Archives."
4 Maloney, *People*, p. 1.
5 The small size of individual islands explains why total land area is only 115 square miles.
6 Maloney, *People*, pp. 2–5, 7.
7 A very short list of scholars with a research interest in the Maldives may be found in *ibid.*, p. 413, and Forbes, "Archives," p. 78.
8 See chapter 1.
9 Forbes, "Archives," p. 75.
10 He was not himself shipwrecked, as Maloney states, *People*, p. 425.
11 There are 376 call numbers in the Bell Collection, one of which catalogues an abandoned Maldives gravestone. The authors did not check out this stone, and rely on Forbes, "Archives," p. 76, for this information. Also deserving of at least a mention is C. W. Rosset, whose visit in the 1880s led to two articles, "On the Maldive Islands," *Journal of the Anthropological Institute*, Vol. 16, 1887, pp. 164–174, and the much longer "Die 14000 Malediven-Inseln," *Mitteilungen der Kais.-Königl. Geographischen Gesellschaft in Wien*, Vol. 39, 1896, pp. 597–637.
12 The *Ta'rikh* covers the period A.D. 1153 to 1821, and can be found in abridged translation in H. C. P. Bell, *The Maldive Islands: Monograph on the History, Archaeology, and Epigraphy*, Colombo, 1940. The *Radavali* dates from the eighteenth century; it too is translated in *ibid.* The full versions (in Arabic) have been available only since 1982. See Hikoichi Yajima, *The Islamic History of the Maldive Islands*, Tokyo, 1982. (Our thanks to Ralph Austen of the University of Chicago for bringing this work to our attention.) In his 1982 fieldwork, Hogendorn found oral evidence concerning cowrie production vague for any period much before about 1900. Oral traditions on the subject appeared to be sparse.
13 H. C. P. Bell, *The Maldive Islands: an Account of the Physical Features, Climate, History, Inhabitants, Productions, and Trade*, Colombo, 1883; Maloney, *People*, pp. 188–195.
14 See Maloney, who has pioneered in these attributions, *People*, p. 414. The references are not with certainty to the Maldives. The islands were probably settled as early as the fifth century B.C., largely from Ceylon but possibly from South India as well. Andrew D. W.

Forbes, "Southern Arabia and the Islamicisation of the Central Indian Ocean Archipelagoes," *Archipel*, Vol. 21, 1981, p. 65. Recent archaeological discoveries reported by the Norwegian explorer Thor Heyerdahl may push back considerably estimates of earliest settlement. Several newly discovered temple structures may be as much as 4,000 years old. See Peter Ford, "Maldives Ruins Suggest Link to Prehistoric Cultures," *Toronto Globe and Mail*, April 1, 1983, p. 9 (brought to our attention by Paul Lovejoy).

15 Maloney, *People*, pp. 414–415; Forbes, "Archives," p. 75; E. H. Warmington, *The Commerce between the Roman Empire and India*, London, 1974, pp. 124–125; Albert Gray and H. C. P. Bell, eds., *The Voyage of François Pyrard of Laval to the East Indies, the Maldives, the Moluccas, and Brazil*, London, 2 vols., 1887 and 1890. Volume 2, part 2, pp. 423–492, is entitled "Early Notices of the Maldives" and includes English translations.

16 Doubtful in our opinion. The Greek word χοιρίναι is too broad a term to be definitely associated with the cowrie, according to our classical dictionaries. See Warmington, *Commerce*, p. 172. F. A. Schilder surveys the classical names for cowries in "Porzellanschnecken," pp. 322–323.

17 Maloney, *People*, p. 415.

18 Sulayman's text is *Akhbar as Sinwa'l Hind*. There are English translations of relevant passages in Maloney, *People*, p. 417 (which we have used) and in Gray and Bell, *Pyrard*, Vol. 2, p. 429. See also Forbes, "Southern Arabia," p. 69, and Heimann, "Small Change," p. 49. There is a short account of Sulayman in the *Encyclopaedia Britannica*, 13th ed., Vol. 11, p. 624, "Geography."

19 Gray and Bell, *Pyrard*, p. 237, describe collection methods. The hint of monopoly would then also be a hint of the long-standing nature of a head tax payable in cowries. Evidence on royal monopoly and the collection of cowries via taxation is reviewed in our later chapters.

20 Al-Mas'udi's text is *Muraj al-Dhanab wa Ma'adin al Jawahir*. The English translation used here is in Gray and Bell, *Pyrard*, Vol. 2, p. 430, quoting the French text, *Prairies d'Or* (see chapter 1, footnote 58). See also Maloney, *People*, p. 417, and Heimann, "Small Change," p. 639.

21 Gray and Bell, *Pyrard*, p. 429.

22 *Ibid.*, pp. 430–431; *Encyclopaedia Britannica*, 1968 edn, Vol. 3, p. 711; Maloney, *People*, p. 418; Yule and Burnell, *Hobson-Jobson*, p. 270; Forbes, "Southern Arabia," p. 69. Al-Biruni's text is *Tarikh al-Hind (A History of India)*. Kânbar is said by Yule to be a misreading of káyar, "coir," which seems reasonable. Cowries actually were exported (still true in the nineteenth century) in small quantities from the Laccadives. These islands, still noted for their coconuts, are far fewer in number than the Maldives, and with a much smaller population. They were inhabited by only 10,000 people at the turn of this century. See De, "Cowry in India," p. 3, and Gardiner, "Maldive Archipelago," p. 328. Maloney, *People*, states that a northern Persian, Abul-Hassan, *c.* 1026, mentions the islands of cowries whence shells are sent to Africa. We have been unable to trace this reference.

23 *Encyclopaedia Britannica*, 1968 ed., Vol. 11, p. 1067; Maloney, *People*, pp. 418–419, whom we have quoted and who follows *al-Idrisi*, trans. S. Maqbul Ahmad, Leiden, 1960, pp. 23–27. See also Gray and Bell, *Pyrard*, Vol. 2, p. 432, whose translation does not indicate so clearly a royal monopoly as that rendered by Ahmad; and Forbes, "Southern Arabia," p. 69.

24 Schneider, *Muschelgeld-Studien*, p. 110.

25 The writers who do not mention the cowrie are cited by Gray and Bell, *Pyrard*, Vol. 2, pp. 433–434, and see Heimann, "Small Change," p. 49. Wang Ta-yuan is noted by Maloney, *People*, p. 117 and also pp. 111, 420. The quotation is found in K. A. Nilakanta Sastri, ed., *Foreign Notices of South India*, Madras, 1939, pp. 292–293.

26 Encyclopaedia Britannica, 13th ed., Vol. 14, pp. 219–220; Bell, *Maldive Islands* (1883), pp. 24–25.

27 The quote (from Gray and Bell, *Pyrard*, p. 444) is an English translation following the

original French rendering from Arabic, *Voyages d'Ibn Batoutah*, ed. and trans. C. Défrémery and B. R. Sanguinetti, Paris, 1858–1859, Vol. 4, p. 122. See also Yule and Burnell, *Hobson-Jobson*, p. 270, and Bell, *Maldive Islands* (1883) which describes Ibn Battuta's stay, pp. 24–25, 117. See also Gibb, *Travels*, chapter 8. We have modernized some spellings in this passage and the one that follows. Ibn Battuta also notes some ceremonial use of cowries in the Maldives (Gray and Bell, *Pyrard*, p. 441).

28 Gray and Bell, *Pyrard*. Mali, in the West African Empire of that name, not of course to be confused with Male, capital of the Maldives.

29 *Encyclopaedia Britannica*, 13th ed., Vol. 14, p. 220.

30 Ma Huan, *Ying-Yai Sheng-Lan*, p. 150; Maloney, *People*, pp. 420–421.

31 Heimann, "Small Change," p. 51, and the sources quoted in his footnote 40, p. 64. For the use of the term "Pei Liu" see Nilakanta Sastri, *Foreign Notices*, pp. 292–293.

32 Gardiner, "Maldive Archipelago," p. 319; Gray and Bell, *Pyrard*, Vol. 2, p. 469. Santo Stefano lived there six months, but unfortunately makes no mention of the shell trade. See R. H. Major, ed. and trans., "Account of the Journey of Hieronimo di Santo Stefano," in R. H. Major, *India in the Fifteenth Century*, London, 1857.

33 De, "Cowry in India," p. 3; Allan, "Coinage," p. 317; Ma Huan, *Ying-Yai Sheng-Lan*, p. 150; our note 31 above; and our discussion of the Bengal market in chapter 1.

34 Schneider, *Muschelgeld-Studien*, pp. 110–111; Quiggin, *Primitive Money*, p. 29.

35 See Heimann, "Small Change," pp. 50, 52. As so often in monetary history, a commodity money is the less workable the more freely it is available. It is then difficult or impossible to prevent unlimited augmentation of the money supply.

36 For the *larin*, see Tim J. Browder, *Maldive Islands Money*, Santa Monica, Calif., 1969 (Browder's pamphlet was brought to our attention by Forbes, "Archives," p. 74 and footnotes); Bell, *Maldive Islands* (1940), Appendix C, "Coinage and Currency of the Maldive Islands;" Bell, *Maldive Islands* (1883), p. 117; Quiggin, *Primitive Money*, pp. 194–196; Gray and Bell, *Pyrard*, Vol. 1, pp. 232–235, 237; and Allan, "Coinage," pp. 319–324. In Frank Perlin's paper, "Money-Use," p. 125, n. 162, there is a highly informative survey from which we shall quote liberally: "By far the best discussion of the *larin* is Wood's excellent introduction and analysis in his catalogue of the Gampola Hoard [Howland Wood, *The Gampola Larin Hoard*, New York, American Numismatic Society, *Numismatic Notes and Monographs*, No. 61, 1934]; a significant number of specimens of the latter are in the American Numismatic Society collection." Raf. van Laere, "The Larin: Trade Money of the Arabian Gulf," *Oriental Numismatic Society*, Occasional paper No. 15, 1980, "mistakenly assumes the shape of the *larin* (a stamped piece of partly flattened wire, usually bent double) to be due to an inability to cut circular coin. In fact, hand cutting techniques were at this time highly skilled, and the problem answered by the *larin* is better explained in terms of increasing speed of production for the huge commercial Indian Ocean market opened up for the coin from the 16th century on. Normally characterized by its high quality silver content, it was surely a response to the need for a standard, reliable trading coinage. It was minted as far north as Tabriz, at Basra, Shiraz, Lar and Hormuz on the Persian Gulf, in Adil Shahi territories (Bijapur Sultanate in peninsular India), Ceylon, the Maldive Islands, and possibly at the V.O.C. mint at Palikot on the Coromandel coast, and in Gujerat. . . . The Portuguese used the *larin* as an accounting unit." The duodecimal system is discussed by Maloney, *People*, p. 134.

37 Browder, *Money*, pp. 5–6, 9, for the *larin* and the first circular coins.

38 Forbes, "Southern Arabia," pp. 72–81, who makes use of the maps and information in G. R. Tibbetts, *Arab Navigation in the Indian Ocean Before the Coming of the Portuguese*, London, 1971. For a discussion of early maritime contacts between Arabia and the East, see G. R. Tibbetts, "Pre-Islamic Arabia and South-East Asia," *Journal of the Malayan Branch of the Royal Asiatic Society*, Vol. 29, No. 3, 1956, pp. 182–208; G. F. Hourani, *Arab Seafaring in the Indian Ocean in the Ancient and Early Medieval Times*, Princeton, 1951;

Hikoichi Yajima, *The Arab Dhow Trade in the Indian Ocean*, Tokyo, 1976; and the discussion of Forbes, "Southern Arabia," pp. 62–66. For shipping see Archibald Lewis, "Maritime Skills in the Indian Ocean, 1368–1500," *Journal of the Economic and Social History of the Orient*, Vol. 16, 1973, pp. 238–264.

39 Forbes, "Southern Arabia," pp. 80–81. The sherds are discussed by John Carswell, "China and Islam in the Maldive Islands," *Transactions of the Oriental Ceramic Society*, Vol. 41, 1975–77, pp. 119–198, with further detail given at a lecture at the University of Manchester in 1977 attended by Forbes ("Southern Arabia," n. 79, p. 77).

40 Philip D. Curtin, *Cross-Cultural Trade in World History*, Cambridge, 1984, pp. 96–97.

41 Al-Mas'udi's observations are noted earlier in this chapter. The trade of Siraf is discussed in Yajima, *Arab Dhow Trade*, pp. 8–10. *Encyclopaedia Britannica*, 13th edn, Vol. 21, p. 228; Major, *India in the Fifteenth Century*, p. 6; Bell, *Maldive Islands* (1940), p. 17; Gray and Bell, *Pyrard*, Vol. 2, pp. 468–469. Circumstantial evidence of extensive contact between the Maldives and Persia is found in the Maldivian use of the silver *larin*, adopted from Persia (and discussed above), and traditions of Persian missionary activity in the islands. Gray and Bell, *Pyrard*, and Gardiner, "Maldive Archipelago," p. 319.

42 Barraclough, *Times Atlas of World History*, pp. 146–147.

43 Leo Africanus, *History of Africa*, Vol. 3, p. 825.

3 The Portuguese domination

1 Major general works on the Portuguese period are Gaspar Correa, who lived many years in India and whose four-volume *Lendas da India* covers the period from 1497 to 1550 (Lisbon, 1858–1865); João de Barros, the administrator and historian, whose four *Decadas* of his *Da Asia* appeared between 1552 and 1615 (long after his death) and are in a large edition published at Lisbon, 1778; Duarte Barbosa, *The Book of Duarte Barbosa*, ed. M. L. Dames, London, 1918; Tomé Pires, *The Suma Oriental of Tomé Pires*, ed. Armando Cortesão, London, 1944; Duarte Gomes Solis, *Alegación en favor de la Compañia de la India Oriental*, ed. Mosés Amzalak, Lisbon, 1955; Frederick Charles Danvers, *The Portuguese in India*, London, 1894; R. S. Whiteway, *The Rise of Portuguese Power in India*, London, 1899; A. H. de Oliveria Marques, *History of Portugal*, New York, 1971; and Bailey W. Diffie and George D. Winius, eds., *Foundations of the Portuguese Empire, 1415–1580*, Minneapolis, 1977. The bibliography in C. R. Boxer, *The Portuguese Seaborne Empire 1415–1825*, London, 1969, is excellent.

2 M. A. H. Fitzler, "Die Maldiven im 16. und 17. Jahrhundert," *Zeitschrift für Indologie und Iranstik*, Vol. 10, 1935–36, p. 219; Gray and Bell, *Pyrard*, Vol. 2, pp. 472–474; Bell, *Maldive Islands* (1883), p. 26; Heimann, "Small Change," p. 51. There is an account of the *cartaz* system in M. N. Pearson, *Merchants and Rulers in Gujarat: The Response to the Portuguese in the Sixteenth Century*, Berkeley, 1976, pp. 39–56.

3 Gray and Bell, *Pyrard*, pp. 472–473; Correa, *Lendas*, Vol. 1, p. 341.

4 Correa, *Lendas*, pp. 341–342; Gray and Bell, *Pyrard*, pp. 473–474; H. C. P. Bell, "Excerpta Maldiviana: The Portuguese at the Maldives," *Journal of the Royal Asiatic Society (Ceylon)*, Vol. 32, No. 84, 1931, p. 79. The crew of a Portuguese ship wrecked in the Maldives in 1503 (presumably before the encounter) was not mistreated (Gray and Bell, *Pyrard*, p. 474). Portuguese attempts to control other lines of commerce are noted by M. N. Pearson, "Corruption and Corsairs in Sixteenth-Century Western India: a Functional Analysis," in Blair B. King and M. N. Pearson, eds., *The Age of Partnership: Europeans in Asia before Dominion*, Honolulu, 1979, pp. 15–41.

5 T. W. Hockly, *The Two Thousand Isles: a Short Account of the People, History and Customs of the Maldive Archipelago*, London, 1935, p. 102; Heimann, "Small Change," p. 51.

6 Barbosa, *Book*, quoted by Gray and Bell, *Pyrard*, Vol. 2, p. 478.

7 De Barros, *Decada III*, quoted by Gray and Bell, *Pyrard*, pp. 484–485.

8 Correa, *Lendas*, Vol. 1, i, p. 341. Other Portuguese notices of the Maldive cowrie trade include A. Nunez and Fernão Lopez de Castanheda, both quoted by Yule and Burnell, *Hobson-Jobson*, p. 270.

9 Pires, *Suma Oriental*, who says that the supplies came from the Maldives. See pp. 93–95. The shells were said to be the only known money in Orissa. Thomas Bowrey, *A Geographical Account of the Countries Round the Bay of Bengal, 1669 to 1679*, Cambridge, 1905, p. 200. For a discussion by an anthropologist of the demand for cowries in this area at about this time, see Heimann, "Small Change," pp. 56–57. Heimann also has a comprehensive table in the same article describing how cowries were counted in Bengal.

10 Perlin, "Money-Use," typescript pp. 8, 95, 96, 100–102. He emphasizes shortages of minted copper coins.

11 We have relied on Perlin's careful work, "Money-Use," p. 96, and the sources quoted there. See also Allan, "Coinage," pp. 317–319; Jean-Baptiste Tavernier, *Travels in India*, 1925, Vol. 1, pp. 23–24; and Peter Mundy, *The Travels of Peter Mundy in Europe and Asia, 1608–1667*, Vol. 2, *Travels in Asia, 1628–1634*, ed. R. C. Temple, London, 1914, p. 311. General information on Indian monetary systems can be found in Simon Digby, "The Currency System," and Irfan Habib, "Monetary System and Prices," in Tapan Raychaudhuri and Irfan Habib, eds., *The Cambridge Economic History of India*, Vol. 1, *c. 1200—c. 1750*, Cambridge, 1982, respectively pp. 93–101 and 360–381.

12 See *Encyclopaedia Britannica*, 13th ed., Vol. 14, pp. 404–405; Kristof Glamann, *Dutch-Asiatic Trade 1620–1740*, Copenhagen, 1958, p. 123. Portuguese presence in Bengal, slight though it was, hampered trade with Chittagong up to 1666, *ibid.*

13 *Encyclopaedia Britannica*, 13th ed., Vol. 3, p. 439.

14 The letter is quoted by Yule and Burnell, *Hobson-Jobson*, p. 270. For loadings at Socotra see Magalhães-Godinho, *Empire portugais*, p. 383, quoting Castanheda and also Duarte Barbosa.

15 Van Santen's work was brought to our attention by Frank Perlin, "Money-Use," pp. 8, 95. As late as 1635, about a tonne of shells was seen coming to Mocha by ship, *ibid.*, p. 95. Via personal communication Philip D. Curtin has given us further information of cowrie shipments toward the Mediterranean surviving the advent of the Europeans. Fernand Braudel, *The Mediterranean and the Mediterranean World in the Time of Philip II*, London, 1973, has a good deal to say about the survival of the Red Sea trade in the seventeenth century.

16 Ryder, *Benin*, pp. 60–61; also Ryder, "Portuguese Trading Voyage," p. 301 ff. Robert Garfield, *A History of São Tomé Island*, unpublished Northwestern University Ph.D. thesis, 1971, is a thorough account of Portugal's new island base.

17 Ryder, *Benin*, p. 61. The Portuguese may have carried a small quantity of shells before the date of the contract, perhaps as early as 1504–1508. See the suggestion by John Vogt, *Portuguese Rule on the Gold Coast*, Athens, Georgia, 1979, p. 70. Pacheco Pereira, in his *Esmeraldo de Situ Orbis* written 1506–1508, mentions neither a trade in *moneta* or plans for one. Schneider, *Muschelgeld-Studien*, p. 124, notes the absence of an early trade.

18 Ryder, *Benin*, and Magalhães-Godinho, *Empire portugais*, p. 383.

19 Ryder, *Benin*. For São Tomé as an off-loading point see Blake, *Europeans in West Africa*, Vol. 1, p. 157; M. Johnson, "Cowrie Currencies," Part 1, p. 34; and Ryder, "Portuguese Trading Voyage," p. 301 ff.

20 Ryder, *Benin*.

21 See chapter 7 for a fuller discussion of the role of winds and currents. The shipment via Portugal instead of direct to Africa is noted by van Emst, "Weg van de Kauri," p. 271.

22 Gray and Bell, *Pyrard*, Vol. 2, p. 485. (400 reis = 1 cruzado = 4 shillings. See Heimann, "Small Change," p. 51.)

23 Schneider, *Muschelgeld-Studien*, p. 121; Gray and Bell, *Pyrard*, Vol. 1, p. 237, quoting A. Nunes in the *Subsidios*, p. 35; Heimann, "Small Change," p. 52.

24 Bal Krishna, *Commercial Relations Between India and England (1601–1757)*, London, 1924, p. 22. See also J. J. A. Campos, *History of the Portuguese in Bengal*, Calcutta, 1979, p. 115.

25 Correa, *Lendas*, Vol. 1, p. 613, quoted by Gray and Bell, *Pyrard*, Vol. 2, p. 474. See also Bell, *Maldive Islands* (1883), p. 26; Maloney, *People*, p. 122. Other sources on the Portuguese in the Maldives are Bell, "Portuguese," and Rosset, "Malediven-Inseln."

26 Fitzler, "Die Maldiven," pp. 224–227; Gray and Bell, *Pyrard*, Vol. 2, pp. 475–476; Bell, *Maldive Islands* (1883), pp. 26–27; Maloney, *People*, pp. 122–123. Fitzler's survey of the rise and fall of Muhammad Ali has detail (often from lesser Portuguese sources) unusual for Maldive economic history. The situation was described by Fitzler as a "Maldivensultan abgeschlossenen Handelsmonopols," p. 224.

27 Correa, *Lendas*, Vol. 2, p. 130; see Bell, "Portuguese," pp. 79–80; Gray and Bell, *Pyrard*, Vol. 2, pp. 474–475; Fitzler, "Die Maldiven," pp. 224–225.

28 Bell, "Portuguese," p. 82.

29 Fitzler, "Die Maldiven," who dates the massacre at 1521, pp. 226, 229; Bell, "Portuguese," pp. 79–83; Maloney, *People*, pp. 122–123; Gardiner, "Maldive Archipelago," p. 319. Some of the dating is controversial by a year or two, as Fitzler explains.

30 Fitzler, "Die Maldiven," pp. 225–234; Bell, *Maldive Islands* (1883), p. 28; Maloney, *People*, pp. 123–124; Bell, "Portuguese," pp. 87–90; Forbes, "Southern Arabia," p. 91.

31 Fitzler, "Die Maldiven," p. 235; Bell, *Maldive Islands* (1883), p. 28; Maloney, *People*, p. 124.

32 Fitzler, "Die Maldiven," pp. 236–237.

33 The two volumes edited by Gray and Bell (*Pyrard*) are the standard source. Earlier versions of Pyrard's manuscript are discussed by H. C. P. Bell, "The Maldive Islands: 1602–1607," *Ceylon Antiquary and Literary Register*, Vol. 1, Nos. 2–4, April 1916, pp. 133–139, 208–212, 266–278.

34 Gray and Bell, *Pyrard*, Vol. 1, pp. 236–240. See also p. 78 for the antagonism shown to Pyrard by the captain and crew of the Portuguese ship from Cochin.

35 *Ibid.*, p. 299.

36 *Ibid.*, p. 327, and the discussion in Heimann, "Small Change," p. 50.

37 Gray and Bell, *Pyrard*, Vol. 1, p. 228; Fitzler, "Die Maldiven," pp. 221, 223.

38 Gray and Bell, *Pyrard*, Vol. 1, p. 228.

39 *Ibid.*, pp. 232–235.

40 Fitzler, "Die Maldiven," pp. 242–243; Bell, "Portuguese," pp. 104–106.

41 Bell, "Portuguese," p. 109.

42 Fitzler, "Die Maldiven," pp. 239–240, 244; Bell, *Maldive Islands* (1940), p. 28; Maloney, *People*, p. 125.

43 Schneider, *Muschelgeld-Studien*, p. 121. For a detailed account of the consequences of the fall of Hormuz, see Niels Steensgard, *Carracks, Caravans, and Companies: the Structural Crisis in the European-Asian Trade in the Early 17th Century*, Copenhagen, 1973, chapter 4 and 7.

44 Bell, *Maldive Islands* (1883), p. 31. Official letters from the sultan to the Dutch in Ceylon were for many years written in Portuguese.

45 The ruins made a vivid impression on nineteenth-century travellers. See C. W. Rosset, "The Maldive Islands," *The Graphic*, October 16, 1886, p. 414.

46 Polanyi, *Dahomey*, pp. 181–182; Ryder, *Benin*, p. 61. See also Ryder, "Portuguese Trading Voyage," and Solis, *Alegación*. Portuguese was of course a *lingua franca* in the West African trade, and other weights and measures as well as those applying to the cowrie had linguistic roots in the language.

47 Curtin, "Wider Monetary World," typescript p. 18; Curtin, *Cross-Cultural Trade*, p. 143.

48 Heimann, "Small Change," p. 52. There is a generous selection of seventeenth-century cowrie exchange rates with copper (cowrie/paisa) and silver (cowrie/rupee), plus methods

of reckoning in Bengal, summarized in Perlin, "Money-Use," typescript pp. 78–80, and Heimann, "Small Change," pp. 53, 57–58.

4 The Dutch and English enter the trade

1 Our main sources on the companies are K. N. Chaudhuri, *The Trading World of Asia and the East India Company 1660–1760*, Cambridge, 1978, and his *The English East India Company: the Study of an Early Joint-Stock Company 1600–1640*, London, 1965; Holden Furber, *Rival Empires of Trade in the Orient 1600–1800*, Minneapolis, 1976; the essays in Leonard Blussé and Femme Gaastra, eds., *Companies and Trade*, The Hague, 1981; Curtin, *Cross-Cultural Trade* (see pp. 155–157 for a passage on the capitalization of the two companies); and C. R. Boxer, *The Dutch Seaborne Empire 1600–1800*, Harmondsworth, 1973, p. 26. For information on the Dutch trade, we have relied heavily on Floris M. Klinkenberg, "De Kaurihandel van de V.O.C.," unpublished M.A. thesis, University of Leiden, 1982. Other sources relied on for the Dutch trade include Gerald J. Telkamp, "Current Annotated Bibliography of Dutch Expansion Studies," *Itinerario*, Leiden, 1978; M. A. P. Meilink-Roelofsz, "Inleiding bij de overzeese geschiedenis in de 17de en 18de eeuw," in *Algemene Geschiedenis der Nederlanden*, Vol. 9, Haarlem, 1980, pp. 420–426; F. S. Gaastra, "De V.O.C. in Azië tot 1680," in *Algemene Geschiedenis der Nederlanden*, Vol. 7, pp. 174–219; and S. Arasaratnam, "The Kingdom of Kandy: Aspects of Its External Relations and Commerce, 1658–1710," *Ceylon Journal of Historical and Social Studies*, Vol. 3, 1960, pp. 109–127.

2 H. C. P. Bell, "Excerpta Maldiviana. No. 11. Dutch Intercourse with the Maldives: Seventeenth Century," *Journal of the Royal Asiatic Society (Ceylon)*, Vol. 32, No. 85, 1932, p. 228.

3 *Ibid.*, p. 229; Bell, *Maldive Islands* (1883), pp. 30, 98.

4 Klinkenberg thesis, p. 67. We have used the average Amsterdam prices of 1650 and 1651 (.47 and .48 guilders respectively) for the calculation. See chapter 5, "Note on method" following Table 5.2, for a description of our methods of calculating cowrie imports and exports. The first appearance of the shells on Netherlands markets may have been a little earlier. See K. Ratelband, ed., *Vijf Dagregisters van het Kasteel São Jorge da Mina (Elmina) aan de Goudkust (1645-1647)*, The Hague, 1953, p. 81; and the mention of cowries in a letter of 1645 from the Dutch governor of Ceylon. Bell, "Dutch Intercourse," p. 233.

5 Glamann, *Dutch-Asiatic Trade*, pp. 20, 22; Bell, "Dutch Intercourse," p. 99.

6 For Goa and Cochin see the explicit mention (probably based on Dapper's *Naukeurige Beschrijvinge*, p. 491, published twenty years earlier) in John Barbot's 1688 manuscript (now being prepared for publication by the Hakluyt Society). The passage differs slightly from the similar one on p. 338 of Barbot's much-altered and updated *A Description of the Coasts of North and South-Guinea*, published as Vol. 5 of A. and J. Churchill, eds., *A Collection of Voyages and Travels*, London, 1732. Glamann says of the early supplies that they were secured "from Coromandel, Bengal, and Ceylon," *Dutch-Asiatic Trade*, p. 22. An independent commercial director for Bengal was appointed in 1655. Before that date, direction was from Fort Geldria on the Coromandel coast, *ibid.*, p. 123.

7 Klinkenberg thesis, p. 32.

8 Bell, "Dutch Intercourse," pp. 232, 239; Bell, *Maldive Islands* (1883), p. 98; Klinkenberg thesis, pp. 43, 62.

9 Bell, *Maldive Islands* (1883), pp. 30–31, 99; Fitzler, "Die Maldiven," p. 630; Bell, "Dutch Intercourse," pp. 230–231, 235–236; Heimann, "Small Change," p. 52; Klinkenberg thesis, pp. 46–49.

10 Klinkenberg thesis, pp. 46–47; Bell, "Dutch Intercourse," p. 230; Heimann, "Small Change," p. 52.

11 "Den Maldiver in den aanbreng van cauris meer en meer te animeeren," Bell, *Maldive Islands* (1883), p. 99; "ons ook seer ernstig recommandeeren de Maldives vaerdaers in alles te carresseeren," *ibid.*; Bell, "Dutch Intercourse," p. 231.

12 This trade had now gone on for "several years consecutively" said Governor van Rhee, in Bell, "Dutch Intercourse," p. 232 and *Maldive Islands* (1883), p. 99.

13 Bell, "Dutch Intercourse," p. 228. In the hundred years after about 1650, the Dutch attempted with some success to implement a closed trading system in the waters around Ceylon and their southern Indian possessions, thus imitating their far more effective policy in the East Indies. For a recent survey, see S. Arasaratnam, "*Mare Clausum*, the Dutch and Regional Trade in the Indian Ocean 1650–1740," paper presented at the International Conference on Indian Ocean Studies, Perth, Australia, 1979.

14 Bell, *Maldive Islands* (1883), p. 98; H. C. P. Bell, "Excerpta Maldiviana. No. 4. A Description of the Maldive Islands: *Circa* A.C. 1683," *Journal of the Royal Asiatic Society (Ceylon)*, Vol. 30, No. 78, 1925, p. 138.

15 Bell, *Maldive Islands* (1883), p. 130; "Portuguese," p. 111.

16 Heimann, "Small Change," p. 65, n. 65, quoting William Foster, ed., *The English Factories in India 1618–1669, a Calendar of Documents in the India Office, British Museum and Public Record Office*, London, *1668–1669*, 1927, pp. 3, 179, 189, 194. Heimann's footnote 66 helpfully works out contemporary rix-dollar, rupee, and shilling exchange rates. One rix-dollar = three guilders = sixty stuivers. There is one statement that cowries at the Maldives themselves (no transport or handling) cost 1.16 to 1.25 rupees in the 1680s. Bowrey, *Bay of Bengal*, p. 219, first footnote.

17 Bell, "Dutch Intercourse," p. 232.

18 Bell, "Description," p. 135; Bell, *Maldive Islands* (1883), p. 99.

19 Bell, "Description," p. 138. According to Heimann, the Dutch were able to increase their profits by shrewd purchases, at favourable terms, of Bengali rice which they then exchanged for cowries. The figures he uses do not, however, appear to deduct transport and other opportunity costs from the postulated net return. "Small Change," p. 65, n. 65.

20 The Klinkenberg thesis, p. 63 ff., discusses the steady growth.

21 Heimann, "Small Change," p. 53.

22 Foster, *English Factories, 1630–33*, 1910, pp. 275, 287; *1634–36*, 1911, p. 176; *1655–60*, 1921, pp. 188, 255 n. 1. Perlin's work led us to the earliest of these references.

23 Ethel Bruce Sainsbury, *Court Minutes of the East India Company*, Oxford, 1907 ff., the four volumes covering 1664 to 1679, *passim*. The hundred-ton order is at p. 256 of the volume *1677–79*, 1938.

24 Hedges, *Diary*, Vol. 3, p. viii.

25 Bell, *Maldive Islands* (1883), p. 430; James Horsburgh, "Some Remarks relative to the Geography of the Maldive Islands, and the Navigable Channels (at present known to Europeans) which separate the Atolls from each other," *Journal of the Royal Geographical Society*, Vol. 2, 1832, pp. 76–77.

26 John Marshall, *Notes and Observations of East India*, ed. S. A. Kahn as *John Marshall in India*, London, 1927 [1677], p. 416.

27 Hedges, *Diary*, Vol. 1, p. 96; Klinkenberg thesis, p. 79; Bell, "Description," pp. 132–133. The shells were taken to Surat for the homeward shipping. We wonder what mechanism establishes the market price for something exacted at gunpoint.

28 Hedges, *Diary*, Vol. 1, p. 190. Hedges, a director of the EIC, was himself on this ship (the *Recovery*), having been superseded due to his running quarrel with Job Charnock. See pp. 2, 5.

29 Susil Chaudhuri, *Trade and Commercial Organization in Bengal 1650–1720*, Calcutta, 1975, pp. 222–223; Hedges, *Diary*, Vol. 1, p. 89.

30 Heimann, "Small Change," p. 52, believes there was some French encroachment on the Maldive trade late in the seventeenth century.

31 The quotation is a translation and paraphrase from the Dutch archives by Om Prakash, "The European Trading Companies and the Merchants of Bengal 1650–1725," *Indian Social and Economic History Review*, Vol. 1, No. 3, 1963/4, p. 47.

32 A statement to this effect is made in Bowrey, *Bay of Bengal*, p. 152. There was a small port at nearby Pipli, but it went out of operation because of silting in about 1670. See Om Prakash, "Asian Trade and European Impact: a Study of the Trade from Bengal, 1630–1720," in Blair B. King and M. N. Pearson, *The Age of Partnership: Europeans in Asia before Dominion*, Honolulu, 1979, p. 51.

33 Alexander Hamilton, *A New Account of the East Indies*, ed. Sir William Foster, London, 1930 [1727], pp. 217–218. Good descriptions can be found in Bowrey, *Bay of Bengal*, pp. 162–163.

34 According to S. Chaudhuri, *Trade*, p. 22. Yule's claim that the Balasore factory was established in January 1651, after some occupation from time to time since 1642 (Hedges, *Diary*, Vol. 3, p. 194, and followed by Hogendorn, "Supply-Side," p. 38) is clearly wrong, says Chaudhuri. There is an historical survey of the English at Balasore in C. R. Wilson, *Early Annals of the English in Bengal*, London, Vol. 1, 1895.

35 Bowrey, *Bay of Bengal*, pp. 162, 183.

36 S. Chaudhuri, *Trade*, p. 87; Prakash, "European Trading Companies," *passim*.

37 We have already noted the purchases at Surat. See also Bowrey, *Bay of Bengal*, p. 219. Prakash, "Asian Trade," p. 58, notes some volume data in the trade from Balasore to the Maldives, which was increasing toward the end of the century. Balasore exported 1,005 tonnes of rice to the Maldives in 1680–81, and 1,879 tonnes in 1697–98. Coarse cotton textile shipments rose from 1,200 pieces in 1680–81 to 2,600 in 1699–1700. Opium exports were 205 lbs. in 1682–83; 369 lbs. in 1697–98. (Some of the data were originally in maunds. There are approximately 82 lbs. to a maund.)

38 Bowrey, *Bay of Bengal*, p. 179, a notice of a Balasore merchantman in the Maldives trade, p. 75, and a report by a Danish warship that five Bengali ships were lying in Balasore Roads with considerable cargoes "from Ceylon and Maldivae Insulae," p. 186.

39 S. Chaudhuri, *Trade*, pp. 73–74, 89–90, 92–93; Prakash, "European Trading Companies," pp. 54–55, who notes that the Maldive market was becoming more attractive to indigenous shipowners being squeezed out of other markets by the European companies' maritime pass system, and the declining interest of local shipowners in making the trip to Ceylon (pp. 49–50); Hedges, *Diary*, Vol. 1, p. 95.

40 Prakash, "European Trading Companies," p. 50.

41 *Ibid.*, especially pp. 38–45. The commerce was apparently an increasing one. Prakash's figures show departures for the Maldives 1680–84 averaging 3.5 annually, with the figure 8.3 for six years between 1697 and 1707, p. 40. See also his "Asian Trade," pp. 58–59.

42 S. Chaudhuri, *Trade*, p. 46; Prakash, "European Trading Companies," p. 55.

43 Horsburgh, "Remarks," p. 77.

44 Bowrey, *Bay of Bengal*, p. 219.

45 Marshall, *East India*, p. 419.

46 "Instructions to Mr. Stanley for the Maldevees," dated 20 Sept. 1682 and quoted in Bowrey, *Bay of Bengal*, p. 219, first footnote; Marshall, *East India*, p. 416; De, "Cowry in India," p. 9.

47 S. Chaudhuri, *Trade*, p. 48.

48 *Ibid.*, p. 47; Bowrey, *Bay of Bengal*, p. 166, n. 2; Hamilton, *East Indies*, p. 541. For the start of the Pilot Service, see Wilson, *Early Annals*, Vol. 1, p. 47.

5 Prosperity for the cowrie commerce

1 John Barbot, *North and South-Guinea*, pp. 338–339. We have modernized some of the spelling. The passage in the 1732 published account is an expansion, possibly by Barbot himself, of that in the French manuscript of 1688.

2 Perlin, "Money-Use," pp. 40–41, 96. A source on Bengal's monetary conditions that we have utilized is Narendra K. Sinha, *The Economic History of Bengal*, Calcutta, 1956–1970.
3 Perlin, "Money-Use," p. 97.
4 Quiggin, *Primitive Money*, p. 193, who notes that large warehouses were used to store the tax collections, which sometimes arrived in boatloads of 50 tons; Yule and Burnell, *Hobson-Jobson*, p. 271; Heimann, "Small Change," p. 57 and 67 n. 102, quoting D. C. Sircar, ed., *Land System and Feudalism in Ancient India*, Calcutta, 1966, p. 49; Perlin, "Money-Use."
5 Sukumar Bhattacharya, *The East India Company and the Economy of Bengal*, London, 1954, p. 189, which describes the important shell works at Dacca and its production of decorative chains and bracelets. This shell works obtained its cowries from Balasore via middlemen.
6 Heimann, "Small Change," p. 66 n. 95.
7 Perlin, "Money-Use," p. 97 n. 33; Khan Mohammad Moshin, *A Bengal District in Transition: Murshidabad 1765–1793*, Dacca, 1973, pp. 119–120.
8 Perlin, "Money-Use," p. 41.
9 *Ibid.*, p. 36; Moshin, *Bengal District*, pp. 118–120.
10 See K. N. Chaudhuri, *Trading World*, especially chapters 9, 11, 12, 14, and 15. For Bengal's rice economy see S. Chaudhuri, *Trade*, Appendix A.
11 Heimann, "Small Change," pp. 59–60, and Graph 1 following p. 13 of the earlier version of this paper, delivered at the International Conference on Indian Ocean Studies, Perth, Australia, 1979.
12 Heimann, "Small Change," p. 60; Sinha, *Bengal*, Vol. 1, pp. 142–144.
13 See footnote 11. The low 1778 cowrie price is an outlier.
14 P. J. Marshall, *East Indian Fortunes: the British in Bengal in the Eighteenth Century*, Oxford, 1976, p. 85, which notes the cowrie cargoes on Bengali ships about mid-century.
15 John Marshall, *East India*, quoted in Bowrey, *Bay of Bengal*, p. 162.
16 Hamilton, *East Indies*, p. 218.
17 *Ibid.*, pp. 192–193.
18 *Ibid.*, p. 218.
19 Prakash, "European Trading Companies," p. 55, and "Asian Trade," p. 59. The bankruptcy at Balasore in 1716 of a local ship just returned from the Maldives, and the public sale of it and its cowrie cargo, is described by Wilson, *Early Annals*, Vol. 2, Part 1, p. 263. For a general account of indigenous sea-borne trade during this period see A. Dasgupta, "Indian Merchants and the Trade in the Indian Ocean," in Tapan Raychaudhuri and Irfan Habib, *The Cambridge Economic History of India*, Vol. 1, *c. 1200–c. 1750*, Cambridge, 1982, pp. 407–433.
20 Bell, *Maldive Islands* (1883), p. 100. Bell's translation of the sultan's letter says "ships from Bellapor and Bengal."
21 Bhattacharya, *East India Company*, p. 124.
22 *Ibid.*, p. 89.
23 *Ibid.*, p. 86. The French had a factory there for many years. Hamilton, *East Indies*, p. 218.
24 Sinha, *Bengal*, Vol. 1, p. 38; Vincent A. Smith, "Political Geography, Government, and Administration," in A. J. Herbertson and O. J. R. Howarth, eds., *The Oxford Survey of the British Empire*, Vol. 2, *Asia*, Oxford, 1914, p. 295.
25 Kalikinkar Datta, "The Dutch Factory at Balasore and Anglo-Dutch Hostilities There in 1786–87," *Indian Historical Records Commission*, Vol. 19, 1942, p. 87.
26 *Ibid.*, p. 86.
27 Thomas Thornton, *Oriental Commerce*, London, 1825, p. 181. Also see pp. 249–250.
28 Boxer, *Dutch Seaborne Empire*, pp. 197, 222–223. A source utilized but not otherwise quoted here is F. S. Gaastra, "De V.O.C. in Azië 1680–1795," in *Algemene Geschiedenis der Nederlanden*, Vol. 9, Haarlem, 1980, pp. 427–464.

29 Klinkenberg thesis, p. 63.
30 Bell, *Maldive Islands* (1883), p. 99; "Dutch Intercourse," p. 138.
31 Klinkenberg thesis, p. 62, and his description of the route from the Maldives to Ceylon, pp. 43–45.
32 Sri Lanka National Archives (S.L.N.A.), H. C. P. Bell Collection, "Missives from Dutch Governors, 1700–1795," English translations, Letters for 1712, 1713, 1715, 1716, 1717, 1718.
33 Bell Collection, "Missives," Letter for 1720. The pattern of departing in November seems to have dated from 1699. A second departure occurred in January. For the timing, see J. R. Bruijn, "Between Batavia and the Cape: Shipping Patterns of the Dutch East India Company." A paper presented at the International Conference on Indian Ocean Studies, Perth, Australia, 1979, p. 4.
34 Bell Collection, "Missives," Letter for 1722. See also a follow-up letter dated December 17, 1722, which calls for the next year's batch to arrive in October and November.
35 *Ibid.*, Letter for 1728.
36 Bell, *Maldive Islands* (1883), p. 100; "Dutch Intercourse," p. 239; Hockly, *Two Thousand Isles*, p. 75, quoting a letter by Governor Loten to incoming Governor Schreuder; VOC 1976 KA 1868, 5 March 1722.
37 Klinkenberg thesis, pp. 46–59. The total weight carried is calculated in Amsterdams ponds on p. 58. See also Bell, *Maldive Islands* (1883), pp. 99–100.
38 Bell Collection, "Missives," Letter dated 1723.
39 H. C. P. Bell speaks of "the disgusted acquiescence of the Maldive Sultan, forced to accept, with very obvious reluctance, the unconscionable bargains made by a fresh European race too powerful to resist . . . grinding terms." "Portuguese," pp. 111–112. He points to huge mark-ups (about 15 to 30 times) between the buying and selling prices of the spices in the voyage of 1727. Bell, *Maldive Islands* (1883), p. 100.
40 Bell Collection, "Missives," Letter dated 1723; Bell, *Maldive Islands* (1883), p. 100.
41 Sinnappah Arasaratnam, *Dutch Power in Ceylon 1658–1687*, Amsterdam, 1958, p. 209, quoting KA 799 fo. 310.
42 Bell, *Maldive Islands* (1883), p. 31.
43 Klinkenberg thesis, pp. 32–33; Prakash, "European Trading Companies," p. 50.
44 Bell, *Maldive Islands* (1883), pp. 98–101; "Description," p. 138; "Dutch Intercourse," p. 228; Datta, "Dutch Factory," pp. 88–89; De, "Cowry in India," p. 10. The argument about complete mastery in the slave trade can be found in WIC 98 (Dutch Archives, The Hague), De la Palma, 26 June 1702: "If your Highnesses were to persist by resolving to be masters of the importation of all, buying them 'a tou prix' [*sic*], we can assure you that in that way we would set the Law to all nations; they would have to regulate themselves to our will, and we would be complete masters of the Slave Trade." Other price data is in Heimann, "Small Change," pp. 53–58, and graph 1 of his Perth Conference paper. In our 1795 price calculation, we used the rix-dollar/rupee exchange rate suggested in "Small Change," p. 65 n. 66. The Dutch also had the influence to redefine the *kotta* of 12,000 cowries at 25 lb., instead of 24 lb. To the extent that shells were purchased by weight instead of tale (rare, we believe), this worked to their advantage. Bell, *Maldive Islands* (1883), p. 119, and "Description," p. 138.
45 Bell, *Maldive Islands* (1883), pp. 99, 100.
46 C. P. Lucas, *A Historical Geography of the British Colonies*, Vol. 1, *The Mediterranean and Eastern Colonies*, Oxford, 1906, p. 129.
47 S.L.N.A., Bell Collection, "Missives from Dutch Governors," Letter for 1721.
48 *Ibid.*, Letter for 1727.
49 *Ibid.*, Letter for 1735.
50 *Ibid.*, "Miscellaneous Extracts," 25.16–22.
51 Bell, *Maldive Islands* (1883), p. 101. Other statements on the supposed Dutch monopoly,

pro and con, may be found in Heimann, "Small Change," p. 53, and the Klinkenberg thesis, p. 60.

52 S.L.N.A., Bell Collection, "Miscellaneous Extracts," 25.16–318C.

53 Bell, *Maldive Islands* (1883), p. 101.

54 The Dutch Company appears to have had a very large final inventory of shells when it was wound up. We cannot at present prove this point but the annual "cowrie purchases" by the V.O.C. in the years just before 1793 are vastly larger than "cowrie sales." As is explained in chapter 7, some part of this represents substandard shells that were sorted and discarded and foreign matter cleaned from the shells. Part of the gap is, however, probably additions to stock. Most of the shells referred to entered England from Germany, as is shown in the series "English Imports from the Continent of Europe" compiled by M. Johnson (not reproduced here).

55 Dutch Gentleman, *Voyage*, pp. 21–22.

56 Useful background sources for this section include Sinha's *Economic History of Bengal*; K. N. Chaudhuri, "European Trade with India," in Raychaudhuri and Habib, *Cambridge Economic History of India*, Vol. 1, pp. 382–407; and Chaudhuri's massive *The Trading World of Asia and the English East India Company*, Cambridge, 1978.

57 Wilson, *Early Annals*, Vol. 2, Part 1, pp. xxxiii–xxxiv.

58 Prakash, "European Trading Companies," p. 62 n. 42. This letter was from the headquarters of the "New" E.I.C. in the short period of joint existence of two companies, old and new. (The final merger was in 1708–09).

59 Examples include the many references in Wilson, *Early Annals*, Vol. 1; Datta, "Dutch Factory," p. 87; Perlin, "Money-Use," p. 95 n. 27 and the archival material quoted there; Holden Furber, *John Company at Work*, Cambridge, 1948, p. 290.

60 Yule and Burnell, *Hobson-Jobson*, p. 271, quoting records at Fort William transcribed by James Long.

61 *Ibid.*, p. 270; Furber, *John Company*, pp. 289–290; Perlin, "Money-Use," p. 9. For a discussion of the rights of E.I.C. captains to import on their personal account, see C. Northcote Parkinson, *Trade in the Eastern Seas 1793–1813*, Cambridge, 1937, p. 201.

62 Thomas Bowrey, *The Papers of Thomas Bowrey*, ed. R. C. Temple, London, 1927, pp. 219–228. The commercial instructions to Captain Tolson of the *Mary Galley*, involving possible calls at Muscat and Batavia and many products, are complex. The ship was, of course, not really a galley as the term is understood today.

63 Sinha, *Bengal*, Vol. 1, p. 52; Bell, "Description," p. 138.

64 Furber, *John Company*, pp. 289–290; Datta, "Dutch Factory," pp. 86–89.

65 Heimann, "Small Change," p. 54 and n. 83, citing Robert Moresby, *Nautical Directions for the Maldiva Islands and the Chagos Archipelago*, London, 1840.

66 Berbain, *Juda*, p. 82.

67 Sinha, *Bengal*, Vol. 1, p. 35; Berbain, *Juda*; Indrani Ray, "The French Company and the Merchants of Bengal (1680–1730)," *The Indian Economic and Social History Review*, Vol. 8, No. 1, 1971, pp. 41–55.

68 Berbain, *Juda*, pp. 82–83. In the Dutch archives Klinkenberg found a survey ("overzicht") of the European cowrie trade, 1730–35 (VOC 7000/KA 12235), that shows exceptionally large French shipments in 1732–33. He believes the figures may be exaggerated, however. See the Klinkenberg thesis, pp. 18–19.

69 Berbain, *Juda*, p. 83; Léon Vignols and Henri Sée, "Les Ventes de la Compagnie des Indes à Nantes (1723–1733)," *Revue d'histoire des colonies françaises*, Vol. 13, No. 4, 1925, p. 491.

70 Vignols and Sée, "Les Ventes," pp. 511–512; S.L.N.A., Bell Collection, "Missives," Letter for 1721; Bell, *Maldive Islands* (1883), p. 99.

71 Bell, *Maldive Islands* (1883), p. 31.

72 VOC 1876 KA 1868.

73 Sinha, *Bengal*, Vol. 1, pp. 35–36.
74 S.L.N.A., Bell Collection, "Miscellaneous Extracts," 25.16–22.
75 Bell, *Maldive Islands* (1883), p. 33; Gardiner, "Maldive Archipelago," p. 320; Lucas, *British Colonies*, p. 126.
76 Lucas, *British Colonies*, p. 126.
77 Sinha, *Bengal*, Vol. 1, p. 36; Berbain, *Juda*, p. 83.
78 Berbain, *Juda*; Sinha, *Bengal*, pp. 36–37.
79 Sinha, *Bengal*, p. 52 n. 11. We believe the 20,000 figure is a misprint for 2,000 (= 50,000 lbs.) Heimann, "Small Change," pp. 53–54 uses 2,000 when quoting this source.
80 Bell, "Description," p. 138.
81 J. Beckmann, *Vorbereitung zur Waarenkunde*, Göttingen, 1793, p. 361, has the Danish figure. The "overzicht" in the Dutch archives noted in footnote 68 shows shipments of moderate size by the Ostend Company in 1734 (Klinkenberg thesis, p. 18). Bell, *Maldive Islands* (1883), p. 31; Berbain, *Juda*, p. 82.

6 Boom and slump for the cowrie trade

1 EIC auctioning early in the nineteenth century is noted by Yule and Burnell, *Hobson-Jobson*, p. 270.
2 Coir exports are mentioned by Parkinson, *Eastern Seas*.
3 The customs records for 1813 are missing, owing to a fire at the Customs House, and are not included in the average. British cowrie export figures between 1810 and 1815 averaged about 5½ tonnes per year. See also M. Johnson, "Cowrie Currencies," Part 1, p. 22.
4 The consequences of the restriction in cowrie imports to Africa are discussed in the framework of an economic model by Jan S. Hogendorn and Henry A. Gemery, "Abolition and Its Impact on Monies Imported to West Africa," in David Eltis and James Walvin, *The Abolition of the Atlantic Slave Trade*, Madison, 1981. It is at this period that "cut money" – silver dollars cut into quarters – began to appear in West Africa.
5 For taxes and tribute, see Yule and Burnell, *Hobson-Jobson*, p. 271; De, "Orissa," p. 15. For estimates of imports see the testimony quoted in De, "Orissa," pp. 18–19. The figures in the testimony are in rupee values. We have converted to tonnes by using an approximate equivalency of 1 rupee = 5,120 shells, or 172 rupees = one tonne (following William Milburne, *Oriental Commerce*, London, 1813, Vol. 2, p. 108.) This is our only volume estimate for the trade to Bengal and Orissa at a time when African imports were moribund. Aside from the Indian demand for cowries as money, and as charms and amulets, one other use was noted by Edouard Foà: "Il n'est pas inutile, peut-être, de dire que le cauris sert, au Bengale, a faire du stuc; on le pile dans un mortier après l'avoir calciné, en y mélangeant du lait caillé et du sucre. Cette pâté, lorsqu'elle est étendue sur les murs et polie, imite parfaitement le mabre," *Le Dahomey*, p. 149.
6 For tax collections in silver, see De, "Orissa," p. 13. For the copper coinage see Furber, *John Company*, pp. 287–289; Sinha, *Bengal*, pp. 143–144; Yule and Burnell, *Hobson-Jobson*; Heimann, "Small Change," p. 60.
7 Furber, *John Company*, p. 289.
8 De, "Orissa," pp. 13–20; Heimann, "Small Change," p. 60. A business decline in northeast India during the 1820s again raised the demand for cowries. (This is not the paradox it seems – depression would tend to create a shortage of the official currency which leaked into tax payments and imports, and cowries were intrinsically more suited to transactions at very low prices than was copper). This interruption in the long-term ebb of shell money in Bengal and Orissa was only temporary. See Heimann, "Small Change."
9 See note 65, chapter 5.
10 Colin W. Newbury, "Prices and Profitability in Early Nineteenth Century West African

Trade," in Claude Meillassoux, ed., *The Development of Indigenous Trade and Markets in West Africa*, London, 1971, p. 92.

11 *Ibid.*

12 The lack of nautical knowledge leading to the surveys is noted by H. T. Fry, "Early British Interest in the Chagos Archipelago and the Maldive Islands," *The Mariner's Mirror*, Vol. 53, No. 4, 1967, pp. 343–356. See especially the comments on the wreck of HMS *Cato*, 50, in the 1780s that prompted the initial interests in charting. There are several references to the expedition itself, the main one being Lieutenant I. A. Young and W. Christopher, "Memoir on the Inhabitants of the Maldiva Islands," *Transactions of the Bombay Geographical Society 1836–1838*, Vol. 1, 1844, pp. 54–86. The captain (Robert Moresby) wrote a far less informative account, "Captain Moresby's Report on the Maldives," *Transactions of the Bombay Geographical Society 1836–1838*, Vol. 1, 1844, pp. 102–108. See also the thesis by W. A. Spray, "Surveying and Charting the Indian Ocean: the British Contribution, 1750–1838," unpublished University of London Ph.D. thesis, 1966, especially chapter 9, "The Arabian Sea, the Maldives and the Vicinity, 1828–1838," pp. 367–396; Maloney, *People*, p. 127; Bell, *Maldive Islands* (1883), p. 36. The survey resulted in the first detailed maps of the atolls and their waters. Forbes, "Archives," p. 75.

13 Young and Christopher, "Maldiva Islands," pp. 82, 85, 86; Thornton, *Oriental Commerce*, pp. 181, 249, 264. Other foreign vessels visiting the islands at this time were from Galle in Ceylon, from the Malabar Coast of India, and from Muscat. (Ships from Malabar and Muscat probably did not carry many cowries in the nineteenth century). Young and Christopher, p. 82.

14 Young and Christopher, "Maldiva Islands," pp. 83–85.

15 *Ibid.*, p. 84.

16 Bell, *Maldive Islands* (1883), p. 101.

17 Young and Christopher, "Maldiva Islands," pp. 71–72.

18 Bell's account of the "doubled" poll tax is in the Sri Lanka National Archives, Bell Collection, 25.16–113, "Diary Notes on Taxation at the Maldives," especially p. 5; Taylor's information is from H. C. P. Bell, *The Maldive Islands, Ceylon Sessional Paper No. 15 of 1921*, Colombo, 1921, p. 34. The same volume has Bell's additional description of taxes on various atolls, 1917–1922: see, for example, pp. 96, 99. Especial thanks to Mohamed Ahmad, who undertook to ask the old people of Mahibadoo Island, Ari Atoll, a series of questions on taxation posed by Hogendorn during the latter's fieldwork of 1982. Rosset, "On the Maldive Islands," p. 168.

19 *Encyclopaedia Britannica*, 13th edn., Vol. 8, p. 835.

20 Not all the shells in Table 6.1 were produced at the Maldives. By the 1840s, occasional lots of *moneta* were coming from other sources as well. Marion Johnson's data show about 45 tonnes imported from the Philippines in both 1846 and 1849, and even more from Singapore in 1847 (66 tonnes) and 1850 (55 tonnes), plus lesser amounts in other years. Some of the shells would have been *moneta*. But a proportion must also have been *Cypraea annulus*, the larger ring-cowrie found most abundantly in East Africa. (*Annulus* became acceptable in West African markets from the mid-1840s, as is discussed later in this chapter.) John Hertz thought the Philippine shells resembled the large Zanzibars rather than the small Maldives. Hertz, "Kauriemuschel," p. 25. "Dutch Gentleman" said the Philippine cowries "don't come up to the *Maldivian*, either in Colour or Clearness," *Voyage*, p. 22.

21 Coincidentally, 1844 was the year of the last known maritime contact between the Maldives and Portugal (until modern times). The convict transport *Prazer e Allegria* went hard aground and broke up; in contradistinction to earlier days, the 104 Portuguese survivors were well-treated. At Male they saw 19 native vessels, including four brigs from Chittagong, in the harbor their kinsmen had once ruled. Bell, "Portuguese," pp. 112–116.

22 Hertz, "Kauriemuschel," pp. 14–29. See pp. 14–15 for mentions of Chittagong. Contrary to

the practice in the Dutch days, the supply of cowries flowing to Ceylon was warehoused there only temporarily for reshipment to Bengal and further re-export from there. Not until about 1840 was it usual for shipments to be sent directly from Ceylon to Europe. See Bell, *Maldive Islands* (1883), p. 105. After that date, as the boom progressed, such direct shipments to Britain from Ceylon grew to fairly substantial proportions. There is further information on the Hertz firm in Hermann Kellenbenz, "German Trade Relations with the Indian Ocean from the End of the 18th Century to 1870," a paper presented at the International Conference on Indian Ocean Studies, Perth, Australia, 1979, p. 10.

23 There is a lengthy discussion of the quantities and values of rice imported to the Maldives from Bengal in Bell, *Maldiva Islands* (1883), p. 107. Rice imports were much larger in value than the next most desired items, cloth and areca nuts. Captain W. F. W. Owen of the Royal Navy had commented a decade before the Hertz visit on the ubiquity of Bengali rice in the Maldive diet: "They import much rice, which enters as a main article of their food in a great variety of messes, and when boiled simply, is used as a substitute for bread. It is also boiled, dried, and then ground into a flour, which is mixed with eggs, honey, or with milk or oil of the cocoa-nut, and thus makes excellent tarts and other dishes." Owen, "On the Same Subject," [the Geography of the Maldiva Islands], *Journal of the Royal Geographical Society*, Vol. 2, 1832, p. 86.

24 Hertz, "Kauriemuschel," pp. 14–15.

25 *Ibid.*, p. 15.

26 Young and Christopher, "Maldiva Islands," p. 85. See also Bell, *Maldive Islands* (1883), p. 104, and Owen, "Same Subject," p. 83.

27 Hertz, "Kauriemuschel," p. 15. Ernst Hieke, *Zur Geschichte des Deutschen Handels mit Ostafrika*, Hamburg, 1939, Vol. 1, p. 73.

28 Hertz, "Kauriemuschel," p. 15.

29 *Ibid.*, and Hieke, *Deutschen Handels*, Vol. 1, p. 73. Melitz thinks one reason *annulus* was unacceptable during much of the trade was that it is less attractive than *moneta, Money*, p. 109. We find it difficult to agree.

30 Hertz, "Kauriemuschel," pp. 15–16. Hertz exaggerated somewhat, we think. A hundredweight of Maldive *moneta* should contain a little less than 45,000 shells (44,800 at 400 to the pound) while various estimates of Zanzibar *annulus* range from 20,000 to 24,000 per cwt.

31 G. S. P. Freeman-Grenville, *The French at Kilwa Island*, Oxford, 1965, p. 120.

32 For the British trade see *ibid.*, p. 114, and Thornton, *Oriental Commerce*, p. 39; a French shipload from north Mozambique in 1776 is noted in the log of a Dutch ship, VOC 90283, 306v.; imports to Bengal from "gulf of Persia and Arabia" are noted by Milburne, *Oriental Commerce*, Vol. 2, p. 143, quoted by Heimann, "Small Change," p. 69 n. 144. The Portuguese shipments from Mozambique are mentioned by Fritz Hoppe, *A África Oriental Portuguesa no tempo do Marquês de Pombal (1750–1777)*, Lisbon, 1970, pp. 76, 136–137, 198, 224, 232, 245, 252 (this page notes both English and French shipments from the Querimba Islands), 269. Hoppe notes what must have been a very occasional shipment from the Querimba Islands via Mozambique to Bahia in Brazil, whence they were sent to the Slave Coast. See p. 227. There is further mention of the Mozambique shipments to India in M. A. H. Fitzler, *Die Handelsgesellschaft Felix v. Oldenburg & Co. 1753–1760*, Stuttgart, 1931, p. 137. For the reverse flow from Bengal to East Africa see Forbes and Ali, "Maldive Islands," p. 228.

33 T. Fowell Buxton, *The Slave Trade*, London, 1838, p. 228.

34 Hertz, "Kauriemuschel," pp. 16–17; Hieke, *Deutschen Handels*, Vol. 1, p. 131; P. Verger, "Influence de Brésil au Golfe du Benin" (letters of dos Santos), pp. 67 ff., in *Les Afro-Américains*, Mémoire d'IFAN 27, Dakar, 1952, p. 67.

35 For types of cargo, see Kellenbenz, "German Trade Relations," p. 6. Direct trade is noted by Curtin, "Wider Monetary World," p. 18. At one point, Robert E. C. Stearns states,

fourteen vessels were engaged in bringing cowries from the East Coast, "Ethno-Concho-logy," p. 302. Hieke, *Deutschen Handels*, Vol. 1, p. 116, discusses the decline of the direct trade.

36 Hieke, *Deutschen Handels*, Vol. 1, pp. 73 ff., 109–113, 118, 124; Kellenbenz, "German Trade Relations," pp. 3, 6, 10; Percy Ernst Schramm, *Deutschland und Übersee*, Braunsch-weig, 1950, pp. 318, 331 ff.; B. Schnapper, *La Politique et le commerce français dans le golfe de Guinée de 1838 à 1876*, Paris, 1961, quoting Loarer, "Rapport commercial sur la côte orientale d'Afrique," p. 123, a manuscript dated 1851 in Arch. CCM, série OK, explorations commerciales; C. W. Newbury, *The Western Slave Coast and Its Rulers*, Oxford, 1961, pp. 57–59. Hieke and Newbury both discuss O'Swald and the direct trade from East Africa.

37 Hertz claimed that the French competition led to a big price rise at the source in Zanzibar, and a decline in the quality of shipments with many dead shells mixed in. An especial surge of demand took place at Zanzibar in 1849, according to Hieke, *Deutschen Handels*, Vol. 1, p. 110. The sudden spurt in shell exports was obvious to any visitor. At the factories of the Europeans (unlike the Maldives) the shells were dried on rooftops, and damaged cowries were used to make a macadam-style pavement for the streets on these buildings. The practice caught on, and before long even the walks and ways by the sultan's palace were paved with the same material. Hertz, "Kauriemuschel," pp. 16, 18. Another difference, compared with the Maldives, was that *annulus* was traded at Zanzibar by weight rather than by number. See Hieke, *Deutschen Handels*, Vol. 1, p. 73. A. G. Hopkins, "Currency Revolution," p. 474, says Régis began to compete "about 1855"; Hertz (p. 18) says 1857. Hieke (p. 129) says the competition from that firm intensified in 1857. Victor Régis was in association with Augustin Fabre & Son. O'Swald sold out their West African cowrie operations in 1869, Hopkins, "Currency revolution," p. 474. Also see Schnapper, *La Politique*, p. 191.

38 See especially Hieke, *Deutschen Handels*, pp. 74–75, 283; Hertz, "Kauriemuschel," pp. 15–16; and Curtin, "Wider Monetary World," p. 18. Interestingly, the British export series shows some significant exports to "Continent of Europe" in the years 1845–1850. This may represent German firms supplementing their own supplies by purchasing at London, and could include some *annulus*.

39 Melitz, *Money*, p. 109, speaks of the strung combination.

40 Hertz, "Kauriemuschel," p. 23, quoting Burton; L. G. Binger, "Transactions, objets de commerce, monnaie des contrées entre le Niger et la Côte d'Or," quoted by Raymond Mauny, *Tableau géographique de l'ouest africain au Moyen Age*, Dakar, 1961, pp. 417, 550; Schneider, *Muschelgeld-Studien*, pp. 169–170, quoting Mischlich and Speith. Schneider (p. 148) says *annulus* had come to be far more plentiful than *moneta* in Togo.

41 Schneider, *Muschelgeld-Studien*, p. 146; A. G. Krause, *Fada Language on the Gabon River in Portuguese West Africa*, Berlin, 1895, p. 371 ff.

42 G. T. Basden, *Among the Ibos of Nigeria*, London, 1921, p. 198.

43 Schneider, *Muschelgeld-Studien*, p. 135, quoting Dr. E. Zingtgraff.

44 The price index is calculated from the data in chapter 9. See also Curtin, "Wider Monetary World," p. 18, and Hopkins, "Currency Revolution," p. 476, where the figures show a slightly greater depreciation. The subject was also treated by Hopkins in his unpublished University of London Ph.D. thesis, "An Economic History of Lagos, 1880–1914," 1964, pp. 170–181. The depreciation of cowries was caused not only by increasing quantities on the supply side, but because of the greater use of dollars and sterling coins, and the stagnation of palm oil prices, which altered demand.

45 Bell, *Maldive Islands* (1883), p. 114. Bell also saw Indian port clearance records (p. 115) that apparently mirrored the decline in cowrie exports. In the five years 1848–52, 241 ships of 15,413 total tonnage entered British Indian ports, sailing from the Maldives. By comparison, in 1856–60 only 168 ships of 13,236 total tons were recorded, a decline of 30% in ships and 14% in tonnage.

46 *Ibid.*, p. 104.
47 Hopkins, "Currency Revolution," pp. 474–475.
48 For the role of Gaiser see Ernst Hieke, *G. L. Gaiser, Hamburg-Westafrika, 100 Jahre Handel mit Nigeria*, Hamburg, 1949, pp. 15–18, 30–32. Hopkins, "Currency Revolution," p. 475, notes that Lagos exported substantial quantities from about the middle 1870s. Most of these exports went to the Niger Delta, where cowrie values were slightly higher than at Lagos.
49 G. W. Neville, "West African Currency," *Journal of the African Society*, Vol. 17, 1918, p. 225.
50 Hopkins, "Currency Revolution," p. 475.
51 Walter Ibekwe Ofonagoro, "The Currency Revolution in Southern Nigeria, 1880–1948," Los Angeles, U.C.L.A. Occasional Paper No. 14, 1976, pp. 14, 29. This paper also appeared under the title, "From Traditional to British Currency in Southern Nigeria: Analysis of a Currency Revolution, 1880–1948," *Journal of Economic History*, Vol. 39, No. 3, 1979, pp. 623–654.
52 Jan S. Hogendorn, *Nigerian Groundnut Exports: Origins and Early Development*, Ibadan and Zaria, 1978, p. 66.
53 Michel Leduc, *Les Institutions monétaires africaines: pays francophones*, Paris, 1965, p. 14.

7 Collection, transport and distribution

1 Hieke, *Deutschen Handels*, Vol. 1, p. 70.
2 Monrad, *Küste von Guinea*, p. 162. For the sake of sailors and citizens of seaports, one hopes the practice reported by Monrad was infrequent.
3 There is no reason to think that "Live Maldives" referred to shells shipped with the living shellfish inside.
4 A fourth method, even more dubious except perhaps to determined anti-Darwinists, is "digging from the ground." "Dutch Gentleman," on p. 19 of his *Voyage*, tells of "prodigious Quantities . . . in the very Ground, being probably deposited there at the time of the Flood, and left there when the Ocean receded from the Land."
5 In addition to the references in chapter 2, see Gray and Bell, *Pyrard*, Vol. 2, pp. 429–432, 485. Captain Alexander Hamilton wrote in 1727 that "the Couries are caught by putting Branches of Cocoanut Trees with their Leaves on, into the Sea, and, in five or six months, the little Shell-fish sticks to those Leaves in Clusters," *East Indies*, p. 192. Finally, Foà wrote in 1895 that the cowries prefer to fix themselves on vegetable debris. The inhabitants of the islands thus cast whole coconut trees into the sea, and pull them in some days later laden with cowries, *Le Dahomey*, p. 147. Compare the reference here to "some days" ("au bout de quelques jours") in contrast to Hamilton's "five or six months." The "tree method" had apparently passed out of use long before Foà's account was written.
6 The full quotation is given in chapter 3, p. 34.
7 Bell, *Maldive Islands* (1883), p. 87. Hogendorn's informants indicated that 20% of that figure would today be considered a very good day's work. But the economic incentive for large output had declined over the intervening hundred years. An old miniature of cowrie fishing was said to be in the collection of Jean, duc de Berry (probably in his illustrated copy of Marco Polo).
8 By 1940 men and boys had dropped out from fishing for the shells. "To the women are left, well-nigh entirely, . . . the collection of cowries." Bell, *Maldive Islands* (1940).
9 Owen, "Same Subject," pp. 82–83. The story is repeated by Hertz, "Kauriemuschel," p. 25, and by "An Officer, Late of the Ceylon Rifles" in his book *Ceylon*, London, 1876, p. 418. Both were obviously following Owen's account.
10 See chapter 2, p. 23.
11 Chapter 2, pp. 24–25. The information that burial preserves the shiny surface better than

Notes to pages 82–85

sun-drying was provided by Mr. Ahmad Shahiku of Male. As Assistant Director of the Ministry of Information and Broadcasting, Mr. Shahiku is interested in the history of the cowrie trade. The Officer of the Ceylon Rifles said in the nineteenth century the shells were piled up to rot, p. 418, but then he also got the fishing method wrong (see note 9).

12 Chapter 3, p. 29; John Marshall, *East India*, p. 416; Hamilton, *East Indies*, p. 192.
13 Bell, *Maldive Islands* (1883), p. 87.
14 Washing is explicitly mentioned by Captain Owen, "Same Subject," p. 83.
15 Bell, "Description," p. 135. (Doubts are expressed below as to the complete accuracy of the months mentioned by this source.)
16 Hedges, *Diary*, Vol. 1, p. 192.
17 Bell, "Description," p. 135. Hogendorn was more sceptical of this figure in his "Supply-side," p. 49, than he is now. Although it is unlikely that the African trade alone would have justified stocks of this size, together with the Bengal trade it might have done.
18 Bell, *Maldive Islands* (1883), p. 87, and "Description," pp. 135, 140. In a letter from Ceylon dated 11 May 1721 (VOC 1956 KA 1848), Governor Rumpf makes reference to corners of the cowrie packages sticking awkwardly above the horizontal layer of cargo, which must refer to the *kottas* loaded for shipment to the Netherlands.
19 Hamilton, *East Indies*, p. 192, and Bell, *Maldive Islands* (1883), p. 102.
20 Hamilton, *East Indies*, p. 192. The rattan sails were succeeded by sailcloth only about 1890 according to Philip K. Crowe, *Diversions of a Diplomat in Ceylon*, London, 1957, p. 290; pp. 289–290 have an interesting description of Maldive boats.
21 Young and Christopher, "Maldiva Islands," pp. 85–86; Bell, *Maldive Islands* (1883), p. 102.
22 Young and Christopher, "Maldiva Islands," p. 86.
23 Reginald Heber, *Narrative of a Journey through the Upper Provinces of India from Calcutta to Bombay 1824–25*, London, 1828, Vol. 1, pp. 19–20.
24 For a tongue-in-cheek account see J. S. Hogendorn, "Research-Trip to the Maldives."
25 Young and Christopher, "Maldiva Islands," p. 85; Bell, *Maldive Islands* (1883), p. 102. João de Barros notes navigation only "during the monsoons, which are seasons of fair winds, regular in their direction, for three months at a time." For the remainder of the year "they do not go to sea," Gray and Bell, *Pyrard*, Vol. 2, pp. 482–483. Notice the discrepancy between these accounts and the earlier statement by the Captain of the *Britannia* (?) that the Bengal shipping departed in November and December; but all clearly point to annual sailings when winds were favorable.
26 For a passage by al-Idrisi in a different translation from that used in chapter 2, employed because it makes the point of a royal monopoly more clearly, see Gray and Bell, *Pyrard*, Vol. 2, p. 432.
27 See chapters 3 and 4; Bell, "Description," p. 135; Hedges, *Diary*, Vol. 1, p. 192.
28 Philalethes, *The Boscawen's Voyage to Bombay*, 1740, p. 52, quoted by Yule and Burnell, *Hobson-Jobson*, p. 271; Abbé Prèvôt, (Abrégé de) *Histoire Générale des Voyages*, Paris, 1780, Vol. 4, p. 82. "Le rois même et les seigneurs exprès des lieux, ou ils conservent des amas de ces fragiles richesses, qu'ils regardent comme une partie de leur trésor."
29 Bell, *Maldive Islands* (1883), p. 101.
30 Hertz, "Kauriemuschel," pp. 14–15. The rice trade is emphasized by Owen, "Same Subject," p. 86.
31 Young and Christopher, "Maldiva Islands," p. 82.
32 Rosset, "On the Maldive Islands," pp. 166–167, and his article "The Maldive Islands," *The Graphic*, Oct. 16, 1886, p. 416. H. C. P. Bell wrote under the heading "Modern Trade, A.D. 1830–80," that "the whole of the export and import trade of the islands is conducted at Male," *Maldive Islands* (1883), p. 101.
33 Bell, "Description," p. 135; *Maldive Islands* (1883), p. 102; Rosset, "The Maldive Islands," p. 416, and "On the Maldive Islands," pp. 166–168; Allan, "Coinage," pp. 313–

322; and Gray and Bell, *Pyrard*, where the system of nobility is discussed at length in various chapters. Heimann, "Small Change," pp. 50–51, points to the prestige value of eating imported rice as a prop to the hierarchy of status. Rosset says there was a 12% tax on imports only, paid in rice, cloth, and cowries.

34 See, for example, Heimann, "Small Change," p. 52.

35 See chapter 2; Barbot, "North and South-Guinea," p. 338; Perlin, "Money-Use," p. 93.

36 Glamann, *Dutch-Asiatic Trade*, p. 25.

37 See the full account of the Indian saltpetre industry in K. N. Chaudhuri, *Trading World*, pp. 336–341, and the table of saltpetre shipments from Bengal, pp. 531–532.

38 Glamann, *Dutch-Asiatic Trade*, p. 25.

39 Information supplied by Femme Gaastra of the University of Leiden, whose students have undertaken studies of how V.O.C. cargo was packed. More often the cowries were carried above the bilge as ballast. Possibly loose ones might have fouled the pumps.

40 Ethel Bruce Sainsbury, *Court Minutes*, p. 395.

41 Klinkenberg thesis, p. 34; VOC 1956 KA 1848, dated 1721. At this time about 30% of the V.O.C. Indiamen sailed for home from ports in Ceylon. Jean Pierre Ricard, *Le Negoce d'Amsterdam*, Rouen, 1723, p. 382.

42 Don Weyers, *Opdract 14*, from VOC 2304 KA 2196, University of Leiden, 1978.

43 Gray and Bell, *Pyrard*, Vol. 1, p. 240. Governor Rumpf's description at Ceylon of horns of packages sticking out from a layer of cargo and requiring mats is an obvious reference to *kottas* of cowries. See note 18.

44 For the problem of adverse winds and currents, see two essays by Philip D. Curtin: "The Slave Trade and the Atlantic Basin: Intercontinental Perspectives," in Nathan I. Huggins, Martin Kilson, and Daniel M. Fox, eds., *Key Issues in the Afro-American Experience*, New York, 1971, pp. 79–80, and "The Atlantic Slave Trade 1600–1800," in J. F. A. Ajayi and Michael Crowder, eds., *History of West Africa*, New York, 1972, Vol. 1, pp. 246–247. The role of maritime technology on the West African coast is surveyed by H. A. Gemery and J. S. Hogendorn, "Technological Change, Slavery, and the Slave Trade," in Clive Dewey and A. G. Hopkins, eds., *The Imperial Impact: Studies in the Economic History of Africa and India*, London, 1978, pp. 255–258.

45 Fernand Braudel, *The Structures of Everyday Life*, Vol. 1 of *Civilization and Capitalism 15th–18th Century*, New York, 1981, p. 419, notes the unsuitability of the Indiamen for the African coast. There were usually thirty or more of the 500-ton class in the E.I.C. fleet toward the close of the eighteenth century, and forty or so of the 800-tonners. These vessels carried a man-of-war's armament, 26 to 32 guns for a 500-tonner, 36 to 38 (a large frigate's battery) for the 800-ton class. Interestingly, these ships were usually not owned by the Company, but were chartered from a ring of private shipbuilders capable of constructing such large craft. See C. Northcote Parkinson, "The East India Trade," in Parkinson, ed., *The Trade Winds: a Study of British Overseas Trade during the French Wars 1793–1815*, London, 1948, pp. 142–145.

46 For duration of the voyage, see Glamann, *Dutch-Asiatic Trade*, p. 26. Dutch shipping patterns are nicely surveyed in Bruijn, "Between Batavia and the Cape," particularly pp. 2–4.

47 Jacques Melitz is not correct in thinking that cowrie transport was mainly via a land route to Western Europe, *Money*, p. 110.

48 Whether the culled larger shells were *moneta* or other varieties deliberately or accidentally included in shipments from the Maldives, is not clear. Nor is it apparent what became of the larger sizes after the garbling. Some were sold to Brazilian ships on the coast, whose captains perhaps knew no better, or perhaps could palm them off along with their tobacco. Very small quantities of cowries were sent to the New World from time to time. These were probably for decorative rather than monetary or other commercial use. The declared value of these cowries was very low, so suggesting another answer to what happened to the large

185

cowries removed from the sorted lots. The same explanation probably accounts for small quantities sent occasionally to Ireland and the Channel Islands. A consignment of 7½ tons sent to the West Indies in 1714 is too large for this explanation to apply; perhaps the West India rum ships carried some cowries to serve as small change on their arrival in Africa. Klinkenberg compiled a series comparing Dutch imports from Asia to Amsterdam with sales at Kamer Amsterdam. The former figure was unsorted, the latter sorted. These data presumably include some transfers from Amsterdam to other *kamers*. Over nine decades of data, they indicate imports of 10,652,743 lbs. and exports of 7,684,994 lbs. An absolute maximum for sorting and cleaning was therefore 27% by weight of the shells originally imported. If the figures are correct, they probably indicate "foulness" (sand content) in the imported shells.

49 PRO T–70, Vol. 25, Oct. 19, 1723. Even in 1734, James Pearce was writing that the Dutch cowries were very good, "clean and garbled. . . . They will do better for us than those in England," PRO C103/130, Aug. 13 and 15, 1734. In T–70, Vol. 22, under the date Dec. 3, 1707, there is a list of goods proper for the market at Whydah: " . . . cowries, ye smaller in size ye better likt by Traders" which suggests that sizes were not well standardized. In T–70, Vol. 23, can be found a comment by Baldwin and Peet at Whydah dated Sept. 10, 1721: "We doubt your Honours will be very great sufferers by the largeness of your Bouges which generally hold out about seventeen pounds to a Grand Cabess, so that at the price they are invoiced for, your Honours give full eighteen pounds for a Man Slave for we are forced to pay fourteen Grand Cabess . . . in Goods you do not pay above Ten Pounds each which is a vast difference, but we humbly hope the next boogees will be better." Our thanks to Robin Law for this reference which suggests a shipment not well sorted.

50 RAC to Directors, United East India Company, T–70, Vol. 24, Sept. 2, 1722.
51 The accounts of the *Prince of Orange* in 1742 include the amount of £15 17s. 5d., "expenses in garbling the cowries brought home loose in this ship from India."
52 Glamann, *Dutch-Asiatic Trade*, pp. 27–28.
53 Surveyed in *ibid.*, p. 5, and the Klinkenberg thesis.
54 Glamann, *Dutch-Asiatic Trade*, pp. 25–26.
55 Our thanks to Femme Gaastra of the University of Leiden for first pointing out to us that cargo was not always divided in the proportions fixed by the V.O.C. charter.
56 Dutch Gentleman, *Voyage to Ceylon*, p. 22. It would be satisfying to know more of these warehouses, but P. van Emst could find no details during his search of the City of Amsterdam archives. "Weg van de Kauri," p. 274, n. 50.
57 Parkinson, "East India Trade," pp. 142, 154–155.
58 Berbain, *Juda*, p. 82. There is more detail in Johnson, Hogendorn, and Lynch, "European Cowrie Trade," *q.v.* The principal foreign buyers in London in the earlier part of the period after the end of the war in 1713 were Portugal and Madeira. In several years they accounted together for more English exports than Africa itself, but after the mid-1720s this market had largely disappeared. In the 1730s and early 1740s, and again at the end of that decade, a market for cowries developed in Flanders. Quantities were usually small, under 10 tonnes, but in 1743 reached nearly 70 tonnes, and in 1748 over 50 tonnes. English trade with West Africa was at a low ebb in the 1740s, owing to the French war and local troubles. See Table 7.1 for British exports to all European destinations, 1700–1790.
59 Prices are from the Royal African Company's invoices, PRO T–70/921–5, K. G. Davies, *The Royal African Company*, London, 1957, p. 357, and occasional ships' books.
60 Lindsell to Royal African Company, RAC (abstract) PRO T–70/19, January 4, 1716–17.
61 James Pearce to Hall, PRO C103/130, August 13 and October 15, 1734.
62 Elizabeth Donnan, *Documents Illustrative of the History of the Slave Trade to America*, Washington, 1931, Vol. 2, pp. 261–262, 309–311, 418, 466, 501, 520. Other references to buying in the Netherlands can be found in Sundström, *Exchange*, p. 94.
63 It was first published in Johnson, Hogendorn, and Lynch, "European Cowrie Trade,"

pp. 266–271. Davies, *Royal African Company*, p. 173 has other references to British cowrie buying in the Netherlands.

64 PRO T–70, Vol. 24, letter of September 21, 1722, and Vol. 25, letter of September 10, 1723. Letters from London are Old Style (O.S.), letters from Amsterdam New Style (N.S.). Holland and Zeeland had adopted the "new" Gregorian Calendar in 1582, but England did not do so until 1752.

65 PRO T–70, Vol. 25, Sept. 13, 1723, and Nov. 26, 1723. The pounds quoted here and henceforth are "Amsterdams ponds," about 10% heavier than one pound avoirdupois. One Amsterdams pond = 0.494 kg. One pound avoirdupois = 0.455 kg. Two thousand Amsterdam ponds are, conveniently, very close to one metric tonne, and a hundred such ponds are close to an English hundredweight (cwt. = 112 English pounds).

66 PRO T–70, Vol. 25, Sept. 13, 1723, Oct. 8, 1723, Oct. 19, 1723. The RAC in this very large transaction used casks containing 48% of the Dutch barrels. PRO T–70, Vol. 924, April 20, 1724. The Dutch themselves sometimes shipped shell in 366 lb. casks. See Ryder, *Benin*, p. 173 n. 2.

67 William Bosman, *A New and Accurate Description of the Coast of Guinea*, London, 2nd edn, 1721, reprinted 1967, p. 349. That sacks were still sometimes used as well as barrels is shown in a ship's account quoted by Berbain, *Juda*, p. 77.

68 PRO T–70, Vol. 25, Oct. 12, 1723. There were 20 stuivers to a guilder, and about 10 guilders to a British pound.

69 PRO T–70, Vol. 25, Oct. 12, 1723; Oct. 19, 1723.

70 *Ibid.*, Oct. 26, 1723. Wilkieson must indeed have believed he was facing competition "unlimited" by the price, as he argued that paying 15 stuivers would not have increased his share of the available shells.

71 His report (*ibid.*) demonstrates how the auctions were conducted in lots. He bought 31 lots, as follows:

12 lots	@ $11\frac{3}{4}$ st.	1 lot	@ $11\frac{1}{2}$ st.
3 lots	@ 12 st.	2 lots	@ $11\frac{5}{8}$ st.
12 lots	@ $11\frac{7}{8}$ st.	1 lot	@ $11\frac{3}{8}$ st.

72 *Ibid.*

73 *Ibid.*

74 *Ibid.*, Nov. 12, 1723. In 15 lots, as follows:

1 lot	@ $11\frac{7}{8}$ st.	3 lots	@ $12\frac{1}{4}$ st.
2 lots	@ $12\frac{1}{8}$ st.	8 lots	@ $12\frac{3}{8}$ st.
1 lot	@ 12 st.		

75 *Ibid.*

76 *Ibid.*

77 *Ibid.*, Nov. 8, 1723 (O.S.).

78 *Ibid.*, Nov. 16, 1723.

79 *Ibid.*, Nov. 23, 1723.

80 *Ibid.*, Nov. 26, 1723.

81 *Ibid.*, and Nov. 22, 1723 (O.S.).

82 *Ibid.*, Nov. 26, 1723.

83 *Ibid.*, and Nov. 22, 1723 (O.S.). It was to be *Sherbro Galley's* third voyage under R.A.C. colors. She was, of course, not really a galley. The name was a convention. Hellevoetsluis, now a very small town, is no longer accessible to ships of any size due to a North Sea flood control project in the Haringvliet arm of the Rhine, and silting.

84 *Ibid.*, Nov. 22, 1723 (O.S.).

85 *Ibid.*, Dec. 7, 1723. All other material in this paragraph is from PRO T–70, Vol. 924, "Charges," under the date April 20, 1724.

86 Evidence elsewhere indicates the shells went via Rotterdam. *Ibid.*, Vol. 25, Dec. 19, 1724.

87 *Ibid.*, Vol. 924, "Charges" and invoice in same volume and under same date. The account

states that the tariff amounted to "$\frac{1}{3}$ additional duty." The original $\frac{2}{3}$ was presumably then an import duty already included in the purchase price. The additional tariff was almost exactly $3\frac{1}{3}$% *ad valorem* on a total f.o.b. value of 43,405.18 for the shipment on the *Sherbro Galley*. For mention of the internal customs at Gouda, see Glamann, *Dutch-Asiatic Trade*, p. 28.

88 PRO T–70, Vol. 924. Transaction costs were thus almost 7% of the original purchase price. The accounts show a 1.5% discount given to the R.A.C. for cash payment ("off for ready money"). They also show the conversion to sterling on the Company's books. The total f.o.b. cost was 44,274 guilders, atop which was the "agio", an exchange rate adjustment of –2108.6. The total of 42,164.14 was valued in the books at £4,054.7s.10d.

89 PRO T–70, Vol. 25, Jan. 7, 1724. Her large cargo of cowries was supplemented by other Dutch goods, including brass kettles, neptunes and pans, knives and sheaths, and gunpowder. Cowries were thus only one of the commodities which were sometimes purchased in Holland at lower prices than in England. In 1730 it was thought that goods obtained there were being shipped onwards from West Africa to the West Indies, which practice was prohibited. The Commissioners for Trade and Plantations made inquiries about this trade. Tinker, who had been the Royal African Company's chief agent at Whydah (and to whom the cowries were consigned in 1723), told them that most ships trading to Africa took in a great part of their loading in Holland; he listed gunpowder, knives, "almost all of the India goods," beads, tobacco pipes, old sheeting, Silesian linen, spirits, and cowries. On the other hand, Humphrey Morice, the leading separate trader, said that, except for gunpowder and spirits, they did not go to Holland for any part of their loading. Silesian linen exported from Hamburg was cheaper in England than in Holland, but iron, beads, and cowries were all cheaper in Holland. In a ship's cargo worth £7–8,000 they did not take from Holland more than £1,000 worth. After 1730 the law was tightened up to prevent these goods from being taken to the West Indies or back to England. In 1735 James Pearce told Thomas Hall that all ships which went to Holland and Guinea were to take on board at least a quarter of their India-goods in London, in case they had to be returned. No such provision is mentioned for cowries. These were very seldom sent back.

90 PRO T-70, Vol. 1225, "3rd Voyage, *Sherbro Galley*."

91 *Ibid.*

92 *Ibid.*, Vol. 25, Feb. 28, 1724.

93 *Ibid.*, April 4, 1724, and Vol. 924, Feb. 28, 1724, and April 4, 1724.

94 *Ibid.*, Vol. 924, July 16, 1724 (O.S.), July 17, 1724, and Aug. 24, 1724 (O.S.). Her sailing directions are particularly complete. "Dispatched from the office for Holland July 16, 1724. Arrived at Hellvoetsluice July 22. Sail'd Aug. 3, Arrived in the Downs Aug. 4. There stopped by the Co. to take in [cargo? supercargo?] for G[old] C[oast]. Sailed Aug. 14."

95 Berbain, *Juda*, p. 77, notes cowries at the bottom of the hold of ships arriving at Whydah.

96 See the *Gentleman's Magazine* for 1731.

97 Berbain, *Juda*, p. 70.

8 Cowries in Africa

1 David Birmingham, "Central Africa from Cameroun to the Zambezi," in Roland Oliver, ed., *The Cambridge History of Africa*, Vol. 3, *c. 1050–c. 1600*, Cambridge, 1977, pp. 546–547. For a concise discussion, see Robert W. Harms, *River of Wealth, River of Sorrow: the Central Zaire Basin in the Era of the Slave and Ivory Trade, 1500–1891*, New Haven, 1981, p. 90.

2 For discussions of the zone in which the cowrie circulated, see the place-names and references in Sundström, *Exchange*, pp. 91–92; Quiggin, *Primitive Money*, especially pp. 30–33, 81–83; Hopkins, *Economic History*, p. 68 and elsewhere in chapters 2, 4, and 6; Hopkins, "Currency Revolution," pp. 471–483; Polanyi, *Dahomey*, pp. 190–191; Hiskett,

"Cowry," pp. 353–358; Jones, "Native and Trade Currencies," pp. 46–50; many references to the southeastern part of the zone in Ofonagoro's two "Currency Revolution" papers; A. J. H. Latham, "Currency, Credit, and Capitalism on the Cross River in the Pre-Colonial Era," *Journal of African History*, Vol. 12, No. 4, 1971, pp. 599–605; and the survey of the northern portions of the zone in Paul E. Lovejoy, "Interregional Monetary Flows in the Precolonial Trade of Nigeria," *Journal of African History*, Vol. 15, No. 4, 1974, pp. 563–585. Though the Senegambia was not in the cowrie zone, it did import substantial quantities in the 1600s and 1700s for shipment 500 miles east to the cowrie-using areas on the upper Niger. See Curtin, "Wider Monetary World," typescript p. 4. Cowries were introduced briefly to Sierra Leone in 1796–97 by the Company's Governor and Council there after their requests for a metallic "mil" piece were ignored by the Directors in London. Cowries were valued at 1,000 to the dollar, double the value of 2,000 to the dollar in the cowrie zone, and showing clearly the isolation of this temporary bastion of the shell money. See David Vice, *The Coinage of British West Africa and St. Helena, 1684–1958*, Birmingham, 1983, pp. 32–33, 136.

3 Hiskett, *Cowry*, pp. 351–353, has a discussion of the linguistics.
4 The Arabic sources are surveyed and quoted in Gray and Bell, *Pyrard*, and in Hiskett's article, as noted in our chapter 1. See also Mauny, *Tableau géographique*.
5 René Caillié, *Travels through Central Africa to Timbuctoo*, London, 1830, Vol. 2, p. 94; Paul E. Lovejoy, "The Role of the Wangara in the Economic Transformation of the Central Sudan in the Fifteenth and Sixteenth Centuries," *Journal of African History*, Vol. 19, No. 2, 1978, p. 181, noting archaeological work at Azalik by S. Bernus and P. Gouletquer; Heinrich Barth, *Travels and Discoveries in North and Central Africa*, London and Gotha, 1857–58, Vol. 5, pp. 22–23; H. R. Palmer, *Bornu, Sahara, and Sudan*, London, 1936, p. 67; and C. W. Newbury, "North Africa and Western Sudan Trade in the Nineteenth Century, a Re-evaluation," *Journal of African History*, Vol. 7, No. 2, 1966, pp. 233 ff, quoting Col. Mircher's information from a Ghadames merchant *c.* 1862.
6 Anne Raffanel, *Nouveau Voyage au pays des nègres*, Paris, 1856, Vol. 1, p. 233; Mungo Park, *Travels in the Interior Districts of Africa*, London, 1799, p. 199n; Oskar Lenz, *Timbuctou*, French edn, Paris, 1887, p. 225; Emile Baillaud, *Sur les routes du Soudan*, Toulouse, 1902, p. 70.
7 René Caillié, *Journal d'un voyage à Timboctou et à Jenne, dans l'Afrique Centrale*, Paris, 1830, Vol. 2, pp. 38, 72; Louis Gustave Binger, *Du Niger au golfe de Guinee par le pays de Kong et le Mossi, par le capitaine Binger*, Paris, 1892, Vol. 1, pp. 207, 498ff; Heinrich Klose, *Togo unter deutscher Flagge*, Berlin, 1899, p. 362ff.
8 Joseph Dupuis, *Journal of a Residence in Ashantee*, London, 1824, p. cxiv.
9 Giovanni Lorenzo Anania, *La Universale Fabrica del Mondo, Overo Cosmografia* [1st edn, 1573; 3rd edn., 1582], ed. Dierk Lange with Silvio Berthoud, "L'intérieur de l'Afrique Occidentale d'après Giovanni Lorenzo Anania (XVIᵉ siècle)," *Cahiers d'histoire mondiale*, Vol. 14, No. 2, 1972, p. 335. We are grateful to John Lavers for drawing our attention to this reference.
10 Hiskett, "Cowry," pp. 346ff. Lovejoy, "Interregional Monetary Flows," is a thorough discussion. See also Lovejoy, "Wangara," p. 190.
11 For Zamfara and Gobir, see Lovejoy, "International Monetary Flows," p. 567, quoting Carsten Niebuhr, "Das Innere von Afrika," *Neues Deutsches Museum*, Leipzig, Vol. 3, Oktober 1790, p. 1003 (Niebuhr got his information from a Hausa slave who had lived in Birnin Zamfara before its destruction in the mid-1760s); and H. R. Palmer, "Western Sudan History: the Raudthat' ul Afkari," *Journal of the African Society*, Vol. 15, No. 59, 1916, p. 269. For Katsina, see Henry Beaufoy, quoted in Robin Hallett, ed., *Records of the Association for Promoting the Discovery of the Interior Parts of Africa*, London, 1967, Vol. 1, p. 184. Mattra, in 1793, also stated that there was no money in circulation there but gold dust and shells (*ibid.*, p. 118), and the use of cowries at Katsina about 1800 is also noted by

C. A. Walckenaer, *Recherches géographique sur l'interieur de l'Afrique septentrionale*, Paris, 1821, quoted by Lovejoy, 'Interregional Money Flows," p. 567. For Adar, see *ibid.*, quoting U. J. Seetzen, "Uber die Phellata-Araber südwärts von Fesan, und deren Sprache, nebst einigen Nachrichten von unterschiedlichen umherliegenden afrikanischen Ländern," *Monatliche Correspondenz zur Beforderung der Erd- und Himmels-Kunde*, Vol. 24, 1811, p. 231. For the taxes, tribute, and trade relations, see Lovejoy, pp. 565, 573, 581.

12 Dixon Denham and Hugh Clapperton, *Narrative of Travels and Discovery in North and Central Africa*, London, 1826, p. 220; Barth, *Travels*, Vol. 2, p. 311; Siegfried Passarge, *Adamaua*, Berlin, 1895, pp. 214, 475ff; Gerh. Rohlfs, "Geld in Afrika," *Petermanns Mitteilungen*, 1889, pp. 187–192; Sundström, *Exchange*, pp. 104, 109n; Schneider, *Muschelgeld-Studien*, pp. 130–131; Gustav Nachtigal, *Sahara und Sudan*, Berlin, 1879, p. 690ff; S. O. Biobaku, *The Egba and their Neighbours*, Oxford, 1957, p. 54; Polanyi, *Dahomey*, p. 661. See also Hiskett, "Cowry," pp. 353–358.

13 Mungo Park, *Journal of a Mission to the Interior of Africa in 1805*, London, 1815, p. 161; and Caillié and Dupuis as cited in notes 7 and 8 above.

14 G. Connah, *Archaeology of Benin*, Oxford, 1975. Connah found only three cowries and a fragment "in poor condition" in layers antedating the Portuguese contact, but suggests that "specimens in earlier deposits may normally have been completely dissolved by the soil" (alternatively, they may never have existed).

15 Ryder, "Portuguese Trading Voyage," p. 301n., quoting Arquivo Historico Ultramarino, Lisbon, São Tomé, caixa 2.

16 Polanyi, *Dahomey*, pp. 126ff., 181, and *passim*. They were observed at Allada inland from Whydah by Catholic missionaries in 1660. See José de Najera, *Espejo Mistico*, Madrid, 1670, Al lector f9v, quoted in Buenaventura de Carrocera, *Mission Capuchina al Reino de Arda*, Vol. 6, 1949, p. 542. (Our thanks to Robin Law for this reference.) We have also relied on Barbot, "North and South-Guinea;" Olfert Dapper, *Naukeurige Beschrijvinge der Afrikaensche gewesten*, Amsterdam, 1688, (probably refers to a date before 1660); John Atkins, *Voyage to Guinea*, London, 1735; and Berbain, *Juda*. For the westward movement see PRO T70/22 f44v (1709), which says the shells were not at Winneba; Johannes Rask, *En kort og Sandferdig rejse-beskrivelse til og fra Guinea*, Trondheim, 1754, p. 84; Dutch Archives, The Hague, VWIS, No. 415, "Only in Apam, Bercou and Accra one uses ... cowries as money." – Our thanks to Michael Doortmont for this reference; Henry Meredith, *An Account of the Gold Coast of Africa*, London, 1812, p. 183; Monrad, *Küste von Guinea*, p. 262; Brodie Cruckshank, *Eighteen Years on the Gold Coast of Africa*, London, 1853, Vol. 2, p. 58. See also G. A. Henty, *March to Coomassie*, London, 1874, p. 260.

17 G. A. Robertson, *Notes on Africa*, London, 1819, p. 297; E. M. Chilver, "Nineteenth Century Trade in the Bamenda Grassfields, Southern Cameroons," *Afrika und Übersee*, Vol. 45, No. 4, 1961, p. 237 (our thanks to A. G. Hopkins for bringing this reference to our attention); Donnan, *Documents*, Vol. 2, p. 529; Lovejoy, "Interregional Monetary Flows," p. 575.

18 Macgregor Laird and R. A. K. Oldfield, *Narrative of an Expedition into the Interior of Africa by the River Niger in the Steam Vessels Quorra and Alburkah in 1832, 1833, and 1834*, London, 1837, p. 341. "[Cowrie] will purchase any article from Eboe to Boosa, and passes current in every part of the interior," Miss Charlotte Maria Tucker, *Abeokuta; or Sunrise within the Tropics*, London, 1854, p. 26; Pierre B. Bouche, *Sept ans en Afrique Occidentale*, Paris, 1885, pp. 198ff; *Petermanns Mitteilungen*, 1861, p. 77.

19 Thomas J. Hutchinson, *Narrative of the Niger, Tschadda and Binuë Exploration*, London, 1855, p. 253.

20 Hiskett, "Cowry," p. 356ff. It should be noted that Hiskett's "first and ... the only concrete evidence of their entry by a direct east to west route" (p. 357) is based on a misreading of Barth. It is almost certain that Barth's reference to the Bahr al Ghazal was to

the source of the natron, and not of the cowries as well; in any event, the reference is to the Bahr al Ghazal that flows into Lake Chad from the northeast, which is north rather than east from Bagirmi. Also Marion Johnson, "Cloth on the Banks of the Niger," *Journal of the Historical Society of Nigeria*, Vol. 6, No. 4, 1973, pp. 353–363; Archibald Dalzel, *History of Dahomey*, London, 1793, p. 135. For other sources on the Oyo, Nupe, and Igbo northern trade in cowries, see Lovejoy, "Interregional Monetary Flows," pp. 569, 574–575, which discusses the relation between palm exports and cowrie imports. Also see Lovejoy for the Niger River trade in cowries. Eighteenth-century Igbo trade is discussed by David Northrup, "The Growth of Trade among the Igbo before 1800," *Journal of African History*, Vol. 13, No. 2, 1972, pp. 221–236. A tale is sometimes quoted that one Hausa word for cowries, *wada*, is derived from the port of Whydah on the Dahomean coast where so many of the shells were imported, thus serving as etymological evidence of a northward flow. E. W. Bovill recounts it thus (*The Niger Explored*, London, 1968, p. 124): "Oudney and Clapperton found that in Hausa they were then [1820s] called *whydah* after the town of that name on the Guinea coast which was the principal port of entry for cowries." Lucie G. Colvin tells it with slight differences ("The Commerce of Hausaland, 1780–1833," in Daniel F. McCall and Norman R. Bennett, eds., *Aspects of West African Islam*, Boston, 1971, p. 123): "Lucas mentioned [in an account published 1791] that the Arabs call the cowries of Hausaland 'Huedah,' which certainly represented 'Whydah,' and which lends credit to this hypothesis [of a northerly flow of shells]." However, the Arabic word *wad'*, meaning cowrie, appears in al-Bakri's manuscript of the year 1068 (see Cuoq, *Sources arabes*, p. 104), 400 years at least before the shells could conceivably have come by sea to Whydah.

21 E. M. Chilver, "Bamenda Grassfields," pp. 233–258.
22 M.-J. Bonnat, "Journal," *L'Explorateur*, 1876; PRO T70/22 f44v; Thomas E. Bowdich, *Mission from Cape Coast Castle to Ashantee*, London, 1819, p. 86. Bowdich wrote that "the currency of Ashantee is gold dust, that of Inta [Gonja], Dagwumba [Dagomba], Gaman [Gyaman] and Kong, cowries ... 16 ackies make an ounce ... eight tokoos [a small berry] are reckoned to the ackie ... five strings of cowries are equal to a tokoo, as at Accra."
23 John Adams, *Cape Palmas to the Rio Congo*, London, 1823, p. 263.
24 Dupuis, *Ashantee*, p. cxiv. While it seems impossible to obtain positive evidence, we will discuss in the next chapter the suggestion that there may have been a single gold–cowrie system from the Niger Bend to the Guinea Coast, operated perhaps by Mandingo traders as attested by Pereira in the first decade of the sixteenth century. This would strengthen the supposition that cowries were already in use on the Benin coast when the Portuguese arrived.
25 Ryder, "Portuguese Trading Voyage," p. 303.
26 *Ibid.*, pp. 297–321, gives details of the voyage.
27 For example, see PRO WIC 1024, encl. in 96, for an estimate of the slave trade at Ardra in 1681: 16,000 pounds of cowries at 80 pounds per slave – 200 slaves.
28 Thomas Phillips, *Journal of a Voyage*, in A. and J. Churchill, eds., *Voyages and Travels*, p.. 227; Barbot, *North and South-Guinea*, p. 348; José de Najera, in de Carrocera, *Mission Capuchina*, p. 542, who wrote that "the only things being valued by these people, and on the whole coast being the snail-shells which they use as money."
29 William Bosman, *Coast of Guinea*, p. 364a.
30 Davies, *Royal African Company*, p. 234.
31 Barbot, *North and South-Guinea*, p. 348. These figures are confirmed by the Royal African Company's invoices and correspondence: 1662–63, 1674, about one-third; 1679 and 1681, when cowries were cheap, about half. See PRO T70/1222, f. 18, f. 101, f. 154, f. 156; T70/65, January 15 and June 13, 1681. Our thanks to Robin Law for these references.
32 Patrick Manning, *Slavery, Colonialism and Economic Growth in Dahomey, 1640–1960*, Cambridge, 1982, p. 44; Dapper, *Naukeurige Beschrijvinge*, p. 491; "When trade is done with cowries, then usually a third is paid in cowries and two-thirds in other merchandise."

33 PRO T70/6.

34 Interestingly, Ashanti, which used a gold-dust currency, appears to have had a similar increasing demand for money. Although cowries and not gold were used as a market currency in markets outside metropolitan Ashanti, gold was actually being imported there in the second half of the eighteenth century, presumably to meet the needs of its expanding economy or reflecting increases in hoarding. See Marion Johnson, "The Ounce," p. 203.

35 Data for the latter part of the seventeenth century is found in Davies, *Royal African Company*, p. 357. See our Table 4.1.

36 Pruneau de Pommergorge, *Description de la Nigritie*, Paris, 1789, p. 204; Berbain, *Juda*, p: 98.

37 Jean Baptiste Labat, *Voyage du Chevalier des Marchais*, Paris, 1730, Vol. 2, p. 109ff. There is reason to doubt the date of des Marchais' information about Dahomey.

38 Barbot, *North and South-Guinea*, Vol. 5, p. 339. This passage did not appear in Barbot's original manuscript, but may have been added by him in a subsequent revision.

39 Writing about the purchase of slaves at Whydah, Barbot says (in French): "... agreeing (for example) for each slave at one Alcoves [*sic*] which is 50 galinas which weigh 60 lbs. (the blacks call Guinbotton which makes 4,000 cowries in number) or 15 iron bars ..." (1688 MS. p. 133)

A few pages later he correctly calculates the *galina* as 200 shells (MS., p. 138), and in his vocabulary (MS., p. 193) he gives the simple numerals, including the confusing (but correct) *oton*, "three" and *aton* "five", and also names for larger cowrie units, including *guinbale*, "4,000 cowries", and *guinbaton*, "20,000 cowries" (thanks to Robin Law for drawing our attention to this vocabulary, and helpful discussion of Barbot's cowries); *guinboton* would thus be 12,000 cowries.

Alcove is only mentioned as a very generalized term for wealth (in Portuguese, it is a kind of basket). From Barbot's text, it could be 4,000 cowries (a *guinbale*), 10,000 cowries (200 × 50), 12,000 cowries (a *guinboton*), or 60 lbs. weight, probably some 20,000 to 25,000 cowries, but possibly fewer if his cowries were as mixed as he describes, and possibly not from the Maldives at all.

The price of a slave in 1681–82 at Whydah can hardly have been as low as 4,000 cowries (equivalent to about 25 shillings); probably it was three times this, a value confirmed by the alternative reckoning in iron bars, usually valued at 5 shillings. This would suggest (unless Barbot's use of the plural *alcoves* was no slip of the pen, and he intended to insert a figure before the word) that the *alcove* or "basket" was 12,000 shells – the same as the Maldives *kotta*. If so, did the Portuguese ever ship cowries to Guinea in the original Maldives packages, and possibly call them *alcoves*?

Whatever the interpretation, it seems that either Barbot could not do simple arithmetic (an unlikely handicap for a successful merchant and navigator), or he could not decipher his notes

40 Berbain, *Juda*, p. 81 and appendix; PRO BT 6/5 f. 23. CO 388 58, letter dated October 31, 1770, f. 27, refers to the same English shipment: "The cowries are of the large sort ... according to the price they cost they may be issued on the coast at half the money the small ones used to go for." There is no indication of where these large cowries came from.

41 Michel R. Doortmont, "De organisetie van de Atlantische Handel in het West Afrikaanse Kustgebied," unpublished thesis, University of Rotterdam, 1984, p. 183; Dutch archives at The Hague, VWIS, No. 415 (*c.* 1786–7), "Only in Apam, Bercou and Accra one uses Maldives and Mozambique cowries as money."

42 Atkins, *Guinea*, p. 112; Labat, *Chevalier des Marchais*, Vol. 2, pp. 109 ff.

43 Mungo Park, *Journal of a Mission*, p. 145. *Cf.* A. E. Mage, *Voyage dans le Soudan occidentale 1863–6*, Paris, 1868, who says that kola was counted like cowries in Segu. But Binger, further south, reports: "In this part of the Soudan, when referring to kola, the first

192

large unit is 100, whereas throughout Samori's state it is only 80." Binger, *Du Niger*, Vol. 1, p. 142.

44 Caillié, *Travels*, Vol. 1, pp. 373, 390.

45 Mage, *Voyage*, p. 171.

46 Lenz, *Timbouctou*, p. 162.

47 Barth, *Travels*, Vol. 4, p. 289 n.; Edmond Caron, *De Saint-Louis au port de Tombouktou*, Paris, 3rd ed., 1893, p. 287: "De Safai à Tombouktou on employe le système decimal."

48 Ch. Monteil, "Le nombre et la numération chez les Mandes," *L'Anthropologie*, in *Soudan et Guinée II*, DA D4 71508, University of Ghana, Legon, p. 498; Solange de Ganay, "Graphes Bambara des Nombres," *Journal de la Société des Africanistes*, Vol. 20, 1950, p. 299. See also M. P. Marti, *Les Dogon*, Paris, 1957, p. 30, recording a symbolic figure representing both Mande and Bambara systems.

49 Einzig, *Primitive Money*, p. 191 ff.; Baillaud, *Soudan*, p. 71.

50 Paul Soleillet, *Voyage à Ségou, 1878–9*, Paris, 1887, p. 235.

51 Park, *Journal of a Mission*, p. 145: "Sixty is called a Mandingo hundred." Binger, *Du Niger*, Vol. 1, p. 162, reports the Mandingo hundred at Benokhobougoula.

52 Maurice Delafosse, *Haut-Sénégal-Niger*, Paris, 1912, Vol. 3, p. 48.

53 Binger, *Du Niger*, Vol. 1, p. 498.

54 *Ibid.*, Vol. 1, p. 309. Delafosse, *Haut-Sénégal-Niger*, p. 48, gives a similar account of terms "in Mandingo and countries under Mandingo influence" for packets of 10, 20, 100, and 200 cowries.

55 A. Mann, "Notes on the Numeral System of the Yoruba Nation," *Journal of the Anthropological Institute*, 1887, pp. 59ff; Hertz, *Kauriemuschel*, p. 23, quoting the *Lagos Almanac*.

56 Barth, *Travels*, Vol. 2, pp. 38ff.

57 Mary F. Smith, *Baba of Karo*, London, 1954, p. 80.

58 Hiskett, "Cowry Currency," p. 355. Simon Lucas, from North Africa at the end of the eighteenth century, believed that merchants at Katsina obtained cowries from "regions nearer the sea" (*Proceedings of the Association for Promoting the Discovery of the Interior Parts of Africa*, London, 1810, Vol. 1, pp. 105ff). See also M. J. E. Daumas and A. de Chancel, *Le Grand Désert: Itinéraire d'une caravane du Sahara au pays des Nègres*, Paris, 1848, p. 241: "Cowries, they tell me, come from the Bahar el Nil [Niger], which runs ten days' journey west of Katsina. The sultan has organized a system of customs posts which prevent individuals from bringing them from the interior without paying enormous duties. He has the monopoly."

59 See, for example, William Allen and T. R. H. Thompson, *Expedition to the River Niger*, London, 1848, Vol. 2, p. 85: "Gori pays an annual tribute of 360,000 to the Filatah king." Also see Lovejoy, "Interregional Monetary Flows," for tribute payments.

60 Nachtigal, *Sahara und Sudan*, Vol. 1, pp. 690ff (quoted and discussed by Hertz, "Kauriemuschel," p. 18); Rohlfs, "Geld in Afrika," and P. L. Monteil, *De Saint Louis à Tripoli par le lac Tchad*, Paris, 1895, both discuss the subject.

61 Ryder, "Portuguese Trading Voyage," pp. 301ff.

62 Thomas J. Hutchinson, *Impressions of West Africa*, London, 1858.

63 Ryder, "Portuguese Trading Voyage," pp. 301ff.

64 See, for example, Bullfinch Lamb in W. Smith, *A Voyage to Guinea*, London, 1744, p. 178.

65 Monrad, *Küste von Guinea*, p. 263.

66 E.g. Hill to Grey, Cape Coast, 24 Apr. 1852 (dispatch quoted in George E. Metcalfe, *Great Britain and Ghana*, London, 1964; W. F. Daniell, "Ethnography of Akkrah and Adampe," *Journal of the Ethnographical Society*, London, 1856.

67 Robertson, *Notes*, p. 274. Cf. Richard Burton, *Wanderings in West Africa*, London, 1863, p. 234 n.

68 Newbury, *Western Slave Coast*, pp. 58ff.

69 Laird and Oldfield, *Narrative*, Vol. 1, p. 166; Samuel Johnson, *The History of the Yorubas*, Lagos, 1921, reprinted London, 1966, pp. 118–119; see also Hertz, "Kauriemuschel," p. 23, quoting the *Lagos Almanac*; Edouard Viard, *Au bas Niger*, Paris, 3rd edn, 1886, p. 231: "The cowries are pierced and threaded in advance in bunches of 1,000" (at Lokoja).
70 Allen and Thompson, *Expedition*, Vol. 1, pp. 350, 460.
71 Dutch Gentleman, *Voyage*, p. 22.
72 Basden, *Ibos*, p. 198; see also the same author's *Niger Ibos*, London, 2nd edn, 1966, where the Igbo cowrie table is correctly given. For a very full account of the Igbo counting systems, see Jeffreys, "Diffusion," pp. 45–53. See also his "The Cowry Shell: A Study of its History and Use in Nigeria," *Nigeria*, No. 15, 1938, p. 224.
73 Jeffreys, "Diffusion". Also see our chapter 1.
74 Dalzel, *Dahomey*, p. 214.
75 J. Alfred Skertchly, *Dahomey As It Is*, London, 1874, p. 28.
76 Schneider, *Muschelgeld-Studien*, pp. 144–145, quoting Peregaux; Bonnat, "Journal," Jan., 1876; PRO T70/22 f44v.
77 R. Buttner, "Bericht von Dr. R. Buttner über eine Reise von Bismarckburg nach Tschautjo und Fasugu," *Mitteilungen aus den deutschen Schützgebieten*, Vol. 4, 1891, pp. 189ff.
78 Frederick E. Forbes, *Dahomey and the Dahomans*, London, 1851, p. 110. This might suggest that the string of 50 in place of 40 was already in use at this date for large transactions, as we know it was in the 1870s.
79 Burton, *Wanderings*, p. 274n.
80 Schneider, *Muschelgeld-Studien*, p. 172.
81 Robert G. Armstrong, *Yoruba Numerals*, Oxford, 1962.
82 Polly Hill, "Notes on the History of the Northern Katsina Tobacco Trade," *Journal of the Historical Society of Nigeria*, Vol. 4, 1968, p. 480.
83 Daumas and de Chancel, *Grand Désert*, p. 239.
84 A. F. Mockler-Ferryman, *Up the Niger*, London, 1892, p. 306.
85 A. F. Mockler-Ferryman, *British Nigeria*, London, 1902, p. 88.
86 Frederick Lugard, *Diaries*, ed. M. Perham and M. Bull, London, 1963, Vol. 4, p. 256.
87 See Sundström, *Exchange*, p. 75, for many references to the cowrie as a unit of account.

9 The cowrie as money: transport costs, values and inflation

1 Bonnat, "Journal," for 1875–6. See also "George Dobson," "The River Volta, Gold Coast, West Africa," *Journal of the Manchester Geographical Society*, Vol. 8, 1892, p. 21: "a canoe 25ft. long by 3ft. wide and 18ins. deep requiring eight men to pole it up." (For the identity of "George Dobson" see Marion Johnson, "M. Bonnat on the Volta," *Ghana Notes and Queries*, No. 10, 1968, p. 6).
2 Dupuis, *Ashantee*, p. cxiv.
3 L. C. Binger, "Transactions, objets de commerce, monnaie, quoted in Mauny, *Tableau géographique*, p. 417, 550; Hertz, "Kauriemuschel," p. 23.
4 Shabeeny, quoted in J. Grey Jackson, *An Account of Timbuctoo and Hausa*, London, 1820, p. 2, says 4 to 5 quintals; Denham and Clapperton, *Narrative*, say 4 cwt.; Caillié, *Journal*, p. 67: 500 lbs.; C. H. Dickson, "Account of Ghadames," *Journal of the Royal Geographical Society*, 1860: 4 cwt.; Rabbi Mordekkai, "Reisen nach Timbuktu," *Petermanns Mitteilungen*, 1870: not over 150 kgs.; Dr. Ollive, "Schilderung von Tendouf," *Petermanns Mitteilungen*, 1880: 3 centner; Col. Mircher, circa 1865 (in C. W. Newbury, "Western Sudan Trade", p. 233): 3 kantar = 150 kgs.; J. L. Miège, *Le Maroc et l'Europe*, Vol. 3, Paris, 1961–62, pp. 85ff: 3 quintals = 154–162 kgs.; *ibid.*, p. 258: 150 kgs.; Frederick Lugard in *Annual Report, Northern Nigeria 1902*: 3–4½ cwt.
5 Barth, *Travels*, Vol. 2, p. 163.

6 Shabeeny in Jackson, *Timbuctoo and Hausa*, p. 2ff.
7 Monteil, *De Saint Louis*, p. 282. This load of 50,000 shells agrees approximately with Barth's estimate that a donkey carried 5,000 to 6,000 kola nuts. Barth, *Travels*, Vol. 5, p. 29. The goatskin bags are noted by Polly Hill, *Studies in Rural Capitalism*, Cambridge, 1970, p. 145; she also discusses the carrying capacity of donkeys. Lugard's cargoes are detailed in Lugard, *Diaries*, Vol. 4, p. 120. See also p. 117: "It is these donkeys that throw everything out. Four more were dying this morning, and had to be left, and one yesterday = 10 loads."
8 Mischlich to German Government, Akte 3832 of 20 March 1903, p. 44, in the German Colonial Archives at Potsdam. (We are indebted to Dr. I. Sellnow for this reference.) Mischlich described 3,000 kola as a "fairly heavy donkey load." This is 1½ times the standard headload of 2,000 kola weighing about 65 lbs.
9 Polly Hill has pointed out to Marion Johnson that merchants using donkeys for transport could also be farmers, in which case the donkeys could be bred on the farm. If the Mossi donkeys used in the Mossi–Salaga–Hausa caravan trade were larger and stronger than the more southerly donkeys, or the farm-bred donkeys of Hausaland, this would account for the higher prices noted in the next sentence of text, and also for the Hausa merchants' preference for Mossi animals.
10 Barth, *Travels*, Vol. 5, p. 29; Binger, *Du Niger*, Vol. 2, p. 103; Lugard, *Diaries*, Vol. 4, p. 192.
11 Dupuis, *Ashantee*, p. cxiv.
12 Meredith, *Gold Coast*, p. 183; Park, *Travels*, p. 199n. This accords with Werner Peukert's statement that in the late eighteenth century one string represented about the minimum subsistence for a day, or rather less. Werner Peukert, *Der Atlantische Sklavenhandel von Dahomey, 1740–1797*, Wiesbaden, 1978, p. 315. The "per diem allowance" at this period seems to have been two strings, whether for European visitors to the capital, hired guards, or porters.
13 Lugard, *Diaries*, passim.
14 C. H. Robinson, *Hausaland*, London, 1896, p. 46. Compare this denouement to the plight of housewives in the German hyperinflation of 1923, said to carry their cash to market in a shopping bag and their purchases home in their purse.
15 Ibn Battuta, *Voyages d'Ibn Battuta*, Vol. 4, Paris, 1922, pp. 122, 435.
16 Leo Africanus, *Description d'Afrique*, Paris, 1956, p. 469.
17 Mahmud al-Kati, *Tarikh al-fattash*, p. 319.
18 Jeffreys, "Marginelle Currency," pp. 143ff.
19 Mauny, "Monnaie marginelloide," pp. 659–669.
20 The late-eighteenth-century inflation, and Bubakr's "currency reform" of 1795, are described in Michel Abitbol, ed. and trans., *Tombouctou au milieu du XVIIIe siècle d'après la chronique de Mawlay al-Qásím b. Mawlay Sulaymán*, Paris, 1982. We are grateful to Liz Hodgkin for drawing our attention to this work. See also Mauny, "Monnaie marginelloide," and Jeffreys, "Marginelle Currency," p. 143ff.
21 Park, *Journal*, p. 161; Caillié, *Journal*, Vol. 2, pp. 220, 426.
22 Charles Monteil, *Djenné*, Paris, 1932, p. 280; Barth, *Travels*, Vol. 5, p. 17; Baillaud, *Soudan*, p. 117.
23 Simon Lucas, in *Proceedings of the Association for Promoting the Discovery of the Interior Parts of Africa*, Vol. 1, p. 186.
24 G. F. Lyon, *Narratives of Travels in Northern Africa*, London, 1819, p. 138; Barth, *Travels*, Vol. 2, p. 161.
25 Al-Kati, *Tarikh al-fattash*, p. 319; Shabeeny in Jackson, *Timbuctoo and Hausa*, p. 2; Park, *Journal*, p. 161; Caillié, *Journal*, Vol. 1, p. 457; Barth, *Travels*, Vol. 5, p. 23; Lenz, *Timbouctou*, Vol. 2, p. 98; J. S. Gallieni, *Voyage au Soudan français, 1879–81*, Paris, 1884, p. 380; Binger, *Du Niger*, Vol. 1, p. 374; G. Jaime, *De Koulikoro à Timbuktu*, Paris, 1894,

p. 219; F. Dubois, *Timbouctou la mystérieuse*, Paris, 1897, p. 179; Captain Lenfant, *Le Niger*, Paris, 1903; P. L. Monteil, *De Saint Louis*, p. 280.

26 Polanyi, *Dahomey*, p. 168.

27 Atkins, *Guinea*, p. 112; Houstoun in 1835 quoted by Donnan, *Documents*, Vol. 2, p. 290; W. Smith, *Guinea*, p. 178.

28 Rask, *Guinea*, p. 257; Rømer, *Nachrichten von der Küste von Guinea*, p. 277.

29 Rask, *Guinea*, p. 84. The system as given by Isert *c.* 1780, though using some different terms and with some different measures, was essentially similar:

1 *cabess* = 2 dollars (the Danish cabess was 2,000 cowries) (? = *ihi*)
4 *cabess* = 1 *gua* = 8 dollars
2 *gua* = 1 *guenno* = 16 ackies = 1 gold ounce
2 *guenno* = 1 *benda* = 2 gold ounces = 32 ackies

Isert, like others of his time, equated the ackie with the silver dollar and with 1/16 of a gold ounce. Silver was over-valued in West Africa as compared with Europe; the silver dollar weighed about ⅞ of a troy ounce. By Isert's time, one troy ounce of gold was equal to 32,000 cowries.

30 Bowdich, *Ashantee*, p. 330.

31 PRO T70/22 f44v. This early eighteenth-century report names the oversize *damba* of the interior the "black man's damba."

32 Marion Johnson, "The Ounce," pp. 202–203. The decline in the real value of cowries was paralleled by a small decline in the real value (as distinct from the gold value) of the trade ounce.

33 Ivor Wilks, "A Note on the Chronology, and Origins, of the Gonja Kings," *Ghana Notes and Queries*, Jan. 8, 1966, p. 28. If there had been an interruption in the flow of gold from the southern goldfields, both the Songhay bid to control the source of their salt supply (normally obtained in return for gold) and the Moroccan invasion of 1591 would be understandable.

34 Bowdich, *Ashantee*, p. 330; Monrad, *Küste von Guinea*, p. 263; Meredith, *Gold Coast*, p. 183.

35 E. Carstensen, *Journal*, Copenhagen, 1965, p. 124; Daniell, "Ethnography," pp. 23–24 (this paper, published in 1856, was actually read in 1852); Barth, *Travels*, Vol. 5, p. 17.

36 Sir Isaac Newton, when Master of the Mint, had calculated a 16:1 ratio between silver and gold; but the silver dollar was the weight of the smaller Spanish ounce, not the troy ounce.

37 G. Nørregard in J. Bronsted, ed., *Vore Gamle Tropenkolonier*, Copenhagen, 1954, Vol. 2, p. 563. Cf. Mungo Park's valuation of dollars at Sansanding in 1805; their worth was high, presumably because they were still quite scarce.

38 Lyon, *Narratives*, p. 138, for Katsina; Denham and Clapperton, *Narrative*, p. 51 of Clapperton's part, at Kano; Hugh Clapperton and R. L. Lander, *Records of Captain Clapperton's Last Expedition to Africa*, London, 1830, p. 59, for Oyo (?); W. Hutton, *A Voyage to Africa*, London, 1821, p. 12, "on the Niger."

39 Tartar Wargee in the *Royal Gazette and Sierra Leone Advertiser*, March 15, 1823 for Timbuktu (not a very good authority); Clapperton and Lander, *Records*, p. 173, for Kano. Clapperton quoted 1,500 to the dollar as "just one half," presumably of the rate he should have had. He also referred to 250,000 cowries as less than 100 dollars. Lander, on the return journey, spoke of 4,000 cowries as "little more than a dollar," perhaps working from the same value. We are grateful to Robin Law for drawing our attention to these values.

40 Cruikshank, *Gold Coast*, Vol. 2, p. 42; Forbes, *Dahomey*, Vol. 1, p. 36; Barth, *Travels*, Vol. 2, pp. 161, 395, and Vol. 5, p. 25.

41 *Gold Coast Blue Book*, "The current value of British coins is 10% above the sterling value, in consequence of gold dust which is the principal currency of the country being £4 per oz. currency, which on being transmitted to England and all expenses being deducted averages about £3 12. 0. per oz. sterling."

42 Timothy F. Garrard, *Akan Weights and the Gold Trade*, London, 1980, pp. 258–259.

43 *Gold Coast Blue Book*, 1855; cf. Daniell, "Ethnography," p. 24.

44 Hopkins, "Currency Revolution," pp. 479–480.

45 Cruikshank, *Gold Coast*, Vol. 2, p. 42.

46 Governor Hill, dispatch dated Cape Coast, April 24, 1852, quoted in Metcalfe, *Great Britain and Ghana*, p. 237; D. Kimble, *Rise of Nationalism in the Gold Coast*, London, 1960, p. 176.

47 *Annual Statement of the Trade and Navigation of the United Kingdom*, 1853, under "British Possessions on the Gold Coast."

48 A. Adumakoh quoting Governor's report, 1859, *Economic Bulletin* (Ghana), Vol. 7, No. 4; Acting Governor Bird, dispatch of January 13, 1860, Admin. 1/456, 12, Ghana National Archives; Executive Council Minutes, July 16, 1861 (our thanks to Mlle. F. Cournaert for this reference); *Gold Coast Blue Books*, 1868 and 1869.

49 E.g. Th. Opoku, "Eines Neger-Pastors Predigtreise durch die Länder am Voltastrom" (1877), *Evangelische Missionmagazin*, Basel, 1885, pp. 270–271; "George Dobson," "River Volta," p. 21; Schneider, *Muschelgeld-Studien*, p. 145, quoting Herr F. Schaenker "from Trepow on the Riga."

50 For a wide sampling of cowrie exchange rates in these years, see Forbes, *Dahomey*, Vol. 1, p. 36; Newbury, *Western Slave Coast*, p. 42; Richard F. Burton, *Mission to Gelele*, London, 1864, p. 143 (Burton also has unusual detail on how prices respond to currency depreciation, as with the fourfold increase in the remuneration of state prostitutes, p. 316); Skertchly, *Dahomey*, p. 28; A. L. Albéca, "L'avenir du Dahomey," *Annales de Géographie*, 1895, p. 185; A.L. Albéca, *Établissements français au Golfe de Bénin*, Paris, 1889, p. 149; Foà, *Dahomey*, p. 148; Schneider, *Muschelgeld-Studien*, pp. 148–149.

51 For exchange rates in the area of Lagos, see especially Hopkins, "Currency Revolution," pp. 476–483; also Newbury, *Western Slave Coast*, p. 58; Hutchinson, *West Africa*, p. 7; Burton, *Wanderings*, p. 234n.; Burton, *Gelele*, Vol. 1, p. 143; Pierre B. Bouche, *Côte des esclaves et Dahomey*, Paris, 1885, p. 198ff.

52 Laird and Oldfield, *Narrative*, p. 166; Allen and Thompson, *Expedition*, Vol. 1, p. 350; A. G. C. Hastings, *Voyage of the Dayspring (1857–9)*, London, 1926, p. 188.

53 Opoku, "Neger-Pastors," pp. 270–271; F. Ramsayer, "Eine Reise im Norden von Asante und im Osten von Volta," *Geografische Gesellschaft zu Jena, Mitteilungen*, Vol. 4, 1886; G. E. Ferguson, "Report of a Mission to the Interior," December 9, 1892, enclosure in a dispatch of Governor Griffith, January 10, 1893, Secret, C.O. 96.230, no. 2199, P.R.O.; Buttner, "Bericht," p. 189ff.; Viard, *Au bas Niger*, p. 231; A. Burdo, *Niger et Benue*, Paris, 1880, p. 137n.; Bonnat, "Journal," Vol. 4, pp. 36–37.

54 Robinson, *Hausaland*, pp. 43–84; Dr. Wolf, "Letzte Reise nach der Landschaft Barbar (Bariba oder Borgu)," *Mitteilungen aus den deutschen Schutzgebieten*, Vol. 4, 1891, p. 1ff.; Mockler-Ferryman, *Up the Niger*, p. 306; *Report on Northern Nigeria*, Cd. 1768, p. 14; Basden, *Ibos*, p. 198.

55 For these figures see W. B. Baikie, "Journey from Bida to Kano," *Journal of the Royal Geographical Society*, 1867, p. 92ff.; Passarge, *Adamaua*, p. 551; Robinson, *Hausaland*, p. 85; P. L. Monteil, *De Saint Louis*, p. 297; Col. Mircher in Newbury, "Western Sudan Trade," p. 233ff.; *Report on Northern Nigeria*, 1902, Cd. 1768, p. 14; Frederick Lugard, *Political Memoranda*, London, 1906, p. 224. Paul Lovejoy believes Baikie is speaking not of gold coins, but silver. See "Interregional Monetary Flows," p. 585. Lovejoy has a table of cowrie equivalencies to silver coins in the nineteenth-century Sokoto Caliphate, in *ibid.*, Appendix A, pp. 584–585, quoting numerous other sources. It will be remembered that the world value of silver fell sharply after 1870. The silver rupee fell from 3 shillings (36 pence) to 1s. 6d. (18 pence), and ultimately to 1s. 4d. (16 pence). See Barth, *Travels*, German edition, Vol. 2, p. 161, and Sundström, *Exchange*, p. 104, for the restraining influence of Bornu's demand.

56 For Timbuktu see Lenz, *Timbouctou*, Vol. 2, p. 162; Jaime, *Koulikoro*, p. 223 n. 1; Caron, *Saint-Louis*, p. 278.
57 Binger, *Du Niger*, Vol. 1, p. 375; Dubois, *Timbouctou*, p. 179; R. Bluzet, "La Region de Timbouctou," *Bull. Soc. Geog. de Paris*, 1895, p. 322ff.
58 P. L. Monteil, *De Saint Louis*, pp. 268, 280; Raffanel, *Pays des nègres*, Vol. 1, p. 233.
59 Mage, *Voyage*, p. 191.
60 Soleillet, *Voyage*, p. 235; Gallieni, *Voyage*, p. 380; Jaime, *Koulikoro*, p. 233 n. 1; Caron, *Saint-Louis*, pp. 278, 287; P. L. Monteil, *De Saint Louis*, p. 280 (values in 1895 were anomalous, owing to the glut of French silver coin); Baillaud, *Soudan*, pp. 70–71.
61 Binger, *Du Niger*, Vol. 1, pp. 27, 54, 162, 191, 206. The apparently round numbers of the exchange rate at Tenetou, Tiong-i, Fourou, and Benkhobougoula are for the actual number of shells; these were locally expressed in Bambara hundreds of 80, and in the case of the last, in Mandingo hundreds of 60 each. Concerning the latter part of the paragraph, Binger wrote (p. 308): "it is impossible to make comparison with silver, as there is none in circulation ... when, in the course of my narrative, I speak of an object which costs 3, 4, 5 francs, that means that, with the number of cowries asked, I could have procured 3, 4, 5 francs in gold dust at the rate of 3 francs per gram."
62 *Ibid.*, Vol. 1, pp. 308, 375, Vol. 2, pp. 103, 142, 166. For the weight of the *barifiri*, see also B. Menzel, *Goldgewichte aus Ghana*, Berlin, 1968, which gives the actual weights of specimens collected at Salaga within a few years of Binger's visit.
63 Wolf, "Letzte Reise nach Borgu," p. 1ff.; Lugard, *Diaries*, p. 192.
64 Daumas and de Chancel, *Grand Désert*, p. 239.
65 The data are compiled from Ryder, "Portuguese Trading Voyage," p. 301; Dapper, *Description*, French ed., Amsterdam, 1686, p. 306; Barbot, *North and South-Guinea*, Vol. 5, p. 339 (Barbot's references to the prices of fowls on the Gold Coast and at Whydah are at pp. 217 and 330); Rask, *Guinea*, p. 257; Berbain, *Juda*; Forbes, *Dahomey*, Vol. 1, p. 110.
66 For economic stagnation, see the work of Colin Newbury, especially "Trade and Authority in West Africa from 1850 to 1880," in L. H. Gann and Peter Duignan, eds., *Colonialism in Africa 1870–1960*, Vol. 1, *The History and Politics of Colonialism 1870–1914*, Cambridge, 1969, pp. 66–99; Newbury, "Prices and Profitability;" and *Western Slave Coast*; and Hopkins, *Economic History*, chapter 4. The import limits beyond which inflation and exchange rate depreciation set in are calculated from data in Hieke, *Deutschen Handels*, Vol. 1, p. 283; *Annual Statement of the Trade and Navigation of the United Kingdom*, 1852–1866, under "British Possessions on the Gold Coast;" and Hopkins, "Currency Revolution," p. 405.
67 These limits might conceivably give some measure of the expansion of the internal exchange economy of the period, but uncertainties concerning the magnitudes involved make the exercise highly speculative. If the local values of cowries imported in any given year of price stability are multiplied by some assumed velocity of circulation, say the 4 or 5 suggested by Jacques Melitz (*Primitive Money*, pp. 61–64), then with $MV = PQ$, the quotient should be a rough measure of growth in the monetized sector. The idea is developed by Webb, "Comparative Study of Money," pp. 455–466. For a similar approach that attempts to measure the total size of the cowrie money stock in Dahomey during the eighteenth century, see Manning, *Dahomey*, p. 44. Manning's tentative suggestion is that the per capita money supply (mainly cowries) may have been close to that of the early twentieth century. Marion Johnson's calculations for the Lagos hinterland suggest that there may have been an actual decline in the local value of circulating money as cowries were replaced by shillings. See "Cowrie Currencies," Part 2, pp. 350–351.

10 The last of the cowrie

1 Sundström, *Exchange*, has a short listing of cowries going out of use, p. 105. For the end on

the Gold Coast see Robert Chalmers, *A History of Currency in the British Colonies*, London, 1893, p. 215.

2 Delafosse, *Haut-Sénégal-Niger*, Vol. 3, p. 48; Elliot P. Skinner, "Trade and Markets Among the Mossi People," in Paul Bohannan and George Dalton, eds., *Markets in Africa*, Evanston, Ill., 1962; Einzig, *Primitive Money*, p. 157.

3 Lugard, *Political Memoranda*, p. 224.

4 M. G. Smith, *Government in Zazzau*, London, 1960, p. 342n.

5 "Langa Langa," *Up Against It in Nigeria*, London, 1922, p. 18. See also A. H. M. Kirk-Greene, "The Major Currencies in Nigerian History," *Journal of the Historical Society of Nigeria*, Vol. 2, No. 1, 1960, p. 140.

6 Hopkins, *Economic History*, pp. 151, 206; Einzig, *Primitive Money*, p. 147. The separation in the import and export trades had taken place much earlier, starting in the 1850s, on the coast of Dahomey and in the area of Lagos. See Manning, *Dahomey*, p. 151.

7 The same conclusion is reached by Sundström, *Exchange*, pp. 105–106, with sources.

8 Birtwistle's report is in the Nigerian National Archives, Kaduna, SNP7/8/1765/1907, p. 16. (Our thanks to Paul Lovejoy for bringing it to our attention.) Birtwistle was a very strong proponent of fixing exchange rates between sterling and cowries.

9 For the end of taxes in cowries at Kano, see Polly Hill, *Population, Prosperity and Poverty: Rural Kano 1900 and 1970*, Cambridge, 1977, pp. 53–54. For the tax payments in Niger, see Stephen Baier, *An Economic History of Central Niger*, Oxford, 1980, p. 106. Hopkins has studied the increasing use of silver coin at the turn of the century in his paper, "The Creation of a Colonial Monetary System: the Origins of the West African Currency Board," *African Historical Studies*, Vol. 3, No. 1, 1970, pp. 101–132; and see Hopkins, *Economic History*, p. 206.

10 Ofonagoro, "Traditional to British Currency," pp. 649–650, quoting CO/520/72 and CO/520/61; Kirk-Greene, "Major Currencies," pp. 140, 148; Basden, *Ibos*, p. 200; Hopkins, "Currency Revolution," p. 483. The average *Cypraea moneta*, at 400 to the pound, weighs about 18 grains, heavier than the original tenth-penny anini, though only about half the weight of the average *annulus* used for money in West Africa.

11 M. Johnson, "Cowrie Currencies," part 2, p. 352; Ofonagoro, "Traditional to British Currency," p. 650; Basden, *Ibos*, p. 199; Einzig, *Primitive Money*, p. 148.

12 Einzig, *Primitive Money*, p. 157; Sundström, *Exchange*, p. 105.

13 Lord Lugard, *The Dual Mandate in British Tropical Africa*, London, 1922, p. 491; see also Quiggin, *Primitive Money*, p. 83. *The Gazetteer of Zaria Province*, London, 1920, states for 1919: "Cowries no longer used as money" (see p. 22). They went completely out of use as currency in East Africa at almost exactly the same time: 1921, according to Forbes and Ali, "Maldive Islands," p. 18.

14 P. L. Monteil, *De Saint Louis*, pp. 269, 280; W. B. Seabrook, *White Monk of Timbuctu*, London, 1934, p. 238; Horace Miner, "The Primitive City of Timbuctoo," *Memoirs of the American Philosophical Society*, Vol. 32, 1953, p. 49.

15 Einzig, *Primitive Money*, p. 157; Manning, *Dahomey*, pp. 19, 254.

16 Basden, *Ibos*, p. 199; Ofonagoro, "Traditional to British Currency," p. 627.

17 Basden, *Ibos*, pp. 196–200; Ofonagoro, "Traditional to British Currency," pp. 639, 649; M. M. Green, *Igbo Village Affairs*, London, 1964, p. 41 n.2; Einzig, *Primitive Money*, p. 148.

18 S. F. Nadel, "A Ritual Currency in Nigeria – a Result of Culture Contact," *Africa*, No. 3, 1937, pp. 488–489; Nadel, *A Black Byzantium*, London, 1942, p. 310; Kirk-Greene, "Major Currencies," p. 140; Melville J. Herskovits, *Economic Anthropology: the Economic Life of Primitive Peoples*, New York, 1965, pp. 249–250. Manning, *Dahomey*, pp. 19, 254, notes a cowrie comeback in that region during the Depression.

19 Ofonagoro "Traditional to British Currency," pp. 624, 627, 650, and sources cited at n. 105, p. 650. Vice, in his *Coinage* catalog, shows the 1/10 penny still minted in large

quantities in 1950, but it was thereafter replaced by an unsuccessful copper coin, the last mintings of which (1956 and 1957) circulated little.

20 Ofonagoro, "Traditional to British Currency," p. 651.
21 *Ibid.*
22 See Hill, *Rural Capitalism*, pp. 139–140; V. Paques, *Les Bambara*, Paris, 1954, p. 42; Marti, *Dogon*, p. 29; Skinner, "Mossi People," p. 262; and B. Holas, *Les Senoufo*, Paris, 1957, p. 72.
23 See J. L. Dougah, *Wa and Its People*, Legon, 1966: 20 to the penny. Other Ghanaian informants, who also mentioned the smuggling, said: 1950, 11.66 to 12.5 to the penny; 1965, 10 to a penny at Wa; and 5–10 to a penny at Lawra. Polly Hill found cowries at Wechau exchanging at 10 to the penny in 1965. We thank these informants, as well as the many others who have taken the trouble to bring or send information about cowrie values, over the space of nearly two decades.
24 Ofonagoro, "Traditional to British Currency," p. 652.
25 Ofonagoro, "Currency Revolution," p. 21.
26 Hopkins, *Economic History*, p. 149; UAC, "The Manilla Problem," *United Africa Company Statistical and Economic Review*, Vol. 3, 1949, pp. 44–56; Ofonagoro, "Currency Revolution," pp. 18–20; Ofonagoro, "Traditional to British Currency," pp. 643–647.
27 The West African Currency Board has been well explored. See especially Hopkins, "West African Currency Board," pp. 101–132; W. T. Newlyn and D. C. Rowan, *Money and Banking in British Colonial Africa*, Oxford, 1954; and J. B. Loynes, *The West African Currency Board 1912–1962*, London, 1962. The French colonial system has received less academic attention. See Leduc, *Institutions monétaires africaines*; and Albert Duchene, *Histoire des finances coloniale de la France*, Paris, 1938.
28 For a calculation of the seigniorage involved in the colonial currency issues, see Jan S. Hogendorn and Henry A. Gemery, "Cash Cropping, Currency Acquisition and Seigniorage in West Africa: 1923–1950," *African Economic History*, No. 11, 1982, pp. 19–23. There is a recent literature on seigniorage, representing a return to a topic that excited much interest in the nineteenth century, cited in *ibid*.
29 The French colonial system was generally very similar to the British; some aspects of it were retained after the francophone states obtained their independence. For particulars (and note Andrew Liddell's comment that "it is not easy to obtain details of the workings of the CFA system") see Andrew Liddell, "Finance Co-operation in Africa – French Style," *The Banker*, September, 1979, p. 105, and January, 1982, p. 41; Robert A. Mundell, "African Trade, Politics and Money," in Rodrigue Tremblay, ed., *Africa and Monetary Integration*, Montreal, 1972, p. 33; "French African Economies – the Empire Stays Put," *The Economist*, July 10, 1982, pp. 66–67; and Patrick and Sylviane Guillaumont, "Zone franc et developpement: les characteristiques de la zone franc sont-elles dissociables?" in Tremblay, *Monetary Integration*, p. 313.
30 The practice is a very old one, with such rooms at Benin described by Ryder, *Benin*, p. 202. Paula Ben-Amos, *The Art of Benin*, London, 1980, p. 10, has a picture of such a floor. The caption notes that "one of the special forms of decoration in a Chief's house used to be embedding the parlour floor with cowrie shells, an earlier form of currency."
31 Lovejoy, "Interregional Monetary Flows," p. 566, discusses the etymology of *kudi*.
32 Heritier, "Des Cauris et des hommes," p. 492.
33 See Abiola Félix Iroko, "Cauris et esclaves en Afrique Occidentale entre le XVIe et le XIXe siècles," paper presented at the Colloque International sur la Traite des Noirs, Université de Nantes, July, 1985, pp. 5–6. A similar tradition is reported by R. Verdier, *Le Pays Kabiyé*, Paris, 1982, quoted by Iroko, p. 11.
34 Einzig, *Primitive Money*, p. 314.
35 Maloney, *People*, pp. 120–121; Heimann, "Small Change," p. 55; Bell, *Maldive Islands* (1940), p. 47; Rosset, "The Maldive Islands," p. 416.

36 From the Indian Customs Records, PRO, and H. C. P. Bell, *The Maldive Islands*, Ceylon
   Sessional Paper No. 15 of 1921, Colombo, 1921, p. 37. Extremely large quantities of cheap
   East African *annulus* were coming to India in the 1880s and 1890s, mainly from Zanzibar
   and mainly to Bombay. The annual average, 1881–82 to 1892–93, was 919 tonnes. The
   much smaller quantities of more expensive Maldive *moneta* (their price was usually more
   than double that of the East African shells) went mostly to Bengal.
37 Records seen in the Republic of Maldives Customs House, Male.
38 As noted in Bell, "Small Notebook A," p. 15.
39 Our thanks to Abdullah Faiz of Kalegefanu Enterprises, I. M. Didi of the firm of that name,
   and A. H. H. Maniku, all of Male in the Maldives, and Phirov Sukhadwala of Coin
   Shellcrafts House, Bombay, for describing the present trade in cowries and the uses to
   which shells are now put.

Bibliography

Abbott, R. Tucker, *Kingdom of the Seashell*, New York, 1982.

Abitbol, Michel, ed. and trans., *Tombouctou au milieu du XVIIIe siècle d'après la chronique de Mawlay al-Qásím b. Mawlay Sulaymán*, Paris, 1982.

Adams, John, *Cape Palmas to the Rio Congo*, London, 1823.

Agassiz, A., "Prof. Agassiz' Expedition to the Maldives," *Geographical Journal*, Vol. 19, No. 4, 1902, pp. 480–483.

Albéca, A. L., "L'Avenir du Dahomey," *Annales de Géographie*, 1895, pp. 166–189.

Albéca, A. L. *Établissements français au Golfe de Bénin*, Paris, 1889.

Allan, J., "The Coinage of the Maldive Islands with some Notes on the Cowrie and Larin," *Numismatic Chronicle*, Vol. 12 (4th series), 1912, pp. 313–332.

Allen, William and T. R. H. Thompson, *Expedition to the River Niger*, London, 1848.

Ames, David W., "The Use of a Traditional Cloth-Money Token Among the Wolof," *American Anthropologist*, Vol. 57, 1955, pp. 1016–1024.

Anania, Giovanni Lorenzo, *La Universale Fabrica del Mondo Overa Cosmographia*, (1st ed., 1573, 3rd ed., 1582). See Dierk Lange with Silvio Berthoud.

Andersson, J. Gunnar, *Children of the Yellow Earth: Studies in Prehistoric China*, New York, 1934.

Annual Statement of the Trade and Navigation of the United Kingdom, various years.

Anstey, Roger, *The Atlantic Slave Trade and British Abolition, 1760–1810*, London, 1975.

Arasaratnam, Sinnappah, *Dutch Power in Ceylon 1658–1687*, Amsterdam, 1958.

Arasaratnam, S., "The Kingdom of Kandy: Aspects of Its External Relations and Commerce, 1658–1710," *Ceylon Journal of Historical and Social Studies*, Vol. 3, 1960, pp. 109–127.

Arasaratnam, S., "*Mare Clausum*, the Dutch and Regional Trade in the Indian Ocean 1650–1740," paper presented at the International Conference on Indian Ocean Studies, Perth, Australia, August 1979.

Armstrong, Robert G., *Yoruba Numerals*, Oxford, 1962.

Atkins, John, *Voyage to Guinea*, London, 1735.

Baier, Stephen, *An Economic History of Central Niger*, Oxford, 1980.

Baikie, W. B., "Journey from Bida to Kano," *Journal of the Royal Geographical Society*, 1867.

Baillaud, Emile, *Sur les routes du Soudan*, Toulouse, 1902.

al-Bakri, *Description de l'Afrique septentrionale*, trans. de Slane, Paris, 1913.

Barbosa, Duarte, *The Book of Duarte Barbosa*, ed. M. L. Dames, London, 1918.

Barbot, John, *A Description of the Coasts of North and South-Guinea*, Vol. 5 of A. and J. Churchill, eds., *A Collection of Voyages and Travels*, London, 1732. (Barbot's 1688 manuscript is being prepared for publication by the Hakluyt Society.)

Bargery, Dr. G. P., *Hausa-English Dictionary*, London, 1934.

Barraclough, Geoffrey, ed., *The Times Atlas of World History*, London, 1979.

Barros, João de, *Decadas, Da Asia*, in Albert Gray and H. C. P. Bell, eds., *Voyage of François Pyrard de Laval*, London, 1890 (orig. 1552–1615. Lisbon edn. 1778).

Barth, Heinrich, *Travels and Discoveries in North and Central Africa*, London and Gotha, 1857–1858.

Basden, George Thomas, *Among the Ibos of Nigeria*, London, 1921.

Basden, George Thomas, *Niger Ibos*, London, 1966.

Baumann, Oskar, *Fernando Póo und die Bube*, Vienna, 1888.

Bean, Richard Nelson, *The British Trans-Atlantic Slave Trade 1650–1775*, New York, 1975.

Beckmann, J., *Vorbereitung zur Waarenkunde*, Göttingen, 1793.

Bell, H. C. P., "Excerpta Maldiviana: No. 4. A Description of the Maldive Islands *circa* A.C. 1683," *Journal of the Royal Asiatic Society (Ceylon)*, Vol. 30, No. 78, 1925, pp. 132–142.

Bell, H. C. P., "Excerpta Maldiviana: No. 10. The Portuguese at the Maldives," *Journal of the Royal Asiatic Society (Ceylon)*, Vol. 32, No. 84, 1931, pp. 76–124.

Bell, H. C. P., "Excerpta Maldiviana: No. 11. Dutch Intercourse with the Maldives: Seventeenth Century," *Journal of the Royal Asiatic Society (Ceylon)*, Vol. 32, No. 85, 1932, pp. 226–242.

Bell, H. C. P., *The Maldive Islands: an Account of the Physical Features, Climate, History, Inhabitants, Productions, and Trade*, Colombo, 1883.

Bell, H. C. P., *The Maldive Islands, Ceylon Sessional Paper No. 15 of 1921*, Colombo, 1921.

Bell, H. C. P., *The Maldive Islands: Monograph on the History, Archaeology, and Epigraphy*, Colombo, 1940.

Bell, H. C. P., "The Maldive Islands: 1602–1607," *Ceylon Antiquary and Literary Register*, Vol. 1, Nos. 2–4, April 1916, pp. 133–139, 208–212, 266–278.

Belshaw, Cyril S., *Traditional Exchange and Modern Markets*, Englewood Cliffs, N.J., 1965.

Ben-Amos, Paula, *The Art of Benin*, London, 1980.

Berbain, Simone, *Le Comptoir français de Juda (Ouidah) au XVIIIᵉ siècle*, Paris, 1942.

Best, Thomas, *The Voyage of Thomas Best to the East Indies 1612–14*, ed. William Foster, London, 1934.

Bhattacharya, Sukumar, *The East India Company and the Economy of Bengal*, London, 1954.

Binger, Louis Gustave, *Du Niger au golfe de Guinée par le pays de Kong et le Mossi, par le capitaine Binger*, Paris, 1892.

Binger, L. G., "Transactions, objets de commerce, monnaie des contrées entre le Niger et la Côte d'Or", *Bulletin de la Société de Géographie commerciale de Paris*, Vol. 12, 1889/90, pp. 77–90.

Biobaku, S. O., *The Egba and their Neighbours*, Oxford, 1957.

Birmingham, David, "Central Africa from Cameroun to the Zambezi," in Roland Oliver, ed., *The Cambridge History of Africa*, Vol. 3, *c. 1050—c. 1600*, Cambridge, 1977.

Blake, John William., ed., *Europeans in West Africa, 1450–1560*, London, 1942.

Blussé, Leonard, "Trojan Horse of Lead: the Picis in Early 17th Century Java," in F. van Anrooij, D. H. A. Kolff, J. T. M. van Laanen, and G. J. Telkamp, *Between People and Statistics: Essays on Modern Indonesian History*, The Hague, 1979.

Blussé, Leonard, and Femme Gaastra, eds., *Companies and Trade: Essays on Overseas Trading Companies during the Ancient Regime*, The Hague, 1981.

Bluzet, R., "La Region de Timbouctou," *Bulletin Soc. Geog. de Paris*, 1895, pp. 374–389.

Bohannan, Paul, "The Impact of Money on an African Subsistence Economy," *Journal of Economic History*, Vol. 19, No. 4, Dec. 1959, pp. 491–503.

Bonnat, M.-J., "Journal," *L'Explorateur*, 1876.

Bosman, William, *A New and Accurate Description of the Coast of Guinea*, London, 2nd ed., 1721, 4th English ed., 1967.

Bouche, Pierre Bertrand, *Côte des esclaves et Dahomey*, Paris, 1885.

Bouche, Pierre Bertrand, *Sept Ans en Afrique Occidentale*, Paris, 1885.

Bovill, E. W., *The Golden Trade of the Moors*, London, 2nd ed., 1968.

Bibliography

Bovill, E. W., *The Niger Explored*, London, 1968.

Bowdich, Thomas Edward, *Mission from Cape Coast Castle to Ashantee*, London, 1819.

Bowrey, Thomas, *A Geographical Account of the Countries Round the Bay of Bengal, 1669–1679*, Cambridge, 1905.

Bowrey, Thomas, *The Papers of Thomas Bowrey*, ed. R. C. Temple, London, 1927.

Boxer, C. R., *The Dutch Seaborne Empire 1600–1800*, Harmondsworth, 1973.

Boxer, C. R., *The Portuguese Seaborne Empire 1415–1825*, London, 1969.

Braudel, Fernand, *The Mediterranean and the Mediterranean World in the Time of Philip II*, London, 1973.

Braudel, Fernand, *The Structures of Everyday Life*, trans. Siân Reynolds, Vol. 1 of *Civilizatior and Capitalism 15th–18th Century*, New York, 1981.

Bronson, Bennet, "Cash, Cannon, and Cowrie Shells: The Nonmodern Moneys of the World," *Field Museum of Natural History Bulletin*, Vol. 47, No. 10, 1976, pp. 3–15.

Bronsted, J., ed., *Vore Gamle Tropenkolonier*, Copenhagen, 1954.

Browder, Tim J., *Maldive Islands Money*, Santa Monica, Calif., 1969.

Brown, Robert, ed., *The History and Description of Africa . . . of Leo Africanus*, trans. Pory London, 1896.

Bruijn, J. R., "Between Batavia and the Cape: Shipping Patterns of the Dutch East India Company." Paper delivered at the International Conference on Indian Ocean Studies Perth, Australia, August 1979.

Burdo, A., *Niger et Benue*, Paris, 1880.

Burgess, C. M., *The Living Cowries*, New York, 1970.

Burton, Richard F., *Mission to Gelele*, London, 1864.

Burton, Richard F., *Wanderings in West Africa*, London, 1863.

Buttner, R., "Bericht von Dr. R. Buttner über eine Reise von Bismarckburg nach Tschautje und Fasugu," *Mitteilungen aus den deutschen Schutzgebieten*, Vol. 4, 1891, pp. 127–189.

Buxton, T. Fowell, *The Slave Trade*, London, 1838.

Cadamosto, Alvise, *Voyages*, ed. G. R. Crone, London, 1937.

Caillié, René, *Journal d'un voyage à Temboctou et à Jenne, dans l'Afrique centrale*, Paris 1830.

Caillié, René, *Travels through Central Africa to Timbuctoo*, London, 1830.

Campos, J. J. A., *History of the Portuguese in Bengal*, Calcutta, 1979.

Caron, Edmond, *De Saint-Louis au port de Tombouktou*, Paris, 3rd ed., 1893.

de Carrocera, Buenaventura, *Mission Capuchina al Reino de Arda*, Vol. 6, 1949.

Carstensen, E., *Journal*, Copenhagen, 1965.

Carswell, John, "China and Islam in the Maldive Islands," *Transactions of the Oriental Ceramic Society*, Vol. 41, 1975–1977, pp. 119–198.

Cassel, Gustav, *The Theory of Social Economy*, New York, 1924.

Chalmers, Robert, *A History of Currency in the British Colonies*, London, 1893.

Chaudhuri, K. N., *The English East India Company: the Study of an Early Joint-Stock Company 1600–1640*, London, 1965.

Chaudhuri, K. N., "European Trade with India," in Tapan Raychaudhuri and Irfan Habib eds., *The Cambridge Economic History of India*, Vol. 1, c. 1200—c. 1750, Cambridge, 1982 pp. 382–407.

Chaudhuri, K. N., *The Trading World of Asia and the English East India Company 1660–1760* Cambridge, 1978.

Chaudhuri, Susil, *Trade and Commercial Organization in Bengal 1650–1720*, Calcutta, 1975.

Chau Ju-Kua, *On the Chinese and Arab Trade in the Twelfth and Thirteenth Centuries*, trans F. Hirth and W. Rockhill, St. Petersburg, 1911.

Chilver, E. M., "Nineteenth Century Trade in the Bamenda Grassfields, Southern Cameroons," *Afrika und Übersee*, Vol. 45, No. 4, 1961, pp. 233–258.

Churchill, Awnsham and John, eds., *A Collection of Voyages and Travels*, London, 1732.

204

Clapperton, Hugh and R. L. Lander, *Records of Captain Clapperton's Last Expedition to Africa*, London, 1830.

Clausen, G. L. M., "The British Colonial Currency System," *Economic Journal*, Vol. 54, No. 213, 1944, pp. 1–25.

Colvin, Lucie G., "The Commerce of Hausaland, 1780–1833," in Daniel F. McCall and Norman R. Bennett, eds., *Aspects of West African Islam*, Boston, 1971, pp. 101–135.

Connah, Graham, *Archaeology of Benin*, Oxford, 1975.

Cooper, Frederick, *Plantation Slavery on the East African Coast*, New Haven, 1977.

Correa, Gaspar, *Lendas da India*, Lisbon, 1858–1864.

Couto, Carlos, *O Zimbo na Historiografia Angolana*, Luanda, 1973.

Crowe, Philip K., *Diversions of a Diplomat in Ceylon*, London, 1957.

Cruikshank, Brodie, *Eighteen Years on the Gold Coast of Africa*, London, 1853.

Crump, Thomas, *The Phenomenon of Money*, London, 1981.

Cuoq, Joseph M., *Recueil des sources arabes concernant l'Afrique occidentale du VIIIe au XVIe siècle*, Paris, 1975.

Curtin, Philip D., "Africa and the Wider Monetary World, 1250–1850," in J. F. Richards, ed., *Precious Metals in the Later Medieval and Early Modern Worlds*, Durham, N.C., 1983.

Curtin, Philip D., *The Atlantic Slave Trade: a Census*, Madison, 1969.

Curtin, Philip D., "The Atlantic Slave Trade 1600–1800," in J. F. A. Ajayi and Michael Crowder, eds., *History of West Africa*, New York, Vol. 1, 1972.

Curtin, Philip D., *Cross-Cultural Trade in World History*, Cambridge, 1984.

Curtin, Philip D., "The Slave Trade and the Atlantic Basin: Intercontinental Perspectives," in Nathan I. Huggins, Martin Kilson, and Daniel M. Fox, eds., *Key Issues in the Afro-American Experience*, New York, 1971.

Daaku, K. Yeboa, "Pre-European Currencies of West Africa and Western Sudan," *Ghana Notes and Queries*, No. 2, May-Aug. 1961, pp. 12–14.

Dalboquerque, Afonso, *The Commentaries of Afonso Dalboquerque*, trans. Walter Birch, London, 1884.

Dalton, George, "Primitive Money," *American Anthropologist*, Vol. 67, 1965, pp. 44–65.

Dalzel, Archibald, *History of Dahomey*, London, 1793.

Daniell, W. F., "Ethnography of Akkrah and Adampe," *Journal of the Ethnographical Society*, London, 1856.

Danvers, Frederick Charles, *The Portuguese in India*, London, 1894.

Dapper, Olfert, *Naukeurige Beschrijvinge der Afrikaensche Gewesten*, door Dr. O. Dapper, Amsterdam, 1668.

Dartevelle, Edmond, *Les "N'zimbu," monnaie du Royaume de Congo*, Bruxelles, *Mémoires de la Société belge d'anthropologie et de pré-histoire*, 1953.

Dasgupta, A., "Indian Merchants and the Trade in the Indian Ocean," in Tapan Raychaudhuri and Irfan Habib, eds., *The Cambridge Economic History of India*, Vol. 1, *c. 1200—c. 1750*, Cambridge, 1982, pp. 407–433.

Datta, Kalikinkar, "The Dutch Factory at Balasore and Anglo-Dutch Hostilities There in 1786–87," *Indian Historical Records Commission*, Vol. 19, 1942, pp. 86–89.

Daumas, Melchior Joseph Eugène, and Ausone de Chancel, *Le Grand Désert: ou, Itinéraire d'une caravane de Sahara au pays des Nègres*, Paris, 1848.

Davies, K. G., *The Royal African Company*, London, 1957.

De, Sushil Chandra, "The Cowry Currency in India," *Orissa Historical Research Journal*, Vol. 1, No. 1, 1952, pp. 1–10.

De, Sushil Chandra, "Cowry Currency in Orissa," *Orissa Historical Research Journal*, Vol. 1, No. 1, 1952, pp. 10–21.

Défrémery, C., and B. R. Sanguinetti, eds. and trans., *Voyages d'Ibn Batoutah*, Paris, 1858–1859.

Delafosse, Maurice, *Haut-Sénégal-Niger*, Paris, 1912.

Bibliography

Del Mar, Alexandre, *Monograph on the History of Money in China from the Earliest Times to the Present*, San Francisco, 1881.

Denham, Dixon and Hugh Clapperton, *Narrative of Travels and Discovery in North and Central Africa*, London, 1826.

Deutsch, J., *Die Zahlungsmittel der Naturvölker in Afrika*, Marburg, 1957.

Dickson, C. H., "Account of Ghadames," *Journal of the Royal Geographical Society* 1860.

Diffie, Bailey W., and George W. Winius, eds., *Foundations of the Portuguese Empire, 1415–1580*, Minneapolis, 1977.

Digby, Simon, "The Currency System," in Tapan Raychaudhuri and Irfan Habib, eds., *The Cambridge Economic History of India*, Vol. 1, *c. 1200—c. 1750*, Cambridge, 1982 pp. 93–101.

Digby, Simon, "The Maritime Trade of India," in Tapan Raychaudhuri and Irfan Habib, eds. *The Cambridge Economic History of India*, Vol. 1, *c. 1200—c. 1750*, Cambridge, 1982 pp. 125–159.

"Dobson, George," "The River Volta, Gold Coast, West Africa," *Journal of the Manchester Geographical Society*, Vol. 8, 1892.

Dodd, Agnes F., *History of Money in the British Empire and the United States*, London, 1911.

Donnan, Elizabeth, *Documents Illustrative of the History of the Slave Trade to America* Washington, 1931.

Doortmont, Michel R., "De organisetie van de Atlantische Handel in het West Afrikaanse Kustgebied," unpublished thesis, University of Rotterdam, 1984.

Dorward, D. C., "Precolonial Tiv Trade and Cloth Currency," *International Journal of African Historical Studies*, Vol. 9, No. 4, 1976, pp. 576–591.

Dougah, J. L., *Wa and Its People*, Legon, 1966.

Drescher, Seymour, *Econocide: British Slavery in the Era of Abolition*, Pittsburg, 1977.

Dubois, F., *Timbouctou la mystérieuse*, Paris, 1897.

Duchêne, Albert, *Histoire des finances coloniale de la France*, Paris, 1938.

Dupuis, Joseph, *Journal of a Residence in Ashantee*, London, 1824.

Dutch Gentleman, *Voyage to the Island of Ceylon on Board a Dutch Indiaman in the Year 1747*, London, 1754.

Dutt, Romesh, *The Economic History of India*, Delhi, 1963 (reprint of 1884 ed.).

The Economist, "French African Economies – the Empire Stays Put", July 10, 1982 pp. 66–67.

Egami, Namio, "Migration of the Cowrie-Shell Culture in East Asia," *Acta Asiatica*, No. 26 1974, pp. 1–52.

Einzig, Paul, *Primitive Money*, London, 1949.

Fah-Hian, *Travels of Fah-Hian*, trans. Samuel Beal, New York, 1969.

Felix, Alonso, Jr., ed., *The Chinese in the Philippines*, Manila, 1966.

Firth, Raymond, ed., *Themes in Economic Anthropology*, London, 1967.

Fischer, Stanley, "Seigniorage and the Case for a National Money," *Journal of Political Economy*, Vol. 90, No. 2, 1982, pp. 295–313.

Fisher, Allan G. B., and Humphrey J. Fisher, *Slavery and Muslim Society in Africa*, London 1970.

Fitzler, M. A. H., *Die Handelsgesellschaft Felix v. Oldenburg & Co. 1753–1760*, Stuttgart 1931.

Fitzler, M. A. H., "Die Maldiven im 16. und 17. Jahrhunder," *Zeitschrift für Indologie und Iranstik*, Vol. 10, 1935–36, pp. 215–256.

Fleischer, H. L., ed., *Abulfedae historia anteislamica*, Leipzig, 1831.

Foà, Edouard, *Le Dahomey*, Paris, 1895.

Forbes, Andrew D. W., "Archives and Resources for Maldivian History," *South Asia*, Vol. 3 No. 1, 1980, pp. 70–82.

Forbes, Andrew D. W., "Southern Arabia and the Islamicisation of the Central Indian Ocean Archipelagoes," *Archipel*, Vol. 21, 1981, pp. 55–92.

Forbes, Andrew and Fawzia Ali, "The Maldive Islands and their Historical Links with the Coast of Eastern Africa," *Kenya Past and Present*, Vol. 11, 1981, pp. 15–20.

Forbes, Frederick E., *Dahomey and the Dahomans*, London, 1851.

Foster, William, ed., *The English Factories in India 1618–1669, a Calendar of Documents in the India Office, British Museum and Public Record Office*, London, *1630–33*, 1910, *1634–36*, 1911, *1655–60*, 1921, *1668–69*, 1927.

Freeman-Grenville, G. S. P., *The French at Kilwa Island*, Oxford, 1965.

Fry, H. T., "Early British Interest in the Chagos Archipelago and the Maldive Islands," *The Mariner's Mirror*, Vol. 53, No. 4, Nov. 1967, pp. 343–356.

Fryer, John, *East India and Persia*, London, 1909.

Furber, Holden, *John Company at Work*, Cambridge, 1948.

Furber, Holden, *Rival Empires of Trade in the Orient*, Minneapolis, 1976.

Gaastra, F. S., "De V.O.C. in Azië 1680–1795" in *Algemene Geschiedenis der Nederlanden*, Vol. 9, Haarlem, 1980, pp. 427–464.

Gaastra, F. S., "De V.O.C. in Azië tot 1680" in *Algemene Geschiedenis der Nederlanden*, Vol. 7, Haarlem, 1979, pp. 174–219.

Gallieni, J. S., *Voyage au Soudan français, 1879–81*, Paris, 1884.

Ganay, Solange de, "Graphes Bambara des Nombres," *Journal de la Société des Africanistes*, Vol. 20, 1950, pp. 295–305.

Gardiner, J. Stanley, ed., *The Fauna and Geography of the Maldive and Laccadive Archipelagoes*, Cambridge, 2 vols.; Vol. 1, 1903; Vol. 2, 1906.

Gardiner, J. Stanley, "The Maldive and Laccadive Archipelagoes" in A. J. Herbertson and O. J. R. Howarth, eds., *Asia*, Vol. 2 of *The Oxford Survey of the British Empire*, Oxford, 1914, pp. 314–329.

Garfield, Robert, *A History of São Tomé Island*, unpublished Northwestern University Ph.D. thesis, 1971.

Garrard, Timothy F., *Akan Weights and the Gold Trade*, London, 1980.

Gazetteer of Zaria Province, London, 1920.

Gemery, H. A. and J. S. Hogendorn, "The Atlantic Slave Trade: a Tentative Economic Model," *Journal of African History*, Vol. 15, No. 2, 1974, pp. 223–246.

Gemery, H. A. and J. S. Hogendorn, "A Note on the Social Costs of Imported African Monies." Paper presented at the annual meeting of the African Studies Association, Houston, Texas, Nov. 5, 1977.

Gemery, H. A. and J. S. Hogendorn, "Technological Change, Slavery, and the Slave Trade," in Clive Dewey and A. G. Hopkins, eds., *The Imperial Impact: Studies in the Economic History of Africa and India*, London, 1978.

Gemery, H. A. and J. S. Hogendorn, eds., *The Uncommon Market: Essays in the Economic History of the Atlantic Slave Trade*, New York, 1979.

Gibb, H. A. R., *The Travels of Ibn Battuta*, Cambridge, 1958.

Gibson, Harry E., "The Use of Cowries as Money during the Shang and Chou Periods," *Journal of the North China Branch, Royal Asiatic Society*, No. 71, 1940, pp. 33–45.

Glamann, Kristof, *Dutch-Asiatic Trade 1620–1740*, Copenhagen and the Hague, 1958.

Gobert, E. G., "Le Pudendum magique et le problème des cauris," *Revue Africaine*, Vol. 95, 1951, pp. 5–62.

Goitein, S. D., *A Mediterranean Society*, Vol. 1, *Economic Foundations*, Berkeley, 1967.

Gold Coast Blue Books, various years.

Grace, John, *Domestic Slavery in West Africa*, New York, 1977.

Gray, Albert, and H. C. P. Bell, eds., *The Voyage of François Pyrard of Laval to the East Indies, the Maldives, the Moluccas, and Brazil*, London, 1887, 1890.

Green, M. M., *Igbo Village Affairs*, London, 1964.

Bibliography

Gregory, C. A., *Gifts and Commodities*, London, 1982.

Grierson, Philip, "The Origins of Money" in George Dalton, ed., *Research in Economic Anthropology*, Greenwich, Conn., Vol. 1, 1978.

Guillamont, Patrick and Sylviane, "Zone franc et developpement: les characteristiques de la zone franc sont-elles dissociables?" in Rodrique Tremblay, ed. *Africa and Monetary Integration*, Montreal, 1972.

Habib, Irfan, "Monetary System and Prices" in Tapan Raychaudhuri and Irfan Habib, eds., *The Cambridge Economic History of India*, Vol. 1, *c. 1200—c. 1750*, Cambridge, 1982, pp. 360–381.

Hallett, Robin, ed., *Records of the African Association 1788–1831*, London, 1964.

Hamilton, Alexander, *A New Account of the East Indies*, ed. Sir William Foster, London, 1930.

Harding, Leonhard, "The West African Trade of Hamburg in the 19th Century," paper given at the St. Augustin (Bonn) Symposium on African Trade, January, 1983.

Harms, Robert W., *River of Wealth, River of Sorrow: the Central Zaire Basin in the Era of the Slave and Ivory Trade, 1500–1891*, New Haven, 1981.

Hastings, A. G. C., *Voyage of the Dayspring (1857–9)*, London, 1926.

Hawkins, E. K., "The Growth of a Money Economy in Nigeria and Ghana," *Oxford Economic Papers*, Vol. 10, No. 3, Oct. 1958, pp. 339–354.

Heber, Reginald, *Narrative of a Journey through the Upper Provinces of India from Calcutta to Bombay 1824–1825*, London, 1828.

Hedges, William, *The Diary of William Hedges, Esq., 1681–1687*, London, 1887.

Heimann, James, "Small Change and Ballast: Cowry Trade and Usage as an Example of Indian Ocean Economic History," *South Asia*, Vol. 3, No. 1, 1980, pp. 48–69.

Heimann, James, "Small Change and Ballast: Cowry Trade and Usage as an Example of Indian Ocean Economic History," paper delivered at the International Conference on Indian Ocean Studies, Perth, Australia, August 1979.

Henty, G. A., *March to Coomassie*, London, 1874.

Herbert, Eugenia W., "Aspects of the Use of Copper in Pre-Colonial West Africa," *Journal of African History*, Vol. 14, No. 2, 1973, pp. 179–194.

Heritier, Françoise, "Des Cauris et des hommes: production d'esclaves et accumulation de cauris chez les Samo (Haute Volta)," in Claude Meillassoux, ed., *L'esclavage en Afrique précoloniale*, Paris, 1975, pp. 477–507.

Herskovits, Melville J., *Economic Anthropology: the Economic Life of Primitive Peoples*, New York, 1965.

Hertz, John E., "Ueber Verwendung und Verbreitung der Kauriemuschel," *Mitteilung der Geographische Gesellschaft in Hamburg*, Hamburg, 1881, pp. 14–29.

Hicks, Sir John, *Critical Essays in Monetary Theory*, Oxford, 1967.

Hieke, Ernst, *G. L. Gaiser, Hamburg-Westafrika, 100 Jahre Handel mit Nigeria*, Hamburg, 1949.

Hieke, Ernst, *Zur Geschichte des Deutschen Handels mit Ostafrika*, Hamburg, 1939.

Hill, Polly, *Migrant Cocoa-Farmers of Southern Ghana*, Cambridge, 1970.

Hill, Polly, "Notes on the History of the Northern Katsina Tobacco Trade," *Journal of the Historical Society of Nigeria*, Vol. 4, 1968.

Hill, Polly, *Population, Prosperity and Poverty: Rural Kano 1900 and 1970*, Cambridge, 1977.

Hill, Polly, *Studies in Rural Capitalism in West Africa*, Cambridge, 1970.

Hiskett, M., "Materials Relating to the Cowry Currency of the Western Sudan – I. A Late Nineteenth-Century Schedule of Inheritance from Kano," *S.O.A.S. Bulletin*, Vol. 29, No. 1, 1966, pp. 122–142.

Hiskett, M., "Materials Relating to the Cowry Currency of the Western Sudan – II. Reflections on the Provenance and Diffusion of the Cowry in the Sahara and the Sudan," *S.O.A.S. Bulletin*, Vol. 29, No. 2, 1966, pp. 339–366.

Hockly, T. W., *The Two Thousand Isles: a Short Account of the People, History and Customs of the Maldive Archipelago*, London, 1935.

Hogendorn, Jan S., *Nigerian Groundnut Exports: Origins and Early Development*, Ibadan and Zaria, 1978.

Hogendorn, Jan S., "A Research-Trip to the Maldive Islands, 1982," *Itinerario*, Vol. 6, No. 2, 1982, pp. 59–67.

Hogendorn, Jan S., "A 'Supply-side' Aspect of the African Slave Trade: the Cowrie Production and Trade of the Maldives," *Slavery and Abolition*, Vol. 2, No. 1, May 1981, pp. 31–52.

Hogendorn, Jan S. and Henry A. Gemery, "Abolition and Its Impact on Monies Imported to West Africa," in David Eltis and James Walvin, *The Abolition of the Atlantic Slave Trade*, Madison, 1981.

Hogendorn, Jan S. and Henry A. Gemery, "Cash Cropping, Currency Acquisition and Seigniorage in West Africa: 1923–1950," *African Economic History*, No. 11, 1982, pp. 15–27.

Hogendorn, J. S. and H. A. Gemery, "Social Saving, Social Cost and Seigniorage of West African Imported Monies: a Survey." Submitted for publication.

Hogendorn, Jan S. and Marion Johnson, "The Cowrie Trade to West Africa from the Maldives in the Nineteenth Century," in G. Liesegang, H. Pasch, and A. Jones, eds., *Figuring African Trade: Proceedings of the Symposium on the Quantification and Structure of the Import and Export and Long Distance Trade of Africa in the 19th Century (c. 1800–1913)*, to be published.

Hogendorn, Jan and Marion Johnson, "A New Money Supply Series for West Africa in the Era of the Slave Trade: the Import of the Cowrie Shell from Europe," *Slavery and Abolition*, Vol. 3, No. 2, 1982, pp. 153–162.

Holas, B., *Les Senoufo*, Paris, 1957.

Hopkins, A. G., "The Creation of a Colonial Monetary System; the Origins of the West African Currency Board," *African Historical Studies*, Vol. 3, No!. 1, 1970, pp. 101–132.

Hopkins, A. G., "The Currency Revolution in South-West Nigeria in the Late Nineteenth Century," *Journal of the Historical Society of Nigeria*, Vol. 3, No. 3, 1966, pp. 471–483.

Hopkins, A. G., *An Economic History of West Africa*, New York, 1973.

Hoppe, Fritz, *A África Oriental Portuguesa no tempo do Marquês de Pombal (1750–1777)*, Lisbon, 1970.

Horsburgh, James, "Some Remarks Relative to the Geography of the Maldive Islands, and the Navigable Channels (at present known to Europeans) which separate the Atolls from each other," *Journal of the Royal Geographical Society*, Vol. 2, 1832, pp. 72–80.

Hourani, G. F., *Arab Seafaring in the Indian Ocean in the Ancient and Early Medieval Times*, Princeton, 1951.

Hrbek, Ivan, "Egypt, Nubia and the Eastern Deserts," in Roland Oliver, ed., *The Cambridge History of Africa*, Vol. 3, *from c. 1050 to c. 1600*, London, 1977.

Hutchinson, Thomas Joseph, *Impressions of West Africa*, London, 1858.

Hutchinson, Thomas Joseph, *Narrative of the Niger, Tschadda and Binuë Exploration*, London, 1855.

Hutton, W., *A Voyage to Africa*, London, 1821.

Hyman, L. H., *The Invertebrates*, Vol. 6, *Mollusca I*, New York, 1967.

Ibn Battuta, *Voyages d'Ibn Battuta*, Paris, 1922.

Ibn Battuta, *Travels in Asia and Africa, 1325–1354*, trans. H. A. R. Gibb, London, 1963.

al-Idrisi, *al-Idrisi*, trans. S. Maqbul Ahmad, Leiden, 1960.

Iroko, Abiola Félix, "Cauris et Esclaves en Afrique Occidentale entre le XVIè et la XIXè siècles," paper presented at the Colloque International sur la Traite des Noirs, Université de Nantes, July 1985.

Isong, Clement Nyong, *Currency and Credit in Nigeria, 1850–1955: a Study of the Monetary*

Bibliography

System of a British Tropical Dependency, and Methods of Mobilizing its Domestic Resources for Economic Development, unpublished Harvard University Ph.D. thesis, 1957.

Jackson, J. Grey, *An Account of the Empire of Marocco*, London, 1814.

Jackson, J. Grey, *An Account of Timbuctoo and Hausa*, London, 1820.

Jackson, J. Wilfrid, "The Money Cowry (*Cypraea Moneta*, L.) as a Sacred Object among North American Indians", *Manchester Memoirs*, Vol. 60, No. 4, pp. 1–10.

Jackson, J. Wilfrid, *Shells as Evidence of the Migrations of Early Culture*, Manchester and London, 1917.

Jaime, G., *De Koulikoro à Timbuktu*, Paris, 1894.

Jeffreys, M. D. W., "The Cowry Shell: A Study of its History and Use in Nigeria," *Nigeria*, No. 15, 1938, pp. 221–256.

Jeffreys, M. D. W., "The Diffusion of Cowries and Egyptian Culture in Africa", *American Anthropologist*, Vol. 50, 1948, pp. 45–53.

Jeffreys, M. D. W., "The Marginelle Currency of Timbuctu," *Bulletin de l'IFAN*, Vol. 15, 1953, pp. 143–151.

Johnson, Harry G., *Further Essays in Monetary Economics*, Cambridge, 1973.

Johnson, Harry G., "Seigniorage and the Social Saving from Substituting Credit for Commodity Money" in Harry G. Johnson, *Further Essays in Monetary Economics*, Cambridge, 1973.

Johnson, Marion, "Calico Caravans: the Tripoli-Kano Trade after 1880," *Journal of African History*, Vol. 17, No. 1, 1976, pp. 95–117.

Johnson, Marion, "Cloth on the Banks of the Niger," *Journal of the Historical Society of Nigeria*, Vol. 6, No. 4, 1973, pp. 353–363.

Johnson, Marion, "Cloth Strip Currencies," Paper presented at the annual meeting of the African Studies Association, Houston, 1977.

Johnson, Marion, "The Cowrie Currencies of West Africa," *Journal of African History*, Part 1, Vol. 11, No. 1, 1970, pp. 17–49, and Part 2, Vol. 11, No. 3, 1970, pp. 331–353.

Johnson, Marion, "M. Bonnat on the Volta," *Ghana Notes and Queries*, No. 10, 1968.

Johnson, Marion, "The Nineteenth-Century Gold 'Mithqal' in West and North Africa," *Journal of African History*, Vol. 9, No. 4, 1968, pp. 547–570.

Johnson, Marion, "Note on Computerising African Trade Statistics," Paper given at the St. Augustin (Bonn) Symposium on African Trade, 1983.

Johnson, Marion, "The Ounce in Eighteenth-Century West African Trade," *Journal of African History*, Vol. 7, No. 2, 1966, pp. 197–214.

Johnson, Marion, Jan Hogendorn and Joanne Lynch, "The European Cowrie Trade," *Slavery and Abolition*, Vol. 2, No. 3, 1981, pp. 263–275.

Johnson, Samuel, *The History of the Yorubas*, Lagos, 1921, reprinted London, 1966.

Johnson, Scott, *Living Seashells*, Honolulu, n.d.

Jones, G. I., "Native and Trade Currencies in Southern Nigeria during the 18th and 19th Centuries," *Africa*, Vol. 28, 1958, pp. 43–54.

Julien, Ch.-A., *Historie de l'Afrique du nord*, Paris, 1961.

al-Kati, Mahmud, *Ta'rikh al-fattash*, Paris, 1913.

Kellenbenz, Hermann, "German Trade Relations with the Indian Ocean from the End of the 18th Century to 1870," paper presented to the International Conference on Indian Ocean Studies, Perth, Australia, 1979.

Kenyon, "The Cowrie Shell in Primitive Currency," *The Numismatist*, 1941, pp. 341–342.

Keynes, John Maynard, *A Treatise on Money*, London, 1930.

Kimble, D., *Rise of Nationalism in the Gold Coast*, London, 1960.

King, Blair B., and M. N. Pearson, eds., *The Age of Partnership: Europeans in Asia before Dominion*, Honolulu, 1979.

Kingsley, Mary, *Travels in West Africa*, London, 1891.

210

Kirk-Greene, A. H. M., "The Major Currencies in Nigerian History," *Journal of the Historical Society of Nigeria*, Vol. 2, No. 1, 1960, pp. 132–150.

Klein, Benjamin, "Money, Wealth, and Seigniorage," in K. F. Boulding and T. F. Wilson, eds., *Redistribution through the Financial System*, New York, 1978, pp. 3–19.

Klinkenberg, Floris M., "De Kaurihandel van de VOC," unpublished University of Leiden M.A. thesis, 1982.

Klose, Heinrich, *Togo unter deutscher Flagge*, Berlin, 1899.

Krause, A. G., *Fada Language on the Gabon River in Portuguese West Africa*, Berlin, 1895.

Krishna, Bal, *Commercial Relations Between India and England (1601–1757)*, London, 1924.

Labat, Jean Baptiste, *Voyage du Chevalier des Marchais*, Paris, 1730.

Labouret, Henri, "L'Échange et le commerce dans les archipels du Pacifique et en Afrique tropicale," in Jacques Lacour-Gayet, ed., *Histoire du commerce*, Paris, 1953, Tome 3, *Le commerce extra-Européen jusqu'aux temps modernes*.

Lacouperie, Terrien de, "The Metallic Cowries of Ancient China," *Journal of the Royal Asiatic Society*, Vol. 20, 1888, pp. 428–439.

Laird, Macgregor and R. A. K. Oldfield, *Narrative of an Expedition into the Interior of Africa by the River Niger in the Steam Vessels Quorra and Alburkah in 1832, 1833 and 1834*, London, 1837.

Lane, E. W., *Modern Egyptians*, London, 1860.

"Langa Langa," *Up Against It in Nigeria*, London, 1922.

Lange, Dierk, with Silvio Berthoud, "L'intérieur de l'Afrique Occidentale d'après Giovanni Lorenzo Anania (XVIe siècle)," *Cahiers d'historie mondiale*, Vol. 14, No. 2, 1972, pp. 298–349.

Latham, A. J. H., "Currency, Credit, and Capitalism on the Cross River in the Pre-Colonial Era," *Journal of African History*, Vol. 12, No. 4, 1971, pp. 599–605.

LeClair, Edward E., and Harold K. Schneider, eds., *Economic Anthropology*, New York, 1968.

Leduc, Michel, *Les Institutions monétaires africaines: pays francophones*, Paris, 1965.

Lenfant, Captain, *Le Niger*, Paris, 1903.

Lenz, Oskar, *Timbouctou*, Paris, 1886–7.

Leo Africanus, *Description d'Afrique*, Paris, 1956.

Leo Africanus – see Robert Brown.

Levtzion, Nehemia, "The Western Maghrib and Sudan," in Roland Oliver, ed., *The Cambridge History of Africa*, Vol. 3, c. 1050—c. 1600, London, 1977.

Levtzion, N. and J. F. P. Hopkins, eds., *Corpus of Early Arabic Sources for West African History*, Cambridge, 1981.

Lewis, Archibald, "Maritime Skills in the Indian Ocean, 1368–1500," *Journal of the Economic and Social History of the Orient*, Vol. 16, 1973, pp. 238–264.

Liddell, Andrew, "Financial Co-operation in Africa – French Style," *The Banker*, September, 1979, pp. 105–111, and January, 1982, pp. 41–43.

Lovejoy, Paul E., ed., *The Ideology of Slavery in Africa*, Beverly Hills, 1981.

Lovejoy, Paul E., "Interregional Monetary Flows in the Precolonial Trade of Nigeria," *Journal of African History*, Vol. 15, No. 4, 1974, pp. 563–585.

Lovejoy, Paul E., "The Role of the Wangara in the Economic Transformation of the Central Sudan in the Fifteenth and Sixteenth Centuries," *Journal of African History*, Vol. 19, No. 2, 1978, pp. 173–193.

Lovejoy, Paul E., *Transformations in Slavery: a History of Slavery in Africa*, Cambridge, 1983.

Lovejoy, Paul E., "The Volume of the Atlantic Slave Trade: a Synthesis," *Journal of African History*, Vol. 22, No. 4, 1982, pp. 473–501.

Loynes, J. B., *The West African Currency Board 1912–1962*, London, 1962.

Lucas, C. P., *A Historical Geography of the British Colonies*, Vol. 1, *The Mediterranean and Eastern Colonies*, Oxford, 1906.

211

Bibliography

Lucas, Simon, see *Proceedings of the Association for Promoting the Discovery of the Interior Parts of Africa.*

Lugard, Frederick, *Diaries*, ed. M. Perham and M. Bull, London, 1963.

Lugard, Lord (Frederick), *The Dual Mandate in British Tropical Africa*, London, 1922 (reprinted 1965).

Lugard, Frederick, *Political Memoranda*, London, 1906.

Lyon, G. F., *Narratives of Travels in Northern Africa*, London, 1819.

McCarthy, D. M. P., "Media as Ends: Money and the Underdevelopment of Tanganyika to 1940," *Journal of Economic History*, Vol. 36, No. 3, 1976, pp. 645–662.

Maffei, J. P., *Opera Omina*, Bergamo, 1747.

Magalhães-Godinho, Vitorino, *L'Économie de l'empire portugais aux XVe et XVIe siècles*, Paris, 1969.

Mage, A. E., *Voyage dans le Soudan occidentale 1863–6*, Paris, 1868.

Ma Huan, *Ying-Yai Sheng-Lan, "The Overall Survey of the Ocean's Shores"* (1433), trans. J. V. G. Mills, Cambridge, 1970.

Maes, Virginia Orr (see Orr, Virginia)

Major, R. H., ed. and trans., "Account of the Journey of Hieronimo di Santo Stefano, a Genovese," in R. H. Major, *India in the Fifteenth Century*, London, 1857.

Major, R. H., *India in the Fifteenth Century*, London, 1857.

Maloney, Clarence, *People of the Maldive Islands*, Madras, 1980.

Mann, A., "Notes on the Numeral System of the Yoruba Nation," *Journal of the Anthropological Institute*, 1887.

Manning, Patrick, *Slavery, Colonialism and Economic Growth in Dahomey, 1640–1960*, Cambridge, 1982.

Manrique, Fray Sebastien, *Travels of Fray Sebastien Manrique, 1629–1643*, ed. C. E. Lugard, Oxford, 1927.

Marco Polo, *The Book of Ser Marco Polo the Venetian Concerning the Kingdoms and Marvels of the East*, ed. and trans. Col. Sir Henry Yule, London, 1929.

Marshall, John, *Notes and Observations of East India*, ed. S. A. Khan as *John Marshall in India*, London, 1927.

Marshall, P. J., *East Indian Fortunes: the British in Bengal in the Eighteenth Century*, Oxford, 1976.

Martens, Dr. E. von, "Ueber verschiedene Verwendungen von Conchylien," *Zeitschrift für Ethnologie*, Berlin, 1872.

Marti, M. P., *Les Dogon*, Paris, 1957.

Matters Affecting the Currency of the British West African Colonies and Protectorates, 1912, Cd. 6426; *Minutes of Evidence*, 1912, Cd. 6427.

Mauny, Raymond, "La monnaie marginelloide de l'ouest africain," *Bulletin de l'IFAN*, Vol. 19, 1957, pp. 659–669.

Mauny, Raymond, "Notes sur Azougui, Chinguetti, et Ouadane," *Bulletin de l'IFAN*, Vol. 17, 1955, pp. 142–162.

Mauny, Raymond, *Tableau géographique de l'ouest africain au Moyen Age*, Dakar, 1961.

Meilink-Roelofsz, M. A. P., "Inleiding bij de overzeese geschiedenis in de 17de en 18de eeuw," in *Algemene Geschiedenis der Nederlanden*, Vol. 9, Haarlem, 1980, pp. 420–426.

Meillassoux, Claude, ed., *L'esclavage en Afrique précoloniale*, Paris, 1975.

Melitz, Jacques, "The Polanyi School of Anthropology on Money: an Economist's View," *American Anthropologist*, Vol. 72, No. 5, 1970, pp. 1020–1040.

Melitz, Jacques, *Primitive and Modern Money*, Reading, Mass., 1974.

Menzel, B., *Goldgewichte aus Ghana*, Berlin, 1968.

Meredith, Henry, *An Account of the Gold Coast of Africa*, London, 1812.

Messier, Ronald A., "The Almoravids: West African Gold and the Gold Currency of the

212

Mediterranean Basin," *Journal of the Economic and Social History of the Orient*, Vol. 17, Part 1, 1974, pp. 31–47.

Metcalfe, George, *Great Britain and Ghana*, London, 1964.

Miège, J. L., *Le Maroc et l'Europe*, Vol. 3, Paris, 1961–62.

Miers, Suzanne, *Britain and the Ending of the Slave Trade*, New York, 1975.

Miers, Suzanne and Igor Kopytoff, eds., *Slavery in Africa: Historical and Anthropological Perspectives*, Madison, 1977.

Milburne, William, *Oriental Commerce*, London, 1813.

Miner, Horace, "The Primitive City of Timbuctoo," *Memoirs of the American Philosophical Society*, Vol. 32, 1953.

Mockler-Ferryman, A. F., *British Nigeria*, London, 1902.

Mockler-Ferryman, A. F., *Up the Niger*, London, 1892.

Monrad, Hans Christian, *Gemälde der Küste von Guinea*, Copenhagen, 1822, Weimar, 1824.

Monteil, Charles, *Djenné*, Paris, 1932 (lst ed. 1903).

Monteil, Charles, "Le nombre et la numération chez les Mandes," *L'Anthropologie*, in *Soudan et Guinée II*, DA D4 71508, University of Ghana, Legon.

Monteil, Parfait Louis, *De Saint Louis à Tripoli par le lac Tchad*, Paris, 1895.

Mordekkai, Rabbi, "Reisen nach Timbuktu," *Petermanns Mitteilungen*, 1870.

Moresby, Robert, "Captain Moresby's Report on the Maldives," *Transactions of the Bombay Geographical Society 1836–1838*, Vol. 1, 1844, pp. 102–108.

Moresby, Robert, *Nautical Directions for the Maldiva Islands and the Chagos Archipelago*, London, 1840.

Moshin, Khan Mohammad, *A Bengal District in Transition: Murshidabad 1765–1793*, Dacca, 1973.

Mukerjee, Radhakamal, *The Economic History of India: 1600–1800*, London, 1945.

Mundell, Robert A., "African Trade, Politics and Money," in Rodrigue Tremblay, ed., *Africa and Monetary Integration*, Montreal, 1972.

Mundy, Peter, *The Travels of Peter Mundy in Europe and Asia, 1608–1667*, Vol. 2, *Travels in Asia, 1628–1634*, ed. R. C. Temple, London, 1914.

Murray, H., *Discoveries and Travels in Africa*, Edinburgh, 1818.

Nachtigal, Gustav, *Sahara und Sudan*, Berlin, 1897.

Nadel, S. F., *A Black Byzantium*, London, 1942.

Nadel, S. F., "A Ritual Currency in Nigeria – A Result of Cultural Contact," *Africa*, No. 3, 1937, pp. 488–491.

Najera, José de, *Espejo Mistico*, Madrid, 1670.

Neville, G. W., "West African Currency," *Journal of the African Society*, Vol. 17, 1918, pp. 223–226.

Newbury, C. W., "North Africa and Western Sudan Trade in the Nineteenth Century, a Re-evaluation,"*Journal of African History*, Vol. 7, No. 2, 1966, pp. 233–246.

Newbury, C. W., "Prices and Profitability in Early Nineteenth Century West African Trade," in Claude Meillassoux, ed., *The Development of Indigenous Trade and Markets in West Africa*, London, 1971.

Newbury, Colin W., "Trade and Authority in West Africa from 1850 to 1880," in L. H. Gann and Peter Duignan, eds., *Colonialism in Africa 1870–1960*, Vol. 1, *The History and Politics of Colonialism 1870–1914*, Cambridge, 1969, pp. 66–99.

Newbury, C. W., *The Western Slave Coast and Its Rulers*, Oxford, 1961.

Newlyn, W. T., "The Colonial Empire," in R. S. Sayers, ed., *Banking in the British Commonwealth*, 1952.

Newlyn, W. T., *Theory of Money*, Oxford, 1971.

Newlyn, W. T. and D. C. Rowan, *Money and Banking in British Colonial Africa*, Oxford, 1954.

Bibliography

Nieburh, Carsten, "Das Innere von Afrika," *Neues Deutsches Museum*, Leipzig, 1790.

Nilakanta Sastri, K. A., ed., *Foreign Notices of South India*, Madras, 1939.

Northrup, David, "The Growth of Trade among the Igbo before 1800," *Journal of African History*, Vol. 13, No. 2, 1972, pp. 221–236.

Nwani, Okonkwo A., "The Quantity Theory in the Early Monetary System of West Africa with Particular Emphasis on Nigeria, 1850–1895," *Journal of Political Economy*, Vol. 83, No. 1, 1975, pp. 185–193. Also see the editors' subsequent apology to Marion Johnson for this article, *Journal of Political Economy*, Vol. 85, No. 4, 1977, p. 876.

Odum, Eugene P., *Fundamentals of Ecology*, Philadelphia, 3rd edition, 1971.

An Officer, Late of the Ceylon Rifles, *Ceylon*, London, 1876.

Ofonagoro, Walter I., "The Currency Revolution in Southern Nigeria 1880–1948," Occasional Paper No. 14, African Studies Center, UCLA, 1976.

Ofonagoro, Walter I., "From Traditional to British Currency in Southern Nigeria: Analysis of a Currency Revolution, 1880–1948," *Journal of Economic History*, Vol. 39, No. 3, 1979, pp. 623–654.

Ojo, G. J. A., *Yoruba Culture: a Geographical Analysis*, Ife and London, 1966.

Oliveira Marques, A. H. de, *History of Portugal*, New York, 1971.

Ollive, Dr., "Schilderung von Tendouf," *Petermanns Mitteilungen*, 1880.

Onions, C. T., ed., *The Oxford Dictionary of English Etymology*, Oxford, 1966.

Opoku, Th., "Eines Neger-Pastors Predigtreise durch die Länder am Voltastrom," *Evangelische Missionsmagazin*, Basel, 1885.

Orr, Virginia, "A Bionomic Shell Study of *Monetaria Annulus* (Gastropoda: Cypraeidae) from Zanzibar," *Notulae Nature*, No. 313, May 29, 1959, pp. 1–11.

Owen, Capt. W. F. W., "On the Same Subject" (the Geography of the Maldiva Islands), *Journal of the Royal Geographical Society*, Vol. 2, 1832, pp. 81–92.

Palmer, H. R., *Bornu, Sahara, and Sudan*, London, 1936.

Palmer, H. R., "Western Sudan History: the Raudthat' ul Afkari," *Journal of the African Society*, Vol. 15, No. 59, 1916, pp. 261–273.

Paques, V., *Les Bambara*, Paris, 1954.

Park, Mungo, *Journal of a Mission to the Interior of Africa in 1805*, London, 1815.

Park, Mungo, *Travels in the Interior Districts of Africa*, London, 1799.

Parker, John, ed., *Merchants and Scholars*, Minneapolis, 1965.

Parkinson, C. Northcote, "The East India Trade," in C. Northcote Parkinson, ed., *The Trade Winds: a Study of British Overseas Trade during the French Wars 1793–1815*, London, 1948, pp. 141–156.

Parkinson, C. Northcote, *Trade in the Eastern Seas 1793–1813*, Cambridge, 1937.

Parkinson, C. Northcote, ed., *The Trade Winds: a Study of British Overseas Trade during the French Wars 1793–1815*, London, 1948.

Passarge, Siegfried, *Adamaua*, Berlin, 1895.

Pearson, M. N., "Corruption and Corsairs in Sixteenth-Century Western India: a Functional Analysis," in Blair B. King and M. N. Pearson, eds., *The Age of Partnership: Europeans in Asia before Dominion*, Honolulu, 1979, pp. 15–41.

Pearson, M. N., *Merchants and Rulers in Gujarat: the Response to the Portuguese in the Sixteenth Century*, Berkeley, 1976.

Pereira, Pacheco, *Esmeraldo de situ orbis*, ed. and trans. G. T. Kimble, London, 1936.

Perlin, Frank, "Money-Use in Late Pre-Colonial India and the International Trade in Currency Media," paper given at the Mughal Monetary Conference, Duke University, June 1981.

Peukert, Werner, *Der Atlantische Sklavenhandel von Dahomey, 1740–1797*, Wiesbaden, 1978.

Philalethes, *The Boscawen's Voyage to Bombay*, 1750.

Phillips, Thomas, "Journal of a Voyage", in A. and J. Churchill, eds., *A Collection of Voyages and Travels*, London, 1732.

214

Pieris, P. E., *Ceylon and the Hollanders 1658–1796*, Tellippalai, Ceylon, 1918.

Pires, Tomé, *The Suma Oriental of Tomé Pires*, ed. Armando Cortesão, London, 1944.

Polanyi, Karl, *Dahomey and the Slave Trade*, Seattle and London, 1966.

Pommegorge, Pruneau de, *Description de la Nigritie*, Paris, 1789.

Prakash, Om, "Asian Trade and European Impact: a Study of the Trade from Bengal, 1630–1720," in Blair B. King and M. N. Pearson, eds., *The Age of Partnership: Europeans in Asia before Dominion*, Honolulu, 1979, pp. 43–70.

Prakash, Om, "The European Trading Companies and the Merchants of Bengal 1650–1725," *Indian Social and Economic History Review*, Vol. 1, No. 3, 1963/64, pp. 37–63.

Prévôt, M. l'Abbé, [Abrégé de] *Histoire Générale des Voyages*, Chapitre II, "Iles Maldives," Paris, Vol. 4, 1780.

Proceedings of the Association for Promoting the Discovery of the Interior Parts of Africa, London, 1810.

Pyrard, François – see Albert Gray and H. C. P. Bell.

Quiggin, A. H., *A Survey of Primitive Money*, New York and London, 1970, first published 1949.

Raffanel, Anne, *Nouveau Voyage au pays des nègres*, Paris, 1856.

Ramsayer, F., "Eine Reise im Norden von Asante und im Osten von Volta," *Geografische Gesellschaft zu Jena, Mitteilungen*, Vol. 4, 1886.

Rask, Johannes, *En kort og sandferdig rejse-beskrivelse til og fra Guinea*, Trondheim, 1754.

Ratelband, K., ed., *Vijf Dagregisters van het Kasteel São Jorge da Mina (Elmina) aan de Goudkust (1645–1647)*, The Hague, 1953.

Ray, Indrani, "The French Company and the Merchants of Bengal (1680–1730)," *The Indian Economic and Social History Review*, Vol. 8, No. 1, 1971, pp. 41–55.

Report from the Select Committee on the West Coast of Africa, various years.

Ricard, Jean Pierre, *Le Negoce d'Amsterdam*, Rouen, 1723.

Richards, John F., "The Early Islamic Monetary Realm in India," paper presented at the Comparative World History Workshop in Pre-Modern Monetary History 1200–1750 A.D., University of Wisconsin, 1977.

Richards, J. F., ed., *Precious Metals in the Later Medieval and Early Modern Worlds*, Durham, N.C., 1983.

Robertson, G. A., *Notes on Africa*, London, 1819.

Robinson, C. H., *Hausaland*, London, 1896.

Rodney, Walter, "Gold and Slaves on the Gold Coast," *Transactions of the Historical Society of Ghana*, Vol. 10, 1969, pp. 13–28.

Rohlfs, Gerh., "Geld in Afrika," *Petermanns Mitteilungen*, 1889, pp. 187–192.

Rømer, L. F., *Nachrichten von der Küste von Guinea*, Copenhagen and Leipzig, 1767.

Roscoe, *The Baganda*, London, 1911.

Rosset, C. W., "Die 1400 Malediven-Inseln," *Mitteilungen der Kais.-Königl. Geographischen Gesellschaft in Wien*, Vol. 39, 1896, pp. 597–637.

Rosset, C. W., "The Maldive Islands," *The Graphic*, Oct. 16, 1886, pp. 413–416.

Rosset, C. W., "On the Maldive Islands," *Journal of the Anthropological Institute*, Vol. 16, 1887, pp. 164–174.

Ryder, A. F. C., *Benin and the Europeans 1485–1897*, London, 1969.

Ryder, A. F. C., "An Early Portuguese Trading Voyage to the Forcados River," *Journal of the Historical Society of Nigeria*, Vol.1, No. 4, 1959, pp. 294–321.

Safer, Jane Fearer, and Frances McLaughlin Gill, *Spirals from the Sea: an Anthropological Look at Shells*, New York, 1982.

Sahlins, Marshall, *Stone Age Economics*, London, 1972.

Sainsbury, Ethel Bruce, *Court Minutes of the East India Company*, Oxford, 1907–1938.

Sakarai, Lawrence J., "Indian Merchants in East Africa," unpublished manuscript.

Bibliography

Savary, J., *Universal Dictionary of Trade and Commerce*, trans. M. Postlethwayt, London, 1751.

Schilder, Franz, Albert, "Die BERGMANNsche Regel bei Porzellanschnecken," *Verhandl. Deutsche Zoologische Gesellschaft Hamburg*, 1956, pp. 410–414.

Schilder, F. A., "Die Ethnologische Bedeutung der Porzellanschnecken," *Zeitschrift für Ethnologie*, 1926, pp. 313–317.

Schilder, F. A., and M. Schilder, "Latitudinal Differences in Size of East Australian Cowries," *The Cowry*, Vol. 1, No. 7, 1964, pp. 100–101.

Schilder, F. A., and Maria Schilder, "The Size of 95,000 Cowries," *The Veliger*, Vol. 8, No. 4, 1966.

Schilder, Maria and F. A. Schilder, "Revision of the Genus *Monetaria (Cypraeidae)*," *Proceedings of the Zoological Society of London*, part 4, 1936, pp. 1113–1135.

Schnapper, B., *La Politique et le commerce français dans le golfe de Guinée de 1838 à 1876*, Paris, 1961.

Schneider, Oskar, *Muschelgeld-Studien*, Dresden, 1905.

Schramm, Percy Ernst, *Deutschland und Übersee*, Braunschweig, 1950.

Seabrook, W. B., *White Monk of Timbuctu*, London, 1934.

Seetzen, U. J., "Uber die Phellata-Araber Südwärts von Fesan, und deren Sprache, nebst einigen Nachrichten von unterschiedlichen umherliegender afrikanischen Ländern," *Monatliche Correspondenz zur Beforderung der Erd-und Himmels-Kunde*, Vol. 24, 1811.

Shannon, H. A., "Evolution of the Colonial Sterling Exchange Standard," *IMF Staff Papers*, Vol. 1, April 1951, pp. 334–354.

Shannon, H. A., "The Modern Colonial Sterling Exchange Standard," *IMF Staff Papers*, Vol. 2, April 1952, pp. 318–362.

Simkin, C. G. F., *The Traditional Trade of Asia*, London, 1968.

Simmel, Georg, *The Philosophy of Money*, London, 1978.

Sinha, Narendra K., *The Economic History of Bengal*, Calcutta, Vol. 1, 1956; Vol. 2, 1962; Vol. 3, 1970.

Sircar, D. C., ed., *Land System and Feudalism in Ancient India*, Calcutta, 1966.

Skertchly, J. Alfred, *Dahomey As It Is*, London, 1874.

Skinner, Elliot P., "Trade and Markets Among the Mossi People," in Paul Bohannan and George Dalton, eds., *Markets in Africa*, Evanston, 1962.

Slimming, David, and Alan Jarrett, *The Cowries of Seychelles*, London, 1971.

Smallwood, H. St. C., "A Visit to the Maldive Islands," *Journal of the Royal Asian Society*, Vol. 48, 1961, pp. 83–89.

Smith, Mary, *Baba of Karo*, London, 1954.

Smith, M. G., *Government in Zazzau*, London, 1960.

Smith, Vincent A., "Political Geography, Government, and Administration," in A. J. Herbertson and O. J. R. Howarth, ed., *The Oxford Survey of the British Empire*, Vol. 2, *Asia*, Oxford, 1914, pp. 242–295.

Smith, W., *A Voyage to Guinea*, London, 1744.

Soleillet, Paul, *Voyage à Ségou 1878–1879*, Paris, 1887.

Solis, Duarte Gomes, *Alegación en favor de la Compañia de la India Oriental*, ed. Mosés Amzalak, Lisbon, 1955 [1628].

Spray, W. A., "Surveying and Charting the Indian Ocean: the British Contribution, 1750–1838," unpublished University of London Ph.D. thesis, 1966.

Spry, J. F., *The Sea Shells of Dar es Salaam: Gastropods*, Dar es Salaam, n.d.

Stearns, Robert E. C., "Ethno-Conchology: a Study of Primitive Money," in *Report of National Museum, 1887*, Washington, 1887.

Steensgard, Niels, *Carracks, Caravans and Companies: the Structural Crisis in the European-Asian Trade of the Early Seventeenth Century*, Copenhagen, 1973.

Stuhlmann, Franz, *Mit Emin Pasha ins Herz von Afrika*, Berlin, 1894.

Sundström, Lars, *The Exchange Economy of Pre-Colonial Tropical Africa*, New York, 1974.

Sylla, Richard, "Monetary Innovation in Economic History," in Paul Wachtel, ed., *Crisis in the Economic and Financial Structure*, Lexington, Mass., 1982

Tavernier, Jean-Baptiste, *Travels in India*, trans. V. Ball, London, 1925 [1676 edition]. We have also used an edition published London, 1684.

Telkamp, Gerald J., "Current Annotated Bibliography of Dutch Expansion Studies," *Itinerario* (Bulletin of the Leiden Center for the History of European Expansion), Leiden, 1978.

Thornton, Thomas, *Oriental Commerce*, London, 1825.

Tibbetts, G. R., *Arab Navigation in the Indian Ocean Before the Coming of the Portuguese*, London, 1971.

Tibbetts, G. R., "Pre-Islamic Arabia and South-East Asia," *Journal of the Malayan Branch of the Royal Asiatic Society*, Vol. 29, No. 3, 1956, pp. 182–208.

The Times Atlas of the World, London, 1980.

Tucker, Miss Charlotte Maria, *Abeokuta; or Sunrise within the Tropics: an Outline of the Origin and Progress of the Yoruba Mission*, London, 1854.

al-'Umari, *Masalik al-absar*, trans. Gaudefroy-Demombynes, Paris, 1927.

UNESCO, *Historical Relations Across the Indian Ocean*, Paris, 1980.

United Africa Company, "The Manilla Problem," *United Africa Company Statistical and Economic Review*, Vol. 3, 1949, pp. 44–56.

van Bentham Jutting, W. S. S., "Vondsten van Tropische Kauri's in Nederland," *Basteria*, Vol. 19, No. 1, 1955, pp. 1–20.

van Dam, Pieter, *Beschryvinge van de Oostindische Compagnie*, ed. F. W. Stapel, s'Gravenhage, 1927–1943.

van Emst, P., "De Weg van de Kauri," *Tijdschrift voor Economische en Sociale Geografie*, Vol. 49, No. 12, 1958, pp. 267–274.

van Laere, Raf, "The Larin: Trade Money of the Arabian Gulf," Oriental Numismatic Society, Occasional Paper No. 15, 1980.

van Opstall, Margaretha E., "Archival Sources in the Netherlands," in Vera Rubin and Arthur Tuden, *Comparative Perspectives on Slavery in New World Plantation Societies, Annals of the New York Academy of Sciences*, special issue, Vol. 292, 1977.

Verdier, R., *Le Pays Kabiyé*, Paris, 1982.

Verger, Pierre, "Influence de Bresil au Golfe du Benin," in *Les Afro-Américains, Mémoire d'IFAN*, Vol. 27, 1952, pp. 67ff.

Viard, Edward, *Au bas Niger*, Paris, 3rd ed., 1886.

Vice, David, *The Coinage of British West Africa and St. Helena 1684–1958*, Birmingham, 1983.

Vignols, Léon, and Henri Sée, "Les ventes de la Compagnie des Indes à Nantes (1723–1833)," *Revue de l'histoire des colonies françaises*, Vol. 13, No. 4, 1925, pp. 489–550.

Vilar, Pierre, *A History of Gold and Money 1450–1920*, London, 1976.

Vogt, John, *Portuguese Rule on the Gold Coast*, Athens, Georgia, 1979.

Walckenaer, C. A., *Recherches géographique sur l'interieur de l'Afrique Septentrionale*, Paris, 1821.

Walls, Jerry G., *Cowries*, Neptune, N.J., 2nd ed., 1979.

Warmington, E. H., *The Commerce between the Roman Empire and India*, London, 1974.

Webb, Jr., James L. A., "Toward the Comparative Study of Money: Reconsideration of West Africa Currencies and Neoclassical Monetary Concepts," *International Journal of African Historical Studies*, Vol. 15, No. 3, 1982, pp. 455–466.

Weyers, Don, *Opdracht 14 VOC 2304/KA 2196*, typescript, University of Leiden, 1978.

Whiteway, R. S., *The Rise of Portuguese Power in India*, London, 1899.

Wilks, Ivor, "A Note on the Chronology, and Origins, of the Gonja Kings," *Ghana Notes and Queries*, 1966.

217

Bibliography

Wilks, Ivor and Phyllis Ferguson, "In Vindication of Sīdī al-Hājj 'Abd al-Salām Shabayni," in Christopher Allen and R. W. Johnson, eds., *African Perspectives*, Cambridge, 1970.

Wilson, C. R., *The Early Annals of the English in Bengal*, London, Vol. 1, 1895; Vol. 2, Part 1, 1900, part 2, 1911.

Winterbottom, Thomas, *An Account of the Native Africans in Sierra Leone*, London, 1803.

Wolf, Dr., "Letzte Reise nach der Landschaft Barbar (Bariba oder Borgu)," *Mitteilungen aus den deutschen Schutzgebieten*, Vol. 4, 1891, pp. 1–27.

Wood, Howland, *The Gampola Larin Hoard*, American Numismatic Society *Numismatic Notes and Monographs*, No. 61, New York, 1934.

Wyrtki, Klaus, ed., *Oceanographic Atlas of the International Indian Ocean Expedition*, Washington, D.C., 1971.

Yajima, Hikoichi, *The Arab Dhow Trade in the Indian Ocean*, Tokyo, 1976.

Yajima, Hikoichi, *The Islamic History of the Maldive Islands*, Tokyo, 1982.

Yang, Lien-Sheng, *Money and Credit in China*, Cambridge, Mass., 1952.

Young, Lieutenant I. A., and W. Christopher, "Memoir on the Inhabitants of the Maldiva Islands," *Transactions of the Bombay Geographical Society 1836–1838*, Vol. 1, 1844, pp. 54–86.

Yu-Chan, Wang, *Early Chinese Coinage*, New York, 1951.

Yule, Col. Henry, and A. C. Burnell, *Hobson-Jobson*, London, 1968 (reprint of 1903 edition).

Index

Index

Baghdad 27
Bagirmi 105
Bahr al-Ghazal r. 190–1
Baillaud, Émile 116
al-Bakri 16
Balasore 42–5, 48, 52, 55, 66, 84, 175;
  Dutch 49, 51; English 54, 55; French 48,
  56, 57; merchants, ships 43, 51
ballast 30, 31, 48, 50, 68, 86, 99, 125, 185
Bamako 142
Bambara country, people 18, 114–5, 128,
  153
Bambara "hundred" (= 80) 115, 117, 129,
  135, 136, 142, 148, 198; "thousand" 116,
  133, 141
Bamenda grassfields 107
Bandar Abbas 26
Bandiagara 142
Banque d'Afrique Occidentale see B.A.O.
B.A.O. (Banque d'Afrique Occidentale)
  154
"bar" currency 124
Barbosa, Duarte 29
Barbot, John 47, 86, 110, 113, 192
barifiri (gold unit) 142
Barros, João de 29, 30, 31, 82
barter trade, West Africa 149
Barth, H. 104, 105, 116, 118, 119, 126, 131
Basden 151, 152, 153
Batavia 37
Batavian Republic (Holland) 54
Bay of Bengal 42, 43, 49, 50, 84; monsoon
  49
beads 188
Begho 136
Beirut 15
Bell, H. C. P. 22, 39, 40, 53, 57, 66, 68, 77,
  81, 82, 84
Bemberike 104
Benares (ship) 66
Bengal: Dutch 29, 31, 51; English 29, 41,
  54; Portuguese 28, 29, 31, 34
    cowrie currency 2, 18, 28, 29, 43, 47,
  64, 65, 77
    cowrie trade 14, 48, 69, 88, 201; import
  via Balasore 42, 43; stocks rundown 69,
  77; Maldives trade 24, 25, 29, 34, 39, 84;
  merchants, ships 34, 41, 43, 48, 54
Benin city, kingdom 2, 18, 30, 106, 166,
  190
Bénin Republic (modern) 10, 104, 156
Benkhobougoula 142
Benue r. 107, 140
Berbain, Simone 56
Bereku 106, 190
Bergman's Rule 11, 162
Beschir, al-Hajj (Bornu) 105
Bida 140, 152

Bight of Benin 110; – and Biafra 123
Bihar 86
Bijapur 29
Bima (rear Makassar) 7
Binger, L. G. 117, 142
Birifor people 155
Birmingham, David 101
Birtwistle C. A. 150
al-Biruni 23–4
Black Volta r. 155
Blackwall (Thames) 91
Blake, chief factor 41
boats, ships, Maldive 39, 42, 49, 84, 175,
  182, 184; "native" 86
Bobo Dioulasso 104, 142
Bole 155
boly cowries (Maldives) 34
Bombay 47, 78, 156, 157, 201
Bonduku 104, 119, 142
Bonnat, M.-J. 125
booty 118
"Borah" (Gujerati merchants) 156
Borgu 127, 155
Borneo 7
Bornu 3, 17, 105, 119, 126, 141
Boscawen (ship) 85
Bosman, W. 134
bosta (100,000 cowries) 25
Boulton and Watt works 65
Bowdich, Thomas 107, 122, 134
Bowrey, Thomas 43, 55
brandy 111
brass 106, 188; currencies 3
Brazil 12, 74, 78, 181; Brazilian
  slave-traders 74
bride-price 152
Bristol 91
Britannia? (ship) 83, 85
brokerage 97
Bruininck, Gov. 49
Bubakr, Pasha (Timbuktu) 131
Bubi people 120
Bukina Faso (Upper Volta) 104
bunch (galinha, 200 cowries) 120,
  121
burgher community, Ceylon 51
Burgess, C. M. 10
Burhanpur 29
burlap gunny sacks 157
Burma 2, 13, 25
Burton, Richard 6, 123, 126
Bussa 104
butter (to Maldives) 43, 48, 82
Buxton, Fowell 73
buzios cowries 29

cabeça, "head" 36
cabess: grand cabess (4,000 cowries) 36,

220

Index

Index

manufactured goods 105
Marginella shells (*koroni*) 130, 131, 144;
  Marginella amygdalla 18
Maria Theresa dollar 69–71
marks, German 150
Marseilles 15, 56, 57
Marshall, John 41, 45, 82
Martens, Dr. von 9, 12
Mary Galley (ship) 55
Masina 115, 133
al-Mas'udi 14, 23, 27, 82
mat, bag (20,000 cowries) 118, 121
Mathura 14
Mauny, Raymond 131
Mauritania 16, 104
Mawlay Ahmad al-Mansur, Sultan
  (Morocco) 16
Mecca 105
Medina, Duke of 35
Mediterranean, eastern 18
Meknes 16
Menomini (American Indians) 13
Meredith, Henry 128
metallic currencies 6, 7, 189; *see also* coin,
  larin, manillas, *pice*, etc.
Middle Belt, Nigeria 152
Middleburg 37; *kamer* 91, 96, 97
Minhaj-us-Siraj 14
mithqal (gold weight unit, usually 72 grains)
  114, 119, 127, 129, 131, 140, 141; silver
  mithqal 130
Mocha 30, 171
mohi coir bag (for cowries) 81
Mombasa 17
moneta (*Cypreae moneta*, money cowrie) 5,
  7, 10–12, 71–3, 75, 78, 104, 126, 127, 146,
  156
monetary factors 144–5; innovation 158;
  policy 64, 132, 139
monetized economy 146
money stock (M) 3, 145–6; *see* quantity
  theory
money supply 198
monopoly: Dutch 39, 40, 41, 52; Maldives 7,
  34, 40, 85, 156, 184; Mamalle 32;
  Portuguese 31, 35; West Africa 3, 193;
  Zanzibar 74
monopsony, Dutch 39, 52, 92; Hamburgers
  (Zanzibar) 74
monsoons 44, 50, 84–5
Monteil, Charles 110, 131
Monteil, P. L. 119
Mopti 104
Moresby, Capt. 66
Morice, Humphrey 99, 188
Morice, M. 72, 73
Morocco 16, 102, 127; invasion of Songhay
  130, 132, 196

Mossi country, people 104, 148, 153;
  donkeys 127–8; traders 126
Mossi "hundred" (100) 117
"mother of cowries" 155–6, 163
Mozambique 7, 12, 71, 73, 114, 181, 192
Mughal empire, emperor 29, 44, 48
Muhammad Ali (Mamalle, Mammali
  Marakkar) 32
Muhammad b. Tughluq, Sultan (Delhi) 24
Muhammad-ul-adil 22
Muslim "hundred" (100) 116, 117, 135
Muslim traders, merchants (West Africa)
  113, 128, 146

Nachtigal, Gustav 119
Nadel, S. F. 152
nafqa (handful of grain) 131
Najera, José de 110
Nantes 56
Nasib Khan, merchant 43
Nawab Nurallah Khan, merchant 43
Nefta 16
Netherlands 45, 63; *see also* Holland
Neville, G. W. 79
New Caledonia 13
New Guinea 13
New Hebrides 13
New Zealand 7
Niamey 104
Niger r. 2, 19; upper 18, 106, 141, 142, 148;
  interior delta 104, 115, 133, 142; bend 15,
  114, 119, 130, 135; middle 18, 102, 104;
  lower 104, 115, 121, 139, 140; delta 99,
  102, 106, 120
Niger colony, modern Republic 118, 148
Niger Company 149
Niger Expedition (1841) 121
Nigeria 118, 138, 148, 150, 153
Nigerian Coinage Ordinance 150
Nikky 104, 109, 127, 128, 129, 142
Nikky *mithqal* 142
Nile r. 26
Nioro 104
Nkonya 107, 122
North Africa 25, 105, 109
North African merchants 2
North America 12
Northfleet (Thames) 91
Nunes, A. 31, 36, 171
Nupe 105, 107, 118, 119, 140, 152, 191

Ofonagoro, Walter 153, 154
ogoji (string of 40 cowries) 117
ogun (20 cowries) 117
oil import 43
Ojibwa (American Indians) 13
okekan ("one bag," 20,000 cowries) 117
olive shells (*Olivella* sp.) 12, 19, 160

226

Index

Robertson, G. A. 106–7
Robinson, C. H. 129
Rodatz, Hans A. 74
Romans 15
Rømer, L. F. 134
Ross, Johannes Matthias 65
Rosset, C. W. 68, 85
rotl ("pound weight", 32 cowries – Bornu) 119
Rotterdam 91; *kamer* 94
Roux de Frassinet, firm 75
Royal African Company *see* R.A.C.
Royal Niger Company 124, 140, 149; *see also* Niger Company
Rumpf, Gov. 57
Ryder, A. F. C. 19, 30, 31, 36, 120
Ryukyu Is. 7, 11, 13

sacks of cowries (= 20,000) 118, 121, 123
Safer, J. F. and F. M. Gill 12
Sage, Walter 11
Sahara 15, 16; cowrie trade 30, 102, 127, 165
St. Malo 33
Salaga 104, 107, 113, 119, 122, 123, 125, 126, 240, 141, 142; Salaga–Hausaland route 109
salt 32, 85; prices 130, 131, 132–3; West Africa 116, 123, 124, 126, 135
saltpetre 48, 86, 185
Sandwich Is. (Hawaii) 13
Sansanding (= Sansani) 106, 131, 133, 142
Sansanne Hausa 104
Sansanne Mango 104
São Jorge da Mina (Elmina castle) 30
São Tomé Is. 30, 109, 171
savanna zone 105, 107
Say 104, 142
scarcity value 127, 130
Schilders, F. A. and M. 10, 11
Schneider, Oskar 9, 12, 13
Segu 115, 132, 133
seigniorage 2–3, 143, 144, 200
Senegal 102; Senegal–Niger region 107
Senufo people, country 153, 155
separate (non-company) traders 99
Seychelle Is. 7, 9
Shabeeny, El Haj 126
Shah Rakh 27
Sharifa, Emir (Kano) 104, 105, 118
Sherbro Galley (ship) 97
Shia Muslims (Maldives) 156
shillings 140, 141, 149, 150
ships 19, 98; Arab 25, 26; Dutch, English 35,. 39, 50, 98, *see also* Indiamen; Indian 41, 43, 84, 180; Maldives *see under* boats; Portuguese 36, 98
ship-trade, West Africa 99

shipwrecks 33, 162, 170, 180
Shiraz 26
Shuja Khan, merchant 43
Siam 29
Sierra Leone 98, 102
Sijilmassa 16
silks 48, 49, 66
silver, depreciation xiii, 40, 48, 158, 197; premium 141
silver coin 65, 123, 133, 148, 150, 197, 198, 199
Singapore 77, 180
Sinha 56, 57
Siraf 23, 27, 170
siya (100 cowries) 25
Slave Coast 19, 66, 110, 112, 156, 181
slave trade, Atlantic 2, 3, 13, 177; expansion 111; Abolition 56, 64, 112, 113, 146, 151
slave trade, internal, West Africa 107, 113, 116, 146; Saharan 104
slave porters 128
slave prices 110–12, 115, 116
slaves as merchandise 104
soa (Akan gold-weight) 135
Socotra 30
Sodre, Vicente 28, 32
Sokode (Togo) 123
Sokoto Caliphate 105, 107
Soleillet, Paul 116
Songhay 16, 28; Askiyas 16; Moroccan invasion 130, 132, 196; salt supplies 130, 196
South Male atoll 82
Spain 63
Spanish ounce 136
spices, spice-trade 37, 39, 49, 51, 89, 177
spirits *see* alcohol
Sri Lanka 20; archives 22
"sterling," Gold Coast 137
stor cabess, grand cabess (4,000 cowries) 134
"string," stringing (cowries) 114, 116, 119, 135, 169, 194; strung cowries 120–3
subsistence costs 195
substantivist school 158–9
"substitute money": *annulus* 73; *Marginella, koroni* 130, 131
sugar labor 109–10
Sulayman al-Tajir ("the merchant") 23
Sulu Is. 7, 13
Sumatra 7, 11, 41
Sunni Muslims (Maldives) 156
supply and demand, cowries 143
Surat 30, 41, 43, 56
Suvadiva atoll *see* Huvadu
Swahili coast, East Africa 102
Sweden 13
Sylhet 29

228

229

833058774